AMERICAN PHILANTHROPIC FOUNDATIONS

PHILANTHROPIC AND NONPROFIT STUDIES

Dwight F. Burlingame and David C. Hammack, Editors

AMERICAN PHILANTHROPIC FOUNDATIONS

Regional Difference and Change

Edited by DAVID C. HAMMACK
and STEVEN RATHGEB SMITH

INDIANA UNIVERSITY PRESS

This book is a publication of

Indiana University Press
Office of Scholarly Publishing
Herman B Wells Library 350
1320 East 10th Street
Bloomington, Indiana 47405 USA

iupress.indiana.edu

The paper used in this publication meets the minimum requirements of the American National Standard for Information Sciences—Permanence of Paper for Printed Library Materials, ANSI Z39.48-1992.

Manufactured in the United States of America

Library of Congress Cataloging-in-Publication Data

Names: Hammack, David C., editor. | Smith, Steven Rathgeb, [date] editor.
Title: American philanthropic foundations : regional difference and change / edited by David C. Hammack and Steven Rathgeb Smith.
Description: Bloomington, Indiana : Indiana University Press, [2018] | Includes index.
Identifiers: LCCN 2018000952 (print) | LCCN 2017059764 (ebook) | ISBN 9780253025432 (eb) | ISBN 9780253025326 (cl : alk. paper) | ISBN 9780253032751 (pb : alk. paper)
Subjects: LCSH: Endowments—United States. | Charities—United States.
Classification: LCC HV97.A3 (print) | LCC HV97.A3 A628 2018 (ebook) | DDC 361.7/6320973—dc23
LC record available at https://lccn.loc.gov/2018000952

1 2 3 4 5 23 22 21 20 19 18

CONTENTS

ACKNOWLEDGMENTS

IN PREPARING THIS BOOK, THE final volume of the Contributions of Foundations project created and funded by the Aspen Institute's former Nonprofit Sector and Philanthropy Research Program, we have incurred many debts—intellectual, institutional, and financial. We gratefully acknowledge those who have helped us. Alan Abramson, as leader of the Aspen program, supported by Rachel Mosher-Williams of the staff and James A. Smith of the research advisory committee, launched these studies and helped see them through to completion. Alan, Rachel, Jim, and the many well-informed foundation leaders and researchers they consulted understood that foundations always face questions about their purposes and their privileges. Surely they did not, just before the Great Recession brought so much attention to America's rising inequality, anticipate the variety of challenges that foundations now face. We hope that this book helps clarify the real questions. A Packard Foundation grant underwrote the Aspen program's support for the project; we are thankful for that support, and we are especially thankful for the foundation's decision, and Aspen's, to leave all aspects of the projects entirely in the hands of the authors and editors.

This book developed alongside two other products of the Contributions of Foundations project. We renew the thanks offered in David C. Hammack and Helmut K. Anheier, *A Versatile American Institution: The Changing Ideals and Realities of Philanthropic Foundations* (Washington, DC: Brookings Institution Press, 2013), and Helmut K. Anheier and David C. Hammack, *American Foundations: Roles and Contributions* (Washington, DC: Brookings Institution Press, 2010). Those books emphasize the long course of development of America's philanthropic foundations and the reality that foundations relate to their many different fields of concern in a variety of ways. Here, we take up a question they left open: How have America's regions and America's foundations related to one another? To answer this large question, we have enlisted a strong group of historians and policy scientists: as editors, we owe each of them thanks for the quality of their work, and for their patience and persistence.

Throughout the entire project, we have learned much through discussions with many others. Here we would particularly thank Putnam Barber, Elizabeth Boris, Kathleen W. Buechel, Emmett D. Carson, Paul DiMaggio, James Ferris, Joel Fleishman, Stanley N. Katz, Ellen Condliffe Lagemann, Kathleen D. McCarthy, Steven Minter, Susan Ostrander, Kenneth Prewitt, Judith Sealander, Jiannbin Lee Shiao, Mark Sidel, Bruce Sievers, Burton Weisbrod, and Julian Wolpert. For their expertise in the law relating to foundations, we are indebted to Paul Feinberg at Case Western Reserve University, Norman I. Silber of Hofstra University, and John Simon of the Yale Law School. We also acknowledge the characteristically exceptional aid provided by four colleagues who have passed away: Peter Dobkin Hall, Barry D. Karl, Richard Magat, and Stanton Wheeler.

The increasing number of individual foundations that make extensive information about their activities available through detailed annual reports, evaluations, and continually improving websites deserve our thanks, and the thanks of all who are interested in American philanthropy. The Foundation Center's carefully constructed samples of grants made by foundations in 2001 and 2005 were again very useful; we are indebted to the center's researchers, especially Sara Englehardt, Steve Lawrence, and Larry McGill. We arranged for all contributors to this volume to have access to these samples. Limitations that derive from the Foundation Center's main purpose—to help foundations work with grantseekers while preserving appropriate anonymity—did impose limits on our ability to answer many questions, especially about the flows of grants across state lines, the exact purposes and fields addressed by grants, and the relationships between grants and a foundation's broader foci.[1] Also valuable was data available to all through the Urban Institute's National Center for Charitable Statistics. The Rockefeller Archive Center and several other important archival research collections did much to underwrite the work reported here by preserving and making available extensive collections of relevant materials. We join all researchers in the hope that more foundations will realize that it is in their own interest to make available an even fuller body of information.

The aim throughout all phases of this project has been to produce work that strikes foundation leaders as fair and representative, and at the same time persuades skeptical researchers and policy analysts. In our effort to achieve this delicate balance, we have had the benefit of many conversations with researchers and foundation leaders at events generously arranged by several sponsors. These include the Aspen Institute, the Pocantico Conference Center of the Rockefeller Brothers Fund, the Rockefeller Archive Center, the Foundation Center, and the Nancy Bell Evans Center on Nonprofits and Philanthropy at the University of Washington Daniel J. Evans School of Public Policy and Governance. We also gained much from discussions organized by the Foundation Center in New York, the Southern California Association of Grantmakers in Los Angeles, the Bradley Center of the Hudson Institute in Washington, DC, the Indiana University Center on Philanthropy in Indianapolis, the Yale Law School in New Haven, and the Mandel Center for Nonprofit Organizations in Cleveland. We have continued to learn much from colleagues and critics at several meetings of the Association for Research on Nonprofit Organizations and Voluntary Action and the International Society for Third Sector Research.

Several people and institutions provided excellent research and editorial support. At Case Western Reserve University, Elise Hagesfeld provided invaluable editorial assistance, Jesse Tarbert raised important points on several topics, and Yuan Liu provided excellent research. At the University of Washington, Beth Lovelady provided excellent research and editorial support. Meghan Mcconaughey at the American Political Science Association also provided very important editorial assistance. Steven Rathgeb Smith also benefited from the financial support of the University of Washington, Georgetown University, American University, and the American Political Science Association in the completion of this manuscript. We want to thank Indiana University Press and our editor, Gary Dunham, for their excellent work. Once again, Loraine Shils Hammack's editorial skill deserves much of the credit for the book's coherence and readability. We have devoted a great deal of our time to this book over the past several years; Loraine Hammack and Penny Smith deserve our humble thanks for their patience as well as for their advice.

David C. Hammack and Steven Rathgeb Smith

Notes

1. Created to aid grant-seekers, this database includes basic information about 124,844 grants of $10,000 or more, awarded to nonprofit organizations and government agencies by a sample of the 1,007 largest private and community foundations in each sample year. For community foundations, it includes only discretionary and donor-advised grants; it omits grants to individuals. The file includes foundation names and states; grant recipient names, cities, states, or countries, units—such as the medical school of a university—as well as, for some grants, information about recipient population groups, grant amounts, grant durations, years authorized, text descriptions, grant purposes, grant population groups, types of support, matching support, and challenge support. The data set uses information provided by the foundations themselves; it does not include field information for each grant, and information on grant purposes and on populations served is quite incomplete. The file offers no information as to the relationship of any individual grant to the granting foundation's larger program. To mask the identity of specific granting foundations, the file includes very limited information on the flows of grants from one state to another.

AMERICAN PHILANTHROPIC FOUNDATIONS

INTRODUCTION

David C. Hammack

FOUNDATIONS AND OTHER ENDOWMENTS REPRESENT both wealth and voice; it follows that they attract critics. When in 2007 we began the studies that culminate in this book, a prominent criticism held that America's foundations had become weak, unimaginative, and ineffective rather than bold, energetic, and venturesome.[1] Ten years later, as the Great Recession that began in 2008 persists amid a return of American inequality to the levels that prevailed in the Gilded Age and the Roaring Twenties, new criticisms appear. Foundations and endowments are now said to hoard money that should be spent on immediate needs; critics add that in pushing to exert greater influence they reinforce inequality when what the nation needs is more equal opportunity.[2]

We offer the studies in this volume as efforts to evaluate these criticisms and to put them into perspective. In assembling the book, we have drawn on both history and the policy sciences. Historians wrote several of the essays that follow this introduction; political scientists and sociologists wrote the others. History, we believe, is particularly important for the study of endowed institutions that are intended to persist over the decades. Historians do their best to understand the actual conditions that shaped past decisions and ambitions. Laws, language, and understandings change, sometimes quite radically. The time-series data that social science requires is never available for long periods. Hence, historical study is essential to efforts to comprehend past purposes and past activities and to assess change over time. Because we agree that all institutions must change with the times, we also believe it is essential to bring the best contemporary analysis to any examination of today's foundations.

Foundation and Endowment Development: A Broad Sketch

America's philanthropic foundations date from the American Revolution. They owe their legal existence to the Constitution's guarantees of property rights, religious liberty, and freedom of speech and to the rights of corporations as affirmed in the Dartmouth College case of 1819. Through these fundamental laws, the United States freed endowed charities from the close supervision that British rule had assigned to the Church of England and other imperial authorities. America's new frame of government made possible independent, self-directing endowments, although regulated to some extent by the states and also, especially from the early twentieth century, by the federal government.

Charitable funds and endowments constitute autonomous sources of initiative to a large extent free of limits that constrain elected governments and profit-seeking businesses. They pursue many distinct, often conflicting, and sometimes controversial purposes. For these reasons, charitable funds and foundations are notable components of American pluralism. Throughout American history, they have pursued causes both religious and secular, both notable and frivolous. Many of their causes have been small, local, uncontroversial, and even peculiar. Other causes have drawn foundations into historic controversies that manifested themselves in regional terms.[3] Over time, some endowed causes have lost favor as other causes gained support.

From the first decades after Americans expelled the government-funded Church of England, special endowments enabled religious communities to thrive throughout the Northeast. With religion came conflict, as well as community. Endowed funds helped Northeastern Protestants bring churches and schools to the West, even as some religious communities rejected the storing of treasure for holy purposes, insisted that "God will provide," and urged leaders and followers alike to take vows of poverty. Early nineteenth-century Presbyterians used their funds to try to hold the nation together despite conflict over slavery,[4] even as Methodist and Congregationalist funds sent missionaries to engage the slaves and urge emancipation. In the nineteenth century, endowed funds underwrote colleges, engineering schools, libraries, and the arts—helping to advance knowledge and secularism while diversifying local economies and building local elites. After the Civil War, the Peabody Fund, one of the first celebrated foundations that operated on an independent basis, distinct from a particular institution or religious group, worked to spread schools through the defeated South. To operate in the South, the Peabody Fund had to acquiesce to local demands that the schools favor white children. Meanwhile, Northern religious funds competed—with very mixed success—for the hearts and minds of southerners, including white Baptists and Methodists as well as the formerly enslaved African Americans.

At the beginning of the twentieth century, advocates for a stronger, more unified sense of American nationality turned to endowed funds when Congress, still deeply divided along lines defined by the Civil War, could not agree to fund education, science, or most celebrations of the nation. Religious endowments continued their work (as they do today), even as funds committed to science rose to prominence, helping to transform medicine and other professions, to build research universities, to separate northern (but not southern) colleges from church sponsorship, and to create a national system of secondary and especially higher education—again contributing to knowledge and opportunity while also building elites. Through the middle of the twentieth century, a number of foundations, located mostly in the Northeast and around the Great Lakes, promoted national standards in public education, public health, and public administration. Often, of course, local and particular regional and religious interests strongly opposed such national standards. Here and there, small numbers of foundations underwrote efforts to encourage labor unions, women's rights, and measures of social and economic reform—and, perhaps more often, to discourage such things.[5] More recently, a few foundations identified with New York, Chicago, and California have backed movements for equal rights regardless of race, religion, gender, or sexual orientation, while some foundations identified with Midwestern and southern states have underwritten campaigns for religious and/or states' rights and charter schools. Throughout the history of the nation—but more in some places than in others—endowed funds provided key support for libraries, museums, orchestras, parks, charitable societies, and other institutions of popular education, and the arts that ornament America's cities despite the absence of government support.

Engaged with fundamental cultural conflicts, America's foundations and endowed funds have always both reinforced and challenged regional identities and regional differences, thus evoking harsh criticism as well as exaggerated praise.[6]

Regionally varying experiences with foundations and endowed funds have no doubt shaped the legislation, the regulations, and the legal decisions that control and constrain foundation activity. Despite the significance of foundations for America's regional differences and despite the many popular and conventional comments about the foundations and

American regions, the topic has never attracted serious attention. This book, the third in a series exploring the roles of foundations in the key fields they have engaged and in American history,[7] offers an ambitious first effort to assess foundation variation across the United States.

On "Foundation"

The classic foundation receives its initial funds from a single donor, but community foundations and some others also seek new contributions, and if they receive sufficient new money each year they qualify for the advantageous tax status of a public charity rather than a private foundation. If they make charitable gifts from financial assets that they hold and invest, both public charities and private foundations enjoy significant tax advantages.

Wealth, permanence, and independence attract critics, who can sometimes take advantage of misperceptions, myths, and misrepresentations. It is often asserted that foundations, defined as substantial funds invested for the support of charitable activities over a sustained period of time, date from actions of such industrial titans as Andrew Carnegie and John D. Rockefeller at the end of the nineteenth century. Yet endowed charitable funds had been active for one hundred years by then. It is not infrequently claimed or assumed that all "real" foundations are limited to secular causes.[8] Yet neither practice nor law requires an American foundation to be nonreligious, and as always, a large share of all foundations continue to be devoted to religious causes.[9] It is said that foundations have abandoned a former commitment to the relief of poverty and disaster. But immediate relief of physical need has never been a chief purpose of American endowments and foundations, which have always chiefly aimed to sustain the activities associated with churches, schools, and other institutions. Recent critics have it that American foundations have mostly given casually and thoughtlessly, taking little care about outcomes. In reality, much foundation-giving has always supported carefully considered initiatives. Not a few of those initiatives enjoyed considerable success, even as many failed. And it is certainly true that some endowments have simply held and distributed money for the use of institutions that a well-informed donor believed would make good use of a flow of income over time.

Observers and critics often note that in the United States, foundation boards can act without reference to legislative majorities or to current markets: if the observer assumes that sovereignty implies a central monopoly over initiatives, such autonomy can seem illegitimate.

American foundations enjoy more autonomy than their counterparts in most other nations, perhaps in all. But they can ignore neither public nor legislative opinion—nor the market. Foundations depend on markets to create and maintain their wealth and to yield income, and to generate the wealth that enables others to help support the causes they champion. Foundations must obey the law in making investments and in making grants. To ignore the opinions of the public and of legislators, regulators, and judges is to put a foundation's future in peril. From time to time, a few foundations—associated with Carnegie, Rockefeller, Ford, Gates, and a few others—have held truly extraordinary amounts of money. But even these foundations have understood that public revulsion can destroy the value of their money. Because a good reputation enhances the value of any grant, foundations have had to learn to take public opinion into account even when pursuing their boldest initiatives. As is increasingly recognized, foundations are most effective when they understand and advance values shared by the people and organizations they support.[10]

Some of the confusion about foundations arises from the fact that many entities that describe themselves as foundations, or are described as such by critics, are not charitable foundations under American law. The word "foundation" has many positive connotations: it can mean fundamental, basic, substantive, consequential, authoritative, principal, and principled. Proclaiming seriousness and credibility, many organizations that have little or nothing to do with endowment-based charitable giving use the term in their names. Hospital systems such as the Cleveland Clinic Foundation mostly lack large endowments. Annual fundraising campaigns in the style of the March of Dimes—originally the National Foundation for Infantile Paralysis—rarely hold and invest large assets over time. The Clinton Foundation is set up as a public charity that annually raises new money from many sources for charitable purposes; it is neither a private foundation nor a community foundation.[11] Foundations that chiefly sell insurance and annuities and manage private—and even charitable—trusts may be commercial rather than charitable. Several large banks and investment companies have, in recent years, created closely tied commercial gift funds that are separately incorporated as public charities, but are by necessity closely associated with their commercial sponsors.

Journalists and critics are tempted to include all the entities noted above as well as many others that hold large amounts of money in discussions of foundations. It can make sense to associate philanthropic foundations with the endowments of charities, such as schools, colleges, universities, medical institutes, and arts organizations that do use their endowment income over time to advance legally recognized charitable purposes. But to conflate foundations and endowed institutions with operating charities that rely overwhelmingly not on endowments but on current income earned through the sale of services and on current fund-raising or with the gift funds controlled by commercial financial institutions—all of which are constrained by their ability to succeed in the current market—makes little sense. It makes even less sense to conflate independent foundations and endowments with the "social welfare" organizations that have recently been used to direct large amounts of money to political candidates, because such actions are explicitly forbidden to legally constituted charities.[12] Political action committees are explicitly devoted to politics, not to the support of charitable services, and generally speaking they do not raise money in order to invest it and underwrite giving over time. A trust fund does not have a charitable purpose unless it is, in effect, a foundation or endowment specifically dedicated to a charity. The same is true of a limited liability corporation (LLC), such as Mark Zuckerberg and his wife, Priscilla Chan, used at the end of 2015 to take hold of most of their Facebook stock. Like other individuals and corporations, Zuckerberg and Chan can invest the wealth in their LLC and in other accounts and funds as they like. Their LLC must pay taxes on its income; and, like others, they can use any of their wealth—including that in their LLC or trust—to make charitable gifts when they choose.[13] Most private giving comes from wealth held in such ways; overall, foundation-giving accounts for only about one-fourteenth of all private giving.[14] Privately held wealth is not charitable until it is given to a charity.

This book emphasizes the foundations that follow federal law that, since the major Tax Reform Act of 1969, has distinguished private foundations that chiefly hold, invest, and distribute significant sums of money for charitable purposes, from public charities, which provide services. Public charities often operate their own schools, hospitals, and other institutions, but they can also constitute community foundations, supporting foundations, and religious funds that mainly raise and invest charitable funds. All public charities seek, accept, invest, and distribute new as well as previous gifts to charitable activities, whether those activities are carried out within the organization itself or by a separate entity. The US Internal Revenue Service uses this language to make the distinction: "Private foundations ... typically have a single major source of funding (usually gifts from one family or corporation rather than funding from many sources) and most have as their primary activity the making of grants to other charitable organizations and to individuals, rather than the direct operation of charitable programs."[15] Under federal law, the IRS does identify some public charities, notably community foundations and supporting funds that resemble foundations, and that we also take into consideration in this book: "[P]ublic charities [that operate in a foundation-like manner] ... have an active program of fundraising and receive contributions from many sources, including the general public, governmental agencies, corporations, private foundations, or other public charities, ... or ... actively function in a supporting relationship to one or more existing public charities."[16] Historians take a long view of the history of region in the United States; policy analysts necessarily focus on specific current laws and regulations. Before the Tax Reform Act of 1969 federal law did not make a strong distinction between a foundation and an endowment fund. With the 1969 law, complaints against the abuse of tax-exempt foundations to advance personal and family and narrow political interests won a clearer distinction between a private foundation that makes grants, and an endowed public charity that provides educational or other charitable services. An operating public charity has many constituents—employees determined to advance their professional reputations, students or patients or clients who seek valued services, new donors who expect their gifts to make a difference. All these constituents have reason to complain when endowed funds are misused.

Some foundation donors and managers chafed against the restrictions imposed after 1969; gradually, they have succeeded in reducing the distinction between "foundations" and service-providing public charities. In an influential decision in the late 1980s, the US courts opened the way for a commercial gift fund to qualify as a tax exempt public charity. It had only to show that it was a distinct entity set up to hold and distribute charitable funds, even if it was controlled by a profit-seeking firm.[17] Through all these changes, it remains true that in general US law leaves a foundation free to determine whether to support causes religious or secular, immediate or fundamental, routine or strategic, charitable or philanthropic—and, if donors grant such power to its board, a foundation may shift support from one cause to another at will.

Today, philanthropic foundations in the United States are notable for their independent control and use of significant charitable funds. Foundations use their funds to support both secular and religious causes, and over time, American legislatures and courts have recognized as charitable a wider and wider array of causes. Charitable funds and foundations grew in numbers throughout the nineteenth century, most of them tied closely to a religious cause or a church-affiliated college. General-purpose foundations first appeared at the beginning of the twentieth century; their numbers grew strongly in the 1920s, the 1940s, and the 1950s. The Tax Reform Act of 1969 led to tighter regulation and, for a few years, to significant taxation of foundation assets: as a result, fewer new foundations appeared in the 1970s and 1980s, and foundation assets declined in purchasing power. But from the 1980s philanthropic grantmaking foundations have grown strongly, despite dips following the stock market gyrations of 2000–01 and 2008–09.

Increasingly prominent and assertive during an era in which the incomes of most Americans have failed to grow, foundations have unsurprisingly attracted criticism. Some critics see foundations simply as exemplifying the increasing inequality of wealth in American society: even as more than half of the nation's people struggle to meet the expenses of family life, health crises, or old age, some extremely wealthy people advance their preferred cultural and civil causes through mega-gifts and endowments. Searching for ways to fund both basic services and signature projects, some government officials ask whether private endowments cannot be recruited to the support of government use—or whether there might not be ways to use foundation assets as venture capital to revive a lagging local economy. Ideological and cultural motives also drive criticism. As foundations have taken up more and more diverse purposes, those who object to some foundation-supported causes protest foundation tax privileges.

Champions and critics of foundations often assert that foundations have different effects in different places. Foundations are sometimes seen as the products of distinctive philanthropic cultures that reflect dominant understandings of how to do good in certain metropolitan areas or in a particular part of the nation.[18] Some foundations seek to intervene in debates over national policies viewed in different ways by groups that are stronger in some states than others. Within states and metropolitan areas, foundations concentrate their offices and their giving in selected localities: critics argue that this reality reinforces differences and inequality among neighborhoods.

How valid are such arguments about foundations and regions? Has the geography of American foundations really changed over time? Where there is change, is it significant? Why is it occurring? Do foundations exhibit different cultures, or support work in different fields, in different parts of the nation? Does the proliferation of foundations make a difference

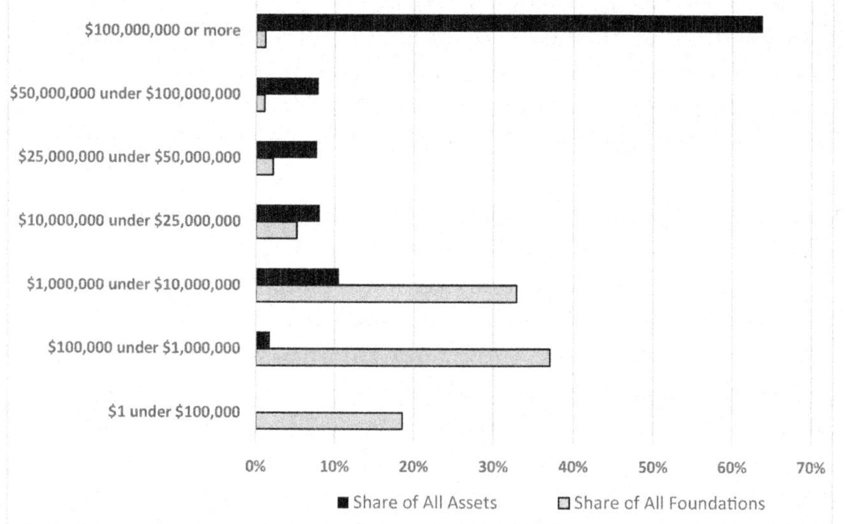

Figure 0.1. Distribution of US Grantmaking Foundations By Asset Size, 2013. *Source:* Calculated from Table 13pf01ta, IRS Statistics of Income Division, July 2013, found at http://www.irs.gov/uac/SOI-Tax-Stats-Domestic-Private-Foundation-and-Charitable-Trust-Statistics.

to the regions, to rural areas,[19] to areas of concentrated poverty? This book offers an initial exploration.

American Foundations in the Second Decade of the Twenty-First Century

American philanthropic and charitable foundations number in the scores of thousands. The Internal Revenue Service count for 2012 (the most recent available as we complete this book) found more than 86,000 foundations: 78,582 independent, 4,218 operating, 2,629 corporate, and 763 community foundations.[20] In addition to the several thousand operating foundations, thousands of substantial endowments, some of them very large, support schools, art museums, libraries, scientific laboratories, and religious institutions in the United States. These funds differ widely in assets: a few hold substantial wealth, but most have under one million dollars. Because there is no practical way to examine all of these funds, and because foundation resources are very unevenly distributed, this book is mostly concerned with the larger funds.

At the high end, in 2012 each of the one hundred largest grantmaking foundations held $721 million or more in assets; altogether, the assets of this one tenth of one percent of all grantmaking foundations amounted to nearly 41 percent of total foundation assets.[21] Another 735 grantmaking foundations held between $100 million and $650 million each, an additional 20 percent of all assets. Altogether, 9 percent of grantmaking foundations held assets of $10 million or more: they accounted for more than 86 percent of the assets of all grantmaking foundations.[22]

The very largest foundations are both concentrated in a few states and widely dispersed. In 2012, twenty-one of the one hundred largest were located in New York, twenty in California, seven in Texas, five in Pennsylvania, and four in Oklahoma. Around the Great Lakes, four operated from Minnesota, three each from Illinois and Michigan, and two each from Indiana and Ohio. In addition to those in New York and Pennsylvania, a number distributed themselves along the East Coast: three in Massachusetts, two in Connecticut, one in New Jersey, two in Maryland, and two in the District of Columbia. Two each in North Carolina and Georgia and one each in Arkansas and Florida joined those in Texas and Oklahoma across the South and the Southwest. Across the Great Plains, the Rockies, and the Pacific Coast, two each in Oregon and Colorado and one each in Nevada and Nebraska joined the large fund totals in California and Washington.

Many of the largest foundations have staffs of ten or more, but the Foundation Center reported in early 2016 that only 730 foundations had staffs of at least five people, while 2,470 had just one to four employees. Each foundation was required by law to give away 5 percent of a moving average of the value of its holdings. By that measure, each of the 835 largest foundations would have given $5 million or more during the year; the largest 39 would each have given between $100 million and more than $1.9 billion. In many states, just a handful of funds hold the lion's share of assets and make the great bulk of all grants, overwhelming the activities of the very large numbers of small funds.

If we focus on the impact that money and effective staff can make, we have to emphasize these big foundations. Some writings about foundations are really only about a still-much-smaller handful of the very largest—about the Rockefeller and Carnegie funds, or about the Ford and the Gates foundations. On occasion, these giant funds stand out and are fair game for critics.[23] Today, a few thousand foundations have quite substantial resources: this book mostly focuses on this larger group.

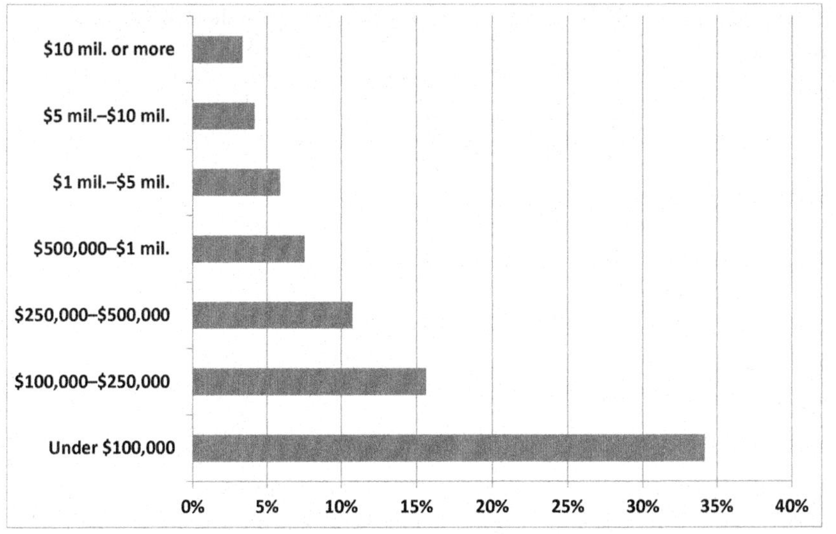

Figure 0.2. Pass-Through Foundations Are Most Commonly Small Foundations. *Source: nccsdataweb.urban.org/kbfiles/638/passThroughFoundations.xls*

If we were to focus on the sheer numbers of individual foundations, we would be examining large numbers of foundations that have small funds and limited expertise, and we would be undertaking a different and more difficult project, one that dealt with small efforts widely dispersed. The *Sesame Street* phrase is apt here: "one of these things is not like the other." The median foundation has less than $1 million in assets; at the 5 percent moving average it is required to spend, on grants and philanthropically engaged staff, less than $50,000 a year. For comparison, the average annual cost of health care insurance for a single family was about $15,000.[24] To do their work of managing assets and making grants, small foundations cannot afford to have their own employees. Many small foundations hold tiny assets: more than one of every three of the very smallest serves a pass-through function, holding gifts only while disbursing them.[25] The amounts given by many smaller foundations exceed the $4,000 in charitable gifts claimed on 6.7 million income tax returns in 2002, but they are orders of magnitude smaller than the distributions from the largest funds. Taken together, the 59 percent of grantmaking foundations that held less than $1 million in 2012 accounted for $12 billion in assets, only 2 percent of grantmaking foundation wealth, less than a third of the assets of the Gates Foundation alone. Foundations that

Table 0.1. Foundations and Educational Endowments $2 Billion or More, by US Region, 2013[26]

Endowed Nonprofit Organizations		Foundations	
New England			
Harvard University (MA)	$32.3		
Yale University (CT)	20.8		
Massachusetts Institute of Technology (MA)	11.0		
Dartmouth College (NH)	3.7		
Brown University (RI)	2.7		
Williams College (MA)	2.0		
Middle Atlantic			
Princeton University (NJ)	18.2	Ford Foundation (NY)	12.3
Columbia University (NY)	8.2	Robert Wood Johnson Foundation (NJ)	10.2
Milton Hershey School (PA)	7.8	Andrew W. Mellon Foundation (NY)	6.2
University of Pennsylvania (PA)	7.7	Bloomberg Philanthropies (NY)	5.4
Cornell University (NY)	4.1	Leona M. and Harry B. Helmsley Charitable Trust (NY)	4.2
University of Pittsburgh (PA)	3.0	William Penn Foundation (PA)	4.1
New York University (NY)	2.9	Rockefeller Foundation (NY)	4.1
Metropolitan Museum of Art (NY)	2.6	Foundation to Promote Open Society (NY)	3.3
Memorial Sloan-Kettering Cancer Center (NY)[27]	2.3	Carnegie Corporation of New York (NY)	3.0
		John Templeton Foundation (PA)	2.6
		New York Community Trust (NY)	2.4
		Richard King Mellon Foundation (PA)	2.3
		The JPB Foundation (NY)	2.3
		The William Penn Foundation (PA)	2.3
		Simons Foundation (NY)	2.2

Table 0.1. *(continued)*

Endowed Nonprofit Organizations		Foundations	
		East North Central	
University of Michigan (MI)	8.4	W. K. Kellogg Foundation (MI)	8.6
Northwestern University (IL)	7.8	Lilly Endowment Inc. (IN)	7.7
University of Notre Dame (IN)	6.8	John D. and Catherine T. MacArthur Foundation (IL)	6.3
University of Chicago (IL)	6.7	Kresge Foundation (MI)	3.5
Ohio State University (OH)	3.1	Charles Stewart Mott Foundation (MI)	2.6
Purdue University (IN)	2.2	The Cleveland Foundation (OH)	2.1
Michigan State University (MI)	2.0	The Chicago Community Trust (IL)	2.1
		West North Central	
Washington University in St. Louis (MO)	5.7	Margaret A. Cargill Foundation (MN)	3.1
University of Minnesota (MN)	2.8	Susan Thompson Buffett Foundation (NE)	2.7
University of Wisconsin Foundation (WI)	2.3	The McKnight Foundation (MN)	2.2
		Greater Kansas City Community Foundation (MO)	2.2
		Ewing Marion Kauffman Foundation (MO)	2.1
		South Atlantic	
Howard Hughes Medical Institute (MD)[28]	18.1	Duke Endowment (NC)	3.4
Duke University (NC)	6.0	Robert W. Woodruff Foundation (GA)	3.1
Emory University (GA)	5.8	Annie E. Casey Foundation (MD)	2.7
University of Virginia (VA)	5.2	John S. and James L. Knight Foundation (FL)	2.4
Johns Hopkins University (MD)	3.0	The Harry and Jeanette Weinberg Foundation (MD)	2.1
University of North Carolina at Chapel Hill & Foundations (NC)	2.4	Wyss Foundation (DC)	2.1

(continued)

Table 0.1. *(continued)*

Endowed Nonprofit Organizations		Foundations	
East South Central			
University of Richmond (VA)	2.0		
Vanderbilt University (TN)	3.7		
West South Central			
University of Texas (Austin) (TX)	9.1	Tulsa Community Foundation (OK)	3.7
Texas A&M University System (TX)[29]	8.1	Walton Family Foundation, Inc. (AR)	2.5
Rice University (TX)	4.8	Charles and Lynn Schusterman Family Foundation (OK)	2.3
		Kimbell Art Foundation (TX)	2.3
Mountain			
Pacific			
Stanford University (CA)	18.7	Bill & Melinda Gates Foundation (WA)	41.3
Kamehameha Schools[30] (HI)	8.1	J. Paul Getty Trust (CA)	11.1
University of Southern California (CA)	3.9	William and Flora Hewlett Foundation (CA)	8.6
University of California, Berkeley (CA)[31]	3.3	David and Lucile Packard Foundation (CA)	6.9
University of California, Los Angeles (CA)[32]	2.6	Gordon and Betty Moore Foundation (CA)	6.4
University of Washington[33] (WA)	2.3	Silicon Valley Community Foundation (CA)	4.7
		California Endowment (CA)	3.7
		Conrad N. Hilton Foundation (CA)	2.4
		Casey Family Programs (WA)	2.1
		James Irvine Foundation (CA)	2.0

held less than $10 million accounted for less than 15 percent of all foundation assets.

Small foundations constitute an interesting social phenomenon. They are important to their donors and they often make a difference to their grantees. As Steven Rathgeb Smith and his colleagues note in this volume, they demonstrate the variety of social, cultural, and religious impulses. But their resources are so small that it is not easy to show that they have a significant impact on local affairs, let alone on the nation as a whole.

Very large foundations are significant, and because their size attracts attention, they are easier to study. The list below shows that large foundations and well-endowed institutions are now widely distributed across the United States. No New England foundation holds $2 billion or more, but that region's considerable number of highly endowed private universities and other institutions rivals the numbers in the Middle Atlantic, Great Lakes, and southeastern states. The South no longer lags far behind in either category, while the Pacific Coast states boast considerably more $2 billion plus foundations than richly endowed private universities. In the Midwest, the Southwest, and the Pacific states, very high endowments are much more likely to be attached to state universities than to their private counterparts.

Why Might Foundations Vary from Place to Place—or Not?

There are both classic and newly asserted economic, legal, religious, and cultural reasons to expect American foundations to vary in numbers, size, purpose, and mode of operation from region to region. There are also reasons to expect that such variations might have decreased in recent decades.

Economy and Wealth

Foundations require concentrated wealth, and wealth has always been distributed very unevenly across the land. Historically, commerce and banking concentrated in the great cities of the Northeastern seaboard, around the Great Lakes, and in a few key river and ocean ports in the West.[34] Historically, agriculture characterized the states of the South, of the Mississippi Valley, and of climate-favored areas elsewhere (Vermont and Upstate New York, the Ohio River Valley, large parts of Michigan and Indiana, California's Central Valley, Oregon's Willamette Valley, and parts of Hawaii). From the end of the Civil War until the 1960s, the South produced little wealth, except in the oil fields of Texas, the real estate booms of Florida, and the processing of select agricultural products—such as tobacco and cotton—into commodities for mass consumption in the Carolinas. Economic conditions have shaped fortunes and political agendas: economic conditions might also be expected to shape philanthropic activity.[35] Despite post–World War II convergence in economic activities and in wealth, inequality among or within regions very likely continues to yield greater disparities in the presence and contributions of foundations.

Over the course of American history, nonprofit organizations have most often been concentrated in relatively well-off, economically complex urbanized areas.[36] For practical reasons, most foundations focus on their home area and locate near the nonprofit institutions they support.[37] Tax-advantaged charitable foundations can give not only for relief of the poor, the distressed, or the underprivileged, but also for causes that are religious, educational, scientific, literary, safety-testing, and cruelty-preventing.[38] We might expect that foundations would support schools, hospitals, and the arts in their home regions, and that foundations committed to particular interpretations of human and civil rights[39] would most likely be found in New York, Chicago, San Francisco, and other cities best known for such commitment.

Religion and Culture

Historically, religious and cultural traditions associated with distinctive approaches to charity and philanthropy have had strong geographic expression across the United States. Peter Dobkin Hall was not the first to see a close relationship between Congregationalists, Presbyterians, Episcopalians, and Quakers—most numerous in New England, the Middle Atlantic, the Great Lakes states, and in the Northwest—and distinctive notions of charity and civic virtue.[40] Writers also discern particular qualities in the religious communities' characteristic of the American South before the Civil War, and argue for the intensification of distinctive Southern religious traits in response to defeat in the Civil War.[41] Catholics, mostly excluded from the American colonies, eschewed both endowments and foundations as they became the nation's largest religious group by the early twentieth century.[42] Jews brought particular charitable traditions, developing them further within the United States. Today, these and many other religious communities are distributed widely and very unevenly across the landscape: their varied ways of preserving belief and community, of raising the next generation, of caring, might well be expected to influence foundations.

Regional religious differences certainly track some long-noted variations among foundations. Presbyterians, Episcopalians, Congregationalists, and other mainline Protestants, who have been among the most prominent creators of philanthropic foundations, are prominent in the North Central states and have a strong presence in the Northeast, around the Great Lakes, and on the West Coast. Evangelical Protestants, who until very recent decades rarely set up foundations, are nearly twice as prevalent in the South as in any other region. In 2000 they exceeded 40 percent of the population in Alabama, Arkansas, and Oklahoma, and also in much of Georgia, Kentucky, north Louisiana, Tennessee, and northern Texas. Catholics have recently begun to make substantial use of foundations. There are more Catholics in the Northeast than all other religious groups combined, but the great waves of European immigration that ended in the 1920s left Catholics concentrated in many industrial areas around the Great Lakes. More recently, Catholic immigrants have often settled in counties on or near the Mexican border, yet in nearly four hundred of the more than a thousand counties of the southern states, Catholics constitute less than one percent of the population. Three-quarters of Utah's residents belong to the Church of Latter-Day Saints, whose members have mostly given through their church and its institutions. Most Jews live in the Northeast, around Cleveland, Detroit, and Chicago, in southern Florida, and in the far Southwest. Jews have been even more inclined than mainstream Protestants to use foundations.[43]

Law and Policy

History launched different parts of the United States on distinctive pathways of law and public policy. We often think of the nation as derived from British political culture, and of American law as developed from the precedents of the English common law. But in New England, early judges and lawmakers saw in the common law more emphasis on community institutions, more acceptance of corporations, and less emphasis on the property rights of male descendants than did their counterparts in New York, Virginia, and most of the South. Hence the New England states—and later Ohio and other places where New Englanders exerted strong influence—were more willing to allow bequests to go to endowments supporting churches, colleges, and libraries rather than to distant nephews.[44] The Confederate states also shared important legal commonalities: their laws supported slavery until they lost the Civil War, then after resisting Reconstruction they enforced legal segregation of African Americans until the 1970s. Southern legal and political systems are said by some to emphasize individualism,[45] by others to empower white male property-owners.

Too often, we forget that the Europeans who conquered and long governed several parts of the United States—Louisiana, much of the Mississippi Valley, and the Southwest—came from the Catholic nations of Spain and France and established legal systems based on civil law. Several recent studies argue that states whose colonial or early settler legal systems derived from English common law still differ systematically from states that started as Spanish, French, or Dutch colonies under civil law. This very general argument engagingly connects the study of economic development within the United States with powerful debates about economic development among nations. "Common law," some hold, "support[s] private market outcomes, whereas civil law seeks to replace such outcomes with state-desired allocations."[46] Particularly relevant to charitable foundations is the related view that the common law tradition offers better security for funds and investors and more autonomy for enterprises and corporations.[47]

An influential analysis in this spirit notes that eighteen states originated in the thirteen British colonies, while Oregon and Washington were initially part of British Canada. Four of the colonies, including New York and New Jersey, had substantial experience of civil law as colonies of the Netherlands and Sweden. As parts of French America, Michigan, Illinois, Indiana, Wisconsin, and Ohio had been under civil law before the Revolution; the same was true of Alabama, Arizona, Arkansas, California, Florida, Louisiana, Mississippi, Missouri, New Mexico, and Texas, which came into the United States from the Spanish and French empires. Settlers brought legal traditions to the other states. Some researchers find that courts are more autonomous, and property rights more secure, in the common law states than in the formerly civil law states.[48]

It is also true that the United States used the considerable powers developed by its federal government during the Civil War to shape the institutions of western territories. As a result, in the states west of the Mississippi, unlike the states of the East Coast, land grant–aided state colleges and universities, state and county hospitals, government-supported agricultural experiment stations and extension services, and national parks and national forest lands have played dominant roles. To the extent that government has done more in the western states, philanthropy has had to do less.

Under American law, legitimate foundation purposes also include "erecting or maintaining public buildings, monuments, or works; lessening the burdens of government . . . [and] defending human and civil rights secured by law."[49] It follows that places that assign fewer tasks to their local governments create fewer opportunities for foundations or other donors. State and local governments draw on widely differing levels of taxable wealth: in 2003, Mississippi, Arkansas, West Virginia, and Montana had total taxable resources per capita of less than $30,000, whereas Delaware, Connecticut, New Jersey, Massachusetts, Wyoming, and Alaska had more than $45,000. One group of states levies taxes at an overall rate of 3.5 percent or less; another group taxes at a level of 6 percent or more.[50] And as Julian Wolpert found in a landmark 1993 study, contributions from donors of all kinds, including foundations, are higher in affluent communities whose governments levy higher taxes.[51]

Reasons to Doubt that Foundations Differ Notably Along Regional Lines

There are reasons to doubt the continuing importance of regional variation among American foundations. Regional differences in the relative importance of different economic activities, and in sheer wealth, declined sharply after World War II. Commercial forces have greatly reduced cultural differences. The increasingly dominant role of the Supreme Court and of the federal government in human rights, health, education, and welfare have made variations among state governments less decisive. Wherever they live, ambitious people seek access to credit, professional reputation, a hearing for their ideas, recognition for their achievements, the opportunity to launch a hit, all on a national and global basis. Some differences persist along all these dimensions. But many problems now appear to be common across the nation: economic inequality, the cost of healthcare, threats to the environment, challenges posed by international trade, and national security. And although many foundations locate near the institutions they support, many have traditionally located in New York, Chicago, and other centers of communication and finance, or in places convenient for their donors or leaders.

As early as 1960, economic geographers were noting changes in the longstanding concentration of manufacturing in the Northeast and around the Great Lakes, and of business and financial services in New York, Philadelphia, Cleveland, and Chicago. Manufacturing was moving south and outside the United States. Business services were becoming more evenly spread across larger cities. Everywhere, agricultural employment was moving toward a tiny fraction of the population. The pyramid-shaped system of cities dominated by New York and Chicago that dated from the 1820s was devolving into a more evenly dispersed network of large, heavily commercial metropolitan areas.[52] During the

1960s, the end of legal racial segregation and the mass adoption of air conditioning reinforced economic changes that were already under way. Southern and western efforts to build great universities and centers for medical and scientific research and the arts pushed the process further. In many ways, the rise of the sunbelt widely celebrated in the 1980s was simply the product of a shift to a much more equal distribution of activities of all kinds.

Claims about the religious, legal, and political sources of regional variation are much debated. Law, politics, religious beliefs, and enthusiasms and ambitions of all kinds clearly shape philanthropy. But *how*, exactly, is difficult to say. Early settlers no doubt influenced early laws, but newcomers brought their own ideas. In many commercial and industrial cities in New England and around the Great Lakes, Catholics outnumbered mainline Protestants by the end of the nineteenth century, building their own institutions and winning positions in city councils, state legislatures, and the courts.[53] In every state the full story is changing and complex: by 2014 the share of the population that claimed to have *no* religious affiliation had risen to 28 percent in the West—and to 19 percent in the South.[54] New York City had been home to 45 percent of US Jews in 1952; by 2000, that share had fallen to just 16 percent.[55]

No doubt, later developments are to some extent the result of dynamics set by the initial selection of legal and organizational pathways. But some paths lead to dead ends or merge into larger streams. Economic convergence can lead to policy convergence. Legislatures and courts change the laws. Rising religious and cultural communities eclipse those that once set standards for emulation and the processes of imitation or institutional isomorphism that lead to the standardization of organizational forms and operations.[56] Once-impressive organizations fade.

The most recent assessment concludes that writing about early southern legal history remains a fragmented enterprise.[57] In the most ambitious effort yet taken to find patterns of variation in state regulation of voluntary associations and nonprofit corporations, Elisabeth Clemens found great variation from state to adjacent state, and much change from year to year.[58] Stanley N. Katz and his associates conclude that "the law of charity should be understood in its relationship, often a collateral one, to developments in the fields of corporations, real and personal property, trusts and wills"—and also in relation to important changes in legal procedures, state laws, and state constitutions.[59]

We have not tried to reconcile possible explanations for regional variation among foundations. We do not see the outlines of a unified field theory of American foundations. The authors of each chapter have, however, had these questions in mind.

Influential discussions of American foundations have advanced several propositions that we recast as questions. Did Andrew Carnegie and John D. Rockefeller create the first foundations in New York and Washington, DC, possibly following examples in Baltimore and Washington? Did foundations once push Eastern initiatives into other American regions? Have distinctive local cultures shaped the philanthropic practices of foundations? Have new, entrepreneurial, technology-based West Coast foundations transformed American philanthropy? More modestly, do American foundations, which account for less than 10 percent of all donations, reinforce distinctive regional patterns of giving?

Some writers see foundations as reinforcing inequality, or even underwriting dynasties;[60] others assert that they can redistribute wealth—or ask them to do so;[61] still others see them as replicating patterns from place to place. Some authors argue that foundations have a comparative advantage over other institutions as social entrepreneurs or institution builders, honest brokers or risk absorbers, or as value conservers. Critics counter that foundations exhibit the disadvantages of insufficiency, particularism, paternalism, and amateurism.[62] Even the richest foundations have insufficient wealth to substitute for modern governments, so it is difficult to see how foundations could make big differences in these ways for ill or for good, but such complaints and expectations deserve close scrutiny.

If foundation giving does have significant effects, foundation locations—as well as the locations of their grantees—might well matter. If foundations support valued institutions—for education, for research, for health, for the arts, for the preservation of religious or cultural values—then places, states, and regions rich in foundations are likely to be rich in such institutions. If foundations can somehow reduce poverty or inequality or racism, or if on the contrary they intensify such maladies, their concentration in some locations could confer advantages or disadvantages that other places will want to examine. If foundations are crucial to sustaining religion or culture or science, those committed to religious, cultural, or scientific enterprises will care where foundations are located. This book seeks to identify the kinds of variations that might be found in foundation characteristics and practices across regions—and also to identify areas in which variations are less important than the commonalities.

The contributors to this volume share a concern with measurement—of resources, of information about the numbers of foundations, about their assets, and about their total giving, by state, county, or zip code. The Foundation Center collects information about grants from a selected set of 1000 of the larger foundations: in preparing this book, all contributors have made use of that data set for the years 2000 and 2005, and found it of some use. In this first chapter, we have examined data from this source and as the notes make clear, many others, to assess current knowledge about differences in foundations from state to state.[63]

Because the Foundation Center data set emphasizes discreet grants without reference to larger programs of giving, uses data from an unspecified set of about a thousand of the larger foundations, and seeks to protect the identities of individual foundations (not easy when a single foundation dominates an entire state, as in Washington, Arkansas, Nebraska, and some other states), its strength is in describing large, general trends. It is a suggestive but incomplete source of information about what foundations are really seeking to accomplish, or about the flow of money across state lines.[64] Information about foundation purposes, or about the ways foundations seek to achieve their purposes, is often difficult to find. Most foundations state their purposes in very general terms—as the law permits, and as makes good sense to boards that wish to preserve their freedom to change purposes from time to time. Some foundations announce broad program objectives, but rarely with great detail about specifics, duration, or resources committed. All the essays in this book go beyond Foundation Center data; each uses varied and distinctive sources.

We *can* say something about the tendencies of foundations in particular places to focus their grants at home or in another direction. We can say something about the fields foundations choose to address. We can offer a variety of perspectives on the signals that foundations seem to send, and can offer some grounded thoughts about how foundation purposes vary from region to region, and how they remain the same regardless of location.

A few foundations have undertaken impressive efforts to evaluate the effectiveness of their giving. But foundations seek to address large, complex, contested fields with limited resources. Most foundation boards are unwilling to divert funds into serious research on the impact of their grants. So while we are learning something about giving strategies that produce results, the available studies do not tell us much about differences in foundation effectiveness from place to place.

Given the complexities—the wide diversity of foundation purposes and approaches, the great variation in foundation roles from one field to another, the large number of pertinent state laws (laws that continue to change from year to year), the lack of adequate sources of data about foundation giving—we have commissioned a diverse range of essays for this volume. All essays make extensive use of the best current data available from the Foundation Center, but the authors have had to recognize the limitations of this and every other data source, and have defined their own foci and developed their own approaches. Several of the essays are based on new data collected mostly in the early 2000s for the purpose. Yet the authors have also worked extensively with one another. The essays on the more easterly regions—by David Hammack on New York, Jessica Elfenbein and Elise Hagesfeld on Baltimore, Elise Hagesfeld and David Hammack on Cleveland, and by Martin Lehfeldt and Jamil Zainaldin on Atlanta and the Southeast—take historical approaches appropriate to clusters of foundations and endowed charities that have long, complicated histories. The essay on Atlanta and the Southeast, by two distinguished scholars and foundation leaders, is one of the first serious efforts to describe the understudied foundations of the South.

The Baltimore and Cleveland essays also seek, in part, to assess recent efforts to use foundations to promote economic development and to improve elementary and secondary education. All authors were very much aware of current interest in what foundations might do to address poverty and economic inequality within their own metropolitan areas; two essays—by Alan Abramson and Stefan Toepler on foundations in the Washington, DC, region and by Heather MacIndoe on metropolitan Chicago—emphasize this question. Peter Frumkin and Heather MacIndoe take the entire state of Texas as their region and ask more comprehensive general questions: what difference do foundations make in the state as a whole? What difference can a state make to its foundations? And how do foundations vary from one part of the state to another? Writing of foundations in Los Angeles, David B. Howard and Helmut K. Anheier ask, in a skeptical spirit, whether foundations are making a measurable difference in that vast city. Are they significant in campaigns to reduce poverty and inequality, or to improve health? Carol J. Silverman and Arleda Martinez show that with regard to foundations Silicon Valley and San Francisco tell a tale of two regions, not one single Bay Area. Steven Rathgeb Smith and his colleagues examine the bifurcated world of Washington State, in which the Bill and Melinda Gates Foundation towers over a lively group of smaller foundations, showing how foundations both have great potential as innovators and face formidable obstacles in promoting social change and policy reform.

This book has come together over a longer span of time than any of us anticipated when we began. As the last of three books produced by the Contributions of Foundations project of the Aspen Institute's Nonprofit Sector and Philanthropy Research Program, it reflects that project's many discussions and debates. As a result, we are confident, this book has a greater unity than most collections of papers.

David C. Hammack is the Hiram C. Haydn Professor of History at Case Western Reserve University. His books include *A Versatile American Institution: The Changing Ideals and Realities of Philanthropic Foundations*; *American Foundations, Globalization, Philanthropy, and Civil Society: Projecting Institutional Logics Abroad* (Indiana University Press); and *Making the Nonprofit Sector in the United States: A Reader* (Indiana University Press).

Notes

1. Influential statements include Christine W. Letts, William Ryan, and Allen Grossman, "Virtuous Capital: What Foundations Can Learn from Venture Capitalists," *Harvard Business Review* 75 (1997): 36–50; Michael E. Porter and Mark R. Kramer, "Philanthropy's New Agenda: Creating Value," *Harvard Business Review* 77 (1999): 121–131; Carl J. Schramm, "Law Outside the Market: The Social Utility of the Private Foundation," *Harvard Journal of Law and Public Policy* 30 (2006): 355; Joel L. Fleishman, *The Foundation: A Great American Secret: How Private Wealth is Changing the World* (New York: Public Affairs, 2009); Mary Ellen S. Capek and Molly Mead, *Effective Philanthropy: Organizational Success through Deep Diversity and Gender Equality* (Cambridge, MA: MIT Press, 2007). For critical responses, see Bruce Sievers, "If Pigs Had Wings," *Foundation News and Commentary* (November–December 1997): 44–46; Stanley N. Katz, "What Does It Mean to Say That Philanthropy is 'Effective'? The Philanthropists' New Clothes," *Proceedings of the American Philosophical Society* 149, no. 2 (2005): 123–31; and Angela M. Eikenberry and Jodie Drapal Kluver, "The Marketization of the Nonprofit Sector: Civil Society at Risk?," *Public Administration Review* 64, no. 2 (2004): 132–40. Others have complained about the purposes to which foundations were putting their resources; an example is Mark Dowie, *American Foundations: An Investigative History* (Cambridge, MA: MIT Press, 2001); for an extended discussion see David C. Hammack and Helmut K. Anheier, *A Versatile American Institution: The Changing Ideals and Realities of Philanthropic Foundations* (Washington, DC: Brookings Institution Press, 2013), Appendix B.

2. On the increase in inequality, see Thomas Piketty and Emmanuel Saez, "Inequality in the Long Run," *Science* 344, no. 6186 (2014): 838–43, and Gabriel Zucman, *The Hidden Wealth of Nations: The Scourge of Tax Havens*, Chicago: University of Chicago Press, 2015). One prominent critique of university endowments is Iowa Senator Charles Grassley, http://www.finance.senate.gov/ranking-members-news/grassley-outlines-interest-in-college-endowments-student

-aid-addresses-colleges-concerns, viewed Oct. 27, 2017; another is Richard Vedder, "Federal Tax Policy Regarding Universities: Endowments and Beyond," *Center for College Affordability and Productivity* (2008).

3. This paragraph makes large claims, supported in some detail in Hammack and Anheier, *A Versatile American Institution*, and in Gareth Jones, *History of the Law of Charity 1532–1827* (Cambridge: Cambridge University Press, 1969). On the limitations English courts can place on foundations, see, for a striking case, Particia L. Garside, *The Conduct of Philanthropy: The William Sutton Trust, 1900–2000* (London: The Athlone Press, 2000).

4. In the 1790s, the Presbyterians of Pennsylvania and New York were making progress in sorting out difficulties that had resulted in part from the pre-Revolution subordination of their denomination to the interests of the Church of England. Denied funds for clergy and the authority to open their own divinity school, Presbyterians had established 150 churches but had found it difficult to educate ministers or to support them in hardscrabble frontier communities or in old age. In 1799 they obtained from Pennsylvania's state legislature a charter for a corporation whose trustees had the authority to accept donations and bequests "for benevolent and pious purposes." Within two years the new fund had gathered some $12,000 in gifts and pledges and was underwriting missions to Native Americans, African Americans, and white settlers in Tennessee and the Carolinas. Soon it was managing real estate in several states, defending property in court, publishing and distributing books, raising funds for theological seminaries in New Jersey and Virginia, subsidizing impoverished congregations, and underwriting travel to Presbyterian assemblies and synods. Closely associated though it was with the institutions of the Presbyterian church in the United States, the Presbyterian "corporation of trustees" exercised distinct responsibilities, with a significant degree of independence from other organs of Presbyterian authority and with a degree of independence from government that Britain would never have permitted. R. Douglas Brackenridge, *The Presbyterian Church (U.S.A.) Foundation: A Bicentennial History* (Louisville, KY: Geneva Press, 1999). Twelve thousand dollars in 1802 is the equivalent of $273,000 in consumer goods or $3 million in unskilled worker compensation in 2014. See "Seven Ways to Compute the Relative Value of a US Dollar Amount—1774 to Present," MeasuringWorth.com, http://www.measuringworth.com/uscompare/result.php?year_source=1802&amount=12000&year_result=2015, viewed Oct. 27, 2017.

5. Richard Magat, *Unlikely Partners: Philanthropic Foundations and the Labor Movement* (Ithaca, NY: Cornell University Press, 1999).

6. For a discussion of this history, see Hammack and Anheier, *A Versatile American Institution*.

7. Helmut K. Anheier and David C. Hammack, *American Foundations: Roles and Contributions* (Washington, DC: Brookings Institution Press, 2010); Hammack and Anheier, *A Versatile American Institution*.

8. In what became an influential 1911 statement, Leonard P. Ayres, the very young leader of the Russell Sage Foundation's Education Department, celebrated "seven great educational foundations" for four qualities: large assets, national or international scope, a very general statement of purpose, and an explicit lack of "religious or ecclesiastical conditions." Leonard P. Ayres, *Seven Great Foundations* (New York: Russell Sage Foundation, 1911), 11–12.

9. American law grants some special privileges to religious institutions, but the same basic laws apply to secular as to religious funds.

10. Rachel Mosher-Williams, Sara Brenner, and Amy Celep, "It's Not Foundation Money but Culture and Talent That Can Change the World," Feb. 10, 2016, https://philanthropy.com/article/Opinion-It-s-Not-Foundation/235257.

11. "Bill, Hillary & Chelsea Clinton Foundation," ProPublica, https://projects.propublica.org/nonprofits/organizations/311580204 (accessed October 27, 2017).

12. Jane Mayer emphasizes the political giving of social welfare organizations in her excellent recent book *Dark Money* (New York: Doubleday, 2016).

13. For discussions of the gift by Zuckerberg and Chan see two articles in the *New Yorker*: John Cassidy, "Mark Zuckerberg and the Rise of Philanthrocapitalism," December 2, 2015 (http://www.newyorker.com/news/john-cassidy/mark-zuckerberg-and-the-rise-of-philanthrocapitalism), and Gillian B. White, "Assessing Mark Zuckerberg's Non-Charity Charity) Dec. 3, 2015 (http://www.theatlantic.com/business/archive/2015/12/assessing-mark-zuckerbergs-non-charity-charity/418719/); also two pieces in the *New York Times*: Jesse Eisinger, "How Mark Zuckerberg's Altruism Helps Himself," December 3, 2015 (http://www.nytimes.com/2015/12/04/business/dealbook/how-mark-zuckerbergs-altruism-helps-himself.html), and Josh Barrow, "Why It's Too Soon to Sour on the Zuckerberg Charity Plan," Dec. 7 (http://www.nytimes.com/2015/12/08/upshot/why-its-too-soon-to-sour-on-the-zuckerberg-charity-plan.html). Important considerations are also raised by Gene Steuerle, "The Zuckerberg Charitable Pledge and Giving from One's Wealth," http://blog.governmentwedeserve.org/2016/01/11/the-zuckerberg-charitable-pledge-and-giving-from-ones-wealth/. All sites accessed on Oct. 27, 2017.

14. The distinctions noted in this paragraph initially eluded even the famous fact checkers at the *New Yorker* in January, 2016; see http://www.newyorker.com/magazine/2016/01/04/what-money-can-buy-profiles-larissa-macfarquhar (accessed October 27, 2017).

15. https://www.irs.gov/charities-non-profits/charitable-organizations/life-cycle-of-a-public-charity-private-foundation (accessed October 27, 2017).

16. https://www.irs.gov/charities-non-profits/charitable-organizations/life-cycle-of-a-public-charity-private-foundation (accessed October 27, 2017).

17. *National Foundation, Inc. v. The United States of America*, 346-85T, (1987), 13 ClsCt 486; https://www.fidelitycharitable.org/docs/Giving-Account-Policy-Guidelines.pdf (accessed October 27, 2017).

18. Peter Dobkin Hall, "Cultures of Trusteeship in the United States," in *Inventing the Nonprofit Sector and Other Essays on Philanthropy, Volunteerism, and Nonprofit Organizations* (Baltimore, MD: The Johns Hopkins University Press, 1992), 135–6; John C. Schneider, "Philanthropic Styles in the United States: Toward a Theory of Regional Differences," *Nonprofit and Voluntary Sector Quarterly* 25 (June, 1996): 190–10.

19. "Baucus Calls on Foundations for More Rural Funding," May 8, 2006, United States Senate Committee on Finance, https://www.finance.senate.gov/ranking-members-news/baucus-calls-on-foundations-for-more-rural-funding (accessed October 27, 2017).

20. "Key Facts on US Foundations 2014 Edition" Foundation Center, http://foundationcenter.org/gainknowledge/research/keyfacts2014/ (accessed October 27, 2017).

21. These numbers include all active grantmaking foundations, including operating foundations, http://foundationcenter.org/findfunders/topfunders/top100assets.html, now available at http://roominginc.org/wp-content/uploads/2014/09/Top-100-funders.pdf (accessed October 27, 2016).

22. The numbers here refer to private or independent foundations that do not operate their own charitable programs. Eleven of the one hundred largest are community foundations (California, Chicago, Cleveland, Columbus, Greater Kansas City, Marin, New York, San Francisco, Silicon Valley, Tulsa), which as public charities are excluded from the data source. Table 1. Domestic Private Foundations: Number and Selected Financial Data, by Type of Foundation and Size of End-of-year Fair Market Value of Total Assets, Tax Year 2012. IRS, Statistics of Income Division, August 2015, http://www.irs.gov/uac/SOI-Tax-Stats-Domestic-Private-Foundation-and-Charitable-Trust-Statistics (accessed October 27, 2017).

23. Some of the most celebrated studies of foundations deal only with the very largest: Horace Coon, *Money to Burn: What the Great American Philanthropic Foundations Do with Their Money* (New York: Longmans, Green, 1938); Waldemar A. Nielsen, *The Big Foundations* (New York: Columbia University Press, 1972); Robert F. Arnove, ed., *Philanthropy and Cultural Imperialism: The Foundations at Home and Abroad* (Boston: G. K. Hall, 1980); Barry D. Karl and Stanley N. Katz,

"The American Private Philanthropic Foundation and the Public Sphere 1890–1930," *Minerva: A Review of Science, Learning and Policy* 19 (1981): 236–70.

24. "Average Family Premium per Enrolled Employee for Employer-Based Health Insurance," Henry J. Kaiser Family Foundation, http://kff.org/other/state-indicator/family-coverage/ (accessed October 27, 2017).

25. IRS data from 2002 analyzed by the National Center for Charitable Statistics; see http://nccsdataweb.urban.org/kbfiles/638/passThroughFoundations.xls.

26. Details of museum assets are from various sources and do not reflect a complete list; hospital finances are complex and we have not identified systematic, comprehensive studies or lists, though such hospitals and hospital systems as Massachusetts General Hospital, the Children's Medical Center of Boston, Children's Healthcare of Atlanta, and the Kaiser Hospitals on the West Coast do seem to have endowments separate from committed retirement funds that might well belong on this chart. We do include the Memorial-Sloan Kettering Cancer Center and the Howard Hughes Medical Institute, which are very similar to operating foundations. University endowment details are from the Center for Measuring University Performance at Arizona State University, *The Top American Research Universities* (Tempe, AZ: The Center, 2014) at https://mup.asu.edu/sites/default/files/mup-2014-top-american-research-universities-annual-report.pdf (accessed October 27, 2017), unless otherwise indicated; details of foundation assets from http://data.foundationcenter.org/#/foundations/all/nationwide/top:assets/list/2013, viewed April 19, 2016. Some college endowments updated to the numbers offered in the *Chronicle of Philanthropy*'s Annual Survey of Charity Endowments, Nov. 18, 2013, available at http://philanthropy.com/factfile/endowment, viewed April 19, 2016.

27. http://philanthropy.com/premium/stats/nonprofit/search.php?category=Arts+and+Cultural+Groups%2C+Public+Broadcasting, viewed April 19, 2016.

28. Howard Hughes Medical Institute Consolidated Financial Statements for the years ended August 31, 2014 and 2013, last accessed April 30, 2016, https://www.hhmi.org/sites/default/files/About/Financials/hhmi-fy2014-audited-statement.pdf.

29. Center for Measuring University Performance at Arizona State University, *The Top American Research Universities*, 66.

30. Kamehameha Schools Report on Financial Activities July 1, 2013–June 30, 2014, http://www.ksbe.edu/assets/annual_reports/KS_Annual_Report_2014.pdf, viewed Oct. 27, 2017.

31. Center for Measuring University Performance (2014), 24.

32. Center for Measuring University Performance (2014), 24.

33. Center for Measuring University Performance (2014), 24.

34. Foundations are likely to have echoed the geographic patterns among business firms. Interbank relationships, for example, long tied banks into tiers, with the banks of small towns linking through deposits and credit relationships with banks in regional capitals, and banks in those capitals linking with money center banks in New York and Chicago. Such relationships were privately arranged before the creation of the Federal Reserve system; since its creation in 1914, Fed branches have to some extent institutionalized such ties. Michael P. Conzen, "The Maturing Urban System in the United States, 1840–1910," *Annals of the Association of American Geographers* 67, no. 1 (1977): 88–108. When bankers and their biggest depositors visited cities in the middle or top tier, they had ready-made connections that could also open doors for their civic, charitable, and philanthropic ambitions.

35. A classic discussion of regional variation in the US economy is Eric Lampard, "The Evolving System of Cities in the United States: Urbanization and Economic Development," in Harvey S. Perloff and Lowdon Wingo Jr., *Issues in Urban Economics* (published for Resources for the Future [Baltimore, MD: Johns Hopkins University Press, 1968), 81–141.

36. Richard D. Brown, "The Emergence of Voluntary Associations in Massachusetts, 1760–1830," *Journal of Voluntary Action Research* II (1973): 64–73; Colin B. Burke, "Nonprofit

History's New Numbers (and the Need for More)," *Nonprofit and Voluntary Sector Quarterly* 30, no. 2 (2001): 174–203.

37. The eighth edition of the *Foundation Directory* (New York: The Foundation Center, 1981), included a list indicating that only one of every four or five foundations "made grants on a regional or national basis," 533–51.

38. https://www.irs.gov/charities-non-profits/charitable-organizations/exempt-purposes-internal-revenue-code-section-501c3, viewed Oct. 27, 2017.

39. See https://www.irs.gov/charities-non-profits/charitable-organizations/exempt-purposes-internal-revenue-code-section-501c3, accessed Oct. 27, 2017, where still other exempt purposes are listed: "lessening neighborhood tensions; eliminating prejudice and discrimination" and "combating community deterioration and juvenile delinquency." There are continual campaigns to redefine the "human and civil rights" that legally constitute "charity" under American law. In the summer of 2015, Charles Koch described his campaign to increase protections for "individual and property rights with equal protection for everyone under the law" and to ensure "free speech and free markets" as seeking to "overcome injustice," just as "the anti-slavery movement, the women's suffrage movement, the civil rights movement" had done. http://www.bloomberg.com/politics/articles/2015-08-04/read-charles-koch-s-speech-to-conservative-mega-donors (accessed October 27, 2017).

40. Hall, "Cultures of Trusteeship in the United States"; see also Schneider, "Philanthropic Styles in the United States."

41. For a review of the literature on this topic, see David C. Hammack, "Nonprofit Organizations, Philanthropy, and Civil Society," in *A Companion to the Gilded Age and Progressive Era*, eds. Christopher McKnight Nichols and Nancy C. Unger (Malden, MA: Wiley-Blackwell, 2016), 215–228.

42. Mary J. Oates, *The Catholic Philanthropic Tradition in America* (Bloomington: Indiana University Press, 1995).

43. Clifford Grammich, *Many Faiths of Many Regions: Continuities and Changes Among Religious Adherents across US Counties*, RAND Labor and Population Working Paper (Santa Monica, CA: RAND Corporation, 2005), 5, 7, 14, 19, 20.

44. Stanley N. Katz, Barry Sullivan, and C. Paul Beach, "Legal Change and Legal Autonomy: Charitable Trusts in New York, 1777–1893," *Law and History Review* 3, no. 1 (1985), emphasizes the difficulties involved in identifying these variations in legal rules and understandings(51–89). Earlier studies include Howard Miller, *The Legal Foundations of American Philanthropy, 1776–1844* (Madison: State Historical Society of Wisconsin, 1961) and Irvin G. Wyllie, "The Search for an American Law of Charity, 1776–1844," *The Mississippi Valley Historical Review* 46, no. 2 (1959): 203–21, which places somewhat less emphasis on "Jeffersonian" politics and more emphasis on varying religious traditions and conflicts. Katz and his colleagues argue that Wyllie and Miller took too limited an approach to understanding legal change.

45. Compare Daniel J. Elazar, *American Federalism: A View From the States* (New York: Thomas Y. Crowell, 1972), with Norman Silber, *A Corporate Form of Freedom: The Emergence of the Modern Nonprofit Sector* (Boulder, CO: Westview Press, 2001).

46. Rafael La Porta, Florencio Lopez-de-Silanes, and Andrei Shleifer, "The Economic Consequences of Legal Origins," *Journal of Economic Literature* 46, no. 2 (2008): 285–322.

47. Porta, Lopez-de-Silanes, and Shleifer, "The Economic Consequences of Legal Origins."

48. Daniel Berkowitz and Karen B. Clay, *The Evolution of a Nation: How Geography and Law Shaped the American States* (Princeton, NJ: Princeton University Press, 2012).

49. https://www.irs.gov/charities-non-profits/charitable-organizations/exempt-purposes-internal-revenue-code-section-501c3 (accessed October 27, 2017).

50. John Mikesell, "Changing State Fiscal Capacity and Tax Effort in an Era of Devolving Government, 1981–2003," *Publius* 37, no. 4 (2007): 532–50.

51. Julian Wolpert, *Patterns of Generosity in America: Who's Holding the Safety Net?* (New York: Twentieth Century Fund, 1993).

52. Harvey S. Perloff, E. S. Dunn Jr., Eric E. Lampard, and R. F. Keith, *Regions, Resources, and Economic Growth* (published for Resources for the Future Baltimore, MD: Johns Hopkins University Press, 1960).

53. Michael McTighe, *A Measure of Success: Protestants and Public Culture in Antebellum Cleveland* (Albany: State University of New York Press, 1994).

54. "Chapter 4: The Shifting Religious Identity of Demographic Groups," PEW Research Center, last modified May 12, 2015, http://www.pewforum.org/2015/05/12/chapter-4-the-shifting-religious-identity-of-demographic-groups/, viewed Oct. 27, 2017.

55. Grammich, *Many Faiths of Many Regions*.

56. Or in the language Paul DiMaggio once used in discussing isomorphism, the "processes of imitation and diffusion" that tend "to make organizations similar to one another are shaped by interorganizational networks"—and in a given time and place the relevant networks may be both multiple and changing. Paul J. DiMaggio, "Comments on 'What Theory is Not'," *Administrative Science Quarterly* 40, no. 3 (1995): 391–97.

57. Warren M. Billings, "Law in the Colonial South," *Journal of Southern History* 73, no. 3 (2007): 603–16.

58. Elisabeth S. Clemens, "The Encounter of Civil Society and the States: Legislation, Law, and Associations 1900–20." National Science Foundation Working Paper SES9911428. http://webcache.googleusercontent.com/search?q=cache:AyFT_rQ5uAgJ:www.ibrarian.net/navon/paper/The_Encounter_of_Civil_Society_and_the_States__Le.pdf%3Fpaperid%3D159070+&cd=3&hl=en&ct=clnk&gl=us, viewed Oct. 27, 2017.

59. Katz et al., "Legal Change and Legal Autonomy," 88.

60. James D. Anderson, *The Education of Blacks in the South, 1860–1935* (Chapel Hill: University of North Carolina Press, 1988); George Marcus and Peter Dobkin Hall, *Lives in Trust: The Fortunes of Dynastic Families in Late Twentieth-Century America* (Boulder, CO: Westview Press, 1992); Mary Anna Culleton Colwell, *Private Foundations and Public Policy: The Political Role of Philanthropy* (New York: Garland, 1993); Sara Diamond, *Roads to Dominion: Right-Wing Movements and Political Power in the United States* (New York: Guilford Press, 1995); Joan Roelofs, *Foundations and Public Policy: The Mask of Pluralism* (Albany: State University of New York Press, 2003).

61. Alan Rabinowitz, *Social Change Philanthropy in America* (New York: Quorum Books, 1990); Susan A. Ostrander, *Money for Change: Social Movement Philanthropy at Haymarket People's Fund* (Philadelphia: Temple University Press, 1995); Julian Wolpert, "Redistributional Effects of America's Private Foundations," in *The Legitimacy of Philanthropic Foundations: United States and European Perspectives*, eds. Kenneth Prewitt, Mattei Dogan, Steven Heydemann, and Stefan Toepler (New York: Russell Sage Foundation, 2006).

62. For an extended discussion, see Hammack and Anheier, *A Versatile American Institution*, Appendix B, on sources.

63. For additional discussion of the Foundation Center data set, see Anheier and Hammack (2010), Appendix A, 403–4. In 2017 the Foundation Center website describes its data on grants as consisting of information from "1,000 of the largest US ... independent, corporate, and grantmaking operating foundations, as well as unrestricted and donor-advised fund grants (when available) for community foundations." It reports information about "domestic and international giving" of this group of 1000 foundations "to organizations by issue, population, and geographic focus." This data set omits "all of the grants" under $10,000. According to the Foundation Center, "[g]iving by these foundations together accounts for more than half of overall US foundation giving each year." The foundation center data set includes information about "the full authorized value of the grant in the year the grant was made, if this information was provided by the foundation," or "the amount paid in the year it was reported." Information about the purposes of grants, the geographic area in which the organizations that

received grants were located, and the population for which the grant was intended, come not from independent analysis, but "from direct reporting of grant-level data to the Foundation Center by foundations, foundation web sites and other public reporting, and from the IRS information returns filed annually by all US foundations." http://data.foundationcenter.org/about.html (accessed October 28, 2017).

64. We also made an effort to use information from Foundation Search, but that source could not provide us with a specific data set—instead, it provides a running report on grants awarded. The running reports can be useful to grant seekers, but because it constitutes neither a defined sample nor a study of the entire universe of all grants by US foundations, we could not use it to establish patterns or trends.

chapter one

NEW YORK FOUNDATIONS

David C. Hammack

New york city remains by far the most important single center of foundation activity in the United States. Even after a relative decline over several decades in numbers, value of grants, and assets, the New York metropolitan region's foundations far surpass those of any other region, and indeed any other state.* New York's foundations remain exceptional in the range of their purposes, in their commitment to national and international initiatives, and in their support of the arts, civil society, public affairs, and the social sciences. Although foundations have grown at a remarkable rate on the West Coast and in parts of the South, the Empire City continues to lead. And because New York continues to house the single largest concentration of big foundations in many fields, it is also home to the nation's largest pools of program officers, subject-area consultants, lawyers, investment managers, accountants, publicists, and other foundation professionals. The Council on Foundations and Independent Sector operate from the Washington, DC, area, but New York remains the base for such key elements of the national foundation infrastructure as the Foundation Center and the Rockefeller Archive Center—which holds records of more than a dozen major foundations, including the Ford Foundation—as well as for key organizations closely allied with foundations in the fields of human rights, the arts, international affairs, and university research.[1]

Large though they are by comparison with foundations elsewhere, New York's foundations are not exempt from the constraints that limit American foundations in general: their resources are small in relation to the fields they seek to address[2] and they are far from unified. Now as in the past, New York's foundations do have certain emphases, but they do not constitute a single force. What Julian Wolpert wrote in 1989 continues to be true: the New York region's "organized philanthropy has little overt coherence, leadership, organizational structure, or visibility ... the vessel has no rudder."[3] In ways that are too often ignored, the foundations of the metropolis continue to be diverse and contentious.

New York foundations and endowments have made significant contributions in many fields. Indeed, New York's foundations played nationally critical roles in establishing the foundation as an organizational resource—a self-governing, long-lasting, if not permanent, fund devoted to purposes very broadly defined as charitable—first as a support for religious, educational, and cultural institutions and causes, and then, from the early twentieth century on, as an open-ended funder of changing groups of institutions and causes. In the first decades of the twentieth century, a celebrated cluster of New York foundations took the lead in building the nation's science-based institutions; unable to continue that role after World War II, New York's funds have helped lead the continuing national effort to keep foundations relevant and effective.

Through its Constitution and the First Amendment, the United States eschewed the ideas of a national church, a national honors list, and a national university, and instead put a premium on the protection of private property. One result has been great and proliferating variety in charities. Over the course of the nineteenth century, sustained and focused giving enabled New York charitable funds to do much to build America's Protestant denominations (evangelical as well as liberal), and to establish nationally prominent colleges, hospitals, libraries, and museums. New York funds continued to support these causes through the first half of the twentieth century, even as some also underwrote notable national and international initiatives in public education, public health, rural development, and social work. As institution builders, the city's funds in these decades underwrote structures vital to medical research and education and to university research in the natural sciences, social sciences, and humanities. In ways that are less widely celebrated, New York funds and endowments also did much to build Jewish organizations in these decades.

In recent decades, most New York City foundations have continued to build institutions and sustain traditions, in a larger and still-growing array of religious and secular communities. Many high-profile New York funds (most famously but by no means exclusively the Ford Foundation) have moved to increase aid, sometimes dramatically, to museums, performance venues, and arts education; to underwrite movements for civil and human rights; to protect the environment; and to improve economic opportunity both in the United States and internationally.

Other forces, and funds located in other parts of the United States, no doubt did more than New York foundations to shape each of these fields, and several of New York's largest and most influential funds owe their origins to other regions, having located in the city chiefly for its centrality in finance and communication. Most New York foundations have had modest aims. New York's foundations have continued to back competing religious communities, competing market- and government-based responses to poverty, and competing ways to improve education or health care. But in the fields emphasized here, New York foundations have contributed decisive impulses of definition or coordination.

Establishing Foundations in New York

New York City's foundations date from the earliest years of America's independence from Britain, and from the beginning they pursued disparate and often rivalrous purposes. By the early decades of the nineteenth century, New York City was home to several of the very largest endowed funds for the support of Protestant denominations, some of the very largest interdenominational Protestant funds, and some of the nation's best-endowed colleges, universities, and arts organizations.[4] Managed by their institutions' boards to contribute to multiple and changing charitable purposes, these funds resembled today's foundations, though they operated within narrower limits. For a century, New York placed more stringent legal controls on a donor's discretion than did Massachusetts and other New England states. When in the late 1880s distant relatives of wealthy donors successfully employed legalities to wrest very large bequests from the New York Public Library and Cornell University, the state's legislature strengthened the rights of donors and allowed the creation of general-purpose foundations. By that time, Pittsburgh's Andrew Carnegie had already launched the philanthropies that built America's distinctive public libraries and evolved into the Carnegie Foundation for the Advancement of Teaching and the more general Carnegie Corporation of New York. And by that time, John D. Rockefeller, who by 1980, like Carnegie, had moved the seat of his business operations to New York by 1880, was already well into his philanthropic career. Carnegie, Rockefeller, and others took advantage of the state's new laws to make New York City the capital of the large, national, general-purpose foundation.

For a hundred years, religion shaped New York philanthropy. In 1817, New York's *Christian Journal and Literary Register* clearly defined the religious and denominational purposes of many early funds: "The Protestant Episcopal Church indeed must have nurseries for Clergymen in theological schools and the means of sending them out as Missionaries, with Bibles, and Prayer Books, and Religious Tracts, or her progress and prosperity will be seriously affected, and her influence confined to a few of the most populous towns."[5] Adherents of the Church of England, wealthy and not so wealthy, taking advantage of royal favoritism during the colonial period, had responded to such calls. Trinity School and King's College, both Anglican, dated from 1710 and 1754 (and benefitted from royal patronage); the Anglican Corporation for the Relief of the Widows and Children of Clergymen in New York received a rare charter in 1769. Following independence and the removal of government support from Church of England, its adherents created the Episcopalian denomination, whose New York members increased support for these charities and funded the creation of many more. By the end of the nineteenth century, Miss Mary A. Edson could leave her million-dollar fortune to twenty-two different Episcopal funds, several of which held considerable endowments. Some of these funds underwrote institutions whose purposes were broadly defined and open to changing interpretation. In addition to Trinity School and Columbia College (successor to King's), Edson's Episcopalian beneficiaries included the General Theological Seminary, the American Church Building Fund, the Cathedral Church of St. John the Divine, the Bible and Common Prayer Book Society, the City Mission Society, the Domestic and Foreign Mission Society, and the Mission for Deaf Mutes. They also included the venerable funds for Aged and Infirm Clergymen and for Indigent Christian Females, Episcopalian Orphanages in New York and Cooperstown, the Adirondack Cottages at Saranac Lake, St. Luke's Hospital, the New York Cancer Hospital, and Women's Hospital.[6]

Presbyterians managed many similar charitable funds and institutions in Philadelphia and Princeton, but in 1818 they organized the "Education Society of the Presbyterian Church in the United States" in New York City, and in the very early 1830s they played a central role in creating the University of the City of New York (now New York University). In 1836, they helped launch Union Theological Seminary in Manhattan.[7] The Methodist Book Concern, which grew large after moving from Philadelphia to New York in 1804, used the considerable sums it earned from the sale of religious materials to aid retired preachers. Combining donations with earned income, by 1844 its value, according to a recent estimate, reached $750,000.[8] An 1884 account added that Daniel Drew—who had once climbed to the top "of the commercial ladder," left "St. Paul's Church, in Fourth Avenue, the Methodist Church at Carmel, Putnam County ... and Drew Theological Seminary" in Madison, New Jersey, as "monuments of his munificence"—died with "next to nothing."[9] New York's nineteenth-century funds most commonly underwrote religious activities, but not in a unifying fashion. Efforts to create interdenominational or nonsectarian Protestant funds proved controversial, and several Protestant denominations built their own endowments in New York.[10] Catholic endowments were conspicuous by their absence; yet by the end of the nineteenth century, land and buildings worth very large sums housed Catholic churches, hospitals, orphanages, clergy, and religious communities.[11] The 1891 Baron de Hirsch Fund for Jewish migrants was the most famous of several early funds for Jewish communal and religious purposes. Like Christians, Jews disagreed among themselves; in the last years of the nineteenth century, New York investment banker Jacob Schiff gave large endowments to Cincinnati's Hebrew Union College (the chief theological school for the Reform movement), to the Conservative Jewish Theological Seminary in New York, and to Harvard University. His most recent biographer sums up Schiff's view: "Reform, a 'healthy liberalism,' saved many Jews from leaving the fold, while Orthodoxy preserved the heritage that nourished Reform."[12]

Protestants also created large, multipurpose interdenominational foundation-like funds, as well as large income-generating buildings in New York City. The American Bible Society, organized in 1816, "secured incorporation . . . in 1841, pursued a new and aggressive policy concerning legacies and annuities after 1848, and amended its charter so that it might 'purchase, take hold and convey or lease certain real estate' in 1852."[13] It invested $300,000 in Bible House in 1853; twenty years later, that building not only housed its printing plant and scores of employees whose annual sales of bibles yielded tens of thousands of dollars, but was also earning rental income "from benevolent societies" of $40,000 annually.[14] The American Tract Society, a less denominational competitor to the Methodist Book Concern, renounced endowment in its early decades, but raised tens of thousands of dollars for investment in the land and the building of Tract House, its own printing and distribution facility, after it consolidated in New York City predecessor entities from the Boston area and other points in the Northeast and moved to a New York City location during the 1820s.[15] In 1895, the Tract Society built one of New York City's tallest new steel-frame skyscrapers in an ultimately unsuccessful effort to shore up its finances.[16] In 1893, John S. Kennedy's nearly $1 million gift of the United Charities Building near Gramercy Park provided more effective underwriting for the (broadly Protestant) Charity Organization Society and many other promoters of self-help for the poor.[17]

Donors to these funds pursued expansive purposes through focused actions. As historian Bertram Wyatt Brown put it, Lewis and Arthur

Tappan and other supporters of the nondenominational funds feared that the Trans-Allegheny West might well be "lost to Catholic, Universalist, anti-Mission Baptist, and other hostile forces." It was in this spirit that they provided key gifts to Oberlin College in Ohio.[18] Congregationalist leader Lyman Beecher endorsed such giving as a way to guard against demagogic irresponsibility: giving through church funds, he insisted, could exert influence "distinct from that of the government, independent of popular suffrage, superior in potency to individual efforts, and competent to enlist and preserve the public opinion on the side of law and order."[19] These funds did not seek to avoid controversy, disagreed among themselves, and had many critics. Denominations also differed on points of doctrine and practice. Before the Civil War, abolitionists complained that the Tract Society's publications avoided direct condemnation of slavery; as northern Protestants grew critical of slavery, southern Baptists, Methodists, and Presbyterians split away from denominational bodies headquartered in New York and Philadelphia. As early as 1831, Mississippi politician and future governor John A. Quitman (born and raised in upstate New York) denounced the "robbery and roguery" of the "stupendous organization of religious societies" that raised money from widows—and sometimes raised critical questions about slavery—from their imposing, well-staffed New York City headquarters.[20]

Donors to hospitals, schools, and libraries also provided substantial funds to support competing priorities, both religious and secular. When his 1868 endowment gave Presbyterian Hospital what was then the largest endowment of any of that denomination's institutions in New York, James Lenox pointed out that other religious communities, including "the Jews, the Germans, the Roman Catholics, and the Episcopalians" had already invested generously in their hospitals.[21] By the 1890s Columbia University (still tied to the Episcopal church) had added to its early college one of the nation's leading collections of endowed professional schools—Medicine (1861), Mines (1863), Architecture (1881), Law (1858), and Education (1889)—and was well into the construction of its impressive Renaissance-inspired campus on Morningside Heights. New York University had similarly added an impressive Bronx campus for its college and for engineering to its older Washington Square facilities, where NYU housed its school of law and its medical connection with the city's Bellevue Hospital. New York, Presbyterian, and Mount Sinai Hospitals were among the nation's best-endowed medical facilities. Also nationally prominent by the end of the century was St. Johns College (a Catholic institution, later Fordham University).

Other nineteenth-century New York institutions reflected commitme to enlightenment ideals rather than religion: the Cooper Union (engine ing and art), Brooklyn's Pratt Institute, and Hoboken's Stevens Institut The names of the technical schools celebrated the names of their founders, as did the New York Public Library, Astor, Lenox and Tilden Foundations (the name under which the New York Public Library was chartered, memorializing founders from 1849, 1870, and 1886).[22] At the end of the century these institutions, along with the Metropolitan Museum of Art and the American Museum of Natural History, were also among the nation's best supported. Although Carnegie Hall, the city's finest concert venue, sought to cover operating costs from ticket sales and rental income rather than from an endowment, it was Andrew Carnegie's 1895 gift that paid for its construction.

It is noteworthy that nonreligious institutions grew in prominence at the end of the nineteenth century, not infrequently through large gifts from people also known for their religious commitments. Morris K. Jesup, now obscure but then one of the city's most prominent philanthropists, was the leading donor to the American Museum of Natural History and its scientific expeditions as well as an important donor to the Metropolitan Museum of Art, the New York Geographical Society, New York's Women's Hospital, Yale University, and Williams College. He also served as treasurer of the John F. Slater Fund "for the industrial education of the Negro," and he personally aided African American churches in the South. During the Civil War he led the US Christian Commission; and later he led and donated large sums to the New York City Mission and Tract Society, to the YMCA, and to Anthony Comstock's Society for the Suppression of Vice.[23] As late as 1908, a well-informed observer could celebrate the New York philanthropy of New Englanders as contributing to "movements for good . . . through the Church, through education, through charity, and for better citizenship"—and also to relieving "starving Ireland and destitute Russia," aiding "education and the moral and industrial uplift of the colored millions of the South," building public libraries and hospitals, bringing to American museums "the most exquisite and inspiring art treasures of Europe," and underwriting far-flung explorations in the interest of science.[24] Other Protestant groups, as well as some Catholics and a number of Jews, could make comparable claims.

Defining their purposes in generous and flexible terms, many of New York City's nineteenth-century religious funds, colleges, hospitals, and arts organizations acted very much like modern foundations. Thanks especially to large gifts from exceptionally wealthy men (and sometimes women, even in an age when women rarely controlled any wealth), New York institutions were amassing impressive endowment wealth as they pursued such conflicting causes as Protestantism and Catholicism, religion and science. Yet to say that many Americans who had made great fortunes placed their foundations in or near New York City is by no means to say that *all* New Yorkers who had made great fortunes created foundations, whether they had launched their successful efforts there or anywhere else. In 1892 more than a third of America's 4,050 millionaires lived the New York City area, but few of them left substantial endowments for charitable purposes. "If only the millionaires of New York would give back to their city and country a small fraction of the wealth which the city and the country have poured into their inflated coffers," wrote Albert Shaw, editor of the prominent *Review of Reviews* (and, as former secretary to the Minneapolis Chamber of Commerce, not a man reflexively hostile to wealth), "many of the darkest problems that now confront and alarm thoughtful and observing men and women would already be half solved."[25]

Large flexible endowments, used to support diverse and changing purposes through religious or somewhat focused cultural institutions, multiplied in New York City over the nineteenth century, but modern foundations, controlled by boards that were free to shift their funds from institution to institution and from field to field, appeared only after the Tilden Will and Cornell bequest imbroglios of the early 1890s prompted change to state law.[26] New York's new law reinforced the city's general financial and communications advantages; Andrew Carnegie and John D. Rockefeller, both of whom operated from New York City rather than their early bases of Pittsburgh and Cleveland, respectively, are only the most famous. The legal change did not motivate these men: by the 1890s, each had already launched substantial initiatives from New York City, including Carnegie's national campaign to create an American system of locally supported public libraries and Rockefeller's multiple campaigns for moral reform and the Baptist Church. Rockefeller's General Education Board dated from 1903 and Carnegie's Foundation for the Advancement of Teaching from 1904; the Rockefeller Foundation began in 1909, and the Carnegie Corporation of New York was established in 1911.

Others came to New York City to manage far-flung businesses and to establish foundations: The Harkness family's Commonwealth Fund had its origin in Cleveland's Standard Oil in 1918; Edward A. Filene brought to New York the part of his Boston retail fortune that created the Twentieth Century Fund (now the Century Foundation) in 1919; and John Markle began to make a fortune in mining and public works in Pennsylvania before establishing the John and Mary R. Markle Foundation Samuel H. Kress started his chain of discount stores in Pennsylvan W. T. Grant launched his chain in New England; they put their fou tions in New York City in 1929 and 1936, respectively. Money for Alfr P. Sloan's foundation (1934) came from Michigan's General Motors; the Andrew W. Mellon Foundation (in New York after 1969, but with key offices there long before) originated in Pittsburgh industry. For several decades, the Duke Endowment for the Carolinas (1924) operated, in considerable part, from offices in New York City. The Ford Foundation followed a long-established pattern when it relocated from Michigan to New York City after World War II.

New Yorkers who had made fortunes at home also created important foundations early in the twentieth century. Two of these have especially strong claims as national pioneers: the Milbank Memorial Fund, first with a general charter, 1906, and the Russell Sage Foundation, first with a broad program as well as a general charter, created by Margaret Olivia Slocum Sage in 1907 with funds from the railroad and financial speculation fortune built by her husband from a New York base. To list only the largest as of 1945, New York was also the place of origin for the fortunes that created the New York (1909) and Surdna (1917) Foundations; several Guggenheim funds (Daniel and Florence, 1925; John Simon, 1925; Murry and Leonie, 1929; and Solomon R., 1937); the John A. Hartford (1929), Clark (1931), Luce (1936), Charles Hayden (1937), Olin (1938), and James (1941) Foundations, and the George F. Baker Charitable Trust (1937).

Foundation donors have often come to New York from other places; the same is true of foundation staffs. The histories of the several Rockefeller and Carnegie foundations, as of the Milbank Memorial Fund, the Russell Sage Foundation, and others, are replete with stories of men and women who came first to a cause or a field of endeavor, and then to a foundation located in New York. The same was also true of those who staffed the city's nineteenth-century religious funds.[27]

Altogether, just before the middle of the twentieth century, nearly half of America's one hundred largest foundations—with reported assets ranging from $10 million to nearly $200 million—clustered in New York City.[28] The city's foundations differed widely in purpose and approach; in many cases one foundation opposed another foundation's aims. Taken as a whole, what did they accomplish? What difference did they make?

The wealthiest and most notable group of New York funds won national prominence between the 1910s and the 1950s as crucial funders of America's new and exceptionally productive research universities and medical centers. The Rockefeller, Carnegie, Milbank Memorial, Russell Sage, Guggenheim, and Twentieth Century funds documented their work in extensive and thoughtful reports.[29] Historians have explored in considerable detail the efforts of these and associated foundations in such fields as the creation of the research medical center,[30] the research university with secure pensions for its faculty,[31] public education,[32] social work,[33] public libraries,[34] public health, and the reform of health care delivery.[35] In these fields, foundation efforts predated significant government funding. And these funds held the largest endowments and the largest share of all foundation assets in the city. They had few rivals elsewhere in the United States, and many rival foundations—most notably perhaps the Julius Rosenwald Fund in Chicago and the Cleveland Foundation—worked closely with them. Opponents of scientific and social research, universal public education, racial equality, and planning (whether urban, regional, or economic), as well as critics of the influence of money in public affairs, objected to the arrogance and influence of metropolitan elites based in New York, even though some of the strongest objections came from other New York funds.[36]

The Rockefeller and Carnegie Foundations, joined after World War II by the Ford Foundation, also played notable and much-debated roles in American philanthropy abroad. Rockefeller and Carnegie had been very significant funders of the League of Nations, of organizations devoted to international cooperation in scientific and medical research, and of public health, welfare, and education. In the 1940s and 1950s the Rockefeller Foundation played a decisive role in the agricultural research behind the so-called green revolution, and was much involved in developing the United Nations headquarters in Manhattan.[37]

Yet it is a mistake to describe the chief foundation-supported international initiatives of the 1920s, 1930s, and 1940s as unified or single-minded. When Rockefeller's China Medical Board built the Peking Union Medical College (PUMC), for example, it was seeking at the same time to advance science and medicine; to add to the prestige of the medical profession; to provide an American competitor to German, French, and Japanese cultural initiatives in East Asia; and to promote Protestant Christianity. When these priorities conflicted and a very effective American leader of the PUMC initiative in Beijing gave less attention to the religious mission, the foundation replaced him.[38]

Moreover, to focus only on the work of broadly mainstream "progressive" funds—whether by praising them, criticizing their limits or mistakes, or damning their efforts altogether—is to misunderstand the

New York City foundation world of the first half of the twentieth c
Many New York foundations continued to adhere to nineteenth-cen
causes. Although the Tract Society and the Methodist Book Concern did eventually move away, other Protestant funds and the American Bible Society remained in New York.[39] When in 1917 the largest Episcopalian fund (for the relief of disabled clergy and their widows and for other denominational purposes) proved uncertain and inadequate, J. P. Morgan and other major donors helped church authorities transform it into a New York–based pension fund operating on insurance principles. In 1906 the Carnegie Foundation for the Advancement of Teaching extended the principle of a retirement fund to professors not tied to a religious denomination, then in 1918 spun that activity off into the Teachers Insurance and Annuity Association (a nonprofit corporation until its quite recent conversion to profit-seeking status).[40] Smaller New York funds continued to underwrite Protestant groups, some of which were affiliated with the Federal Council of Churches located in New York from 1908. This grew into the National Council of Churches in 1950; two years later it moved into new premises near Columbia University and the Union Theological Seminary. Funds devoted to Jewish religious and specifically Jewish communal service also grew, as did the endowments of Jewish universities, hospitals, and other institutions. Catholic endowments, however, lagged. As late as 1946 physical plants constituted 86 percent of the assets of Catholic liberal arts colleges, which "often refer[red] to their 'living endowment' in the form of contributed services of members of the religious orders."[41]

Some of the most prominent general-purpose funds did make cautious and limited, though significant, investments in fields often characterized as liberal, including regional planning, certain approaches to international relations, and the struggle for racial equality.[42] More often, these fields attracted support from smaller funds imbued with religious values, as in the case of the Phelps-Stokes Fund (established in 1911), which focused more directly on African, African American, and Native American concerns. During the 1910s and 1920s the New York Foundation provided some of the most consistent and influential support for the National Association for the Advancement of Colored People (NAACP) and the Urban League.[43] A few small funds embraced frankly activist progressive agendas, funding organizing campaigns, action research, and other activities in support of racial minorities and workers and winning attention that far outweighed their size: the Stern Fund (1936), the William C. Whitney (1937) and Field (1940) Foundations, the Robert Marshall Civil Liberties Trust (funded in 1943), the Emil Schwartzhaupt

Foundation (1950), the New World Foundation (1954), and the Samuel Rubin Foundation. One of the earliest, most liberal, and smallest foundations, the American Fund for Public Service (1922), nicely raises the question of what is and is not a New York City foundation: although it derived from a Wall Street fortune and had headquarters in an office near Union Square on West Thirteenth Street, its founder lived on Cape Cod, incorporated it in Delaware, and appointed an initial board that included several members from Chicago.[44] Other smaller funds, including the JM Foundation of New York (1924) and Smith Richardson Foundation of Westport, Connecticut (1935), were equally passionate and effective in support of conservative movements.[45]

Many notable midcentury New York foundations pushed neither a religious nor a political perspective, nor the construction of new science-based institutions: taking a more modest approach, they committed themselves to particular fields of research and teaching. In this respect, New York stood out for the wide range of fields taken up by its funds. Cleveland might be notable for funds directed to medical research and music and Chicago and Western Michigan for funds concerned with the welfare of farmers and with local institutions in higher education and the arts, but by the third decade of the twentieth century, New York funds were taking up a very wide spectrum of causes. Some of the oldest foundations—Milbank Memorial, Lillia Babbitt Hyde (1924), Markle, John A. Hartford, Josiah Macy, Jr. (1930), and Booth-Ferris[46]—joined the Carnegie Corporation, the Rockefeller Foundation, and the Commonwealth Fund in underwriting research in medicine and public health. Such national medical research funders as the National Foundation for Infantile Paralysis and the American Foundation for the Blind also operated from New York. The Research Corporation (dating from 1912) used patent royalties to fund scientific research; the Chemical Foundation[47] and the Camille and Henry Dreyfus Foundation underwrote research in chemistry. The Engineering and Harry Frank Guggenheim Foundations underwrote engineering research. The Russell Sage, the Laura Spelman Rockefeller Memorial, and the W. T. Grant Foundations supported social science research—joined by the Sloan Foundation's commitment to economics and the Viking (later, Wenner-Gren) Foundation's close engagement with anthropology. Supporting the arts were the Chaloner Prize Foundation (dating to 1890), and the Samuel H. Kress, Julliard Musical, and Solomon R. Guggenheim Foundations, among others. Endowments for the American Academy in Rome were held in its New York foundation.

It is easy to lump together all funds that supported research, medicine, and education, but in fact they often differed significantly among themselves—and not infrequently, the same foundation pursued competing if not conflicting agendas. While the Rockefeller Foundation often moved to raise the research of American universities to world-leading levels, the General Education Board, like the Carnegie Foundation for the Advancement of Teaching, pushed for more inclusive (and less "academic") programs in middle schools and high schools.[48] While the Carnegie Corporation, the Rockefeller Foundation, and the Commonwealth Fund worked to raise the standard of American medical research, disseminate the best research through a hierarchy of hospitals, and raise the prestige and the incomes of well-trained doctors, the Commonwealth Fund also joined the Milbank Memorial Fund, the Russell Sage Foundation, and others in seeking to assure that the best possible medicine would be available to everyone, regardless of location or ability to pay.[49] For decades the Metropolitan Museum of Art, like the Kress Foundation, emphasized the art of Greece, Rome, medieval churches, and the Old Masters; the Museum of Modern Art and the collections that came eventually into the Guggenheim and the Whitney museums promoted art of the twentieth century.

In addition to their early commitment to religion, New York funds continued to underwrite local, and quite traditional institutions. The Winifred Masterson Burke Relief Foundation maintained facilities in White Plains for the "relief of worthy men and women"; in 1951 it became the Burke Rehabilitation Hospital. The Edna McConnell Clark Foundation long aided local youth-serving organizations in Cooperstown and New York City; the Surdna Foundation continued to provide general operating support to "local educational and charitable organizations"; the large Charles Hayden Foundation built settlement houses and camps for boys in New York and Boston; and the James Foundation, also very large, gave to major institutions devoted to liberal Protestantism, education, and social service.[50] For decades, the Murry and Leonie Guggenheim Foundation provided free dental care to tens of thousands of New York City children. A number of other New York funds continued the ancient practice of giving directly to the needy.[51] From 1948 to 1997 the Vincent Astor Foundation concentrated its substantial gifts on institutions Mrs. Brooke Russell Astor considered to be the city's "crown jewels"—the American Museum of Natural History, the Metropolitan Museum of Art, the New York Public Library, the New York Zoological Society, Rockefeller University, and South Street Seaport.[52]

In short, New York's twentieth-century funds varied widely in focus, approach, and commitment. The same was equally true of New York

City's increasingly well-endowed universities and colleges, hospitals and clinics, museums and concert halls. Focusing on the tension between national and local concerns just after the end of this period, in 1989 Julian Wolpert observed that "[p]hilanthropy in New York, more so than in other metropolitan areas, faces conflicting demands as the capital of the international and U.S. donor community as well as a prominent support base for its own immediate region." The evidence Wolpert reviewed indicated that within the region, foundations sought in particular to "sustain the major institutions in the arts, education, and health care." He did detect a shift after the 1970s toward addressing the needs of "minority populations, poverty among the elderly and children, gender concerns, and severe social problems." Despite this shift, he concluded, foundations had "not been an influential voice of the Region's intellectual and moneyed elite on controversial issues of local government policy on homelessness and racial and ethnic disparities in quality of life." And he asked whether the region's foundations were "so diverse" and their resources so limited that they could "only contribute marginally to the solution of the 'big' problems."[53] Yet we should add that several of the large funds that had long underwritten New York institutions did eventually spend out their money and close (including the James, Murray and Leonie Guggenheim, and Vincent Astor foundations), and that others, including Edna McConnell Clark and Surdna, were turning themselves into national leaders in the movement to make foundations more entrepreneurial even as Wolpert wrote.

Twenty-First-Century New York Foundations

The current size of the New York City region's foundation world is evident in a few numbers. More than one hundred twenty New York foundations hold assets of $100 million or more: in the Los Angeles, San Francisco, Chicago, and Houston metropolitan areas, the comparable numbers are between twenty and forty.[54] In 2000, a Foundation Center study concluded that the New York metropolitan area (defined to include the five boroughs of the city itself and three New York state counties to the north, and thus omitting the New York region counties on Long Island and in New Jersey and Connecticut) was home to more than 5,700 active foundations, or just over one in ten US grantmakers. Despite some relative decline, New York City foundations continued to lead the nation: they hold 17 percent of all US foundation assets, and account for 17.5 percent of all foundation giving. With its universities, hospitals, museums, libraries, and national offices, New York has an exceptional concentration of well-funded public charity nonprofits, yet gifts from Manhattan foundations equal 10 percent of total public charity revenue for these organizations (the equivalent number in Philadelphia, Chicago, and Houston is 4 percent, in Los Angeles 5 percent, and in San Francisco 6 percent).[55] And the *growth* of New York City's total foundation giving in the 1990s exceeded that of "all *states* outside of New York." New York City's historic foundations are very well known, but in 2000 almost 40 percent of the metropolitan region's largest foundations were less than ten years old.[56]

Basic numbers also make evident the prominence of New York funds in several fields; a few details indicate their increasing diversity of purpose within each field. Year after year, New York City is home to a full third of the fifty largest US foundations giving abroad or giving to support the study of international affairs. A quarter of all giving by New York area foundations goes to international and foreign activities. No other metropolitan region has a comparable concentration. Together, the Washington, DC, and Baltimore regions house many international donors, but most work with government money or locate near federal offices in hopes of influencing national policy. Los Angeles, Silicon Valley, Massachusetts, and Illinois each have four or five of the leading foundation donors to international affairs: the New York region has more than twenty. New York's international funds range from the long-established Ford and Rockefeller foundations, the Carnegie Corporation of New York, and the Rockefeller Brothers Fund to the Foundation to Promote Open Society, the Open Society Institute, Jennifer and Peter Buffett's NoVo Foundation, and the Deutsche Bank and Pfizer foundations. The announced aims of their grant-making programs in recent years have included raising knowledge of China among the American public, building civil society in Eastern Europe, encouraging economic development in broad terms, and improving life chances for girls from poor families in Africa and parts of Asia. Reinforcing New York's centrality in international grantmaking are smaller funds devoted to improving American perceptions of, and relations with, many particular nations.[57]

With fourteen of the fifty largest foundation donors, the New York City region also leads in funds providing grants to civil rights and social action organizations. San Francisco and Silicon Valley, taken as a single area, follow with a total of eight. The other large donors in these fields are widely scattered, with just three each in Michigan and Washington, DC, and no more than two in any other state. In this field the leading New York foundations range from Ford, Carnegie, Rockefeller, Rockefeller Brothers, and Robert Sterling Clark to the Foundation to Promote Open Society, the Open Society Institute, NoVo, and Overbrook (which describes itself as a "progressive family foundation that supports organizations advancing human rights and conserving the natural environment"[58]). From time to time these funds have expressed concern about the rights of members of racial minorities and (regardless of race) women; those who are gay, lesbian, or transgender; workers; the poor; the mentally ill or limited; and religious dissenters.

New York City is also home to a quarter or more of the fifty largest foundation donors to the arts, each of which gives a steady $10 million to$40 million dollars or more annually. Many of these, including the Ford Foundation, the Foundation to Promote an Open Society, the Andrew W. Mellon Foundation, the Andy Warhol Foundation for the Visual Arts, the William Randolph Hearst Foundation, and the Shubert Foundation, take the entire nation as their area of work, though they give somewhat more within the region than outside. Like foundations in other fields, they vary widely in focus, from Mellon's emphasis on high scholarship to Warhol's support for new artists to Shubert's commitment to legitimate theater. Some of the New York funds active in the arts also pursue strong social agendas, but others emphasize the arts for their own sake. The only other substantial concentration of national funders in the arts is in California, and it involves eight to ten foundations, divided between the Los Angeles region, Silicon Valley, and San Francisco. Many of these, like their one or two counterparts in each of a dozen other states, focus chiefly on building up museums and performance centers in their own communities.[59]

In the field of health, the New York metropolitan region—if we count the three or four large health-funding foundations in nearby New Jersey and Connecticut—also accounts for between a quarter and a third of the fifty largest foundation donors. California's contingent of thirteen in this field is split between Silicon Valley and Los Angeles. Apart from North Carolina's three, no other state is home to more than two. In this field, as in elementary and secondary education, libraries, and international giving, the Bill and Melinda Gates Foundation, located in Seattle, Washington, deploys by far the largest sums given by any single foundation. But Gates has no counterparts in its own region.[60] Among the New York funds concerned with health, several—including Robert Wood Johnson in nearby New Jersey, Rockefeller, Milbank Memorial, and other longstanding funds—have been seeking the general reform of health care. Others narrowly target the care and cure of people afflicted with particular diseases, or manage the charitable distribution of expensive drugs for the "big pharma" companies.

The prominence of the New York region's foundations in higher education helps explain why it is also home to many of that field's key nongovernment institutions. The Social Science Research Council, the social science–supporting Russell Sage and Alfred P. Sloan Foundations, the humanities-leaning American Council of Learned Societies, the art-history supporting Kress Foundation, and the Andrew W. Mellon Foundation (one of the most prominent funders of university research in the humanities and social sciences), all dating from the first few decades of the twentieth century, remain in New York City. Also remaining in the New York region are the foundation-created, now self-sustaining Educational Testing Service (ETS), so important to college, graduate school, and professional school admissions, as well as the Teachers Insurance and Annuity Association (now serving employees of nonprofits as well as professors). Not far from ETS in New Jersey are the graduate student–supporting Woodrow Wilson Foundation, the Institute for International Exchange, and the well-endowed Institute for Advanced Study, all largely funded by foundations.

In elementary and secondary education, public affairs, community improvement, and religion, the New York metropolitan region also has the largest single number of foundations but by a smaller margin, and other states also have notable concentrations of leading donors. In 2011, California matched New York's total of eleven of the fifty largest foundation donors to K–12 education; Texas had six and Colorado had four. Seven New York funds were among the top fifty in religion: they were joined by six from California; four each from Texas, Minnesota, and Michigan; and three in Tennessee.[61] Among the largest New York foundation givers in this field in 2011 were two funds of Protestant origin, the Henry Luce Foundation and the Carnegie Corporation of New York, and three Jewish funds: Regals, Tova, and American Friends of Yeshiva Aish Hatorah. Robert W. Wilson was a major donor to the American Civil Liberties Union (ACLU), the Environmental Defense Fund, the Nature Conservancy, and the New York Public Library, but he also made a multimillion dollar gift to the Catholic Archdiocese of New York.[62] More generally, in 2013 Cardinal Dolan announced that the Archdiocese was launching four endowments, for Catholic schools, parish religious education, new parishes and those that serve the poor, and programs directed toward people in their teens and twenties.[63]

Table 1.1. New York and Other Foundations among the Top Fifty in Giving across Focus Areas, 2011

	Abroad	Internat'l Affairs	Civil Rights	Arts	K–12	Health	Public Affairs	Comm. Improv't	Religion	Total
NY	17	18	14	13	11	12	10	9	7	111
CA	9	8	11	11	11	13	8	5	6	82
MI	2	1	3	2	2	2	5	5	4	26
TX	3	1	2	3	6	2	1	2	4	24
PA	2	2	1	3	1	0	3	5	1	18
MA	2	4	2	1	1	0	1	1	2	14
IL	1	4	2	1	2	2	1	1	0	14
NC	0	0	2	1	1	3	2	3	1	13
GA	2	1	1	1	0	2	1	1	2	11
FL	2	0	1	2	0	2	2	0	2	11
MN	1	0	0	3	0	0	0	3	4	11
AR	1	0	1	2	1	1	2	2	0	10
WA	1	0	2	0	1	1	2	2	0	9
DC	2	1	3	1	0	0	0	0	0	7
OH	0	0	0	0	0	1	2	3	1	7
MO	1	0	0	2	1	0	1	1	1	7
TN	0	0	0	1	1	0	0	2	3	7
CO	0	0	1	0	4	0	0	0	0	5
WI	0	0	1	1	2	0	0	0	1	5
OK	1	0	0	0	0	1	1	0	2	5
NJ	0	0	2	1	0	0	0	0	1	4
CT	0	0	0	0	2	1	1	0	0	4

Source: foundationcenter.org/findfunders/statistics/, accessed in May 2014. In 2017 this data is available at http://data.foundationcenter.org/about.html#api, as indicated in the references to the previous few pages.

New York Approaches to Foundation Philanthropy

Greater New York foundations have become so various that they cannot be said to subscribe to a single regional culture and cannot operate as a unit. Dedicated to disparate purposes, managed by people devoted to distinctive missions, deeply engaged in separate and distinctive worlds of religious faith, practical affairs, the social sciences, the natural sciences, the humanities, and the arts, New York foundations have little in common.

Francie Ostrower documented some notable disparities in a remarkable study of wealthy New York donors at the end of the twentieth century. In a carefully nuanced analysis, she showed that religious commitment mattered greatly to many donors. "For Protestants," she concluded, "religious affiliation was tied to making major donations to a church." Catholics emphasized "giving to schools at the precollege level." Jewish donors gave most strongly to social services, especially through "Jewish-affiliated" federated funds. Some of the wealthiest Jewish donors made their biggest gifts to non-Jewish universities and cultural institutions, she adds, in this way conforming to a general norm. Yet nearly half of these Jewish donors—but none of the leading non-Jewish donors to universities and cultural institutions—also made a very large gift to organizations devoted to "rights, advocacy, and policy."[64] The categories Protestant, Catholic, and Jewish are of course internally complex, and only begin to indicate the elements of New York's diversity.

Ostrower also examined the significance of gender to donors. She began by quoting Kathleen McCarthy's observation that women have "most often turned to nonprofit institutions and reform associations as their primary points of access to public roles." She also notes that traditional roles have given wealthy women direct contact with childrearing, education, and social services, while denying men access to such experience. Wealthy women, she found, were about as likely as men to give to colleges and universities, more likely to give to social welfare organizations (especially those that serve children), and less likely to give to hospitals. She added that religion, ethnicity, education, and other factors also affected women's philanthropy. "The relation of gender to giving and volunteering," she concluded, "may be among the most dynamic" and rapidly changing of all relationships in philanthropy.[65] What was broadly true of wealthy women's recent philanthropy has been true for the larger New York funds created by women. The Milbank Memorial, the Russell Sage Foundation, the Wallace Foundation, and others noted in this chapter owe their existence and their emphasis on public health, social work, social research, and education to their female founders.[66]

In the past forty years, only the largest challenges to their home region have led substantial groups of New York funds to coordinate their activities. The New York City fiscal crisis of the 1980s and the 2008 collapse of the international financial system centered on Wall Street inevitably jolted charitable funds and endowments. Both led a select number of New York foundations to underwrite studies and to convene discussions.[67] The attack on New York's World Trade Center on September 11, 2001, and the flooding caused by Hurricane Sandy in 2011 did induce many New York foundations to make unusual contributions to immediate relief, and also to fund studies and convene discussions. Corporate foundations have not been discussed earlier in this chapter because they did not emerge as distinctive elements of New York philanthropy, but corporate foundations do emphasize gifts to social welfare causes as well as to education. It was corporate foundations, together with corporations, individuals, and those who wished to express solidarity with the metropolis, that provided the bulk of the private funds gathered to relieve suffering after the 9/11 attack and in Hurricane Sandy.[68]

Throughout their history, many foundations located in New York have operated very much in the spirit now celebrated as venture philanthropy; indeed, many donors have located foundations in New York because the city's location at the center of the nation's networks of finance, communication, and publication facilitated close relationships with grantees. As Christine Letts and her associates have argued, and as Steven R. Smith shows in his discussion of the case of Seattle later in this volume, a venture philanthropist works as a partner with its grantees, provides sustained technical and capacity building assistance, and actively helps grantees implement their programs.[69] Venture philanthropy entails a committed, long-term approach to grantmaking, setting clear expectations for performance, sometimes underwriting operating expenses, and requiring grantees to meet performance targets and over time to seek autonomy and sustainability. For a grantee, it can mean that failure to meet a target results in the loss of a funding stream. Some current venture philanthropists have initially, at least, emphasized organizational growth, popularity, and sales of services and goods more than their predecessors, and put less emphasis on redefining the roles of government. But the difference is a matter of degree.

Venture philanthropic qualities have characterized many New York City foundation efforts from the nineteenth century to the present. Because their funds have always been severely limited in relation to their ambitions, foundations have always sought leverage. In the nineteenth century, this was true of Protestant denominations and of bible and tract societies, as well as of colleges, museums, and libraries. Examples of venture philanthropy by the Carnegie Foundation include investments in public libraries that were to be maintained by taxes, in pensions unencumbered by religious tests for college professors that were to be funded by the professors themselves and their schools, and in the Educational Testing Service, which worked with colleges and charged students a fee for taking its college-entrance tests. Rockefeller initiatives that fit the venture philanthropy pattern range from investments in public health programs (to be funded over the long term through taxes), the operations of the modern medical center (to be funded through insurance paid for by patients, employers, and eventually taxes), and in a range of cases ranging from the building of modern, science-based professions (ultimately paid for by fees for professional service and by taxes), the institutions of international standard-setting in science, technology, and public services (funded by industry and government), to the so-called green revolution (funded by government and then by earnings from increased crop production). Sustained commitment, provision of technical assistance, clear performance targets, conditions for grant renewal, and grants for operations as well as programs characterized important grantmaking by the Milbank Memorial, Russell Sage, New York, Commonwealth Fund, Alfred P. Sloan, W. T. Grant, Markle, Daniel and Florence Guggenheim, Josiah Macy, and many other New York foundations of the first half of the twentieth century. In the wake of new restrictions on foundation grantmaking imposed by the Tax Reform Act of 1969, two New York foundation leaders, John Simon of the Taconic Foundation and Lou Winnick of the Ford Foundation, reinvented the program-related investing approach that had been important to nineteenth-century housing reform and early twentieth-century social welfare grantmaking.[70]

Venture philanthropy is typically identified with recent, often high-tech, West Coast fortunes.[71] Yet several of New York City's newly established foundations have also achieved prominence for their support of venture philanthropy or what is often referred to as "impact investing." Expanding on earlier Taconic and Ford initiatives, the F. B. Heron Foundation has further developed and promoted the impact investing approach.[72] The Edna McConnell Clark Foundation restructured procedures to press grantmakers to meet specific performance targets. The Clark Foundation used performance targets to guide the early intervention approach of the Harlem Children's Zone. The younger Robin Hood Foundation only funds the most effective nonprofits, provides substantial technical assistance, and on occasion cancels grants early if it deems grantees to be underperforming. The Acumen Fund, incorporated in 2001, funded by the Rockefeller Foundation, Cisco Systems, and three wealthy individuals, and celebrated in a Harvard Business School case and in the *Stanford Social Innovation Review*, uses the venture approach very broadly as it invests in profit-seeking firms, nongovernmental organizations (NGOs), and social entrepreneurs around the world.[73] Finally, the Bloomberg Philanthropies, in 2012 one of the largest and most influential foundations in the United States, has also engaged in significant venturing. In addition to some notable program-related investments, Bloomberg joined with an investment bank and with governments to adapt the British concept of "social investment bonds" to the financing of services to released prisoners: if recidivism declines, government will share some of the savings with investors who organized and paid for the services.[74]

If there is a characteristic New York version of venture philanthropy, it might embrace the Bloomberg social investment bond approach, the commitment to systematic analysis and wide publication exemplified by the Wallace Foundation's engagement with the problem of leadership in elementary and middle schools, the Milbank Memorial Fund's intensive work with state legislatures seeking ways to improve health policy, the Clark Foundation's examinations of the effectiveness of the social initiatives it has been funding, and the Robert Wood Johnson Foundation's sustained effort to publicize detailed analyses of its interventions in the delivery of health care.[75] The information-rich approach to venturing is, in fact, a New York tradition that dates to the nineteenth-century underwriting of Protestant colleges in Ohio and the West, YMCAs, and public libraries; to the earliest years of several Carnegie and Rockefeller initiatives; and then to the pre–World War II work of the Milbank Memorial, Russell Sage, and Century (which then called itself the Twentieth Century Fund) Foundations.

Foundations can relieve need, separately from government or by supplementing government. Foundations can also act philanthropically, innovating by influencing social perceptions and ways of working, or encouraging original achievement in science, the arts, society, or in policy. And foundations can preserve traditions, protect private assets devoted to public purposes, and promote valued beliefs. Some argue that foundations should emphasize relief of need to such an extent that their chief purpose is to redistribute wealth to the poor. Others insist that foundations should chiefly build institutions, helping them absorb risks and conserve both assets and core values. Still others ask that foundations above all support social entrepreneurship, responding to needs and problems that are beyond the reach of market firms and government agencies.[76]

For more than two hundred years, New York City's foundations have sought to do all these things. Some New York funds have always been among the nation's largest, but they have never had sufficient resources to relieve poverty through direct gifts, and only a minority of the smaller funds have given priority to charity in that sense. New York's most influential funds have acted philanthropically to promote valued beliefs and causes. Religious and broad enlightenment values—sometimes working in concert, sometimes at cross-purposes—dominated through the nineteenth century; scientific and universalistic social goals (not infrequently in high tension with religious purposes and the aspirations of professionals in medicine, science, and education) rose to the fore in the early twentieth century. The range has only grown wider and wider in recent decades. Perhaps because the city is at the nexus of America's financial, communications, marketing, and international linkages, New York's foundations have been remarkable for their successes in building institutions and institutional networks. They have also made very considerable investments in original achievement in a wide and expanding array of fields.

This is a good place to return to the initial point, that much philanthropy that is arranged in New York reflects fortunes and ambitions developed elsewhere. A particularly notable current instance is offered by David H. Koch. In large part through his foundations, David Koch has given very generously to New York institutions over the past twenty years. Through his foundation and directly he has given or pledged $100 million to New York–Presbyterian Hospital, $66.7 million to the Memorial Sloan Kettering Cancer Center, over $26 million to the Hospital for Special Surgery, $20 million for the David H. Koch Dinosaur Wing of the American Museum of Natural History, $65 million to the Metropolitan Museum of Art, and $100 million to the State Theater at Lincoln Center. He is also a passionate believer in free societies, and a major donor to the Cato Institute, the Reason Foundation, and the Americans for Prosperity Foundation; the conservative movement counts his foundation as an important source of support. Koch grew up in Kansas and after his graduation from the Massachusetts Institute of Technology, Kansas was where he saw extraordinary early success in growing the family business. His foundation is located, like those of others in his family, in Wichita.[77] Yet in 2014 *Crain's New York Business* concluded that he was the most reliably connected of all of New York City's leaders, in the sense that his "seniority, participation in transactions and shared board relationships" gave him unsurpassed ability to connect with others who were also highly influential.[78]

Sometimes conservative by one standard or another, sometimes creative, sometimes progressive, often in conflict with one another, sometimes not even located in New York City, New York foundations resist efforts to define them more precisely. New York foundations do generally seek to make good use of the advantages the metropolis offers as a center of finance, of communication, of national and international travel, and of expertise in an astonishingly wide range of fields. New York also has a long tradition as a place that tolerates difference. We might conclude that New York foundations have in common an ambition to use money and the many advantages of a New York location to advance a cause.

David C. Hammack is the Hiram C. Haydn Professor of History at Case Western Reserve University. His books include *A Versatile American Institution: The Changing Ideals and Realities of Philanthropic Foundations*; *American Foundations, Globalization, Philanthropy, and Civil Society: Projecting Institutional Logics Abroad*; and *Making the Nonprofit Sector in the United States: A Reader.*

Notes

* With special thanks to pioneer researcher Julian Wolpert; Steven Lawrence, Loren Renz, and others at the Foundation Center; and to Case Western Reserve University research assistant Yuan Liu.

1. In a thoughtful 1989 essay, Julian Wolpert wrote that the New York region had "a well-deserved reputation as the world and national capital, but also as a generous supporter of an immense variety of local nonprofit services in the arts, education, health, and social services." Julian Wolpert, *Philanthropy in the New York Region: Its Accomplishments, Shortcomings, and Challenges, 1979–89* (New York: New York Regional Association of Grantmakers, 1989), 1.

2. For a general discussion of this point, see the introduction to this book. As Wolpert wrote, in New York (as elsewhere), "[t]he public does not fully appreciate . . . how limited are philanthropy's current resources relative to public sector budgets and how limited are both public and philanthropic allocations relative to the enormity of even local and immediate needs." *Philanthropy in the New York Region*, 19.

3. In 1989, Wolpert wrote that "the lack of apparent coherence and leadership in the philanthropic community severely limits its ability to participate more fully as an active participant in the Region's civic life." *Philanthropy in the New York Region*, 21.

4. For a general overview of nineteenth-century foundations and quasi-foundations, see David C. Hammack and Helmut K. Anheier, *A Versatile American Institution: The Changing Ideals and Realities of Philanthropic Foundations* (Washington, DC: Brookings Institution Press, 2013), chapter 2.

5. Church at Canadaigua, Ontario County, State of New-York, "Protestant Episcopal Church at Canadaigua," *Christian Journal and Literary Register*, no. 1 (January 22, 1817): 14. http://books.google.com/books?id=aagQAAAAIAAJ&dq=The+Christian+Journal,+and+Literary+Register&source=gbs_navlinks_s.

6. Printed record of *Fairchild v. Edson, Appeal from New York Supreme Court First Department, New York Court of Appeals*, 1894.

7. "Address of the Board of Directors of the Presbyterian Education Society to the Christian Public," *Journal of the American Education Society* (November 1831), 153. This document makes clear the challenge facing a historian of foundations: on one page it asserts that the society was "[w]ithout permanent funds, and without chartered privileges of any kind," so that it depended only on current gifts and "must live or die, according as those shall decree by whom it is supported." (154). Yet it goes on to report that what amounts to 38 percent of the parent American Education Society's total income in three months of 1831 came from what apparently were in fact permanent funds: $344.50 from interest on scholarship endowments, $221.72 from dividends and interest on funds, and $135.00 in repayments of loans (168). On New York University, see Edwin G. Burrows and Mike Wallace, *Gotham: A History of New York City* (New York: Oxford University Press, 1998), 531; on Union Theological Seminary, see http://www.utsnyc.edu/about/history-mission/timeline.

8. Richard Carwardine, "Trauma in Methodism: Property, Church Schism, and Sectional Polarization in Antebellum America," in *God and Mammon: Protestants, Money, and the Market,*

1790–1860, ed. Mark A Knoll (New York: Oxford University Press, 2001), 196. By the decades after the Civil War the Methodist Book Concern had become large enough to suffer serious internal fraud; see John Lanahan, *The Era of Frauds in the Methodist Book Concern at New York* (New York: Methodist Book Depository, 1896). Google eBook viewed online at https://books.google.com/books?id=_4USAAAAYAAJ&printsec=frontcover&source=gbs_ge_summary_r&cad=0#v=onepage&q&f=false.

9. Willard W. Glazier, *Peculiarities of American Cities* (Philadelphia: Hubbard Brothers, 1884), 293.

10. On the difficulty of sustaining interdenominational Protestant funds, see Mark A. Noll, *God and Mammon: Protestants, Money, and the Market, 1790–1860* (New York: Oxford University Press, 2001). The 1904 *annual report of the American Baptist Home Mission Society* (New York) reported that six of its "permanent funds" held just under $1.4 million: *Seventy-Second Annual Report of the American Baptist Home Mission Society* (New York: American Baptist Home Mission Society, 1904), 6, https://babel.hathitrust.org/cgi/pt?id=wu.89077047116;view=1up;seq=7. An account of Dutch Reformed funds is included in David D. Demarest, "Educational Institutions, Boards, Missions," in *The Reformed Church in America: Its Origin, Development and Characteristics* (New York: Board of Publication of the Reformed Church in America, 1889), chapter 5, https://ia902605.us.archive.org/1/items/reformedchurchinoodema/reformedchurchinoodema.pdf; the 1922 fifth edition of Charles Edward Corwin, *A Manual of the Reformed Church in America 1628–1922* (New York: Board of Publication and Bible-School Work of the Reformed Church in America, 1922), lists Rutgers University (New Jersey), Union, Hope, and Central colleges (New York, Michigan, and Iowa, respectively), two theological seminaries, several schools in New York City and elsewhere, and a dozen charitable, mission, education, and publication societies as beneficiaries. The manual also notes that the Board of Direction of the Corporation of the Reformed Church in America, incorporated in 1819, had in 1922 "control of the Widows' Fund, the Disabled Ministers' Fund, and as the agent of the General Synod . . . of the professorial endowments, certain scholarships, and other funds" and gave the assets controlled by this Board of Direction as totaling a million dollars or more (98–99).

11. Mary J. Oates, *The Catholic Philanthropic Tradition in America* (Bloomington: Indiana University Press, 1995).

12. Naomi Cohen, *Jacob H. Schiff: A Study in American Jewish Leadership* (Lebanon, NH: University Press of New England, 1999), 100. Orthodox Jews, who had counted the Jewish Theological Seminary as belonging to their community, did not hesitate to object to Schiff's support for the Conservative movement. Arthur A. Goren, *New York Jews and the Quest for Community* (New York: Columbia University Press, 1970) provides a classic analysis of disagreements and tensions among the city's Jewish residents in the first decades of the twentieth century.

13. Peter J. Wosh, *Spreading the Word: The Bible Business in Nineteenth-Century America* (Ithaca, NY: Cornell University Press, 1994), 178.

14. John Francis Richmond, *New York and Its Institutions, 1609–1871* (New York: E. B. Treat, 1872), 122.

15. For the American Bible Society and the American Tract Society, see David Paul Nord, *Faith in Reading: Religious Publishing and the Birth of Mass Media in America* (New York: Oxford University Press, 2004), chapters 4 and 5.

16. As the society stated in the year the building opened, it funded this building by "mortgaging the lot." It added, "[t]here is good reason to hope that the gift of this ground to the Society by its founders will become the means of furnishing an endowment" whose earnings would "supplement the gifts of its members and friends and be a pledge for the execution of any trusts committed to it by legacy or otherwise." Moses King, *King's Photographic Views of New York* (New York, 1895), 326.

17. Page Putnam Miller, "United Charities Building," in *Landmarks of American Women's History* (New York: Oxford University Press, 2003), 68–77. For a contemporary photograph, see King, *Photographic Views*, 571. On September 14, 2014, the *Wall Street Journal* reported that

the three charities that shared ownership (the Community Service Society, the Children's Aid Society, and the New York City Mission) had sold the building for $138 million.

18. The Tappan Brothers made their fortune from the New York City base of R. G. Dun & Co., the pioneer business credit reporting firm. Bertram Wyatt-Brown, *Lewis Tappan and the Evangelical War Against Slavery* (New York: Atheneum, 1971).

19. Lyman Beecher, "A Reformation of Morals Practicable and Indispensable, A Sermon delivered at New Haven on the evening of October 27, 1812," Lyman Beecher, *Sermons Delivered on Various Occasions* (Boston: T. R. Marvin, 1828), 86, quoted in David Sehat, *The Myth of American Religious Freedom* (New York: Oxford University Press, 2010), 58.

20. John Francis Hamtramck Claiborne, *Life and Correspondence of John A. Quitman* (New York: Harper & Brothers, 1860), 109. On conflict over slavery in the Protestant tract societies, see John R. McGivigan, *The War against Pro-Slavery Religion: Abolitionism and the Northern Churches, 1830–1865* (Ithaca, NY: Cornell University Press, 1984) and Anne M. Boylan, *Sunday School: The Formation of an American Institution, 1790–1880* (New Haven: Yale University Press, 1990).

21. *Richmond, New York and Its Institutions*, 364. By the late 1870s, Mount Sinai's assets included buildings valued at more than $350,000, permanent funds of nearly $100,000 or more, and a lease for a large parcel of land on Fifth Avenue at Sixty-Seventh Street for $1 a year. Mount Sinai was already becoming an internationally significant research and teaching hospital. Mount Sinai Hospital, *Annual Report* (New York, 1879), 16.

22. Harry Miller Lydenberg, "A History of the New York Public Library, Chapter XV, Consolidation," *Bulletin of the New York Public Library, Astor, Lenox and Tilden Foundations* 25, no. 1 (1921), 3–38.

23. "Morris Ketchum Jesup," in Henry Hall, *America's Successful Men of Affairs: The City of New York* (New York: New York Tribune, 1895), 351; Winthrop Packard, "The New England Society in the City of New York," *New England Magazine* 37, no. 5 (January 1908), 534–40.

24. Packard, "The New England Society," 543.

25. American Millionaires. The *Tribune*'s List of all Persons in the United States Reputed to be Worth a Million or More," *New York Tribune Monthly* 4 (June 1892). An extensive, systematic historical investigation of a statistically random sample of 124 of the men and women listed in the *Tribune's* 1892 list of millionaires found no evidence of a gift or bequest from more than half; Merle Curti, Judith Green, and Roderick Nash, "Anatomy of Giving: Millionaires in the Late 19th Century," *American Quarterly* 15, no. 3 (Autumn 1963): 416–35. Albert Shaw, "American Millionaires and Their Public Gifts," *American Review of Reviews* 7, no. 37 (February 1893): 60.

26. Barry Sullivan, Stanley N. Katz, and Capt. Paul Beach (1985), "Legal Change and Legal Autonomy: Charitable Trusts in New York, 1777–1893," *Law and History Review* 3, no. 1 (1985): 51–89.

27. Patricia L. Rosenfield, *A World of Giving: Carnegie Corporation of New York, A Century of International Philanthropy* (New York: Public Affairs Books, 2014), provides many examples. Writing of the American Bible Society in the first half of the nineteenth century, Wosh, *Spreading the Word*, notes that "only one-quarter of the forty managers whose origins can be documented grew up in New York City" (39); a larger share came from New England, and nearly a fifth came from overseas.

28. For a discussion of sources, see Appendix A.

29. The Carnegie Foundation for the Advancement of Teaching (from 1906), the Rockefeller Foundation (from 1913; see www.rockefellerfoundation.org/about-us/annual-reports), the Carnegie Corporation of New York (from 1916), and the John Simon Guggenheim Foundation published detailed annual reports. The Russell Sage Foundation's Leonard Ayres and the Carnegie Corporation's Frederick P. Keppel published influential essays on foundations in 1911 and 1930, respectively. Other notable insider accounts include works by Russell Sage's John Glenn, Lillian Brandt, and F. Emerson Andrews (1947), by Rockefeller fund leaders Abraham Flexner (1952),

Raymond D. Fosdick (1952), Dean Rusk (1961), and Warren Weaver (1967); and by Gerald White Johnson (1948) and Adolf A. Berle (1969) on the Twentieth Century Fund.

30. Steven Wheatley, *The Politics of Philanthropy: Abraham Flexner and Medical Education.* (Madison: University of Wisconsin Press, 1988).

31. Ellen Condliffe Lagemann, *Private Power for the Public Good: A History of the Carnegie Foundation for the Advancement of Teaching* (Middletown, CT: Wesleyan University Press, 1983).

32. Pamela Barnhouse Walters and Emily A. Bowman, "Foundations and the Making of Public Education in the United States, 1867–1950," in *American Foundations: Roles and Contributions*, eds. Helmut K. Anheier and David C. Hammack (Washington, DC: Brookings Institution Press, 2010), 31–50.

33. David C. Hammack and Stanton Wheeler, *Social Science in the Making: Essays on the Russell Sage Foundation, 1907–47* (New York: Russell Sage Foundation, 1994), and Wolfgang Bielefeld and Jane Chu, "Foundations and Social Welfare in the 20th Century," in Anheier and Hammack, *American Foundations*, 158–81.

34. George Bobinski, *Carnegie Libraries: Their History and Impact on American Public Library Development* (Chicago: American Library Association, 1969); Abigail A. Van Slyck, *Free to All: Carnegie Libraries and American Culture, 1890–1920* (Chicago: University of Chicago Press, 1998).

35. Daniel M. Fox, "Foundations and Health: Innovation, Marginalisation and Relevance since 1900," in Anheier and Hammack, *American Foundations*, 120–40.

36. For an account emphasizing the progressive agenda of New York and allied foundations in this era, see Olivier Zunz, *Philanthropy in America: A History* (Princeton, NJ: Princeton University Press, 2009). For an overall assessment with extensive references, see Hammack and Anheier, *A Versatile American Institution.*

37. Steven Heydemann with Rebecca Kinsey, "The State and International Philanthropy: The Contribution of American Foundations, 1919–1991," in Anheier and Hammack, *American Foundations*, 205–36.

38. Qiusha Ma, "The Rockefeller Foundation Builds a Johns Hopkins School of Medicine in Asia: The Peking Union Medical College, 1900–1937." PhD diss., Case Western Reserve University, 1995.

39. Protestant funds included the American Missionary Association of the Board of Home Missions of the Congregational Christian Churches, the Jarvie Commonweal Service of the Board of National Missions of the Presbyterian Church, and John D. Rockefeller Jr.'s Sealantic Fund (the last of these largely devoted to the education of Protestant ministers). If we follow the Regional Plan of New York and extend "New York" to Connecticut, the Edward W. Hazen Foundation of Haddam (1925) should be included as a notable supporter of efforts to sustain a significant role for religion—largely Protestant—in higher education, until it ceded this role to the Danforth Foundation in the 1950s. Carnegie's Church Peace Union also pursued its objectives through religious entities, in this case from all religious traditions; in the 1960s, according to Merrimon Cuninggim's *Private Money and Public Service: The Role of Foundations in American Society* ([New York: McGraw-Hill, 1972], 144), the Booth-Ferris Foundation was also underwriting "theological education" as well as other causes. Shelby Harrison and F. Emerson Andrews, *American Foundations for Social Welfare* (New York: Russell Sage Foundation, 1946); Rockefeller Archive Center, "A Guide to the Sealantic Fund Records," http://dimes.rockarch.org/FA265/biohist, viewed October 26, 2017.

40. "Report of the Committee on Church Pension Fund," *Journal of the General Convention of the Protestant Episcopal Church in the United States of America 1919* (1920), 516–21; Church Pension Group Annual Report 2008, https://www.cpg.org/linkservid/15D58845-B798-962A-D55634ACC1DC1872/showMeta/0/?label=Aboutus%2D2008%20Annual%20Report.

41. University of the State of New York, *Bulletin* (1945), 16. By comparison, physical plants accounted for only half of the total assets of all the state's institutions of higher education; a

all assets were in endowment funds (15). https://www.google.com/search?tbm=bks&hl=en&q=%22often+refer+to+their+%E2%80%98living+endowment%E2%80%99+in+the+form+of+contributed+services+of+members+of+the+religious+orders%22+%281945%29 (accessed October 26, 2017).

42. Zunz, *Philanthropy in America*; on regional planning, see Hammack and Wheeler, *Social Science in the Making.*

43. Nancy J. Weiss, "Long-Distance Runners of the Civil Rights Movement: The Contribution of Jews to the NAACP and the National Urban League in the Early Twentieth Century," in *Struggles in the Promised Land: Towards a History of Black-Jewish Relations in the United States,* ed. Jack Salzman (New York: Oxford University Press, 1997), 142; http://nyf.org/files/2013/08/100-Years-Taking-Risks-That-Matter.pdf.

44. Karen Trahan Leathem, "Edith Rosenwald Stern," in *Notable American Women: A Biographical Dictionary,* ed. Susan Ware, vol. 5. (Cambridge, MA: Harvard University Press, 2004), 612–13; Gloria Garrett Samson, *The American Fund for Public Service: Charles Garland and Radical Philanthropy, 1922–41* (Westport, CT: Greenwood, 1996); essays by Susan Ostrander and Robert A. Bothwell in *Foundations for Social Change: Critical Perspectives on Philanthropy and Popular Movements,* ed. Daniel R. Faber and Deborah McCarthy (Lanham, MD: Rowman & Littlefield, 2005); and for the New World Foundation, http://newwf.org/milestones/founding-story/.

45. John J. Miller lists the John M. Olin and Smith Richardson funds as among the most effective contributors to the conservative movement he chronicles in *A Gift of Freedom: How the John M. Olin Foundation Changed America* (New York: Encounter Books, 2006), 7. The other conservative funds listed here were located in Arlington, Virginia; Pittsburgh, Pennsylvania (3); Ann Arbor, Michigan; Wisconsin (2); St. Louis, Missouri; Wichita, Kansas (2); Oklahoma; and southern California.

46. Judith S. Jacobson, *The Greatest Good: A History of the John A. Hartford Foundation* (New York: John A. Hartford Foundation, 1984).

47. Kathryn Steen, "German Chemicals and American Politics, 1919–22," in *The German Chemical Industry in the Twentieth Century,* ed. John E. Lesch (New York: Springer, 2000), 323–45.

48. Walters and Bowman, "Foundations and the Making of Public Education."

49. Fox, "Foundations and Health."

50. For these funds, see the relevant entries in Harrison and Andrews, *American Foundations for Social Welfare* and Cuninggim, *Private Money and Pubic Service.*

51. The Havens Relief Fund Society, the Fur Trade Foundation, the Lillia Babbitt Hyde Foundation, the John B. Pierce Foundation, and the Booth-Ferris Foundation fit this description. Merrimon Cuninggim observed (*Private Money and Public Service,* 150) that the W. Alton Jones, Altman, Robert Sterling Clark, Edward E. Ford, and Ambrose Monell foundations could all be described as making "grants to worthy institutions and charitable agencies" that did not "catch much of the public eye or … take on a distinctive coloration." The John B. Pierce Foundation's distinction lay in its pursuit of traditional aims through research on heating, ventilation, and sanitation—the business of its donor. Harrison and Andrews, *American Foundations for Social Welfare.*

52. John Stinson and Liavon Yurevich, "Summary" and "Historical Note," in "Detailed Description of The Vincent Astor Foundation Records, c1900–1998," Vincent Astor Foundation Records, Manuscripts and Archives Division, The New York Public Library.

53. Wolpert, *Philanthropy in the New York Region,* 9, 13, 16, 17.

54. Data compiled from GuideStar.org, 2013. The endowments of more than six hundred New York region nonprofits, including public charities as well as foundations, exceeded one hundred million dollars. Foundations and public charities located in New Jersey and Connecticut would add to these totals. A similar pattern emerges from the Foundation Center's "Top 100" list of foundations by assets in spring, 2014, reflecting annual report numbers from 2012 and 2013: of that list's seventy funds with assets exceeding one billion dollars or more, fourteen were located in

New York and one in nearby New Jersey; eight were in the Los Angeles area; seven around San Francisco Bay; four in Houston/Galveston; two each in Baltimore, Chicago, Denver, the Detroit area, Indianapolis, Kansas City, Minneapolis, Philadelphia, Pittsburgh, Seattle, and Tulsa; and one in each of another fourteen cities. "Foundation Stats," Foundation Center, accessed May 20, 2014, http://foundationcenter.org/findfunders/topfunders/top100assets.html.

55. Calculated from IRS data in http://nccsweb.urban.org/PubApps/geoSearch.php (accessed May 20, 2014). The Gates Foundation makes an exception of Seattle, where foundation giving is equal to 46 percent of all public charity revenue.

56. New York Metropolitan Area Foundations, "Highlights" (New York: The Foundation Center, 2002).

57. "Top 50 US Foundations Awarding Grants for International Affairs, circa 2011," FC Stats: The Foundation Center's Statistical Information Service (foundationcenter.org/findfunders/statistics/). Viewed May 20, 2011; see also http://data.foundationcenter.org/#/fc1000/subject:international_affairs/all/top:foundations/list/2011, viewed Oct. 26, 2017. A few examples among many include the American Ireland Fund, the Belgian American Educational Foundation, the French-American Foundation, the Kosciuszko Foundation, the Polish Institute of Arts and Sciences of America, and the United States-Japan Foundation.

58. "Top 50 US Foundations Awarding Grants for Civil Rights and Social Action, circa 2011," from FC Stats: The Foundation Center's Statistical Information Service, (foundationcenter.org/findfunders/statistics/), viewed May 20, 2014. The Overbrook Foundation (website), accessed June 25, 2014, http://www.overbrook.org/.

59. "Top 50 US Foundations Awarding Grants for Arts and Culture, circa 2011," (http://data.foundationcenter.org/#/fc1000/subject:arts/all/top:foundations/list/2011), viewed Oct. 26, 2017. Compare "Top 50 US Foundations Awarding Grants for Performing Arts, circa 2011," also from FC Stats.

60. "Top 50 FC 1000 Foundations Awarding Grants for Health, 2011," http://data.foundationcenter.org/#/fc1000/subject:health/all/top:foundations/list/2011. Viewed Oct. 26, 2011.

61. "Top 50 FC 1000 Foundations Awarding Grants for Education, 2011," http://data.foundationcenter.org/#/fc1000/subject:education/all/top:foundations/list/2011, viewed Oct. 26, 2017.

62. http://www.milliondollarlist.org/donors/robert-w-wilson-charitable-trust, viewed May 22, 2014. This site is maintained by the Indiana University Lilly Family School of Philanthropy; see https://philanthropy.iupui.edu/research/million-dollar-list/index.html.

63. "Cardinal Dolan's Column," *Catholic New York*, http://www.archny.org/news-events/columns-and-blogs/cardinal-dolans-column/?i=27815 (accessed January 10, 2013).

64. Francie Ostrower, *Why the Wealthy Give: The Culture of Elite Philanthropy* (Princeton, NJ: Princeton University Press, 1995), 53–64.

65. Ostrower, *Why the Wealthy Give*, 69, 85, and chapter 3 passim.

66. On Russell Sage, see Ruth Crocker, *Mrs. Russell Sage: Women's Activism and Philanthropy in Gilded Age and Progressive Era America* (Bloomington: Indiana University Press, 2006).

67. Charles Brecher and Raymond D. Horton, *Power Failure: New York City Politics and Policy since 1960* (New York: Oxford University Press, 1993); Alan S. Blinder, Andrew W. Loh, and Robert M. Solow, eds., *Rethinking the Financial Crisis* (New York: Russell Sage Foundation, 2012).

68. For an overview of corporate foundation work nationally, see "Key Facts on Corporate Foundations" (New York: Foundation Center, 2012). On 9/11 and Hurricane Sandy, see Rick Schoff, *September 11: The Philanthropic Response* (New York: Foundation Center, 2004), and Steven Lawrence, *Philanthropy and Hurricane Sandy: A Report on the Foundation and Corporate Response* (New York: Foundation Center, 2014).

69. Christine W. Letts, William P. Ryan, and Allen Grossman, *High Performance Nonprofit Organizations: Managing Upstream for Greater Impact* (New York: Wiley, 1999). Steven Smith's suggestions for these pages were very helpful.

70. *New Options in the Philanthropic Process: A Ford Foundation Statement of Policy,* New York, 1968, quoted at https://www.missioninvestors.org/system/files/tools/history-of-pris-ford-foundation.pdf; see Hammack and Wheeler, *Social Science in the Making.*

71. Celebrated examples include Seattle's Social Venture Partners (socialventurepartners.org), San Francisco's Roberts Enterprise Development Foundation (redf.org), and Silicon Valley's Skoll Foundation (skollfoundation.org) and Omidyar Network (omidyar.com).

72. Clara Miller, "The World Has Changed and So Must We," in Federal Reserve Bank of San Francisco and Low Income Investment Fund, *Investing in What Works for America's Communities* (San Francisco: Federal Reserve Bank, 2012), 226–35.

73. Alnoor Ebrahim and V. Kasturi Rangan. "Acumen Fund: Measurement in Impact Investing (A)." Harvard Business School Case 310-011, September 2009. (Revised May 2011); Hima Batavia, Justin Chakma, Hassan Masum, & Peter Singer, "Market-Minded Development," Stanford Social Innovation Review, Winter 2011, https://ssir.org/articles/entry/market-minded_development, viewed Oct. 26, 2017.

74. For example, Bloomberg Philanthropies invested five million dollars in Little Sun, a profit-seeking producer of solar-powered lamps for sub-Saharan Africa ("Bloomberg Philanthropies Makes $5 Million Impact Investment in Little Sun, Creators of Solar-Powered Lamps Delivering Light to Off-Grid Populations in Africa," Bloomberg Philanthropies, April 23, 2014, http://www.bloomberg.org/press/releases/bloomberg-philanthropies-makes-5-million-impact-investment-little-sun-creators-solar-powered-lamps-delivering-light-grid-populations-africa/). In a social impact bond effort, Bloomberg collaborated with the Goldman Sachs investment bank, the Manpower Demonstration Research Corporation (MDRC) nonprofit research and evaluation think tank, and two nonprofits that aid adults leaving Rikers Island, a New York City prison. Goldman Sachs loaned $9.6 million to MDRC, which in turn selects and supervises nonprofits to work with ex-prisoners. Bloomberg Philanthropies is guaranteeing $7.4 million of the loan; if the recidivism rate falls by 10 percent, City of New York funds will repay the loan; if the recidivism rate falls further (saving money that would otherwise have been spent on imprisonment), the bank will make a profit (Caroline Preston, "Getting Back More Than a Warm Feeling," *New York Times,* Nov. 8, 2012), available at http://www.socialimpactexchange.org/sites/www.socialimpactexchange.org/files/NY%20Times_ABLE_Getting%20Back%20More%20Than%20a%20Warm%20Feeling.pdf, viewed Oct. 26, 2017.

75. See wallacefoundation.org/; on R. W. Johnson, see James R. Knickman and Stephen L. Isaacs, "The Robert Wood Johnson Foundation's Efforts to Improve Health and Health Care for All Americans," in Anheier and Hammack, *American Foundations;* on Milbank, see Fox, "Foundations and Health"; emcf.org.

76. David C. Hammack and Helmut K. Anheier, "Foundations in the United States," chapter 1 in Hammack and Anheier, *A Versatile American Institution.*

77. Jane Mayer, *Dark Money: The Hidden History of the Billionaires Behind the Rise of the Radical Right* (New York: Doubleday, 2016), discusses the philanthropy of David Koch (147ff.).

78. http://www.kochfamilyfoundations.org/FoundationsDHK.asp; Miller, *A Gift of Freedom;* Crain's New York Business, "Crain's Most Connected New Yorkers: David H. Koch," accessed October 4, 2017, http://mycrains.crainsnewyork.com/most-connected/public/profiles/david-h-koch/reliability.

chapter two

PHILANTHROPIC FUNDS IN BALTIMORE

Jessica I. Elfenbein and Elise C. Hagesfeld

ENDOWMENTS, FEDERATED GIVING ORGANIZATIONS, AND foundations are all methods of creating sustainable, independently managed financial support for charitable purposes. Baltimore's history is rich with a multiplicity of funds that support the philanthropic and charitable activities of its citizens, from the creation of landmark institutions like the Johns Hopkins University (JHU) to the progressive agenda of the Baltimore Alliance of Charitable and Social Agencies, to the particular purposes of corporate and family foundations.

Baltimoreans' philanthropic efforts have expressed themselves in four overlapping phases. From the early nineteenth century through the Civil War period, wealthy donors provided substantial endowments for individual institutions that functioned like modern supporting foundations. These donations created the financial underpinnings of the Peabody Institute and JHU, which helped to shape the fabric of the city itself. In the period from the 1880s through the early twentieth century, the new scientific philanthropy began to express itself through Baltimore's active Charity Organization Society. In the 1920s, the Baltimore Alliance of Social and Charitable Agencies, the Associated Jewish Charities, and Catholic Charities helped lay the groundwork for the federated charity movement. These organizations functioned to some degree like the modern community foundation—meeting community needs and creating greater impact by aggregating multiple smaller donations for grantmaking. The modern philanthropic foundation, including family, corporate, and community foundations, took hold in Baltimore only after World War II. This chapter examines philanthropic funds in part to illustrate the development of charitable forms and organizations unique to Baltimore. It also helps to demonstrate how individuals and institutions in Charm City pioneered new forms of philanthropic giving and provided a training ground for individuals and institutions which rose to national prominence in the foundation world.

Baltimore's endowed funds have most often supported particular local purposes, frequently in a distinguished fashion. Donors gave to advance secular and religious causes to which they were deeply committed. By the late nineteenth century, the city's millionaires were unusually numerous and generous.[1] One hundred years later, as Baltimore became largely a branch office town, civic leaders undertook an economic development campaign to attract philanthropic foundations with national or international portfolios, including the the Annie E. Casey Foundation and George Soros' Open Society Institute.

The Baltimore region has a distinctive and noteworthy philanthropic tradition, including the creation of JHU, the Enoch Pratt Free Library, the Peabody Institute, the Sheppard-Pratt Hospital, the Walters Gallery, the Baltimore Museum of Art, the Associated Jewish Community Federation of Baltimore, The Harry and Jeanette Weinberg Foundation, and, more recently Michael Bloomberg's extraordinary additions to the resources of JHU.[2] It also includes notable milestones in the histories of Episcopalians, Methodists, Quakers, Unitarians, Catholics, and Jews. Over time, Baltimore's philanthropic funds have emphasized specific purposes, especially education, health care, social services, and economic development. The funds have encouraged collaboration, public and private partnerships, community outreach, and other creative strategies intended to improve social and economic life in the city. Like every locale, Baltimore has place-specific attributes. Although European and African settlement began in 1729, Baltimore began to grow only after the American Revolution. With its harbor on the Chesapeake Bay and the enterprise that made the Baltimore and Ohio (B & O) one of the nation's first valuable railroads, Baltimore became an important commercial center and saw spectacular growth from 1830 to 1880. As a city with a kind of schizophrenia about region, it developed northern industries with a special affinity for southern markets. In the characteristic fashion of important market cities everywhere, Baltimore honored the views of those who contributed to its prosperity, including Quakers and Unitarians, even as it was friendly to the culture of its most important customers in the South. For much of the nineteenth century, the railroad was *the* determining factor in the creation of the fortunes that ultimately produced philanthropic activity. Maryland's location as a border state, Baltimore's prominence as a major hub for free and enslaved blacks in the period before the Civil War, and its reputation afterward as a city with strong African American culture, also explain some of the city's philanthropy.

Baltimore's early religious diversity resembled that of Philadelphia. In 1789 it became home to the first Catholic bishop in the United States, and prior to 1860, it hosted strong Episcopalian, Presbyterian, Baptist, Methodist, Quaker, and Jewish communities. Recognizing the deep local divisions over race, both before and after the Civil War, philanthropy played a role in constructing largely segregated arrangements in health care, education, and social welfare. In the later part of the twentieth century and in the early twenty-first century, philanthropic efforts in Baltimore have increasingly focused on addressing those deep divisions in the city's population and the resulting gaps in economic, social, and physical well-being. Through modern independent, family, corporate, and community foundations, philanthropists today seek ways to respond to the needs of Baltimore and its citizens by supporting economic development, cultural enrichment, social service innovation, and a multiplicity of other special purposes.

Early Nineteenth-Century Philanthropists and Endowed Institutions

The most famous nineteenth-century Baltimore philanthropy was the work of such donors as George Peabody, Johns Hopkins, Enoch Pratt, and Mary Elizabeth Garrett, and of extraordinary institutional leaders, including Daniel Coit Gilman, John M. Glenn, Mary Richmond, and Henrietta Szold. Through the colleges, hospitals, arts, and social service organizations they endowed and led, these philanthropists set the precedent for later generations.[3] Endowed institutions functioned in much the same way that a supporting foundation might today: then as now, each donation provided both sustaining funds and public awareness, encouraging others to add their support. A healthy endowment signaled that regardless of how new or innovative the institution, it was likely to continue for a long time to come.

Johns Hopkins created a new model for higher education in the United States with his large endowment of JHU: a comprehensive research university, possessed of sufficient assets to underwrite research as well as teaching, and able to shift resources from one field to another as knowledge grew. At JHU, Daniel Coit Gilman was a key leader in the creation of the research university, an institutional form that would spread across the country. Gilman, along with John M. Glenn, Mary Richmond, and Henrietta Szold, also helped create modern social service fund-raising and service-delivery systems. Szold applied what she had learned in Baltimore's remarkable Jewish community to contribute to both the development of

Reform Judaism in the United States and the creation of Hadassah in 1912, the Women's Zionist Organization of America. Baltimore's early philanthropists created innovative institutions, convened networks of interested organizations and individuals, collected and disseminated information about community priorities, and designed systems to improve society, often making their vision a reality. In many ways, they functioned like modern foundations, investing in sometimes specific, sometimes broad initiatives in their own community that would perpetuate their values into the future.

George Peabody was not a native Marylander; however, his gifts provided a model for future giving in Baltimore and throughout the United States. Born in 1795 in Danvers, Massachusetts, Peabody's philanthropy was remarkable in many ways: his giving was not religiously motivated; he was especially devoted to communities that were formative for him—including his childhood home and Baltimore, where "he made his money"; and, finally, Peabody had a powerful-yet-simple desire to "be useful to mankind."[4] His interests were broad: education, science, and safe, affordable, and decent housing for working-class people. Peabody lived in Baltimore for more than two decades, from 1815 to 1837, while he worked in partnership with Elisha Riggs, a native Marylander, with whom he formed a prosperous trading house that provided his first fortune. In describing his Baltimore connections, Peabody explained: "I have ever felt as I now feel, and as I am sure I shall ever feel—an adopted son of Maryland, and proud of my citizenship. . . . The early history of my connection with Baltimore . . . will make me feel a great interest in her prosperity, and consequently in the success of those institutions which must always have a strong influence on the welfare and happiness of her citizens."[5] From Baltimore, Peabody left for London where he opened one of the first American financial firms. Using his vast European commercial contacts, he expanded booming American companies, such as Robert Garrett and Company, a Baltimore firm, and started the company that would later become the famed financial House of Morgan.[6]

Although Peabody did not return to the States for sixteen years, he kept abreast of major developments in Baltimore, and knew that the city's "cultural and educational development had not kept pace with her remarkable commercial and economic growth." Beginning in 1851, he seriously considered what he might do to address that situation. Following a visit from prominent Baltimorean Reverdy Johnson and James Watson Webb, a New York journalist and diplomat, Peabody ratcheted up his gifts to Baltimore in the mid-1850s. He shared with Johnson and Webb his hope for creating an educational institution in Baltimore and sought their advice. Johnson returned to Baltimore, carrying Peabody's plan to John Pendleton Kennedy—who became one of the chief promoters of the Peabody Institute in Baltimore. After his talks with Johnson, Kennedy wrote in his diary, "I will endeavor to plan something on a munificent scale which may serve to educate a large number of students in the most useful arts and sciences."[7]

In 1856, when Peabody had "relished the accumulation of wealth and its attendant power and influence," yet "grown weary of riches and material possessions," he made his first trip back to the United States after an absence of almost two decades.[8] Removed from the day-to-day management of his business, he began to distribute his enormous wealth. Ultimately, Peabody's lifetime philanthropies totaled more than $7 million, distributed both in Europe and the United States.[9] Unlike many before him, Peabody's gifts were not made in the form of bequests to be given after his death. Interested in seeing his philanthropy actualized during his lifetime, he gave gifts while he was alive, presaging the philanthropy that would later be practiced by donors like Mary Elizabeth Garrett, Julius Rosenwald, and George Soros.[10]

The purpose of Peabody's 1856 visit was to gather prominent Baltimoreans, including John Pendleton Kennedy, Reverdy Johnson, and Charles James Madison, to form a board of trustees for the Peabody Institute. Peabody himself imagined a library, a music academy, a lecture series, an art gallery, and public classes, especially catering to children in the city schools. The trustees were charged with implementing his vision, realized in 1857 when Peabody gave a remarkable $300,000 gift to establish the Peabody Institute. In today's dollars, the Peabody Institute gift would be worth over $8 million.[11]

Though Baltimore's Peabody Institute was shaped by George Peabody's vision, it was his trustees who executed the plan. In making his decision to create the Peabody Institute, he considered that there were people who were as ambitious to ameliorate poverty and suffering as he had been to accumulate his riches. He assembled a group of these men and entrusted to them the business of investing his money in social and charitable purposes to "accomplish the greatest good of humanity." After turning the burden of charitable management over to his trustees, Peabody described feeling that "there was a higher pleasure and a greater happiness than accumulating money, and that was derived from giving it for good and humane purposes."[12]

It took a full decade for the institute to open. First the financial panic of 1857 halted the project. Then, the trustees themselves were paralyzed by their divided loyalties during the Civil War. At its opening in 1867, the Peabody Institute featured a library, courses of lectures, an academy of music, an art gallery, and student prizes. It was a major cultural achievement of its time.[13] Baltimore school children had the day off from school and the international press covered the event, which Peabody himself attended.

The gift of the Peabody Institute paralleled James Smithson's gift toward what became America's national museum, the Smithsonian; Stephen Girard's gift of Girard College, an orphanage and school for boys in Philadelphia; and the endowment of the Boston Public Library by Joshua Bates. Even relative to these, the Peabody Institute was "grander in its original design than any previous benefaction in America." By 1869, two years after its opening, Peabody's contributions to the institute totaled $1.4 million. As importantly, the Peabody Institute became the root of other great benefactions to Baltimore, including the Enoch Pratt Free Library and JHU.[14] Today, the Peabody Institute is part of JHU and is considered the first music conservatory founded in the United States.

Meanwhile, just as the Peabody Institute opened in Baltimore, George Peabody was making an even larger and more significant gift. A northerner, he was concerned about the plight of the South after the Civil War. On February 8, 1867, he founded a new type of philanthropy in the Peabody Fund for Southern Education to reflect his awareness of that region's enormous need for improved education. Peabody's education fund aimed to reconcile the "nominally reunited country."[15] The day he founded the fund, he gathered a group of prominent national leaders and, to their astonishment, announced that he would give $2 million, one-half of his entire fortune, to "re-establish the educational system of the South, if these men would accept and administer the gift."[16] The group was so moved that they prayed together, consecrating themselves to the task of the gift's "wise expenditure." Peabody's gifts to the Southern Education Fund were intended to "promote and encourage the intellectual, moral, and industrial education of the Southern states."[17] His willingness to work with state and local governments on building the educational infrastructure of the South provided a model for later philanthropists to follow, including his decision to support segregated institutions. Peabody's use of what would be known as a matching grant made his gift contingent on local investment of dollars and demonstration of political will. By providing initial funds to build a school building, for example, the foundation's gifts inspired the local community to vote for taxation that would be necessary to maintain the school once it was open. Peabody's funding also subsidized the early hires of teachers who were graduates of newly created teacher training programs called "normal schools." These subsidies were made in the hope that the local community would see the benefit of having expert instructors in their classrooms and would continue to hire additional qualified teachers in the future.[18]

The Peabody Education Fund created a model of foundation philanthropy that is often credited to the Rockefeller and Carnegie Foundations at the turn of the twentieth century. Peabody identified a broad field of interest—creating an entirely new educational system for the South after the Civil War. He appointed prominent men of affairs, including several US presidents, justices of the US Supreme Court, university presidents, and notable businessmen to manage and to make the most effective distribution of funds from his $3 million donation. The fund's board of trustees was often called "the most distinguished group which ever administered a public or private trust."[19] They were an indication of Peabody's own view that his gift "should be placed in the hands of men primarily of vision who were in the habit of surveying large fields, making decisions and trusting to others as to ways and means of carrying them out."[20]

Peabody had his fund work closely with local and state governments, using grants to persuade local communities to establish their own tax-supported public school systems.[21] This strategy was emulated by Andrew Carnegie in his national campaign to put libraries in towns across the United States. He was inspired by Peabody's example of marrying the power of charitable giving to public investment.[22] Peabody's work in the South also spawned other important initiatives, including the John F. Slater Fund, the Anna T. Jeanes Fund, and the founding of Tulane University.[23] Peabody showed how personal wealth could be effective in both creating local charitable institutions and encouraging major regional policy change.

By the 1850s, Baltimore's community of philanthropists supported several innovative institutions, most of them secular. One of the earliest such initiatives, in 1844, was the construction of the Athenaeum Building to house The Maryland Historical Society, for which donors raised $35,000. Moses Sheppard founded the Sheppard Asylum in 1852 to provide a facility in which humane and scientifically supported treatments for the mentally ill might be developed. When he died in 1857, Sheppard left a bequest of $750,000 for the asylum's further support it.[24] William Walters amassed another of Baltimore's leading nineteenth-century fortunes, earning his first wealth as a grain merchant. Walters, like Johns Hopkins, entered the whiskey business. By the 1850s he owned the largest wholesale liquor business in the nation. In time, Walters bought banking and railroad interests and assembled an impressive art collection. His son, Henry Walters, was said to be the South's wealthiest man. Henry spent $1 million a year building the Walters' art collection; he also opened his galleries to the public in a much more ambitious way.[25] The younger Walters acquired three contiguous properties in fashionable Mount Vernon and built suitably impressive homes in which to display his collections, granting both the properties and artwork to the city of Baltimore on his death in 1931.[26] They became the Walters Art Gallery in 1934, which continues to be free and open to the public.

Johns Hopkins was also a transplant. Born outside of Annapolis in the 1790s to a large, devout Quaker family, Hopkins came to Baltimore in 1812 after his family emancipated their slaves at the command of their religious meeting. He joined his uncle's grocery business, helping to keep it profitable during the war with the British. He soon started Hopkins Brothers, a wholesale company, earning his first fortune selling "Hopkins Best" whiskey—an enterprise for which he "later expressed regret."[27] Much of Hopkins's wealth derived from the B & O Railroad, the potential of which he quickly saw and "enthusiastically invested in … eventually becoming the company's largest stockholder and most powerful board member." During John Work Garrett's presidency of the B&O, his family, in their roles as civic leaders, steered Baltimore's commercial future as he managed the railroad's affairs.[28]

Garrett also hosted George Peabody when he visited in 1866 for the Peabody Institute's opening and again six months later. During those visits, Garrett brokered conversations between Peabody and Johns Hopkins as Hopkins sought advice on disbursing his great wealth.[29] Peabody's consultations moved Hopkins to draft a will through which he created a board of trustees for his philanthropic enterprises. By July 1867, bills to incorporate Hopkins's benefactions reached the Maryland legislature.[30] When he died in 1873 on Christmas Eve, at age seventy-eight, Hopkins left $7 million of his $8 million estate for the creation of a hospital and university. His bequest was in the form of B & O, bank stocks, and real estate, which was the largest philanthropic gift ever given in the United States.[31]

In addition to funding JHU, Hopkins planned to endow a hospital, then an unpopular choice for a philanthropic gift since "philanthropists then, as now, invested in causes that had a good chance of transforming society for the better." In the 1880s when the Johns Hopkins Hospital finally opened, "there was little reason to think that medicine … would offer such change."[32] While the processes of disease were beginning to be understood, this new knowledge had largely failed to change the practice of medicine in hospitals. In part this was because hospital patients were mostly people of the lower classes who could not afford a private doctor for a home visit. Hospitals were seen as places for the poor, disabled, and others who lacked family support or resources. In this context, Hopkins's gift was ambitious and eleemosynary, seeking to provide a venue for the development of advanced medical training and treatment while aware that on a day-to-day basis, the hospital would be treating Baltimore's poorest people. Connected to the creation of the hospital and the university was a plan to have a medical school, but the trustees found themselves short on funds.

John Work Garrett, also a JHU trustee, was himself a notable local philanthropist who supported Baltimore's fledgling YMCA and the Peabody Institute, to which he contributed statues and friezes.[33] A regular contributor to relief during Baltimore's frequent smallpox epidemics, Garrett also financed lectures and exhibits across the community and acquired exotic animals for the Baltimore Zoo. Eventually, Garrett amassed a fortune of almost $17 million. By the mid-nineteenth century, Garrett's in-town mansion, where Peabody stayed when he visited Baltimore in 1866 and 1867, had become known as "a center of innovative philanthropy in the United States."[34] While certainly not inevitable, this function makes sense because, for much of the nineteenth century, Baltimore was reputed to have among the highest concentrations of millionaire philanthropists in the country.[35]

When Garrett died in 1884, his estate was equally divided among his three children, two sons and a daughter, who inherited real estate holdings totaling more than 2,500 acres of land.[36] Mary Elizabeth Garrett was, like her father, an enthusiastic supporter of many Baltimore causes, especially those that helped women; but like her father, she did not create foundations to reach her philanthropic goals. She supported groups like the Maryland Prisoner Aid Society, the Northeastern Day Nursery, the Baltimore Orphan Asylum, the Society for the Prevention of Cruelty to Animals (SPCA), and the Shelter for Aged Colored People. In 1866 she joined the board of the Baltimore Woman's Industrial Exchange. Early on, she tried to convince the trustees of JHU to admit women students, her "first stab at what would become her trademark 'coercive philanthropy' to change institutional male-dominated policy in order to advance women's status and opportunities."[37] Garrett "fine-tuned the art of 'coercive philanthropy.'" She did not simply give money away; she, like those who create foundations, carefully controlled how it was spent. She used her wealth as a bargaining chip, often a blatant bribe, encouraging policy change to achieve gender parity at male-run institutions. Although Mary Garrett's approach was effective only as long as she, the donor, enforced her wishes, foundations are often created as a means of vesting donor funds in an independent corporation that has the power to determine which organizations will be the recipients of grants and under what circumstances. JHU's trustees could have chosen to walk away from Garrett's gifts, though to do so would have had significant political, social, and institutional consequences.[38]

Garrett, together with other Baltimore women, "dreamed a daring dream—to organize a national network of women to raise $100,000 to open JHU's stalled medical school. But they insisted on one very specific condition: that women students be admitted to the new school on the same terms as men." The effort, known as the Women's Medical School Fund, succeeded in raising more than $100,000. Mary Garrett offered an additional $100,000 to sweeten the deal. Her gift represented "an unprecedented philanthropic offer to a university from one of the country's wealthiest women. ... It was more than quadruple what the average male wage earner in the United States could expect to earn in a lifetime."[39] Unfortunately, the JHU trustees told Garrett and others leading the Women's Medical School Fund that they needed to raise an incredible $500,000—the equivalent of approximately $13 million in 2013.[40] Thirty-eight-year-old Mary Garrett then offered $306,977 of her own funds, thus making the long-awaited medical school a reality. This magnificent gift to JHU in 1893 allowed for the erection of a new medical school to "honor the vital role women had played in calling attention to the sorry state of American medicine and in revolutionizing medical education and training."[41] It followed one Garrett had given just two years earlier to Baltimore's innovative Bryn Mawr School for Girls.

Mary Garrett was not her family's only philanthropic woman. Her sister-in-law, Mary Frick, began to memorialize her husband in the 1880s, first by establishing the thirty-bed Garrett Sanatorium for Children in Mount Airy, Maryland, and then by creating the Robert Garrett Fund for the Surgical Treatment of Children, thus laying the foundation for a children's medical and surgical center at Johns Hopkins Hospital.[42] Like the funds given by Mary Garrett and John Work Garrett, Mary Frick's contributions were gifts to operating charities rather than foundations in a strict twentieth-century sense.

Mercantile and commercial endeavors rather than heavy industry provided the corpus of Baltimore's nineteenth-century wealth. This is not only true for Johns Hopkins, George Peabody, and the Walters family, but also for the Abell Family, for whom the *Sun* newspapers generated wealth, and

Baltimore merchants, including Eugene and Joshua Levering, who accumulated their fortune through coffee and tea brokering. Among the early philanthropic efforts of these wealthy Baltimoreans was coming to "the relief of the Johns Hopkins University to tide it over the period when the Baltimore and Ohio railway's financial troubles cut off the University's income." An 1893 *New York Review of Reviews* article noted that there were then about fifty-five large fortunes of a million dollars or more in Baltimore, though "generally speaking" not belonging to "multimillionaires."[43] These fortunes were "accumulated slowly by old-fashioned business care and sagacity." The list included Hopkins and Enoch Pratt and noted that about half of the (mostly) men on the list were of a "recognized disposition to be generous, whether they have actually made very large gifts or not."[44] Still, it was Mary Elizabeth Garrett's contribution to JHU to open the medical school's enrollment to women that was the most notable of all the benefactions occurring on the eve of the article's publication, an especially significant contribution as it was a case of one woman explicitly helping other women.[45]

The Charity Organization Society and Federated Giving: New Tools for Community Investment

Social and political issues also emerged from industrialization and urbanization. In the first two decades of the twentieth century, poverty, driven by cyclical unemployment, unregulated markets, and lack of education, was exacerbated by poor housing and sanitation, a lack of access to health care and an unsafe food supply. These ills were further intensified by successive waves of immigration and continuing racial segregation and sparked an active debate within the philanthropic community about the best ways to address them. While large foundations like the Rockefeller Foundation, the Russell Sage Foundation, and the Carnegie Corporation of New York began to form in part to support efforts in researching both the scope of these problems and their solutions, the leadership in many cities across the country recognized that action must be taken. Progressives sought to meet the challenges of the burgeoning urban landscape with all means available—including the private charitable sector and government reforms.

Existing charitable organizations tried to relieve the immediate pain of hunger, homelessness, illness, and poverty that seemed only to be growing. The charity organization movement, begun in London in 1869, was embraced and quickly replicated in many American cities, including Baltimore. Pioneering an allegedly scientific philanthropy to separate the worthy from the unworthy poor, organizers began using the case work method to look into the personal circumstances of each individual or family seeking aid. These societies sought to coordinate the work of numerous philanthropic organizations to avoid duplication, root out impostors, and encourage the thorough investigation of all petitions for help. Most importantly, those engaged with scientific philanthropy began to collect data on who was receiving aid and why, in an attempt to coordinate a community-wide approach that would be tailored to meet the existing need. Thus, scientific philanthropy began as a revolt against what was perceived as the old-fashioned spendthrift almsgiving that provided the same meager benefits to all poor people, without regard to their individual situations, thereby failing to address the root causes of poverty.[46] It was an attempt to prevent poverty and its attendant miseries by meeting individual needs before people fell into destitution, thus avoiding the need for a dole altogether.[47]

In Baltimore, coordinated relief started in 1870 with the Association for the Improvement of the Condition of the Poor (AICP), whose organizers drafted a constitution outlining policies intended to encourage the practice of scientific philanthropy. Unfortunately, a gap between policy and practice quickly arose, establishing the AICP almost entirely as an almsgiving society. Critics of the AICP in 1881 organized the Charity Organization Society (COS) in a second, more successful effort to practice scientific philanthropy. Daniel Coit Gilman, president of JHU, was the force behind its organization.[48] He and the other founders wanted the Baltimore COS to act as a central bureau to organize charity. They hoped that the COS would educate and improve those who *had not*. They anathematized indiscriminate almsgiving. While the COS did not distribute alms, it connected those who were deemed *deserving* with assistance. COS leaders believed that by eliminating duplication, fraud, and waste, community resources would increase.[49] They participated in the Baltimore Alliance of Social and Charitable Agencies, which published a monthly magazine titled *City & State: A Maryland Journal of Social Progress* in order to highlight the activities and publish the findings of the more progressive agencies.

By 1885, focused on rationalizing the provision of social services by various groups within the city, the Baltimore COS evolved into a vital force in the field of social welfare. Wishing to "remove much of the sentiment from the administration of charity," its leaders worked to make giving an efficient business transaction, insisting on efficiency and economy in the practice of charity.[50] The COS "considered as sheer waste" and "looked with abhorrence" on random almsgiving.[51] They developed a cadre of volunteer visitors to investigate individuals seeking aid. They had 236 volunteers by 1890 and 310 by 1893.[52] These visitors were to assess each family's circumstances and the legitimacy of their needs as well as provide useful advice and link the family with services when appropriate. The Baltimore COS included black and white volunteers and clients. In 1904, 27 percent of the cases COS investigated came from the African American community at a time when they made up about 15 percent of the city's population. Among the COS representatives was Sarah Fernandis, a black graduate of the New York School of Philanthropy and a pioneering social worker, who would go on to found the first black settlement house in the United States in nearby Washington, DC.[53] The activities of the COS and its friendly visitors, along with the growing settlement house movement, were the predecessors of the profession of social work which began to emerge in the first two decades of the twentieth century.

Baltimore's COS served as an incubator for individuals who would go on to transform the country's approach to social problems through the education and support of schools of social work, pioneering social science research, and national foundation leadership. In the 1890s, the Baltimore director of the COS, Amos Warner, taught one of the first courses in the administration of scientific charity in the country at JHU. Mary Richmond, the pioneer of the case work method of social work and one of the most influential individuals in the emerging social work field, began her work within the Baltimore COS, succeeding Warner as director in 1891. In 1907, she went on to head the Field Department of the Russell Sage Foundation, which supported the development and curricula of some of the earliest and best schools of social work across the country, including those at Columbia University in New York, Western Reserve University in Cleveland, and Washington University in St. Louis.[54] Under Mary Richmond's direction, the Russell Sage Foundation also engaged in groundbreaking social science research surveys that provided definitive proof of the scope and scale of social and urban problems that informed the legislative agenda of progressive politicians through the 1930s.[55]

At the center of the new scientific philanthropy was the drive to coordinate community efforts in addressing social problems. Along with the formation of the COS and private charitable foundations, Baltimore was also home to an innovative group of federated funding organizations in the late nineteenth- and early twentieth-centuries. Representing Catholic and Jewish constituencies, these groups used annual community-wide fund-raising campaigns to aggregate many smaller gifts into a large fund. Although they were public charities rather than private foundations, these groups appointed boards of trustees as representatives of diverse constituencies to oversee grant distribution to other charitable organizations, thereby functioning very much like the modern community foundation. Groups like the Federated Jewish Charities, the United Hebrew Charities, the Associated Catholic Charities, and the Baltimore Alliance of Social and Charitable Agencies all functioned with keen awareness of the emerging movement toward scientific philanthropy. By supporting only established charitable organizations that could demonstrate their effectiveness, federated funders helped to legitimize certain institutions, in part to eliminate repeated charitable appeals from multiple smaller organizations and misguided approaches to social problems that wasted scarce charitable dollars. Both private foundations and federated funders shared this quest for efficiency and effectiveness in philanthropy, and both relied on a growing team of experts from the increasingly professional and specialized fields of medicine, social science, and education.

Baltimore continued to lead the way in experimenting with methods for addressing the needs of its increasingly diverse population. The expanding Jewish community focused the majority of its efforts on creating agencies to coordinate support for charitable organizations serving its own community members. The new federated Jewish charities functioned much as community foundations would later: by accumulating a large pot of resources in a yearly fund drive that were then distributed to selected nonprofit organizations delivering direct services. Even today, the Associated Jewish Community Federation of Baltimore is among the largest grantmakers in the metropolitan area, along with other federated funders like the United Way and Catholic Charities. The city's expanding Jewish and Catholic population shaped a great deal of the philanthropic landscape in the last quarter of the nineteenth century and throughout all of the twentieth century.

In the mid-nineteenth century, American Jewish communities began formally organizing charitable institutions to serve coreligionists in need. In 1843, Baltimore's Jews organized the Hebrew Assistance Society, a group dedicated solely to helping poor Jewish people.[56] When the group renamed itself the Hebrew Benevolent Society in 1856, the *Baltimore American* reported, "Inasmuch as we know, no Jew has ever asked for assistance from the general charity fund. The Jews take care of their own poor and contribute to poor of all religions."[57]

The year 1882 was critical to the development of both Baltimore's Jewish community and its charities. According to Baltimore native and JHU professor of political economy Jacob H. Hollander, until then the city's Jewish population was "homogenous—made up of German immigrants and their descendants. ... Such differences as existed were economic, intellectual and social. In charitable affairs, benefactors and beneficiaries differed in degree rather than in kind."[58] That changed when the infamous May Laws enacted in Russia in 1882 drove tens of thousands of Jews from villages and towns in the Pale of Settlement—an area that now corresponds to parts of western Russia, Poland, Lithuania, Ukraine, Moldova, and Belarus. As a major East Coast port city, Baltimore received many Eastern European immigrants. The Russian and Eastern European immigrants and their destitution on arrival forever changed Baltimore's Jewish landscape.[59]

The numbers are staggering. Baltimore's Jewish population was about 10,000 in 1880. Over the next ten years, more than 24,000 Jews landed in Baltimore. Not all stayed, but by 1887 the city's Jewish population was up 50 percent to 15,000. Between 1891 and 1898 another 17,367 Jews arrived. By the beginning of the twentieth century Baltimore was home to 25,000 Jews. The annual Jewish immigration to Baltimore in the 1890s was roughly 2,000, a number that rose to 5,000 a year between 1900 and 1905. Immigration may have peaked in 1907 when, in a single year, 6,065 Jews arrived. By 1910, there were 45,000 Jewish Baltimoreans.[60]

Baltimore's Jewish charitable landscape in the 1880s featured a number of organizations started by German Jews as a form of self-help for other German Jews. As Eastern Europeans arrived, Baltimore's established Jewish community, according to Hollander, responded to "stricken humanity. But as the situation lost its bitter novelty and the burden settled in onerous pressure, benevolence waned, and something akin to patronage grew."[61] No longer were the charitable groups a place where more prosperous Jews relieved the misfortunes of others, but, rather where the fulfillment of religious obligation to participate in charity became a "tax-like charge for the infinite relief of the misery and dependence of a distinct class, different in speech, tradition and origin, uncouth in arrival and unwelcome in presence, whose only claim was a tenuous tie of emotional appeal and an identical negation in religious belief."[62]

Though strife between and among Jewish groups in Baltimore—caused by factors ranging from language barriers and differences in religious observances to workplace disputes—defined much of the period between the 1880s and 1920s, there were sincere efforts at help. As Eastern European Jews arrived in stunning numbers, established German speaking Jews in Baltimore and throughout the country offered assistance.[63] In 1890 the Baltimore branch of the Baron de Hirsch Fund, created specifically for the purpose of aiding new Jewish immigrants from Eastern Europe with job training, general education, and training in modern agricultural methods, began to support local initiatives.[64] Among other efforts, this fund gave $700 to Henrietta Szold's night school for Russian immigrants.[65]

At the very end of the nineteenth century, many American Jewish communities began systematizing community-wide fundraising operations and apportioning contributions to affiliated organizations through federated charities that provided a full range of communal services from cradle to grave.[66] In 1902, a full dozen years after new immigrants created the Friendly Inn, some in Baltimore's uptown community began promoting the consolidation of Jewish charities when leaders of twelve "older Jewish charitable organizations ... formed by the German Jews" met together, excluding the charities founded by the more recent immigrants.[67] In 1906, the Federated Jewish Charities (FJC), the first of Baltimore's two Jewish federations, was founded.[68] Louis H. Levin, the editor of the *Jewish Comment*, a Baltimore Jewish weekly, was hired as executive secretary. Levin had worked through the newspaper to advocate for the federation of the city's German Jewish charities as a means to stem "waste and irritation."[69]

Before the FJC's founding, the leadership of the various groups that made up its membership were "to a large extent, identical." Yet, the agencies "bore no well-defined relation, the one to the others."[70] The boards of these group were "regarded much as a title of nobility, to be held and enjoyed by the incumbent for this lifetime, and after his death to descend to his eldest son, to be by him in turn held for life."[71] As the aim for these groups was to raise money as reliably as possible, keeping a well-defined set of the financial elite as their leadership was undoubtedly effective. Neither community engagement nor mutual obligation on a broad scale were especially important. Rather, the groups' managements became "practically self-perpetuating and accountable only to themselves."[72] The FJC changed everything. From its inception, the new organization rotated its officers and provided much needed oversight for the constituent agencies.[73] Also, after the FJC's creation, gifts were given by individuals rather than in the name of a business firm, as they had been previously.

The FJC modeled modern practices in charitable work. In 1908, for example, the FJC president remarked that, because "a well-ordered household becomes a philanthropic no less than a business corporation, the Federation has submitted its financial operations to professional auditors, and has proffered the same facilities to its constitutional societies, thus ensuring a new degree of fiscal precision and an initial step toward a uniform system of institutional accounting."[74] Viewing itself as a "friend, mediator, guide, and supervisor," the FJC's leaders pointed out that "the public hardly realizes how the Federation prevents the multiplicity of demands that were so constant in prefederation times."[75] The FJC replaced volunteer workers with "expert paid workers in very many branches of social endeavor."[76] Interested in the systematic solicitation of the entire Jewish community, Levin created a comprehensive list of the Jews of Baltimore because he believed that the FJC's first work was "that of a collection agency, and its prospects depend on the success of the committees in getting subscriptions. The work is tedious."[77] In his efforts at mass fundraising, rather than in creating or operating a foundation, Levin mined the *City Directory* "from cover to cover, taking out every Jewish name uptown and downtown," an effort that resulted in a list of between five and ten thousand names.[78] Volunteer solicitors successfully canvassed the city. In its first year, contributions increased an average of more than 50 percent over previous contributions. A mail campaign was attempted, but cost and insufficiency caused its quick demise.[79] Subscriptions to the new organization exceeded $62,000, "a sum greater than that heretofore raised by all the beneficiary organizations."[80]

In a 1910 assessment of the contribution made by Jewish federations locally and nationally, its president, Eli J. Frank, said the FJC "as an improved fiscal device ... is essentially a Jewish invention and bids fair to constitute the great distinctively Jewish contribution to modern charity organization."[81] The model had yet to be adopted by any non-Jewish group, but was being studied to see if it was applicable.[82] Noting that the model varied from one Jewish community to the next, Frank reported that Baltimore's emphasis was on "direct giving to the exclusion of all other means of raising money."[83]

Jacob Epstein was Baltimore's most prominent Jewish philanthropic leader. A Lithuanian immigrant, Epstein, through the success of his Baltimore Bargain House wholesale operation, became one of the city's wealthiest citizens and a key player in the city's Jewish community.[84] In 1907 Epstein announced interest in establishing a Jewish Home for Consumptives, a sanitarium for the treatment of poor Jews suffering from tuberculosis. Epstein gave $35,000, with an additional annual contribution of $500 for Mount Pleasant (as the seventy-nine-acre Reisterstown-based Jewish Home for Consumptives came to be known).[85] Though active in the FJC from the beginning, Epstein understood its exclusionary nature. He called a meeting to "consider the advisability of uniting all the constituent societies of down town."[86] He hoped that by "uniting these societies schnorring, balls, picnics and raffles would be done away with and the duplication of work stopped, while the Jewish community would be made to feel its responsibility of helping the needy and suffering all the stronger."[87] The result was the organization of the United Hebrew Charities (UHC), which formally began in 1908 with no assets and constituent agencies all in a deficit position, headquartered in the heart of Baltimore's Eastern European Jewish shtetl.[88] In 1910, President William Levy, a German Jew, described the UHC's work as "composed entirely of benevolent societies which were established principally by coreligionists of foreign birth." It had, he said, "the approval and support of our older citizens, and the state recognizes the good it does by contributing toward the maintenance of two of its constituent societies."[89] By 1911 the UHC had about 4,000 contributors (more than twice as many as the FJC), the majority of whom, though poor, gave as "a duty and a pleasure." Most liked the UHC because through it they "assist[ed] all the various institutions, which they could not do with their limited means, if each was managed independently."[90] Jacob Epstein was very committed to the UHC and likely its biggest donor, giving $1,500 in 1917 and $2,500 the following year.[91]

For the FJC's leaders the creation of the UHC allowed the federation model to be applied "to the organizations established, and most largely maintained and officered, by the more recently arrived of our coreligionists."[92] FJC President Eli Frank argued—perhaps spuriously—that in 1906, when the FJC was created, the downtown charities "had not yet reached the stage of development in the methods either of their conduct or of their support that would then have warranted their inclusion in the Federation."[93] Their quick adaptation was "little short of phenomenal." By having two groups of federated charities, Frank concluded, "The Jewish charities of this city are thus substantially completely federated, but in the form of two distinct and independent Federations, each appealing separately to the public for the support of the societies affiliated with it."[94] The existence of the two groups marked "a transition stage in our development." It was Frank's "pious wish that the complete unification of all our charitable affairs" be consummated.[95]

Those supporting uniting the federations disdained the practice of dividing coreligionists and recognized the finite number of prospective donors. Solomon Ginsberg, the UHC's first president in 1907 and among its last in 1917, reported pointedly, "We all must admit it to be a fact that the man who contributes to the United Hebrew Charities is as a rule also a contributor to the Federated Charities or to other charities, while the man who gives to neither charity gives no charity."[96] By 1910 the UHC president reported "the kindly feeling now existing among the Jewish charitable organizations of our city [that] will ultimately lead to one large and stronger organization." The FJC's president noted "that the time is not far distant when this will be accomplished."[97]

A 1919 Amalgamation Committee featuring members from each federation wrestled with issues presented by the member agencies. In 1920, with leaders of the FJC and UHC present, Louis Levin casually asked what they thought of bringing the groups together. "Both sides roared 'Never!' Smiling broadly Levin said, 'Hurrah, gentlemen, do you realize that this is the first time that you have ever agreed on any subject?'"[98] In 1920 the Maryland legislature passed a bill amalgamating the two groups into Associated Jewish Charities. Levin was the association's first executive director, an accomplishment referred to as his "master work."[99]

In 1920, the Amalgamation Committee fund-raised jointly, resulting in pledges of $422,600 from 11,700 donors, including more than $21,000 from Jacob Epstein. Bills to satisfy the pledges went out in the name of the Associated Jewish Charities.[100] Interestingly, the AJC's report on subscribers contained over twelve thousand names of Baltimore Jews, nearly twice as many as appeared on the combined lists of the FJC and UHC. Eighteen agencies operated under the association's auspices.[101]

Louis H. Levin outlined new targets for fund-raising, including young working women. He believed that "workingmen, too, are in position to affect powerfully the pace of our development."[102] Early goals of the association included the eradication of disease, the healthy birth and development of children, the spread of education, the abolition of impossible housing conditions, and the improvement of recreational facilities.[103] These goals, Levin believed, were shared by "the religionist, the nonreligionist, the conservative, and the radical."[104] He was convinced that "our very cooperation on a broad platform will only demonstrate that fundamentally we have so much in common that we can take our differences with humor rather than with tragedy."[105] Within a decade after the creation of the Associated Jewish Charities, Jewish individuals—many of Eastern European immigrant origin—rose from their early poverty to accumulate great wealth through ventures in industry, commerce, real estate, and finance. Like their fellow well-to-do Baltimoreans, they began to found their own philanthropic foundations to pursue specific charitable purposes.

The Catholic community in Baltimore generally preferred direct institutional support through decentralized fund-raising rooted in church-based appeals. It also supported campaigns by religious orders responsible for specific institutions like schools, orphanages, or relief societies. But efforts by Catholic lay people in conjunction with clergy in other large cities began to push Baltimore's Catholics to consider participating in community-wide federations and philanthropic planning. At the meeting of the Baltimore COS in 1900, Thomas Mulry, the lay leader of the St. Vincent de Paul Society of New York City, stated that "the platform of charity is broad enough for Hebrew, Protestant, and Catholic to meet on and work together for the amelioration of God's poor. We are no less earnest in adherence to our particular belief because we work with those of other creeds for the common good."[106]

Eventually this spirit of cooperation was incorporated into the Catholic leadership of Baltimore as the rising tide of immigrants in the period highlighted the insufficiency of Catholic resources to address the needs of growing populations. Most Catholic institutions had neither endowments nor savings, leaving them entirely dependent on the annual benevolence of surrounding parishes for their operating expenses.[107] Efforts to organize Catholic giving and institutional decision-making began in 1907 under the auspices of Robert Biggs, lay leader and president of the Baltimore Society of St. Vincent de Paul, who began a central bureau of Catholic charities. Biggs worked to coordinate relief efforts between agencies and hired the first full-time social worker among Catholic organizations to investigate cases and provide needy families with referrals to the appropriate agencies. Much of the work of the St. Vincent de Paul Society was directed and completed by lay leaders, but in 1921 a new bishop named Michael James Curley was appointed. In an attempt to bring charitable matters under his direct control, the bishop appointed Reverend Edwin Leonard to establish the archdiocesan bureau of Catholic Charities, which replaced the Central Bureau of the St. Vincent de Paul Society, effectively forcing Biggs's retirement. The change in leadership created a public controversy, but the upshot was the successful transfer of oversight of Catholic charitable institutions from an independent religious order that gave lay leadership a great deal of autonomy to the religious hierarchy of the diocese.[108] Reverend Leonard centralized decision making among the clergy, and the St. Vincent de Paul Society "became little more than a volunteer force for the implementation of decisions made in the Bureau's office."[109] Bishop Curley's actions fit squarely within a pattern of the church hierarchy replacing and overriding lay leadership at the diocesan and national levels. The National Conference of Catholic Charities, which was founded in 1910 and led by many active lay leaders—including growing numbers of Catholic women and social workers—was largely taken over by male clergy in the 1920s.[110] In Baltimore, the resurgence of the St. Vincent de Paul

Society and the reengaging the laity in issues of outreach and assistance to the poor and dependent would have to wait until the Great Depression. In the intervening years, however, the Catholic Charities behaved like other federated philanthropies, raising large sums each year, distributing grants to organizations meeting their community's needs, and disseminating information on how those monies were spent.

Foundation Philanthropy Gains Prominence

Beyond the work of the Associated Jewish Charities of Baltimore and JHU, neither of which fully qualify as twentieth-century foundations, Charm City's philanthropic landscape came to include a great variety of independent philanthropic foundations, community foundations, and federated funders. The National Center for Charitable Statistics lists over three hundred private foundations that are incorporated in the Baltimore area, with assets ranging from over $2 billion (Annie E. Casey Foundation) to assets of just over $10,000 (The First Mariner Charitable Foundation).[111] Among all of these philanthropic foundations are examples of corporate foundations like the A. S. Abell Foundation; family foundations that have a connection to faith traditions like the Marion I. and Henry J. Knott Foundation, the Joseph and Harvey Meyerhoff Family Charitable Funds, and The Harry and Jeannette Weinberg Foundation; foundations with individual donors and special purposes like the Emanuel Chambers Foundation, which was centered on supporting education and healthcare for the African American community; independent national foundations like the Open Society Institute and Annie E. Casey Foundation; and the Baltimore Community Foundation, which is focused on supporting education and neighborhood development in the city. In the period from the 1930s to the 1990s, the number of foundations in Baltimore increased and came to reflect the growing diversity and prosperity of some of its citizens. These foundations pursued (and some continue to pursue) multiple purposes, such as supporting education and healthcare, youth programs, arts and culture, social services, environmental conservation, and community development. They reflect the city's changing population, supporting activities that specifically target Baltimore's Jewish, Catholic, and African American communities as well as the general population.

At the heart of it, foundations see themselves as investing scarce resources where they will do the most good—through identifying key nonprofit organizations that are engaged in their fields of interest and using grants to support those efforts. In contrast to the audacious vision of the Peabody Fund for Southern Education and others founded with a view to transform systems and innovate institutions, foundations created from the mid-twentieth century onward generally "seek leverage within current systems" and "look for ways to do more with less."[112] The purposes and practices of Baltimore's twentieth-century foundations, while ambitious, are tailored to the complicated economic, social, technological, and cultural landscapes in which they and their grant recipients function.

The story of the A. S. Abell Foundation is illustrative. The foundation began in 1953 with a $100,000 gift from the A. S. Abell Company, modest even by midcentury standards. The intention of the foundation at its inception was to perpetuate the already active philanthropy of Harry C. Black, chairman of the board of the A. S. Abell Company, which owned the Sun Papers—two of Baltimore's three daily newspapers—and a board member of Fidelity and Deposit Company, a bond firm in which Black's family had the controlling interest. Although he "enjoyed a reputation as a leading philanthropist … his reputation was characterized by a certain unorthodoxy."[113] As an individual donor, Black contributed to JHU, the Peabody Institute, the Enoch Pratt Free Library, South Baltimore General Hospital's library, and the Baltimore chapter of the American Red Cross. An opponent of prohibition, he organized and hosted an annual luncheon for newspaper business colleagues which he called "Beer among the Daffodils" from the repeal of prohibition until his death at age sixty-nine in 1956.[114] So short was Black's tenure as president of the Abell Foundation that it is absent from his news obituary in the *New York Times*. Still, Black's ecumenical and egalitarian approach to philanthropy was clearly communicated to the board. Gifts went to arts and cultural organizations, educational institutions, to the United Negro College Fund of Baltimore, the Jewish Federation, and Catholic Charities.[115]

Between 1953 and 2008, the Abell Foundation gave over $186 million to public education, human services, and community development in Baltimore. It expanded dramatically in 1986 when Time-Mirror purchased the A. S. Abell Company's outstanding stock, increasing the foundation's assets tenfold to $112 million. Professional leadership then passed to Robert C. Embry as president, and Gary Black Jr., the grand-nephew of Harry C. Black. At the end of 2009 the foundation's assets were $180 million, and it had sharpened its focus to support activities within the city of Baltimore that address urban poverty, unemployment, crime, and lack of access to education.[116]

Family foundations also appeared on Baltimore's philanthropic landscape in the second half of the twentieth century. For example, in 1977 the Marion and Henry Knott family began a local philanthropic foundation.

Born in 1906, Henry Knott, a Baltimore native, worked in his father's construction business in the 1920s. "Henry became a brick contractor and made his fortune as a no-nonsense businessman whose various enterprises built thousands of homes, offices, and shopping centers in the Baltimore area."[117] In 1946, he developed his first town-house neighborhood in east Baltimore, followed by more home and apartment construction jobs. Prefabricated wall panels sped up construction. Meanwhile, Marion Burk moved to Baltimore from Richmond, Virginia, and married Henry in 1928. The Knotts had thirteen children, twelve of whom lived to adulthood. Explicit in its focus on Catholic affairs, "The Marion I. & Henry J. Knott Foundation is a Catholic family foundation committed to honoring our founders' legacy of generosity to strengthen our community."[118] The foundation began eighteen years before Henry's death in 1995. By then it had given away about $140 million, much of it to Roman Catholic institutions. The long roster of recipients included Loyola College, his alma mater; the Baltimore Symphony Orchestra; the Baltimore diocesan hospitals, to which he donated money for treating the poor; the University of Notre Dame; parochial schools; and the Johns Hopkins Oncology Center.[119] The Knott Foundation, "a vehicle to teach his children how to stay involved in the community," has a "family only" board of trustees.[120] In 1995, the Knotts had fifty-five grandchildren and fifty-one great grandchildren. To serve as a board member, an individual must be a lineal descendant of Henry and Marion Knott or the spouse of a lineal descendent and attend a year of training sessions.[121]

So prevalent and popular had family and corporate foundations become that by 1983, the Association of Baltimore Area Grantmakers (ABAG) was founded to provide a variety of technical and other assistance to a dozen members. Founding members believed they could work more effectively if they knew the broader funding community, knew the issues surrounding different program areas, such as education and workforce development, and worked together to solve problems. In three decades, membership multiplied more than tenfold to 135 funders comprised of private and community foundations, donor-advised funds, and corporations with strategic, ongoing grant-making programs concerned with local and regional issues.[122]

The Meyerhoff family and its Joseph and Harvey Meyerhoff Family Charitable Funds, a group of Baltimore-based family foundations, provide an example of the impact of successful Eastern European Jews in the city's philanthropic landscape in the second half of the twentieth century and beyond. Joseph Meyerhoff emigrated from Russia in 1907 at age seven and became, like Henry Knott, a major real estate developer. By the time of his death at the age of eighty-five, he had built more than 15,000 homes in the Baltimore area as well as 17,000 apartments in Maryland, Florida, Pennsylvania, and Georgia.[123] A former president of the National Association of Home Builders, Meyerhoff's Magna Properties also built nineteen shopping centers in various states. A generous philanthropist in Baltimore and Israel, he was a major donor to the Baltimore Symphony Orchestra. His single largest gift was $10 million toward the $23 million cost of building the Joseph Meyerhoff Symphony Hall, which was completed in 1982 and seated 2,500.[124] A music lover, Meyerhoff served as president of the Baltimore Symphony Orchestra. His charitable giving also included the Baltimore Museum of Art, the Baltimore Opera, and the Peabody Institute, which, by the mid-twentieth century, had morphed into a music conservatory. On the national and international stage, Meyerhoff served as a national general chairman of the United Jewish Appeal. At the time of his death he was chairman of the Palestine Economic Corporation, which encouraged private investments in Israel, having earlier served as president. In addition, in Israel he also served on the board of Tel Aviv University, Hebrew University, the Technion, and the Weizmann Institute of Sciences.[125] Harvey "Bud" Meyerhoff, Joseph's son, was instrumental in the building of the United States Holocaust Memorial Museum. Bud Meyerhoff is also a supporter of JHU and its hospital, as well as the Johns Hopkins Health System. Through their foundations, the Meyerhoffs have been major supporters of higher education in the Baltimore region and in Israel. Terry Meyerhoff Rubenstein, Bud's oldest child, serves as the executive vice president of the funds.[126]

The Meyerhoffs share much in common with The Harry and Jeannette Weinberg Foundation in their interest in charitable giving in Baltimore and in Israel, although the scale of the Weinberg Foundation dwarfs almost all other local family foundation work. Founded in 1959 and based in Baltimore, the Weinberg Foundation has assets of over $2 billion and is one of the nation's largest private foundations.[127] Harry Weinberg emigrated to Baltimore from Galicia in the Austro-Hungarian Empire in 1911, at the age of three. Because his family needed his income, Harry Weinberg's formal schooling lasted only six years, most of them spent in "disciplinary classes." Weinberg "made a fortune in sensing an opportunity in businesses that others had given up on."[128] He was particularly successful in the transit field, where he bought up privately owned municipal transit companies, and in real estate, especially in Baltimore and Hawaii. When he died in 1990, at age eighty-two, he left nearly a billion dollars to the foundation. When his will was probated, the Weinberg Foundation had become one of the twelve largest charitable trusts in the country.[129] His foundation provides funding to organizations in Hawaii, Maryland, and Israel.

An example of a foundation on a smaller scale, but one that was also driven by strong donor intent, the Emanuel Chambers Foundation was endowed in 1945 by the bequest of Emanuel Chambers, a black steward for more than thirty years at two of the most prominent businessmen's social clubs in Baltimore. In addition to serving at table, Chambers was also a concierge, personal secretary, and trusted confidante to many of the leading businessmen, attorneys, and physicians of the city.[130] Over three decades at the clubs, Chambers "earned a reputation for solving the problems of the club members that became legendary. In fact it was generally believed there was nothing Emanuel couldn't do."[131] From procuring tickets to sold-out performances, to hiding club members whose wives (or other women) were searching for them, to helping members get train tickets at a moment's notice, Chambers was, by all accounts, a resourceful, discreet, and hardworking man who came to be a good friend to many. By living on his wages and investing his tips with his broker, a club member, Chambers managed to amass a fortune, leaving over $150,000—the equivalent of approximately $2 million in today's dollars—to his foundation, which was established to "advance and promote the physical, mental, moral, and social condition of the inhabitants of Baltimore regardless of race, color, or creed."[132]

In practice, the board of trustees, made up of Chambers's personal friends, used his foundation to support the welfare of black Baltimoreans, including scholarships for black students to attend college and support for visiting nursing care and hospital care for black patients. The Emanuel Chambers Primary Care Center at Johns Hopkins Hospital was named in his honor in 1973. His portrait hangs in the hospital, and his photograph is now part of an online exhibit, curated by JHU, titled "The Indispensable Role of Blacks at Johns Hopkins."[133] At the unveiling of his portrait in Johns Hopkins Hospital in 1965, Stuart Olivier, a financier and the president of the foundation's board of trustees, remembered Emanuel as a savvy investor, a true friend to those in need, and a person who was "dedicated to the service of mankind."[134] Openly weeping at moments while he delivered his speech in tribute to his friend, Olivier concluded that, although Chambers "had no education, was no bank president nor president of a university," he had amassed "a fortune larger than the combined membership of the club members he waited on," and was "one of nature's finest and truest gentlemen."[135] In 1973, the Chambers fund, then with assets of $580,000—a little more than $3 million today—closed and distributed its principal to the institutions that it had long been in the habit of supporting, most prominently Johns Hopkins Hospital, Provident Hospital, the Instructive Visiting Nurse Association, and Morgan State College, the largest historically black college in Maryland.[136]

George Soros is another Jewish immigrant who created a large philanthropic foundation. Born in Hungary in 1930, Soros emigrated to the United Kingdom before coming to New York in 1956 where he entered the world of finance, amassed extraordinary wealth and gained access to world leaders. His fortune comes from his own hedge fund, the Quantum Fund. According to the Carnegie Endowment of Peace's Morton Abromowitz, Soros became, like the Rockefellers, Henry Kissinger, Bill Gates, and only a handful of others, a "private citizen who had his own foreign policy." By the close of the twentieth century, Soros was annually nominated for the Nobel Peace Prize.[137] Like Carnegie, Rockefeller, Rosenwald, and, closer to home, Peabody and Garrett, Soros's philanthropy is hands-on in his policy-shaping work. Soros began his philanthropy on the world stage. He concluded that it would be a logical extension of his philanthropy to "go from helping to establish open societies where they had been absent to defending them where they existed."[138] Soros was mindful of the fact that the United States was home to hundreds of thousands of nonprofit organizations. He was not interested in duplicating the work of other groups. In an "it takes a village" effort, Soros brought together eight "thought leaders" (including Bard College president Leon Botstein and several notable philosophers) to discuss approaches and programs in America at a philosophers' weekend.[139] Participants identified objectives of philanthropy and discussed the possibility of targeting a particular city for a high concentration of programs and assistance, determining to "select an urban center that might serve as a social laboratory where programs could be tested to reveal useful approaches or flawed hypothesis." Having decided on a field office in the United States, the foundation's staff looked for a city from which to "learn more about the dynamics in play in urban centers that result in persistent poverty and injustice and then invest significant charitable funds to address their root causes." After exploring a number of cities, including New Haven, Connecticut, and San Antonio, Texas, Baltimore was chosen because it was "a city with typical problems" which had "the resolve to address them." Of Soros's Open Society Institute (OSI) offices, OSI Baltimore is the only one in the United States "that directs its work solely to solve problems in one city."[140] Soros liked Baltimore's size (then about 650,000 inhabitants) and its then mayor, Kurt L. Schmoke.[141]

In 1996, Soros opened the only OSI field office in the United States in Baltimore to work on three intertwined problems: drug addiction, mass incarceration, and issues that kept young people from succeeding as students and citizens. Soros's approach, and that of OSI Baltimore, is to look for "the root causes of problems."[142] The OSI Baltimore office is staffed by local residents with the autonomy to make decisions about program priorities and funding. In the early years, the work cost about $13 million per year and focused on five areas, each with its own program officer: drug addiction treatment, criminal justice, workforce development, education and youth, and access to justice.[143] For a decade, Soros was the sole funder of OSI Baltimore. Since 2006, the organization has sought other investors to support the work. Still, thus far, Soros himself has contributed more than $60 million to Baltimore through OSI, the single largest outside philanthropic investment in Baltimore's history.[144]

Soros expresses OSI's impact on Baltimore as follows: "We are making some progress because we are tackling the root causes of the big problems facing Baltimore and other cities."[145] Among his innovations is the Baltimore Community Fellowship program through which more than one hundred people have each received $48,000 in fellowships for their eighteen-month effort to address a social concern. According to Soros, these fellows "can show tangible results for their work in Baltimore."[146] Soros has committed to continue investing in OSI Baltimore in the future, pledging to match contributions on a one-to-one basis. His effort of involving local funders has thus far included 225 people and organizations who have invested over $14.5 million. While Soros sees this as a solid start, he knows that impact and sustainability depend on many more donors getting involved.[147] Soros's philosophy is based on two propositions. The first is that in situations that have thinking participants, "the participants' view of the world is always partial and distorted. That is the principle of fallibility." The second is that "these distorted views can influence the situation to which they are related because false views lead to inappropriate actions. That is the principle of reflexivity. For instance, treating drug addicts as criminals creates criminal behavior."[148]

In addition to the bold systems thinking of George Soros and OSI, Baltimore in the late-twentieth and early twenty-first centuries is lucky to have the Annie E. Casey Foundation (AECF) which, with assets of $2.8 billion, is one of the largest foundations based (though not born) in Baltimore.[149] Established in 1948 by Jim Casey and his siblings, the foundation was named in honor of their mother, who, as a young widow, raised them alone. The fortune that supports AECF had its origins on the West Coast. In 1907 Jim Casey began a messenger service to help support his mother and siblings. In time, that small family business became United Parcel Service (UPS), the global million-dollar enterprise.[150] Unmarried and childless, by 1948 Casey's wealth far exceeded his personal needs. That year, he and his siblings began the charitable foundation in their mother's name. The central organizing principle was based on his belief that "the future chances of kids depends largely on whether their parents—their families—are able to provide emotionally, ethically, and materially."[151] The Casey Foundation's concerns first found expression in funding a summer camp for disadvantaged children in Seattle for two decades. When Jim Casey stepped down as the chief executive officer of UPS in the mid-1960s, he turned his focus on AECF and launched Casey Family Programs in 1966 as an independent operating foundation to provide direct services to foster youth and families while promoting improvements in child welfare practice and policy. After UPS moved its headquarters to the East Coast, Casey sponsored similar programs in New England. These later became known as Casey Family Services. Today they are the foundation's child welfare agency, providing direct services to thousands of children and families in New England and Maryland. When Jim Casey died in 1983 at the age of 95, he left a significant amount to the AECF. Eleven years later, at the invitation of Baltimore's mayor, Kurt Schmoke, AECF relocated from Greenwich, Connecticut, to Charm City.

Both the Annie E. Casey Foundation and the OSI relocated to Baltimore in the 1990s in part because of the unique opportunity that the city provides to conduct research on innovative approaches to urban problems. A cooperative city government, a world-class university, healthcare systems, and a population characterized by both wealthy professionals and those in dire poverty in inner city neighborhoods provide the mix of resources and needs that these organizations hoped would provide a fruitful testing ground for potential solutions to complex problems. In its past and present, Baltimore has been the site of philanthropic innovation.

Conclusion

In the 2010s, philanthropic foundations in Baltimore are a mixed group. Some are homegrown, created out of fortunes made over the last century. Others are national foundations that have chosen to relocate to Baltimore in the closing decades of the twentieth century because the city embodies the kinds of challenges these foundations were established to address, and, often, because of the proximity and relative affordability of Charm City to Washington, DC, and the government and policy centers there.[152] Foundations have worked in tandem with local groups and organizations to pursue diverse agendas that include initiatives like needle exchanges and the decriminalization of some street drugs and the expansion of anchor institutions and family economic self-sufficiency strategies, innovative social policies that continue a tradition begun 150 years ago with the creation of enterprises like the Peabody Institute, the Pratt Library, and JHU. In a recent article, Tim Armbruster, former president of the Goldseker Foundation, stated that "the shift from an industrial to a service-based economy has thrust nonprofits and philanthropy into a major role in civic leadership and life, meds and eds [health care and higher education] in particular are the region's intellectual and economic drivers."[153] Still, a recent study examining economic development in Baltimore counters that the leadership of foundations, while particularly useful around advocacy for issues relating to poverty, education, and social services, has not successfully replaced corporate leadership in terms of its capacity to drive economic development.[154] Regardless, foundations and federations continue to be at the center of what helps to shape Baltimore as a city and a community, and as "an incubator of activism and philanthropy"[155]

JESSICA I. ELFENBEIN is Professor of History at the University of South Carolina. She directed the award-winning public history project, *Baltimore '68: Riots and Rebirth.*

ELISE C. HAGESFELD, PhD is a lecturer in history at Case Western Reserve University in Cleveland. She brings over a decade of experience as a development professional in the nonprofit sector to her scholarship.

NOTES

1. Albert Shaw, "American Millionaires and Their Public Gifts," *New York Review of Reviews,* February 1893, 58.

2. Michael Barbaro, "$1.1 Billion in Thanks from Bloomberg to Johns Hopkins," *New York Times,* January 26, 2013, http://www.nytimes.com/2013/01/27/nyregion/at-1-1-billion-bloomberg-is-top-university-donor-in-us.html.

3. See David C. Hammack and Helmut K. Anheier, "American Foundations: Their Roles and Contributions to Society," in *American Foundations: Roles and Contributions,* eds. Helmut K. Anheier and David C. Hammack (Washington, DC: Brookings Institution, 2010), 3–28, for an overview of the foundation field. For an extended discussion of the roles of nineteenth-century funds and endowments, see David C. Hammack and Helmut K. Anheier, *A Versatile American Institution: The Changing Ideals and Realities of Philanthropic Foundations* (Washington, DC: Brookings Institution Press, 2013), 19–42.

4. Franklin Parker, *George Peabody: A Biography* (Nashville, TN: Vanderbilt University Press, 1971), ix.

5. "George Peabody at Baltimore," *New York Daily Times*, February 4, 1857, 2.

6. Kathleen Waters Sander, *Mary Elizabeth Garrett: Society and Philanthropy in the Gilded Age* (Baltimore: Johns Hopkins University Press, 2008), 14.

7. Parker, *George Peabody*, 27, 57–58, 69, 88–89.

8. Sander, *Mary Elizabeth Garrett*, 54.

9. Sander, *Mary Elizabeth Garrett*, 54.

10. Sander, *Mary Elizabeth Garrett*, 54.

11. Parker, *George Peabody*, 57–58, 89, and Sander, *Mary Elizabeth Garrett*, 55. Information on the worth of historical currency is based on the rate of inflation according to the Consumer Price Index, and can be found at www.measuringworth.com.

12. Parker, *George Peabody*, 166.

13. Parker, *George Peabody*, 87, 89, 90.

14. Parker, *George Peabody*, 87, 90, 91.

15. Parker, *George Peabody*, x.

16. "Peabody Foundation Led Way 60 Years Ago," *New York Times*, February 6, 1927, 10.

17. The Peabody Education Fund operated from 1867 until 1914 and first funded a comprehensive survey of the needs of public school education, which revealed the need for adequate systems and for adequately trained teachers. As a result, the foundation had two primary tasks: creating local public school systems where they did not exist, and creating the means for adequately training public school teachers. This led to the 1875 creation of the Peabody Normal School in Nashville, Tennessee. Ironically, by accomplishing these tasks, the Peabody Education Fund created a third group of new educational problems—namely that normal schools required instructors who were prepared to teach public school teachers. After a nine-year study was completed in 1914, the George Peabody College for Teachers was created in Nashville. By the 1920s, Peabody College drew students from thirty-eight states and nine foreign countries. "Peabody Foundation Led Way 60 Years Ago," *New York Times*, February 6, 1927, 10; and Parker, *George Peabody*, 160–61.

18. Pamela Barnhouse Walters and Emily Bowman, "Foundations and the Making of Public Education in the United States, 1867–1950," in Hammack and Anheier, *A Versatile American Institution*, 31–51.

19. "Peabody Foundation Led Way 60 Years Ago," *New York Times*, February 6, 1927, 10.

20. "Peabody Foundation Led Way 60 Years Ago," 10.

21. For a fuller discussion of the role of philanthropic foundations in the transformation of American public education, see Eric Anderson and Alfred A. Moss, *Dangerous Donations: Northern Philanthropy and Southern Black Education, 1902–30* (Columbia: University of Missouri Press, 1999); Peter Max Ascoli, *Julius Rosenwald: The Man Who Built Sears, Roebuck and Advanced the Cause of Black Education in the American South* (Bloomington: Indiana University Press, 2006); Walters and Bowman, "Foundations and the Making of Public Education." For more on George Peabody and his philanthropic endeavors, see Leonard P. Ayres, *Seven Great Foundations* (self-pub., 1911); J. L. M. Curry, *A Brief Sketch of George Peabody, and a History of the Peabody Education Fund through Thirty Years* (New York: Negro Universities Press, 1898); and George A. Dillingham, *The Foundation of the Peabody Tradition* (Lanham, MD: University Press of America, 1989).

22. George Peabody. Maryland State Archives. http://msa.maryland.gov/msa/speccol/photos/philanthropy/html/peabody.htm.

23. Parker, *George Peabody*, 162.

24. Bliss Forbush, *Moses Sheppard: Quaker Philanthropist of Baltimore* (Philadelphia: J. B. Lippincott, 1968); Bliss Forbush, *The Sheppard and Enoch Pratt Hospital, 1853–1970: A History* (Philadelphia: J. B. Lippincott, 1971). The hospital opened in 1891, when the income from Sheppard's original gift was sufficient to support operations. It continues to serve people with mental illness in Maryland as the Sheppard and Enoch Pratt Hospital, now over 120 years old.

25. Sander, *Mary Elizabeth Garrett*, 28, 30.

26. "The History of the Walters Art Museum," Walters Art Museum website, accessed September 20, 2013, www.thewalters.org/about/history.

27. Sander, *Mary Elizabeth Garrett*, 14.

28. Sander, *Mary Elizabeth Garrett*, 20–21, 23, 29.

29. Sander, *Mary Elizabeth Garrett*, 55.

30. Parker, George *Peabody*, 166; Scott M. Cutlip, *Fundraising in the United States: Its Role in America's Philanthropy* (New Brunswick, NJ: Rutgers University Press, 1965), 248. Cutlip mentions this connection between Peabody, Hopkins, and Garrett and discusses the lasting impression these large gifts left in the community of Baltimore. By 1920, the Johns Hopkins University and the medical school were struggling financially due to a reluctance of trustees to make a public appeal for funds even though their endowment had been significantly depleted in the panic of 1880. The community assumed that the institutional endowment was large enough to sustain the school and hospital in perpetuity (247–55).

31. Interestingly, earlier in 1873, Cornelius Vanderbilt had endowed a university in Nashville in his name for "just" $1 million. Sander, *Mary Elizabeth Garrett*, 94.

32. Sander, *Mary Elizabeth Garrett*, 157–58.

33. Daniel Coit Gilman, *The Launching of a University, and Other Papers; A Sheaf of Remembrances* (New York, 1906), 27–40.

34. Sander, *Mary Elizabeth Garrett*, 29.

35. Albert Shaw, "American Millionaires and Their Public Gifts," *New York Review of Reviews*, February 1893, 58.

36. Sander, *Mary Elizabeth Garrett*, 73, 110–11, 120–21.

37. Sander, *Mary Elizabeth Garrett*, 73, 110–11, 120–21.

38. On the politics of foundations' giving and their use to social movements, see David C. Hammack, "American Debates on the Legitimacy of Foundations," in *The Legitimacy of Philanthropic Foundations: United States and European Perspectives, ed. Kenneth Prewitt, Mattei Dogan, Steven Heydemann, and Stefan Toepler* (New York: Russell Sage Foundation, 2006); J. Craig Jenkins and Abigail Halci, "Grassrooting the System? The Development and Impact of Social Movement Philanthropy," in *Philanthropic Foundations*, ed. Ellen Condliffe Lagemann (Bloomington: Indiana University Press, 1999), 229–56; Mark Dowie, *American Foundations: An Investigative History* (Cambridge, MA: MIT Press, 2001); and Alice O'Connor, "Foundations, Social Movements, and the Contradictions of Liberal Philanthropy," in Anheier and Hammack, *American Foundations*, 328–46.

39. Sander, *Mary Elizabeth Garrett*, xii, 2–3, 122, 134, 160, 179. Other sources relevant to philanthropy and higher education include Bruce A. Kimball and Benjamin Ashby Johnson, "The Beginning of 'Free Money' Ideology in American Universities: Charles W. Eliot at Harvard, 1869–1909," *History of Education Quarterly* 52 (2012): 222–50; Bruce A. Kimball and Benjamin Ashby Johnson, "The Inception of the Meaning and Significance of Endowment in American Higher Education, 1890–1930," *Teachers College Record* 14, no. 10 (2012): 114.

40. The relative value of the gift in today's dollars was calculated used the change in the rate of inflation as reflected by the Consumer Price Index. See www.MeasuringWorth.com (October 2, 2013).

41. Sander, *Mary Elizabeth Garrett*, 182.

42. Sander *Mary Elizabeth Garrett*, 217.

43. Shaw, "American Millionaires," 58.

44. Shaw, "American Millionaires," 58.

45. Shaw, "American Millionaires," 58.

46. Jessica Elfenbein, *The Making of a Modern City: Philanthropy, Civic Culture, and the Baltimore YMCA* (Gainesville: University Press of Florida, 2001), 42–43. For an extended discussion of the emergence of the Charity Organization Society and the ways in which scientific

philanthropy differed from what had come before it, see James Leiby, *A History of Social Welfare and Social Work in the United States* (New York: Columbia University Press, 1978), 111–35.

47. "Constructive Philanthropy," *City & State: A Maryland Journal of Social Progress* 1, no. 4 (May 1919): 2.

48. A contemporary wrote of Gilman, "Baltimore's debt to him is deep and lasting. He helped to model her charter, he was a cooperator in her charities and her philanthropies, and was an adviser and more than an adviser in promoting her educational welfare.... The Peabody Institute, the Enoch Pratt Free Library, the Samuel Ready Orphan School, the McDonogh School, the Mercantile Library, the Municipal Art Society, the Reform Leagues in city and state, the Charity Organization Society, and the public schools, all to a greater or less extent, received impulse or profit from his cooperation." Charles M. Andrews, "Daniel Coit Gilman, LL.D.," *Proceedings of the American Philosophical Society* 48, no. 193 (September–December 1909): lxviii.

49. Constitution of the COS (1885), in Charles Hirschfeld, *Baltimore, 1870-1900: Studies in Social History* (Baltimore: Johns Hopkins University Press, 1941), 139–40.

50. Hirschfeld, Baltimore (1941), 142.

51. Hirschfeld, *Baltimore*, 142.

52. Hirschfeld, *Baltimore*, 141, 145.

53. Alvin B. Kogut, "The Negro and the Charity Organization Society in the Progressive Era," *Social Service Review* 44, no. 1 (March 1970): 11–21.

54. For more on Mary Richmond and her work at the Baltimore COS and the Russell Sage Foundation, see Sarah Henry Lederman, "Philanthropy and Social Case Work: Mary E. Richmond and the Russell Sage Foundation, 1909–28," in *Women and Philanthropy in Education*, ed. Andrea Walton (Bloomington: Indiana University Press, 2005), 60–80. It is interesting to note that all three of these schools of social work continue to be at the forefront of their disciplines, ranking in the top ten of the graduate schools of social work in the *US News and World Report*.

55. For more on the Russell Sage Foundation and its role in the development of social work as a discipline, see John M. Glenn, Lillian Brandt, and F. Emerson Andrews, *Russell Sage Foundation, 1907–47* (New York: Russell Sage Foundation, 1947); David C. Hammack and Stanton Wheeler, *Social Science in the Making: Essays on the Russell Sage Foundation, 1907–72* (New York: Russell Sage Foundation, 1994); and Alice O'Connor, *Social Science for What? Philanthropy and the Social Question in a World Turned Rightside Up* (New York: Russell Sage Foundation, 2007).

56. E. Digby Baltzell, Allen Glicksman, and Jacquelyn Litt, "The Jewish Communities of Philadelphia and Boston: A Tale of Two Cities," in *Jewish Life in Philadelphia, 1830–1940*, ed. Murray Friedman (Philadelphia: Institute for the Study of Human Issues, 1983), 305. Boston's United Hebrew Benevolent Association began in 1864. Philadelphia's United Hebrew Charities was founded in 1869.

57. Isaac M. Fein, *The Making of an American Jewish Community: The History of Baltimore Jewry from 1773 to 1920* (Philadelphia: Jewish Publication Society, 1971), 74. The quote cited appeared February 21, 1856. The experience of Baltimore's Jewish community is consistent with the argument made by Charles Liebman that a high priority for American Jewish philanthropy through the 1960s was to raise the standing of the Jewish community, and the acceptance of Jewish professionals, by funding excellence and making excellent health care and other services, including access to arts education and arts experiences, available to everyone. See Charles S. Liebman, "Leadership and Decision-Making in a Jewish Federation: The New York Federation of Jewish Philanthropies," *American Jewish Yearbook* 79 (1979): 3–76.

58. Federation of Jewish Charities (hereafter FJC), 1st Joint Report, 1908, 6, Archives of the Associated Jewish Charities of Baltimore (hereafter Associated), Box 23, Jewish Museum of Maryland (hereafter JMM).

59. FJC 1st Joint Report, 1908, 6–7, Associated, Box 23, JMM.

60. The immigration figures are taken from Fein, *Making of an American Jewish Community*, 143, 149. The population figures are taken from Earl Pruce, *Synagogues, Temples and Congregations of Maryland, 1830–1990* (Baltimore: Jewish Historical Society of Maryland, 1993), 176.

61. FJC 1st Joint Report, 1908, 6–7, Associated, Box 23, JMM.

62. FJC 1st Joint Report, 1908, 6–7, Associated, Box 23, JMM.

63. On arrival in Baltimore, differences between the Eastern European and Russian newcomers and their more settled coreligionists appeared unbridgeable. Yet, time eliminated much of the difference. In 1900, three-fourths of Baltimore's Jews of German descent engaged in mercantile pursuits while three-fifths of Russians worked as artisans. By 1924, however, there was "not much of an occupational distinction" among the 67,500 German and Russian Jews who comprised Baltimore's Jewish population. Fein, *Making of an American Jewish Community*, 223.

64. The Baron de Hirsch Fund, a foundation, was incorporated in New York State in 1891 to serve Jews fleeing Eastern Europe and migrating to the United States. The fund offered protection for immigrants through port work, relief, temporary aid, promotion of suburban industrial enterprises, removal from urban centers through the Industrial Removal Office, land settlement, agricultural training, and trade and general education. In 1894, the Baron de Hirsch Agricultural College was opened in Woodbine, New Jersey—the first school in the United States to impart secondary education in agriculture. During the Nazi era, the fund spent large sums of money for German Jewish relief. Later, its chief activity was support of the Jewish Agricultural Society, created in 1900 by the fund and its European counterpart, the Jewish Colonization Association, to promote the Jewish farm movement. "Baron de Hirsch Fund: Genealogical Finding Aid," JewishGen website, accessed October 4, 2004, http://data.jewishgen.org/wconnect/wc.dll?jg~jgsys~ajhs_pb~r!!277.

65. Fein, *Making of an American Jewish Community*, 142, 144, 154, 172. Cyrus Adler lived in Baltimore between 1883 and 1893. He later served as president of both the Jewish Theological Seminary and Dropsie College.

66. Boston created a Federation of Jewish Charities in 1895. Philadelphia came on line in 1901. Baltzell, Glicksman, and Litt, "The Jewish Communities of Philadelphia and Boston," 305.

67. Fein, *Making of an American Jewish Community*, 214.

68. The Federation of Jewish Charities' founding charities were Hebrew Hospital and Asylum Association, Hebrew Ladies Sewing Circle, Hebrew Orphan Asylum, Hebrew Ladies Orphan Aid Society, Hebrew Benevolent Society, Maccabeans, Hebrew Free Burial Society (which M. S. Levy represented), Hebrew Ladies Sewing Society, Council Milk and Ice Fund, Hebrew Education Society (which Julius Levy represented), and Daughters in Israel. Alexandra Lee, *Vision: A Biography of Harry Friedenwald* (Philadelphia: Jewish Publication Society of America, 1964), 181.

69. Levin, one of fourteen children, worked as a bookkeeper at Strauss Brothers before attending law school, and becoming the editor of the *Comment*. Alexandra Lee Levin, *Dare to Be Different: A Biography of Louis H. Levin of Baltimore, A Pioneer in Jewish Social Service* (New York: Bloch, 1972), 49.

70. FJC AR 1909, 5–9, Associated, Box 23, JMM.

71. FJC AR 1909, 5–9, Associated, Box 23, JMM.

72. FJC AR 1909, 5–9, Associated, Box 23, JMM.

73. FJC AR 1909, 5–9, Associated, Box 23, JMM.

74. FJC 1st Joint Report, 1908, 4–5, Associated, Box 23, JMM.

75. Although this is not an uncommon fundraising claim, and one often subject to hyperbole, in the case of the FJC it seems to have been true. Rather than annual campaigns on behalf of a dozen organizations, the FJC had only one each year. FJC, 1912 AR, 6, Associated, Box 23, JMM.

76. FJC, 1912 AR, 6, Associated, Box 23, JMM.

77. Levin, *Dare to be Different*, 49–50.

78. A letter to Cyrus Adler from Harry Friedenwald, dated November 29, 1907, described Eli Frank as "a young lawyer—a graduate of the Johns Hopkins University and of the University of Maryland Law School." He was then on the faculty of the law school. He was described as having "deep interest in Jewish matters," borne out by his service on the board of the Hebrew Hospital and as an officer of the FJC. JMM, Friedenwald Collection, 1984.23, Box 13; Levin, *Dare to Be Different*, 50; and JMM, Associated, Box 4, Minutes FJC, October 15, 1906.

79. FJC 1st Joint Report, 1908, 10, Associated, Box 23, JMM.

80. JMM, Associated, Box 4, Minutes FJC, November 25, 1906.

81. Levin, *Dare to be Different*, 49–50.

82. FJC, 1910 AR, 4, Associated, Box 23, JMM.

83. FJC, 1910 AR, 4, Associated, Box 23, JMM.

84. A letter to Cyrus Adler from Harry Friedenwald dated November 29, 1907, described Epstein as "an emigrant from Russia about 1881." By 1907, he was "one of the leading merchants in the city had . . . very active in all Jewish charities. . . . He has considerable political influence." JMM, Friedenwald Collection, 1984.23, Box 13.

85. JMM, Associated, Box 4, Minutes, FJC, April 11 and June 1907; Isidor Blum, The Jews of Baltimore(Baltimore-Washington 1910), 103, and Letter from Leonard Weinberg, President, Mount Pleasant, to Mrs. William Levy, December 14, 1931, Levy Collection, JMM, Box 22.

86. Fein, *Making of an American Jewish Community*, 223–24. For more information on Epstein, see also Lester Levy, *Jacob Epstein* (Baltimore: Maran Press, 1978).

87. Epstein was on the FJC board as early as 1907. FJC Minutes, January 20, 1907, JMM, FJC, Box 4. "Schnorring" here translates as constant, shameless begging.

88. UHC Annual Report, 1917, Associated, Box 22, 6–7. Those present were Jacob Epstein, Joseph Castelberg, M. S. Levy, Gershon Schwartz, Lewis Putzel, Israel Levinstein, Tanchum Silberman, Adolph Kres, Paul S. Levy, Meyer L. Bloom, Jonas Greenblatt, Louis Hurwitz, A. J. Sugar, M. E. Senkow, Ephraim Macht, Samuel Singer, Jacob Rab, and Solomon Ginsberg.

89. *In Memoriam Michael Simon Levy and Betsy Levy* (Baltimore: Lord Baltimore Press, 1912), 15; and "Progress of United Hebrew Charities," *Baltimore American*, December 17, 1911.

90. "Progress of United Hebrew Charities," 168.

91. UHC AR 1917, 168, Associated, Box 22, JMM.

92. FJC, 1910 AR, 4, Associated, Box 23, JMM.

93. FJC, 1910 AR, 4, Associated, Box 23, JMM.

94. FJC, 1910 AR, 4, Associated, Box 23, JMM.

95. FJC Annual Report, 1909, Associated, Box 23, 5.

96. UHC Annual Report, 1917, Associated, Box 22, 11–12, 169; and Fein, *Making of an American Jewish Community*, 216.

97. "Charitable Work Among Hebrews," *Baltimore American*, December 5, 1910.

98. Levin, *Dare to Be Different*, 219.

99. Levin, *Dare to Be Different*, 219.

100. FJC, Minutes, May 4, 1920; July 19, 1920; December 9, 1920. Associated, Box 8, JMM.

101. The other officers of the Associated were Emil Crockin, first vice president; Walter Sondheim, second vice president; Albert Hutzler, treasurer; and Mayer L. Bloom, assistant treasurer. "Subscribers to the Associated Jewish Charities of Baltimore," 1921, 4–5. Associated, Box 2, JMM.

102. FJC, 1916 AR, 9–10, Associated, Box 23, JMM.

103. FJC, 1916 AR, 9–10, Associated, Box 23, JMM.

104. FJC, 1916 AR, 9–10, Associated, Box 23, JMM.

105. "Abstract of Report of Secretary, Louis H. Levin," January 18, 1920. Associated, Box 8, JMM.

106. Mary J. Oates, *The Catholic Philanthropic Tradition in America* (Bloomington: Indiana University Press, 1995), 52.

107. Oates, *The Catholic Philanthropic Tradition in America*, 99–100.

108. Dorothy M. Brown and Elizabeth McKeown, *The Poor Belong to Us: Catholic Charities and American Welfare* (Cambridge, MA: Harvard University Press, 1997), 59–60.

109. Thomas W. Spalding, *The Premier See: A History of the Archdiocese of Baltimore, 1789–1989* (Baltimore: Johns Hopkins University Press, 1989), 335–37.

110. Brown and McKeown, *The Poor Belong to Us*, 62–65.

111. "Our Members," The Association of Baltimore Area Grantmakers (website), accessed September 23, 2013, http://www.abagrantmakers.org/?page=Member_List; "Private Foundations in Baltimore City, MD, 2011–2012," National Center for Charitable Statistics, accessed September 28, 2013, http://nccsdataweb.urban.org/PubApps/geoShowOrgs.php?id=C24510&code=C24510&v=pf.

112. Hammack and Anheier, *A Versatile American Institution*, 118.

113. "A Brief History," Abell Foundation website, accessed October 30, 2009, http://www.abell.org/aboutthefoundation/history.html.

114. "Harry Black, 69, of Sunpapers Dies," *New York Times*, November 26, 1956, 27, http://www.nytimes.com/1956/11/26/archives/harry-black-69-of-sunpapers-dies-board-chairman-of-abell-company-in.html.

115. "A Brief History," Abell Foundation website, last accessed July 19, 2010, http://www.abell.org/aboutthefoundation/history.html.

116. "A Brief History," Abell Foundation website, last accessed July 19, 2010, http://www.abell.org/aboutthefoundation/history.html.

117. "Henry Knott Sr., 89, Maryland Developer," *New York Times* (Late Edition, East Coast), November 29, 1995, D19.

118. "About the Knott Foundation," The Marion I. and Henry J. Knott Foundation home page, accessed November 9, 2017, http://www.knottfoundation.org/.

119. "Henry Knott Sr., 89, Maryland Developer," D19.

120. Harlan, Heather. "Brick by Brick: Knotts Have a Tight Hold on City's Past, Future." *Baltimore Business Journal*, October 11, 2004, sec. Commercial Real Estate. https://www.bizjournals.com/baltimore/stories/2004/10/11/story3.html.

121. "Family Legacy," The Marion I. and Henry J. Knott Foundation home page, accessed October 24, 2017, http://www.knottfoundation.org/about/family_legacy.

122. "Our Members," The Association of Baltimore Area Grantmakers, accessed November 28, 2017, http://www.abagrantmakers.org/page/Member_List.

123. "Entrepreneur Joseph Meyerhoff, 85, Known for His Philanthropy, Dies." *The Washington Post*. February 5, 1985.

124. "Joseph Meyerhoff, Developer, Was an Active Philanthropist," *New York Times* (1923–Current file), February 5, 1985.

125. "Joseph Meyerhoff, Developer, Was an Active Philanthropist," *New York Times* (1923–Current file), February 5, 1985.

126. "About Us," Joseph and Harvey Meyerhoff Family Charitable Funds, accessed November 28, 2017, http://www.meyerhoffcharitablefunds.org/about-us.

127. "Company Overview of the Harry and Jeanette Weinberg Foundation Inc.," Bloomberg.com, November 9, 2017, http://investing.businessweek.com/research/stocks/private/snapshot.asp?privcapId=4890850.

128. Glenn Fowler, "Harry Weinberg, 82, Businessman in Transit and Real Estate, Is Dead," *New York Times*, November 6, 1990, http://www.nytimes.com/1990/11/06/obituaries/harry-weinberg-82-businessman-in-transit-and-real-estate-is-dead.html.

129. Glenn Fowler, "Harry Weinberg, 82, Businessman In Transit and Real Estate, Is Dead," *New York Times*, Nov. 6, 1990.

130. Francis F. Beirne, *The Amiable Baltimoreans* (Baltimore: Johns Hopkins University Press, 1984), 281–83.

131. "Modest Means Grew to Major Gift Giving: One-Time Poor Boy Emanuel Chambers Built a Fortune through Frugality and Wise Investment. He Used It to Benefit City Institutions

and Those in Need," *Baltimore Sun*, February 9, 1997, accessed September 18, 2013, http://articles.baltimoresun.com/1997-02-09/features/1997040006_1_emanuel-mckim-hopkins-hospital.

132. The estimate of Chambers's bequest in contemporary dollars is based on the rate of inflation in the consumer price index between 1945 and 2013. See http://www.Measuringworth.com. (September 18, 2013).

133. "The Indispensable Role of Blacks at Johns Hopkins" can also be seen online at http://bfsa.jhu.edu/exhibits/exhibit-list/ (accessed November 9, 2017).

134. "Emmanuel Chambers Estate Is Now Worth Half-Million," *Baltimore Afro-American*, June 6, 1965, A6.

135. "Emmanuel Chambers Estate Is Now Worth Half-Million," *Baltimore Afro-American*, June 6, 1965, A6.

136. "Emanuel Chambers Fund Closed Out with $580,000," *Baltimore Afro-American*, February 17, 1973, D34.

137. Michael T. Kauffman, *Soros: The Life and Times of a Messianic Billionaire* (New York: Random House, 2002), xiii.

138. Kauffman, *Soros*, 304.

139. Kauffman, *Soros*, 304.

140. http://www.soros.org/initiatives/baltimore/about (accessed July 2, 2010).

141. Kauffman, *Soros*, 307.

142. http://www.soros.org/initiatives/baltimore/about (accessed October 24, 2017).

143. Kauffman, *Soros*, 307.

144. http://www.soros.org/initiatives/baltimore/about (accessed July 2, 2010).

145. Lorraine Mirabella, "The Business of Doing Good Works," *The Baltimore Sun*, September 12, 2010, A3.

146. Lorraine Mirabella, "The Business of Doing Good Works," *The Baltimore Sun*, September 12, 2010, A3.

147. Lorraine Mirabella, "The Business of Doing Good Works," A3.

148. Lorraine Mirabella, "The Business of Doing Good Works," A3.

149. http://www.aecf.org/AboutUs/~/media/PDFFiles/AECF_2010_Financial_Statements.pdf (accessed July 18, 2011).

150. Wolfgang Saxon, "James E. Casey Is Dead at 95; Started United Parcel Service," *New York Times*, June 7, 1983, http://www.nytimes.com/1983/06/07/obituaries/james-e-casey-is-dead-at-95-started-united-parcel-service.html.

151. "Our History," Annie E. Casey Foundation (website), accessed October 30, 2009, http://www.aecf.org/about/history/.

152. "City Chosen for Anti-Drug Effort Soros Initiative: A Focus on Treatment of Individuals and Correction of Related Problems," *The Baltimore Sun*, August 5, 1997 (http://articles.baltimoresun.com/1997-08-05/news/1997217031_1_drug-abuse-drug-treatment-drug-problem).

153. Paul Sturm, "Baltimore Is a City That Gives and Gives and Gives," *BMORE Magazine*, August 3, 2010. http://www.bmoremedia.com/features/bmorephilanthropy080310.aspx.

154. David Connolly, Hal Wolman, Katherine Pearson, and Royce Hanson, *Corporate Citizenship and Urban Problem Solving: The Changing Civic Role of Business Leaders in American Cities* (Washington, DC: Brookings Institution, 2006), http://www.brookings.edu/research/reports/2006/09/useconomics [September 18, 2013]).

155. Sander, *Mary Elizabeth Garrett*, 29.

chapter three

THE WASHINGTON, DC, REGION'S MODEST FOUNDATION SECTOR

Alan J. Abramson and Stefan Toepler

THE LEVEL OF FOUNDATION ACTIVITY in the Washington, DC, region presents a puzzle. Ordinarily, a wealthy region like Washington, DC, would be expected to have a large foundation community with high levels of foundation assets and grantmaking. Surprisingly, however, Washington's foundation sector is only of moderate size. What accounts for the relatively modest size of the foundation community? How does Washington's status as a national and international capital affect foundation activity? How can this city's foundations make the best use of their modest resources? This chapter will address these and other related questions.

To deepen our understanding of foundations in Washington, DC, we rely heavily on a broad range of data from the Foundation Center, official US government sources, and interviews with leaders of Washington's foundation community. Unfortunately, there are few previous studies of DC's foundations to draw on; so in this chapter, we present an early analysis that others will want to build on.

What our analysis suggests is that Washington's foundation sector has been significantly shaped by the region's status as the nation's capital. The federal government has been a major engine of growth for the region's economy, with many of the area's residents working directly or indirectly for the federal government.[1] Consequently, the region has not been home to many jobs in manufacturing or other nongovernmental industries.

The upshot of this economic development pattern is that Washington, DC, has been a region with a sizeable middle class, anchored by a significant number of federal employees and a substantial wealthier class, made up of lawyers, consultants, and other professionals engaged in government-related work but employed in the private sector. However, both historically and today, the region's economy has supported relatively few of the mega-wealthy who are likely to establish large foundations. Thus, reflecting its government-dominated economy and as detailed below, the Washington area has a moderate-sized foundation sector and none of the large, mega-foundations found elsewhere.

Overall, US foundations account for only a small portion—roughly 3 percent—of total nonprofit revenue.[2] Because Washington's foundation sector is moderately sized, and because it is interested in supporting many national and international organizations, the region's foundations provide exceptionally modest funding for nonprofits serving Washington residents. Foundations based outside of Washington, DC, send money to the region mostly to support the area's many national and international nonprofit organizations rather than to support the region's locally oriented nonprofits. The overall reality is that Washington is more a conduit for foundation funds headed elsewhere than a final destination for these funds.

Looking to the future, local leaders who want to strengthen the role of foundations in Washington, DC, should step up efforts to capture the region's significant wealth for philanthropy. Without a more intensive effort to increase the wealth that goes to philanthropy in this region, the wealth is likely to be consumed, willed to future generations, or lost to other purposes. In addition, foundations should redouble their monitoring of community needs and tracking of government, nonprofit, and business efforts to address these needs so that foundations can determine where they can add the most value. Individual foundations can also pool their funds into collaborative initiatives, such as the existing Washington AIDS Partnership, to stretch the modest resources they have available.

As should be clear, the subject of this chapter is foundations in Washington, DC. We focus largely on grant-making foundations that have their own endowments. Nonprofits that have "foundation" in their names but that are largely grant-seeking rather than grant-making institutions are not included. Generally, we use the US government's definition of the Washington, DC, metropolitan area as our geographic area of interest. This definition, which has changed somewhat over time, currently includes twenty-two counties and cities in the District of Columbia, Maryland, Virginia, and West Virginia.[3]

Portrait of the Washington Area Foundation Sector

No Mega-Foundations

In addition to the overall modest size of Washington's foundation sector, it is also the case, as noted above, that there are no exceptionally large foundation in the Washington area. No Washington foundations appear in the list of the nation's fifty largest foundations, and only two area foundations—the Freedom Forum at number eighty and the Jack Kent Cooke Foundation at number ninety-eight—were among the nation's hundred largest foundations as of 2013.[4] Lacking a marquee funder with national name recognition—such as Ford or Rockefeller in New York, Gates in Seattle, or Getty in Los Angeles—the Washington, DC, metro area is home to a broad and interesting mix of midsized foundations.

Two of the most locally active, independent foundations are the Morris and Gwendolyn Cafritz Foundation and the Eugene and Agnes E. Meyer Foundation. Some of the more significant foundations in Washington, DC, make national grants in specific program areas: for example, the Public Welfare Foundation focuses on criminal and juvenile justice and workers' rights, and the Jack Kent Cooke Foundation focuses on scholarships for needy high school, college, and graduate students. The Fannie Mae and Freddie Mac Foundations have been among the most important corporate funders in recent decades, although their grant-making programs have been restructured in recent years because of their parent companies' financial problems. The World Bank also operates a relatively large local giving program, but does not operate an independent foundation. The Case Foundation represents the area's technology wealth, as does Venture Philanthropy Partners (VPP), which employs a "venture philanthropy" approach that allows VPP to be highly engaged with its grantees.[5] The region's most significant operating foundations are the Freedom Forum, which provides funding for the Washington-based Newseum, and the nationally oriented Howard Hughes Medical Institute, which is a foundation in all but its tax designation.

These foundations are part of a Washington, DC, foundation community that, in 2010, consisted of 1,512 foundations with some $13 billion in assets and grantmaking of $878 million.[6] As shown in table 3.1, as of 2010, the area foundations with the largest assets were the Freedom Forum (with $867 million), the Morris and Gwendolyn Cafritz Foundation (with $649 million), the Diana Davis Spencer

Table 3.1. Largest Washington Area Foundations by Assets and Giving, 2010

Rank	Foundation	Assets	Rank	Foundation	Giving
1	The Freedom Forum, Inc. (DC)	$867,021,671	1	The Community Foundation for the National Capital Region (DC)	$62,969,894
2	The Morris and Gwendolyn Cafritz Foundation (DC)	649,238,051	2	The Freedom Forum, Inc. (DC)	41,126,918
3	Diana Davis Spencer Foundation (MD)	609,202,819	3	The Ellison Medical Foundation (MD)	38,964,726
4	Jack Kent Cooke Foundation (VA)	554,365,737	4	Arthur S. DeMoss Foundation (DC)	35,271,848
5	The J. Willard and Alice S. Marriott Foundation (MD)	523,637,528	5	New Mighty Foundation (DC)	29,177,945
6	The Sherman Fairchild Foundation, Inc. (MD)	486,855,838	6	Public Welfare Foundation, Inc. (DC)	23,476,197
7	Public Welfare Foundation, Inc. (DC)	468,558,354	7	The Morris and Gwendolyn Cafritz Foundation (DC)	23,041,084
8	The Community Foundation for the National Capital Region (DC)	368,358,325	8	The Sherman Fairchild Foundation, Inc. (MD)	22,935,740
9	Glenstone Foundation (DC)	351,452,960	9	Jack Kent Cooke Foundation (VA)	19,020,073
10	The Gottesman Fund (DC)	258,945,062	10	The Mitchell P. Rales Family Foundation (VA)	18,602,779
11	Arthur S. DeMoss Foundation (DC)	238,121,792	11	Robert H. Smith Family Foundation (VA)	16,667,520

Table 3.1. *(continued)*

Rank	Foundation	Assets	Rank	Foundation	Giving
12	Charles G. Koch Charitable Foundation (VA)	206,497,763	12	Freddie Mac Foundation (VA)	14,052,127
13	The Claude Moore Charitable Foundation (VA)	196,055,172	13	The Gottesman Fund (DC)	13,921,375
14	Eugene B. Casey Foundation (MD)	192,976,735	14	The Wyss Foundation (DC)	13,237,330
15	Eugene and Agnes E. Meyer Foundation (DC)	179,496,020	15	Searle Freedom Trust (DC)	12,365,616
16	The Laszlo N. Tauber Family Foundation (MD)	169,104,893	16	The J. Willard and Alice S. Marriott Foundation (MD)	12,303,959
17	Wallace Genetic Foundation, Inc. (DC)	167,962,024	17	Charles G. Koch Charitable Foundation (VA)	12,257,639
18	Wallace Global Fund II (DC)	163,297,650	18	Wallace Global Fund II (DC)	10,835,023
19	Freddie Mac Foundation (VA)	130,155,024	19	Sheila C. Johnson Foundation, Inc. (VA)	8,910,805
20	Searle Freedom Trust (DC)	121,297,567	20	Eugene and Agnes E. Meyer Foundation (DC)	8,489,825
	Total	$6,902,600,985		Total	$437,628,423

Source: Washington Regional Association of Grantmakers, "Our Region, Our Giving: Philanthropy in the Greater Washington Region," Foundation Center, Washington, 2012.

Foundation (with $609 million), the Jack Kent Cooke Foundation (with $554 million), and the J. Willard and Alice S. Marriott Foundation (with $524 million). In terms of giving, the largest Washington area foundation by far is the Community Foundation for the National Capital Region. With grants of $63 million in 2010, its giving was over 50 percent greater than that of the next two foundations, the Freedom Forum ($41 million) and the Ellison Medical Foundation ($39 million). Other top local givers include the Arthur S. DeMoss Foundation ($35 million), New Mighty Foundation ($29 million), and Public Welfare Foundation ($23 million).

In some ways, the structure of the Washington, DC, foundation field resembles the structure of the foundation community on a national level. For example, foundation assets are heavily concentrated both nationally and in the Washington region. As shown in table 3.1, the twenty largest Washington-based foundations in 2010 controlled assets of $7 billion, or over half of all local foundation assets. Likewise, with $437 million in grants, the twenty largest foundation-givers accounted for half of all grant-making by foundations located in the DC metro area.

The composition of Washington-area foundations by type—independent, corporate, community, and operating—also parallels the composition for the nation as a whole. Nationally, nine out of ten foundations are independent foundations that, in 2009, controlled more than 80 percent of all foundation assets and a little less than three-quarters of total foundation-giving. Though small in numbers, corporate and community foundations each accounted for 9 percent of giving nationally. Community foundations held 8 percent of all foundation assets; corporate foundations 3 percent, and operating foundations that also make grants held the remaining 6 percent.[7]

As shown in table 3.2, a similar pattern holds in the Washington area for the breakdown of foundation activity by foundation type. In 2009, independent foundations in the DC area accounted for about 90 percent of all foundations, nearly three-quarters of all giving, and a little less than 80 percent of assets. Assets held by Washington-area corporate foundations matched the national figure of 3 percent, but corporate giving was only 6 percent compared to the national level of 10 percent. Washington-area community foundations held less than half the share of assets that community foundations control nationally but had higher levels of giving with over 10 percent. Operating foundations, reflecting the size of the Freedom Forum, accounted for a disproportionally high share of regional foundation assets.

Table 3.2. DC Metro Foundation Financials, by Foundation Type, 1999, 2004, and 2009

1999	Number	%	Assets	%	Giving	%
Independent Foundations	830	86.7%	$6,425,124,450	75.5%	$358,987,332	69%
Corporate Foundations	36	3.8%	$661,231,148	7.8%	$93,752,389	18%
Community Foundations	6	0.6%	$146,127,915	1.7%	$33,661,638	6.5%
Operating Foundations	85	8.9%	$1,281,753,780	15.1%	$33,810,108	6.5%
Total	957		$8,514,237,293		$520,211,467	

2004	Number	%	Assets	%	Giving	%
Independent Foundations	1,216	88.9%	$8,072,672,363	72.9%	$536,731,074	68.8%
Corporate Foundations	36	2.6%	$703,107,863	6.4%	$99,131,483	12.7%
Community Foundations	4	0.3%	$819,530,913	7.4%	$71,747,528	9.2%
Operating Foundations	112	8.2%	$1,474,842,646	13.3%	$72,661,157	9.3%
Total	1,368		$11,070,153,785		$780,271,242	

2009	Number	%	Assets	%	Giving	%
Independent Foundations	1,312	89.2%	$9,254,491,281	78.3%	$665,460,626	73.6%
Corporate Foundations	44	3.0%	$367,843,493	3.1%	$54,701,719	6.0%
Community Foundations	6	0.4%	$393,102,222	3.3%	$97,118,645	10.7%
Operating Foundations	109	7.4%	$1,804,809,508	15.3%	$87,443,588	9.7%
Total	1,471		$11,820,246,504		$904,724,578	

Source: The Foundation Center's Statistical Information Service. Aggregate Financial Information for Foundations in the Washington, DC, Metropolitan Area, circa 1999, 2004, and 2009.

Rapid Growth

While still of moderate size, the Washington foundation sector grew at a rapid pace between 1999 and 2009, as reflected in table 3.2. According to Foundation Center data, the number of foundations grew from 957 to 1,471;

assets rose from $8.5 billion to $11.8 billion; and giving increased from $520 million to $905 million. Commensurate with the overall growth of the US foundation community, foundation-giving by Washington-area foundations thus increased by an average of 7.4 percent per year from 1999 through 2009, or by 3.7 percent per year after adjusting for inflation.

Especially noteworthy was the growth in giving by independent foundations that increased from approximately two-thirds of all local foundation-giving in 1999 to nearly three-quarters of foundation-giving in 2009. With assets increasing by 28 percent over this period, community foundation-giving grew even more strongly. Community foundations more than tripled their giving in five years—from $34 million in 1999 to $72 million in 2004, and then grew to $97 million in 2009. Corporate foundation-giving, by contrast, fared less well. Although this type of giving increased from $94 million to $99 million between 1999 and 2004, its share of all local foundation-giving dropped from 18 percent to 12.7 percent during these five years. By 2009, corporate foundations' shares of total giving had halved again—to 6 percent—with a decline in giving to $55 million.[8] Much of the recent decline in corporate foundation assets and giving was due to the dissolution of the Fannie Mae Foundation in early 2007.[9]

Modest Relative Size of Foundation Sector

In light of the significant wealth in the Washington area, we might expect the area's foundation sector to be larger than the foundation communities in many other areas. However, while Washington ranked second among twenty-five large areas in per-capita income in 2009, it ranked only fifteenth among twenty-five large areas in foundation assets per capita and thirteenth in foundation-giving per capita. This is illustrated in table 3.3.

Consistent with the observation that Washington is a wealthy area with a modest size foundation sector is the finding that Washington's wealth does not translate into foundation-giving as much as it does in other areas. As shown in table 3.4, among twenty-five large areas, DC ranked nineteenth in terms of foundation-giving relative to income.

The region's major community foundation, the Community Foundation for the National Capital Region (CFNCR), is relatively large compared to other area foundations. The foundation's giving of $90 million in 2009 was more than double the giving of any other local foundation. However, compared to other community foundations around the United States, the DC-area community foundation is only of moderate size. This is shown in table 3.5.

Besides being a small community relative to its income, Washington's foundations are also small in relation to the size of the region's nonprofit

Table 3.3. Foundation Assets and Grants per Capita, 2009

	Income, Per Capita* ($)	Ranking	Foundation Assets, Per Capita** ($)	Ranking	Foundation-Giving, Per Capita*** ($)	Ranking
Atlanta	37,101	24	1,648	20	133	17
Boston	53,553	3	3,145	8	262	5
Chicago	44,379	11	2,491	14	218	9
Cincinnati	37,967	21	1,376	22	126	19
Cleveland	39,451	20	3,111	9	213	10
Dallas	41,764	16	1,704	19	126	20
Denver	46,611I	6	2,610	13	149	16
Detroit	37,927	22	1,751	18	130	18
Houston	46,570	7	1,878	17	124	22
Kansas City	40,438	18	2,713	12	198	11
Los Angeles	42,784	12	3,096	10	178	12
Miami	42,764	13	1,645	21	125	21
Milwaukee	42,303	14	3,208	7	258	6
Minneapolis	45,811	9	3,940	6	243	7
New York	52,037	4	4,898	4	449	3
Philadelphia	46,075	8	3,001	11	298	4
Phoenix	34,452	25	8,264	2	52	24
Pittsburgh	42,298	15	4,398	5	242	8
Portland, OR	39,568	19	2,086	16	161	14
San Diego	45,706	10	877	24	61	23
San Francisco	59,993	1	6,297	3	503	2
Seattle	50,378	5	12,177	1	1,021	1
St. Louis	40,728	17	1,167	23	161	15
Tampa	37,632	23	365	25	30	25
Washington, DC	56,984	2	2,158	15	165	13

* Bureau of Economic Analysis. US Department of Commerce. 2009.
** Population Estimates. US Census Bureau and Foundation Center's Statistical Information Service. Foundation Assets: The Foundation Center's Statistical Information Service.
*** Population Estimates. US Census Bureau and Foundation Center's Statistical Information Service. Foundation-Giving: The Foundation Center's Statistical Information Service.

and governmental sectors and its overall economy (see table 3.6). Thus, the assets of Washington foundations are 22.8 percent of the region's nonprofit sector expenses, which puts the region twelfth among the nation's fifteen largest areas. Similarly, total foundation assets in the region amount to 13.2 percent of the region's government GDP, with the region ranking twenty-third out of twenty-five on this measure. Finally, foundation assets

Table 3.4. Index of Foundation-Giving Relative to Income

Metropolitan Statistical Area (MSA)	
Seattle	20.3
New York	8.6
San Francisco	8.4
Philadelphia	6.5
Milwaukee	6.1
Pittsburgh	5.7
Cleveland	5.4
Minneapolis	5.3
Boston	4.9
Chicago	4.9
Kansas City	4.9
Los Angeles	4.2
Portland, OR	4.1
St. Louis	4.0
Atlanta	3.6
Detroit	3.4
Cincinnati	3.3
Denver	3.2
Washington, DC	3.1
Dallas	3.0
Miami	2.9
Houston	2.7
Phoenix	1.5
San Diego	1.3
Tampa	0.8

Sources: Bureau of Economic Analysis, US Department of Commerce. 2009 Population Estimates. US Census Bureau and Foundation Center's Statistical Information Service. Foundation Assets: The Foundation Center's Statistical Information Service.

are 2.9 percent of the region's overall GDP, placing the region twenty-first out of twenty-five regions on this measure.

Context: Factors Shaping Foundation Activity in the National Capital Region

Why does the Washington-area foundation sector take the form it does? What explains the modest overall size of Washington's foundation community? What are the major contextual factors influencing the activities, strategies, and impacts of Washington foundations? In particular, the

Table 3.5. CFNCR Giving Compared to Other Community Foundations

Rank	Foundation	Total Giving ($ millions)
1	Greater Kansas City Community Foundation	$183.5
2	Silicon Valley Community Foundation	$154.3
3	Tulsa Community Foundation	$153
4	The Community Foundation for Greater Atlanta	$142.1
5	California Community Foundation	$129.2
6	The New York Community Trust	$123.4
7	The Chicago Community Trust	$110.6
8	Foundation for the Carolinas	$89.9
9	The Community Foundation for the National Capital Region	$89.8
10	Boston Foundation	$82.5
11	The Columbus Foundation	$79.8
12	Community Foundation of Texas	$76.1
13	The San Francisco Foundation	$75.6
14	The Cleveland Foundation	$75
15	Community Foundation for Southeast Michigan	$67.3
16	The Greater Cincinnati Foundation	$65.1
17	The Oregon Community Foundation	$60.7
18	Greater Houston Community Foundation	$55.5
19	Marin Community Foundation	$54.8
20	The East Bay Community Foundation	$50.7
21	The Seattle Foundation	$48
22	Community Foundation of Middle Tennessee	$46.9
23	The San Diego Foundation	$40.3
24	Community Foundation of Greater Memphis	$40
25	The Community Foundation Serving Richmond and the Central Denver Foundation	$38.6

Source: The Foundation Center's Statistical Information Services, "25 Largest Community Foundations by Total Giving, 2009."

development of the region's foundation community has been shaped by the pattern of local economic development; the area's status as the nation's capital; the fact that the Washington region is a large, growing, wealthy area; and the diversity and divisions within the region.

However, before considering the factors behind the surprisingly moderate dimensions of Washington's foundation community, it is important to note that its modest size should not be attributed to a lack of generosity from the area's residents, at least according to the *Chronicle of Philanthropy*'s 2012 study of generosity in America. This study found that,

Table 3.6. Washington, DC, Foundation Assets Relative to Size of Nonprofit and Governmental Sectors and Overall Economy, Compared to Other Regions

Foundation Assets as % of MSA's GDP			**Foundation Assets as % of MSA's Govt GDP**			**Foundation Assets as % of MSA's Nonprofit Sector Expenses**		
Rank	MSA	%	Rank	MSA	%	Rank	MSA	%
1	Seattle	18.1%	1	Seattle	153%	1	Seattle	216.3
2	Pittsburgh	9.3%	2	Pittsburgh	111.2%	2	Los Angeles	105.4
3	San Francisco	8.1%	3	San Francisco	93.4%	3	New York	93.2
4	New York	7.7%	4	New York	82.1%	4	Denver	66.8
5	Minneapolis	6.8%	5	Minneapolis	71.4%	5	Kansas City	57.1
6	Cleveland	6.3%	6	Milwaukee	70.8%	6	Minneapolis	54.8
7	Milwaukee	6.1%	7	Los Angeles	62.1%	7	Chicago	50.1
8	Kansas City	5.4%	8	Cleveland	60.8%	8	Philadelphia	43.1
9	Los Angeles	5.4%	9	Philadelphia	59.4%	9	Atlanta	40.5
10	Philadelphia	5.3%	10	Boston	58.9%	10	Cleveland	34.6
11	Boston	4.8%	11	Chicago	52.1%	11	Phoenix	25.4
12	Chicago	4.7%	12	Kansas City	46.5%	12	Washington, DC	22.8
13	Denver	4.4%	13	Denver	45.4%	13	San Francisco	12.8
14	Detroit	4.2%	14	Detroit	42.7%	14	Tampa	9.5
15	Portland, OR	4.0%	15	Portland, OR	40.2%	15	Portland	6.8
16	Miami	3.6%	16	Houston	40.1%			
17	Atlanta	3.4%	17	Dallas	37.6%			
18	Dallas	3.1%	18	Atlanta	34.9%			
19	Cincinnati	3.0%	19	Cincinnati	32.4%			
20	Houston	3.0%	20	Miami	32.3%			
21	Washington, DC	2.9%	21	St. Louis	25.2%			
22	St. Louis	2.6%	22	Phoenix	18.4%			
23	Phoenix	1.9%	23	Washington, DC	13.2%			
24	San Diego	1.6%	24	San Diego	8.6%			
25	Tampa	1.0%	25	Tampa	7.9%			

Nonprofit data were drawn from the National Center for Charitable Statistics (http://nccs-data.urban.org/index.php); MSA GDP from the Bureau of Economic Analysis (https://www.bea.gov/regional/index.htm); and foundation assets from the Foundation Center's Statistical Information Service (now at http://data.foundationcenter.org/).

after excluding taxes, housing, and other necessary expenses, people living in the DC metro area contributed 5.5 percent of their income to charities. In fact, Washington ranked as the second most generous of twenty-five large Metropolitan Statistical Areas (MSAs) after Atlanta.[10] The median charitable contribution in the Washington, DC metro area was $3,006, compared to a national median of $2,564.[11]

Economic Development Driven by Government

Although the Washington area is wealthy and its residents are comparatively generous, the region's foundation community is underdeveloped. Regional economic development patterns have produced many wealthy residents, but few have huge megafortunes that endow large foundations. How did this happen?

Washington's prosperity has developed around its major industry, the federal government.[12] Today, government accounts for 22 percent of the area's economy, which is a much larger percentage than in any other large metropolitan areas (see table 3.7). The region benefits from the presence of a large government-employed middle class and a sizeable group of professionals—lawyers, consultants, lobbyists, contractors, and others—whose income also derives from government-related work.

The Washington region has never previously had significant manufacturing or other industries that helped individuals amass great fortunes in other areas. Before Washington's selection as the nation's capital, the area had only a modest level of economic activity. In fact, in many ways, Washington—especially the central governmental area—is a "created" city, carved out of the banks of the Potomac River when the city was chosen as the new home of the federal government.[13]

Early hopes that Washington would become a commercial center were dashed when the silting of the Potomac River made shipping difficult and the port of Georgetown lost out to the emerging port of Baltimore, forty miles to the northeast.[14] Thus, rather than a national commercial center, in the 1800s Washington's economy consisted of locally oriented real estate firms, flour mills, breweries, cotton companies, and utilities as the major industries outside the federal government.[15]

The region's economy grew with the expansion of the federal government. The City Beautiful Movement of the early 1900s, which brought parks and other amenities to Washington, furthered the region's attraction as a place of learning and culture, and it helped fuel population growth and the real estate and tourism industries. However, many of the new Washingtonians were not well-connected to the community. Washington's Episcopal Bishop Satterlee articulated the difference in 1905: "A new type of residents are [*sic*]

Table 3.7. Government Percentage Share of Metropolitan Area GDP, 2009

Washington, DC	21.9%
San Diego	18.1%
Seattle	11.9%
Kansas City	11.7%
Tampa	11.3%
Miami	11.2%
St. Louis	10.5%
Cleveland	10.4%
Phoenix	10.2%
Portland	9.9%
Atlanta	9.8%
Detroit	9.7%
Denver	9.6%
Minneapolis	9.5%
New York	9.4%
Cincinnati	9.3%
Chicago	9%
Philadelphia	9%
Los Angeles	8.8%
San Francisco	8.7%
Milwaukee	8.5%
Pittsburgh	8.3%
Boston	8.2%
Dallas	8.2%
Houston	7.6%
US Metropolitan Portion	12.5%

Source: Bureau of Economic Analysis, US Department of Commerce, 2009.

gathering in Washington, who, while they bring wealth, magnificence, and luxury to the capital of the country, are, as a rule, actuated by no sense of civic, moral, or religious obligation regarding the welfare of the community, and it is a very serious question whether the material advantages that they bring are any compensation for the atmosphere of careless irresponsibility which they create."[16] In the late twentieth century, the Washington area did become a hub of digital communication, information technology, and internet commerce, although the region's high-tech industry has had its ups and downs, as reflected in the changing fortunes of America Online (AOL).

Table 3.8. Wealth Patterns, Washington Compared to National

Household (HH) Net Worth	Percentage of Households		Average HH Net Worth ($Thousands)		Average Age Head of Household	
	Washington, DC	Nation	Washington, DC	Nation	Washington, DC	Nation
$1,000,000–$4,999,999	8.53%	5.77%	$1,966.9	$1,915.1	55.2	57.5
$5,000,000–$9,999,999	1.19%	0.61%	$7,085.6	$7,153.2	55.9	56.5
$10,000,000–$19,999,999	0.42%	0.27%	$14,022.9	$13,484.9	57.4	58.1
$20,000,000 or more	0.12%	0.12%	$36,521.2	$39,579.0	53.6	60.5

Source: John Havens and Paul Schervish, "Wealth Transfer Estimates: 2001 to 2055 Washington D.C. Metropolitan Area," Center on Wealth and Philanthropy, Boston College, July 26, 2006.

The upshot of this economic development pattern is that Washington has a large number of moderately wealthy residents. Compared to national patterns, Washington's wealth is concentrated in the moderately high-income classes. Slightly more than 9.7 percent of the region's households have a net worth between $1 million and $10 million, compared to 6.4 percent of households nationally, as shown in table 3.8.

Interestingly, Washington's wealthiest residents are relatively young compared to the wealthiest at a national level. Households with $20 million or more in net worth are, on average, seven years younger in Washington than in the United States overall, as also shown in table 3.8.

National and International Capital

The fact that Washington is the nation's capital has affected much of the regional economy's growth and the development of significant wealth—but not huge, mega-wealth—in the area. This pattern of regional wealth has yielded a modest-sized foundation sector.

Washington's status as a national and international hub has probably attracted some foundations—like the Howard Hughes Medical Institute—to the area so they could be close to federal policymakers and important national facilities like the National Institutes of Health. Others, like the Annie E. Casey Foundation, chose neighboring and more affordable Baltimore as a location for similar reasons (see Baltimore chapter in this volume). For the most part, national foundations prefer to set up satellite offices to liaise with national and international institutions rather than moving their headquarters to the Washington region.

However, the fact that Washington is the nation's capital has affected foundation activity in some negative ways as well. Because of the peculiarities of the US Constitution, citizens of the District of Columbia have incomplete control of their own local political affairs and also do not have representatives with full voting power in either the US House or Senate. The city won limited home rule in the early 1970s when residents gained the right to elect their own mayor, but checks on local authority remain in place. For example, even today Congress retains the right to overturn any law passed by the district's government.

The shackles on local leaders have contributed to local elites disengaging from local issues. Why should wealthy Washingtonians get involved in addressing local problems if federal officials can step in at any time and negate their efforts? Wealthy residents do not focus their foundation dollars on local needs in part because they are not engaged in local issues. District residents have often had to look beyond City Hall, Washington-based foundations, and other local institutions toward Congress and the president for help in addressing local problems.

The disengagement of local elites has also been fostered by the perceived incompetence of the district's government and other important area organizations, including the local United Way. Even though the district's government has control of significant resources to address social needs, local elites and their foundations have been reluctant to partner with the government because it has often been seen as ineffective or even corrupt. Thankfully, the performance levels of the district's government and the local United Way have improved in the last decade.

Perhaps especially relevant for the region's foundation community is the fact that, as the nation's capital, Washington, DC, is populated not only by the usual array of local nonprofits but also by a broad range of national and international nonprofits that have far-flung clients. In fact, national and international nonprofits make up a larger portion of the Washington-area nonprofit sector than locally focused nonprofits. As shown in table 3.9, total expenses of Washington area nonprofits were $28.8 billion in 2000, with nonprofits serving local residents accounting for 44 percent of total expenditures, and nonprofits predominantly engaged in national and international activities making up 56 percent of overall expenses.

Similar to the profile of the national nonprofit sector, Washington's locally oriented nonprofit sector is dominated by health, education, and human service organizations. Local, private nonprofit hospitals—including

Table 3.9. Composition of DC Metropolitan Nonprofit Sector as Compared to the United States, 2000, selected fields.

	US Total		DC Total		DC Local Nonprofits			DC National/Int'l Nonprofits		
	Expenses	%	Expenses	%	Number	Expenses	%	Number	Expenses	%
Arts and Culture	$19,004	2.6%	$2,490	8.6%	540	$934	7.3%	320	$1,556	9.7%
Higher Education	$75,957	10.4%	$2,909	10.1%	13	$2,546	19.9%	4	$363	2.3%
Other Education	$33,216	4.5%	$1,967	6.8%	891	$909	7.1%	374	$1,058	6.6%
Hospitals	$320,225	43.8%	$3,985	13.8%	34	$3,647	28.5%	1	$338	2.1%
Other Health	$122,947	16.8%	$3,338	11.6%	424	$1,694	13.2%	517	$1,644	10.3%
Environment	$6,736	0.9%	$1,269	4.4%	121	$579	4.5%	194	$690	4.3%
Human Services	$100,258	13.7%	$6,062	21.0%	1318	$1,792	14.0%	579	$4,270	26.6%
International	$10,661	1.5%	$909	3.2%	0	$0	0.0%	385	$909	5.7%
Public/Societal Benefit	$35,571	4.9%	$5,660	19.6%	517	$572	4.5%	1032	$5,088	31.7%
Religion	$6,181	0.8%	$137	0.5%	210	$92	0.7%	101	$45	0.3%
Mutual Benefit	n/a	–	$119	0.4%	14	$40	0.3%	19	$79	0.5%
Total	$730,756	100.0%	$28,845	100.0%	4082	$12,806	100.0%	3526	$16,040	100.0%
in millions										

Sources: Nonprofit Roundtable 2005, Table 2.3; Wing et al., 2008, Table 5.9.

the teaching hospitals at Georgetown University and George Washington University; the nationally recognized Children's National Medical Center; and local community hospitals, such as Sibley Memorial, Maryland's Suburban Hospital, and Northern Virginia's Inova System—are the largest type of locally oriented nonprofits in the Washington area. Universities and other higher education institutions—including Georgetown, George Washington, American, Howard, Catholic, and Gallaudet Universities—are in second place.

In some contrast, Washington's large national and international nonprofit sector is dominated by public and societal benefit, human services, and other health organizations, as shown in table 3.9. For the most part, this portion of Washington's nonprofit sector reflects the heavy presence of national umbrella and advocacy organizations in the nation's capital. As discussed further below, Washington's large national and international sector is a magnet for both local and national foundation dollars and contributes to the reality that the region is a significant conduit—rather than a final destination—for foundation dollars, and runs a net philanthropic deficit.

Large, Growing, Wealthy, and Diverse Region

Also important for the Washington foundation community is the fact that it is situated in a large, growing, wealthy, and diverse area. In 2010, the Washington, DC, metropolitan area was the seventh largest MSA in the country, with a population of 5.6 million people.[17] Among the fifteen largest MSAs, Washington was the sixth fastest growing MSA in the United States from 2000 to 2010, with a population increase of 16.4 percent. The Washington region had a per-capita income of $57,000 in 2009, the second highest among the twenty largest metropolitan areas. In 2011, Washington was home to six of the top ten US counties in terms of median household income.[18]

However, the Washington area is by no means uniformly wealthy. In fact, the region is divided on a variety of dimensions. Like almost all US metro area foundation communities, an important part of the context for Washington's foundations is the fragmentation of the region into multiple state and county jurisdictions. The district, Maryland, and Virginia—or DMV in the local vernacular—all have their own particular governance structures and different political cultures. Within Maryland and Virginia, counties are critical political subdivisions.

Wealth is distributed very unevenly throughout the area. Western counties within the region are especially prosperous, while the eastern part of the area has a high poverty rate. These divisions result in a mismatch between available resources and needs. In the west, Loudon, Fairfax, Arlington, Prince William, and Fauquier Counties in Virginia, and Montgomery County in Maryland are among the wealthiest US counties, all with median household incomes above $90,000 in 2011.[19] In contrast, as of the 2010 Census, 30 percent of the children in the District of Columbia lived in poverty, mostly in the eastern portions of the city.[20]

Besides great differences of wealth within the region, there is diversity on other dimensions as well. The area has large African American, Latino, and immigrant populations. Washington ranks seventh in the country among metro areas for the size of its Asian population, and the region had the fifth largest growth in black population during 2000–2007.[21] Washington is also home to many immigrants from a broad range of countries. One study stated that the impressive population growth of 1.6 million people that took place between 1985 and 2007 was entirely the result of international migration.[22]

Impacts on Foundation Activities

Limited Foundation Support for Local Nonprofits

How have these important contextual factors shaped the activities of Washington's foundations? With local assets of relatively modest size, there has been a longstanding concern that limited local foundation resources have been overstretched by the presence of numerous national and international organizations that provide additional funding choices for foundations in the Washington area. Reflecting these concerns, the Meyer Foundation commissioned the Foundation Center to closely examine the funding patterns of local foundations.[23] As shown in table 3.10, the Foundation Center's study confirmed that nonprofit service providers that focus on local residents do not benefit from the vast majority of local foundation resources. In fact, the area's twenty-six largest foundations devoted only about one-third (33.2 percent) of their grant allocations to locally focused organizations and a little over one-quarter (25.9 percent) to national or international organizations, while 41 percent of grant dollars went outside the local area.

While it is common for large foundations to allocate funding outside their home regions, generally, smaller foundations practice charity at home with their limited resources. However, just like Washington's larger funders, the area's other, smaller foundations devoted only about one-third (33.4 percent) of their grant dollars to strictly local purposes. National and international organizations received slightly less than one-fifth

Table 3.10. Geographic and Programmatic Foci of Local Foundation-Giving, 2006

	Local Recipients' Focus		**Nonlocal Recipients**
	Local	National/ International	
Large Funders	$114,292,292	$89,014,640	$141,028,739
%	33.2%	25.9%	41.0%
Small Funders	$71,705,207	$39,109,868	$103,589,626
%	33.4%	18.2%	48.3%
Large Funders:			
Arts & Culture	14.1%	36.7%	n/a
Education	17.3%	19.4%	n/a
Health	16.9%	3.9%	n/a
Environment	5.4%	11.2%	n/a
Human Services	33.3%	11.3%	n/a
International	–	7.9%	n/a
Public/Societal Benefit	10.1%	8.3%	n/a
Religion	2.7%	0.6%	n/a

Source: Foundation Center, 2009.

(18.2 percent) of grant allocations of smaller foundations, and about half, or 48.3 percent, of grants went to out-of-area recipients.[24] A possible explanation for this finding is that giving by small foundations reflects family philanthropy, which incorporates a broader set of motivations (e.g., alumni giving to universities outside the area) than just a commitment to local charity. Unfortunately, a breakdown of the purposes of out-of-area giving that could provide more clues on this issue is not available.

However, the Foundation Center study did provide information about the programmatic focus of locally oriented nonprofits that received grants from larger local foundations.[25] Of the local-purpose grants, the largest amount of grant dollars—one-third—went to the human services field. This was followed by education and health (17.3 percent and 16.9 percent, respectively), arts and culture (14.1 percent), public and societal benefit (10.1 percent), and the environment (5.4 percent). As these local funding foci indicate, large, grant-making, Washington-area foundations emphasized service to economically disadvantaged and ethnic and racial minority populations. This reflects Washington's racial diversity as well as its emergence as a major immigration hub in recent years.[26]

The nationally and internationally oriented giving by these large local foundations had a significantly different pattern than their local giving. Compared to their local giving, these foundations devoted a much larger portion of their national and international funding to arts and culture, international purposes, and environmental activities, and gave a much smaller percentage of their funding to human services, as shown in table 3.10.

The high percentage of local foundation funding going to national arts organizations reflects the presence of large-scale national cultural institutions in Washington, including the Smithsonian Institution, the National Gallery of Art, and the John F. Kennedy Center for the Performing Arts—all of which are government organizations. Some national organizations, such as these cultural institutions, may provide direct benefits to local residents, and foundation grants supporting such organizations may be intended for local as well as national purposes. However, the overall findings suggest that a large share of the local philanthropic resources is not primarily geared toward addressing local community needs. Whether the Washington region, with its dual nonprofit sectors, constitutes an outlier in this respect, however, cannot be established for certain in the absence of comparable data for other metro areas.

Net Philanthropic Deficit

As it turns out, local foundation funding is actually the smallest part of total foundation funding flowing into the region. In fact, the Washington area is a major importer of philanthropic funds. As shown in table 3.11, grant recipients in the Washington metro area attracted close to $1.7 billion in grant support from the nation's largest foundations in 2005. Of this amount, only $166 million, or one out of every ten grant dollars, came from local, Washington-area foundations. A much greater amount, $1.5 billion, came from foundations outside the area. To put this in further perspective, the Washington region attracted more than 10 percent of the $16.4 billion dollars that the nation's largest foundations distributed in grants in 2005.

Table 3.12 provides a breakdown of the geographic focus of Washington-area recipients for grants of $50,000 or more gifted from foundations based outside Washington. More than $1 billion, or three-quarters of the incoming foundation grants, went to national organizations; another 20 percent was sent to organizations with international purposes; and a mere 3 percent went to locally oriented organizations. Thus, despite the large overall flow of foundation funding in the area, like some other regions, Washington generates a net philanthropic deficit, with more local foundation dollars going to out-of-area purposes than out-of-area foundation dollars flowing into the

Table 3.11. Foundation Funding to DC MSA Recipients, 2005

	Non-Local Foundations	%	Local Foundations	%	Total	%
DC	$1,069,987,338	71.2%	$104,189,765	62.7%	$1,174,177,103	70.4%
MD	$78,682,069	5.2%	$22,818,082	13.7%	$101,500,151	6.1%
VA/WV	$354,283,593	23.6%	$39,050,334	23.5%	$393,333,927	23.6%
Total	$1,502,953,000		$166,058,181		$1,669,011,181	

Source: Authors' calculations, based on Foundation Center data.

Table 3.12. Non-Local Foundation Funding Flows, by Geographic Programming Focus of Recipients, 2001

Geographic Focus of Funding Recipients	Amount of Funding Received from Nonlocal Foundations	%
Local Focus	$48,746,080	3%
National Focus	$1,091,091,857	77%
International Focus	$284,398,876	20%
Total	$1,424,236,813	

Source: Authors' calculations, based on Foundation Center data.

region for local uses. The major funding coming into the Washington region has little impact on local residents, and the Washington area serves more as a conduit or gateway for philanthropic flows to national and international destinations than an end destination itself.

Recommendations for Strengthening Washington's Foundation Sector

What to do? A major goal of this chapter is to stimulate further thinking about the future course of foundation philanthropy in the Washington region. In light of the area's great wealth but modest foundation resources, what strategies should Washington's foundation leaders pursue to maximize the impact of existing foundation resources and expand the funds that will be available in future years?[27]

Capture New, Young Wealth for Philanthropy

As described in previous sections, the Washington region has an abundance of young, wealthy residents. In the years ahead, there is the potential for significant increases in regional philanthropy, including foundation-giving, if this wealth can be captured for philanthropy. However, for this potential to be realized, there should be a concerted, intentional effort to guide the abundant regional wealth to local philanthropy, or it is likely to be spent elsewhere—on consumption, bequests to heirs, government taxes, or even perhaps for philanthropy in other regions, where Washington's wealthy have vacation or retirement homes.

Leaders of Washington's foundation and philanthropic community can play a role in reaching out to the young and middle-aged wealthy to give funds in Washington. Several organizations—the Washington Regional Association of Grantmakers, the CFNCR and other regional community foundations, Venture Philanthropy Partners, and numerous donor advisor groups—seem especially well-positioned to lead the effort to expand local philanthropy. However, these organizations may need to reallocate existing resources—or raise additional support—in order to prioritize this kind of outreach.

Educate Foundation Donors, Boards, and Staff around Foundation Strategy

Foundation resources are precious, and they must be used strategically to ensure they achieve the maximum good. With foundation funds in relatively short supply in the Washington area, the need for thoughtfulness in the use of local foundation resources is especially great. While many Washington foundations are led by experienced, skilled grantmakers, the Washington foundation community should ensure that local foundation donors, board members, and staffers who are newer to the field have access to—and use—high-quality information regarding best practices in foundation grantmaking. This education can draw on both local and national resources, such as the programs of the Washington Regional Association of Grantmakers, the GrantCraft initiative of the Foundation Center, and the Grantmaking School at Grand Valley State University.

Identify Strategic Niches

For Washington foundations, developing a strategic approach to grantmaking may mean identifying special niches where they can address emerging social needs and make a contribution—even with limited resources—in program areas that are receiving limited attention. Adopting this kind of strategic approach may lead, for example, to more foundation support for nonprofit advocacy that can influence public policy and thereby leverage even larger amounts of government funding. Strategic philanthropy may also lead to increased support for small and medium-sized human service organizations and less funding for large, established nonprofit institutions, such as hospitals, universities, and museums, that have other large funding sources.

Of course, some Washington foundations are already practicing this kind of strategic philanthropy. The Consumer Health Foundation focuses on racial and social equity in the health field; the Meyer Foundation helps to strengthen the leadership capacity of nonprofit executives; and the Moriah Fund seeks to advance social justice. In fact, it is interesting to note that Washington-area foundations have allocated the largest portion of their funding to education and human services, while nationally it is education and health rather than human services that receive the bulk of foundation funding.[28]

Collaboration among Foundations

Strategic Washington-area foundations should also look for opportunities to collaborate with one another to maximize their impact. In fact, Washington foundations already have a track record in this area. The Washington AIDS Partnership is an initiative of the Washington Regional Association of Grantmakers through which foundations pool their funds to award more than $1 million annually to local organizations involved with HIV/AIDS prevention and care. Similarly, the Community Development Support Collaborative was a consortium of local and national funders that allocated more than $17 million over fifteen years to neighborhood revitalization in Washington, DC, before it closed in December 2011.[29] The Partnership for Prince George's County is a geographic-focused collaborative to address limited knowledge about and limited giving in the county. The Partnership was incubated at the Washington Regional Association of Grantmakers and now resides at the Community Foundation for Prince George's County. Washington funders will want to explore other opportunities for collaborative initiatives.

Expand Partnerships with Government and Corporations

Washington-area foundations should consider collaborations not only with each other, but with government agencies and corporations as well. Government in the District of Columbia now seems like a more reliable partner than previously, and local foundations should explore opportunities to expand their partnerships with local government. Some local governments have now established offices within government to liaise with foundations and other nonprofits and facilitate expanded partnerships (e.g., Fairfax County's Office of Public Private Partnerships and the District's Office of Partnerships and Grant Services).

Washington foundations can also play a role in deepening the engagement of the strong local business community in addressing regional social problems. With the weakening of the United Way in recent decades, the business community seems somewhat less engaged than it previously was, and there may be a role for foundations in reaching out to corporations for collaborative initiatives that have the benefit for foundations of leveraging their own modest resources. The Washington Regional Association of Grantmakers recently established an Institute for Corporate Social Responsibility in conjunction with Johns Hopkins University to deepen the connection between philanthropy and the business community and facilitate more successful partnerships to address community needs.

Expand Foundation Intelligence Gathering

More generally, with their limited resources, Washington foundations need the best possible information about where their resources are most needed and can make the most difference. Foundations should keep careful track of emerging social problems—like the suburbanization of poverty—and be mindful of where government is—and is not—addressing social needs. This kind of information should then guide foundation funding decisions.[30]

Increase National and Local Foundation Funding for Local Work

Local foundation leaders who are concerned with local problems have long recognized that many of their local and national foundation colleagues devote much of their Washington funding to organizations with national or international—rather than local—focus. Figuring out how to get more foundation funding to address local needs is a difficult but important challenge that deserves continuing attention. Local leaders may need to do more to emphasize to both locals and outsiders that the region is an area not only of tremendous wealth but of significant need and that it has the capacity to make good use of its philanthropic resources.

Some national funders have been and will continue to be attracted to addressing local Washington area needs in order to mount demonstration programs that get the attention of national policymakers. Local leaders will obviously want to track these kinds of projects and ensure that the initiatives provide maximum benefit to local residents and institutions.

Make Full Use of Foundation Assets

Finally, foundations should be encouraged to make full use of their financial and other assets to support their missions. Traditionally, foundations in Washington and around the country have been content to advance their social objectives by paying out the legally required 5 percent of their assets in grants every year. In recent years, there has been growing interest in having foundations take an expanded view of their assets and encouraging them to use their assets to make loans, loan guarantees, and, more generally, invest their assets in ways that will advance their missions. Foundations should also make use of their nonfinancial resources—including their convening power—to advance their missions.

Concluding Thoughts

As described in the pages above, the Washington area is a region of great wealth but of limited foundation activity. The region's status as a national and international capital has helped to fuel significant economic growth but not amass great megafortunes, especially going back in history. What in current-day Washington seems like a large foundation would only qualify as a small- or medium-sized grant-making institution in many other big cities. Reflecting their modest size, Washington foundations have had only limited impact on the region's many social problems. Foundations based outside the region have sent grant money to Washington more to support national and international organizations and causes than nonprofits serving local residents.

For those who care about Washington's foundation sector, the challenge for the years ahead is to make the best use of existing foundation assets and capture additional resources for these important institutions. This chapter offers some suggestions about possible strategies for the future. There is great potential for Washington foundations to play an expanded role in the years to come in addressing important regional issues. Whether this potential is realized remains to be seen.

Alan J. Abramson is Professor of Government and Politics in the Schar School of Policy and Government at George Mason University. He is also Founding Director of Mason's Center for Nonprofit Management, Philanthropy, and Policy.

Stefan Toepler is Associate Professor of Nonprofit Studies in the Schar School of Policy and Government at George Mason University in Virginia. He is coeditor of *Private Funds, Public Purpose: Philanthropic Foundations in International Perspective* and *The Legitimacy of Philanthropic Foundations: United States and European Perspectives*, among others.

Notes

1. Overall, in 2007, 18.9 percent of all employees in the Washington metro area worked for all levels of government, which is 75 percent higher than the mean of 11.3 percent of employees that work for government in the twenty-five largest metro areas. *State and Metropolitan Data Book*, 2010, "Metropolitan Areas—Employees and Earnings by Selected Major Industries: 2007, Table B-12.

2. According to the Urban Institute, 2011 revenues for reporting public charities break down as follows: 47 percent from fees for service; 33 percent from government fees and grants; 13 percent from private contributions, including individual, foundation, and corporate donations; and 7 percent from other sources. According to Giving USA, the components of 2011 private contributions are 73 percent from individuals; 14 percent from foundations; 8 percent from bequests; and 5 percent from corporations. Thus, private foundations account for about 3 percent of total revenue of reporting public charities. "Reporting public charities" include organizations that filed IRS Forms 990 and had $25,000 or more in gross receipts; excluded are small organizations and most religious organizations which do not file tax returns. Sarah L. Pettijohn, "The Nonprofit Sector in Brief: Public Charities, Giving, and Volunteering, 2013" (Washington, DC: Urban Institute), available at http://www.urban.org/UploadedPDF/412923-The-Nonprofit-Sector-in-Brief.pdf (February 7, 2014); *Giving USA: The Annual Report on Philanthropy for the Year 2011, Executive Summary* (Chicago: Giving USA Foundation, 2012).

3. The twenty-two jurisdictions currently included in the Washington-Arlington-Alexandria Metropolitan Statistical Area are: the District of Columbia; Calvert, Charles, Frederick, Montgomery, and Prince George's Counties in Maryland; Arlington, Clarke, Fairfax, Fauquier, Loudoun, Prince William, Spotsylvania, Stafford, and Warren Counties in Virginia; Alexandria, Fairfax, Falls Church, Fredericksburg, Manassas, and Manassas Park cities in Virginia; and Jefferson County in West Virginia. US Executive Office of the President, Office of Management and Budget, OMB Bulletin No. 10-02, December 1, 2009, available at https://obamawhitehouse.archives.gov/sites/default/files/omb/assets/bulletins/b10-02.pdf (accessed October 18, 2017).

4. Ranking is based on financial data in the Foundation Center's database as of January 28, 2013. http://data.foundationcenter.org/.

5. For more on the venture philanthropy approach, see Christine Letts, William Ryan, and Allen Grossman, "Virtuous Capital: What Foundations Can Learn from Venture Capitalists," *Harvard Business Review* (March–April 1997): 36–44.

6. Washington Grantmakers, *Our Region, Our Giving: Philanthropy in the Greater Washington Region* (Washington, DC: Foundation Center, July 2012), 2.

7. Foundation Center, http://data.foundationcenter.org/.

8. FC Stats: The Foundation Center's Statistical Information Service (http://data.foundationcenter.org/ "Aggregate Financial Information for Foundations in the Washington, DC, Metropolitan Area, circa 1999, 2004, and 2009."

9. When Fannie Mae shut down its separate corporate foundation, it continued some of its charitable giving from within the corporation so there was not a complete loss of philanthropic activity. See David S. Hilzenrath and Amy Joyce, "Fannie Mae Shuts Down Foundation: Big Local Donor to Move In-House," *Washington Post*, February 24, 2007.

10. "Generosity in America's 50 Biggest Cities: A Ranking," *Chronicle of Philanthropy*, August 23, 2012: B6.

11. "How America Gives: Exploring Philanthropy in Your State, City, and Neighborhood," *Chronicle of Philanthropy*, accessed August 20, 2012, available at http://philanthropy.com/.

12. Thus, on the East Coast, the federal government is concentrated in Washington; academic, defense, and medical research is focused in Boston; and foundations are strongest in New York and to a lesser extent in Connecticut and Pennsylvania. The authors are grateful to David Hammack for pointing out these different regional foci.

13. James Sterling Young, *The Washington Community, 1800–28* (New York: Harcourt, Brace, and World, 1966), 17.

14. Keith E. Melder, *City of Magnificent Intentions: A History of Washington, District of Columbia* (Washington, DC: Intac, 1997), 91–95.

15. Constance McLaughlin Green, *Washington: A History of the Capital, 1800–1950* (Princeton, NJ: Princeton University Press, 1962), 2, 9–34.

16. Green, *Washington: A History of the Capital, 1800–1950*, 193.

17. United States Census Bureau, "Table 20. Large Metropolitan Statistical Areas—Population: 1990 to 2010," available at http://gsbs.uthscsa.edu/images/uploads/Metro1.pdf (accessed October 18, 2017).

18. "Highest Income Counties in 2011," *Washington Post*, available at http://www.washingtonpost.com/wp-srv/special/local/highest-income-counties/ (accessed January 28, 2013).

19. *Washington Post*, "Highest Income Counties in 2011."

20. US Census Bureau, "Child Poverty in the United States 2009 and 2010: Selected Race Groups and Hispanic Origin," American Community Survey Briefs, November 2011, 9, available at https://www.census.gov/prod/2011pubs/acsbr10-05.pdf (accessed October 18, 2017); and US Census Bureau, "Areas with Concentrated Poverty: 2006–2010," American Community Survey Briefs, December 2011, 8, available at https://www.census.gov/library/publications/2011/acs/acsbr10-17.html (accessed October 18, 2017).

21. William H. Frey, Alan Berube, Audrey Singer, and Jill H. Wilson, *Getting Current: Recent Demographic Trends in Metropolitan America* (Washington, DC: Brookings Institution, 2009), 12.

22. Lisa A. Sturtevant, and Yu Jin Jung, "Domestic Migration To and From the Washington DC Metropolitan Area: 1985–2007" (Technical Report No. 4). George Mason University Center for Regional Analysis.

23. Foundation Center, "Giving by Foundations in the National Capital Region: How Much Stays Local?," March 2009 revised edition.

24. Foundation Center, "Giving by Foundations."

25. Foundation Center, "Giving by Foundations."

26. Foundation Center, "Key Facts on Washington, DC, Area Foundations," June 2007. Available at http://foundationcenter.issuelab.org/resource/key-facts-on-washington-dc-area-foundations.html (accessed October 18, 2017).

27. While the authors of this chapter are generally sympathetic to the goal of growing foundation resources in the years ahead, this chapter is not the venue for exploring the pros and cons of expanding the Washington area foundation sector. We include our thoughts about growing foundation resources for the sake of those who believe this is an important objective.

28. Foundation Center, "Key Facts on Washington, DC, Area Foundations," June 2007. Available at http://foundationcenter.issuelab.org/resource/key-facts-on-washington-dc-area-foundations.html (accessed October 18, 2017).

29. The Washington Regional Association of Grantmakers is continuing some of the work of the collaborative through its Affordable Housing Action Team, which seeks to grow the number of funders who are knowledgeable about and committed to supporting the growth of affordable housing in the Washington region.

30. For example, the Washington Regional Association of Grantmakers currently reaches out to a broad range of experts to educate its member foundations.

chapter four

NORTHEASTERN OHIO'S COLLABORATIVE FOUNDATIONS

Elise C. Hagesfeld and David C. Hammack

> Cleveland would cooperate even if it had to be genteelly clubbed into doing it, Cleveland would be neighborly, Cleveland would give till it hurt. . . . The city government cooperates with the private foundation; the art museum with the art school, the Playhouse and the public library; and the newspapers cooperate with everything in sight, provided it is not subversive or injurious to business. The good Clevelander, before turning out his light to get into bed, asks himself: "Have I cooperated today or have I failed?"
>
> R. L. Duffus, "Cleveland: Paternalism in Excelsis," 1928[1]

Introduction

Does regional location shape the aims and ambitions that donors assign to charitable foundations? In the 1920s, the prominent New York journalist Robert L. Duffus argued that for northeastern Ohio, the answer was yes. Region—more precisely, the cultural history of a region's elites—did, he insisted, make a difference. Because Cleveland had been home to some of the most discussed and imitated of all American foundation donors—such as John D. Rockefeller; but also the Harkness family, who were donors of the Commonwealth Fund and of the extensive undergraduate houses at Harvard and colleges at Yale; the founding donors of the Cleveland Museum of Art; and the creators of the community foundation and the modern community chest—Duffus had a point. At the same time, Duffus carefully acknowledged that he was ignoring the majority of

Cleveland's people: "By Cleveland, in this connection and in most other connections that get into the newspapers and have speeches made about them," he wrote, was generally meant "Nordic Cleveland—the leaders of the approximately 30 percent of the population who are native-born whites of native parentage."

We could more accurately rephrase Duffus to say that in the first half of the twentieth century, many of the wealthy Clevelanders who took their cultural cues from New England and the American Northeast emphasized civic "cooperation." Along with their families, they maintained for several generations philanthropic practices that had helped to build so many Protestant churches and colleges in Ohio in the nineteenth century. Yet, despite their prominence, these people represented a minority of the Protestant community in the Cleveland region. Duffus ignored Cleveland's large Catholic and Jewish communities, whose members emphasized distinctiveness as well as cooperation; he also ignored the reality that some Protestants and Jews favored foundations and endowments, while Catholics and evangelical Protestants did not. He also paid no attention to the several remarkable individualists who had also established foundations in the region. Cleveland and northeastern Ohio were changing rapidly in the 1920s and have continued to change. Here as elsewhere, over time, foundations have also developed and changed.

If northeastern Ohio's communities have shaped its foundations, we can further ask what foundations have done to define the region's character. They have, it seems, underwritten the region's nationally prominent nonprofit organizations in medicine and the arts, organized charity, religion, and higher education; built connections between northeastern Ohio and New York, New England, the US South, and overseas; and supported efforts to address the region's religious and racial conflicts. Some foundations are now seeking out the challenges of globalization, economic discontinuity, and educational underachievement. The latter are big challenges, indeed.

Northeastern Ohio donors have directed their foundations to support a remarkable range of special causes. Some of the largest donors—not only John D. Rockefeller, but also members of the Harkness, Brush, Knight, Gund, Timken, Mandel, Lewis, and many other families—have devoted their foundations more to national and international causes than to the region where they assembled their fortunes. Others have focused more specifically on religious causes. Altogether, the range and complexity of foundation activities and ambitions make it very difficult to provide a summary assessment of their contributions, but there are significant areas in which foundations have helped to set the region's agenda.

Northeastern Ohio: Economy and Society

We take northeastern Ohio as our region because it is a densely settled geographic area that is economically and socially integrated in many ways.[2] It is difficult to define as a region; like other metropolitan areas in the United States, it is internally fragmented in political and social terms and deeply tied into much larger economic, social, and political units. Fifty years ago, the visionary regional planner Constantine Doxiadis—who embraced a notion of pioneering geographer Jean Gottman that suggested a continuous megalopolis extended from Manchester, New Hampshire, to Northern Virginia—discerned a tight-knit region that bordered the southern shores of the Great Lakes from southern Wisconsin to Cleveland, Ohio, and on down to southwestern Pennsylvania. Doxiadis also saw extensions emanating from this region across southern Ontario, along the New York Thruway to Albany and the Hudson River, and along the northern edge of Lake Ontario and down the St. Lawrence to Montreal. In this vast urban system, greater Cleveland (which included the central city, as well as Youngstown, Akron, Canton, Sandusky, and all their suburbs and rural fringes) served as a key node, its center the largest place in an area that stretched eastward beyond Pittsburgh. Analysts continue to find this notion useful and can see evidence for it not only in the transport and communication lines and patterns of housing density that underlie a more recent Regional Plan Association map, but also in a satellite photograph of lights visible at night.

Altogether, this greater Cleveland–northeastern Ohio region embraced 3.9 million people in 2010, ranking it with greater Minneapolis and Seattle at the top of a group tied for twelfth-largest metro region in the United States.[3]

Northeastern Ohio's location has created many opportunities to gain wealth. By the 1850s a web of canals, railroads, and telegraph lines already provided this area with cheap, reliable connections to New York, Philadelphia, and Baltimore; to the Alleghenies, Michigan, Illinois, Wisconsin, and Minnesota; to eastern Canada; to central and southern Ohio; and down the Ohio and Mississippi Rivers to St. Louis, New Orleans, and the Gulf of Mexico. People and capital flowed west through this web. Moving east were goods from the Great Lakes—initially just lumber, fish, pigs, and cattle, but soon expanded to fruit, meat, grains, rails, girders for bridges and buildings, equipment for factories and offices, sewing machines, bicycles, pumps, engines, tires, household appliances, and then a rapidly expanding array of manufactured goods.

Working closely with investors from Massachusetts, Connecticut, and New York, northeastern Ohio entrepreneurs built harbors, canals, and ships; bridges, railroads, and rolling stock; and equipment for factories, farmers, and builders, offices, and homes. Through such firms as Republic Steel, Youngstown Sheet and Tube, Cleveland Cliffs, North American Coal, Standard Oil, and Dow Chemical, investors quickly gained control of much of Appalachia's coal, Michigan and Minnesota's iron and copper ores and chemicals, and Pennsylvania and Ohio's oil. For about a hundred years, northeastern Ohio built an unusually diverse and steadily growing manufacturing economy. Cleveland's notable corporate law firms and commercial banks served the steel and metal goods and chemical and paint manufacturing plants of their own city and also those in Akron, Canton, Massillon, Wooster, Lorain, and Youngstown. They also served the grain-processing, farm-implement, and tire factories of Akron, as well as Standard Oil. Taking advantage of their strategic location, northeastern Ohio merchants helped build national systems for making and distributing, clothing, eyeglasses, and other goods.

The advantages to location in northeastern Ohio persuaded entire firms to relocate to northeastern Ohio from Massachusetts, Connecticut, New York, and New Jersey. Workers came with them: skilled workers in metal, wood, and cloth, as well as unskilled workers from town and countryside in the United States—and also from Germany, the Austro-Hungarian Empire, Poland, and Russia. Seasoned workers in commerce and many teachers and religious workers came from New England, the Middle Atlantic, Germany, and Central and Eastern Europe. The region also attracted a steady flow of technicians, scientists, musicians, architects, and designers trained in Europe as well as the American Northeast. By the 1870s some of Cleveland's steel mills were employing thousands. As its industries grew, unskilled workers left Appalachian coal mines and Alabama cotton fields to take northeastern Ohio's factory jobs. After World War I, Cleveland's East Side and adjacent suburbs attracted so many African Americans that many came to call the city "Alabama North."[4]

From the Civil War to the Great Depression, northeastern Ohio grew more rapidly than the rest of the United States. But after World War II—and emphatically from the 1960s—the region's economy went into a difficult period of reorientation. By the 1970s, it cost less to make basic forms of iron, steel, and many other manufactured products in Asia and then ship them through the St. Lawrence Seaway to the Port of Cleveland, than to make them in the region from still-abundant Great Lakes ores and Appalachian coal. Manufacturing's decline has been steep, but it remains important. Even today—as civic leaders tout Cleveland's hospital, medical research, and medical equipment industries and the city retains an unusually large concentration of law firms and business consultancies—northeastern Ohio businesses continue to manufacture a wide variety of goods and coordinate much of the production in Europe, Central America, and Asia.[5]

Northeastern Ohio forms a social and cultural unit as well as an economic one. At the once-contested border where the early American nation fought and traded with Native American tribes, the French, and British Canadians, the region drew its initial population from New England and New York. By the late nineteenth century, German was widely taught in public schools, Catholics constituted the region's largest single religious group, and Cleveland was becoming home to one of the world's largest Jewish communities.[6] Great numbers of African Americans joined the mix through the Great Migration of the 1920s, 1930s, and 1940s.[7] More recently, the entire multicounty region has remained one of the most densely settled areas in North America, with notable and growing concentrations of Hindus, Buddhists, and Muslims, as well as people from Asian countries, such as India and China, and from Latin America—particularly Puerto Rico and Mexico.

Rivalries among particular places continue to divide this region. Residents of Akron, Canton, and Youngstown insist that their cities are quite distinct from Cleveland; many towns in Lake, Geauga, Portage, and Medina Counties feel quite independent of the main urban centers. Students at Oberlin and the College of Wooster often have no sense that they are in Cleveland's suburbs even though some of their teachers live in the central city and its inner suburbs.[8]

Within Cleveland's city limits, neighborhoods on the east and west sides of the Cuyahoga River consider themselves very different from one another. Religious and racial distinctions remain strong. African Americans concentrate on Cleveland's east side and in several of its eastern suburbs. Many think of the city's west side population as predominantly Catholic and Central European, yet non-Catholics are also numerous in several west side and western suburban neighborhoods, and Catholics are numerous throughout the region. Jewish synagogues are scarce west of the Cuyahoga, but many have moved to suburbs to the southeast.

Despite its divisions—or possibly because its divisions are not only deep but also numerous—the region has also pioneered effective approaches to intergroup cooperation. The Catholic diocese has worked to mitigate rivalries imported from Europe, with considerable success despite the persistence of ethnic parishes.[9] The Community Chest–United Way movement, largely invented in Cleveland in 1913, has always raised and distributed funds for Catholic, Jewish, and Protestant human service agencies, as well as the charities of other major religious traditions.[10] Since 1936, the Anisfield-Wolf Award, managed by the Cleveland Foundation, has honored writers from across the nation for contributions to interracial and interreligious understanding.[11] The majority of the region's most prominent nonprofits—the Cleveland Orchestra,[12] the Cleveland Museum of Art, the Cleveland Foundation, the Catholic Diocese of Cleveland,[13] the Jewish Community Federation of Cleveland,[14] the Cleveland Museum of Natural History, University Hospitals, the Cleveland Clinic, and, in the business association field, Team NEO and its sponsors and the foundation-supported Fund for Our Economic Future[15]—engage people from most or all of the region's nine counties and beyond.

Northeastern Ohio Foundations before 1970

Diversity in the purposes of foundations and endowments appeared early in the region's history. The New Englanders and New Yorkers who organized northeastern Ohio's nineteenth-century economy brought with them practices and connections to charitable funds. Their schools and seminaries benefitted from some of the earliest foundation-like charities based in New York, Philadelphia, and New England, including the American Education Society, the Society for the Promotion of Collegiate and Theological Education at the West, the Home Mission Board, the College Board of the Presbyterian Church, and the American Baptist Home Mission Society.[16] The American Bible Society, the American Tract Society, the Sunday School Union, and the church-building and clergy-support funds of the main Protestant denominations subsidized the provision of buildings and reading material for Protestant churches.[17] Until the late twentieth century, Protestant donors received much more prominent attention in published sources—general-circulation newspapers and magazines, journals of professional societies, annual reports, and memorials printed by charities and collected by public libraries—than Jewish or Catholic donors, partly, perhaps, because the latter preferred to keep a low profile. But northeastern Ohio's Jews brought powerful philanthropic traditions with them from their first arrival to Cleveland during the 1830s.[18] The region's Catholic institutions, like Catholic institutions elsewhere in the United States, depended on Catholic endowments and donors in France and Austria-Hungary to help staff parishes, religious communities, schools, and hospitals.[19]

By 1900, substantial northeastern Ohio trust funds supported a wide range of purposes and institutions. Protestants funded not only academies and colleges, but also small hospitals and clinics, orphanages, city missions, and YMCAs.[20] Catholics built parish churches and schools, St. Vincent

Hospital, academies, and seminaries. After the Civil War, the Jewish fraternal organization B'nai B'rith raised sufficient funds from Jewish communities across the North and the South to build an orphanage in Cleveland that would serve the entire Jewish population east of the Mississippi. The local Jewish community created charitable and educational institutions and responded to the influx of refugees who sought safety and opportunity in the United States from the 1880s on.[21]

Northeastern Ohio's strong institutional ties to religious and cultural as well as business communities in New England, the Mid-Atlantic, and Europe reinforced its diversity. Divided by religious and cultural loyalties, nineteenth-century Ohio favored local and denominational initiatives that created dozens of small colleges, in contrast to the emphasis in southern states, Michigan, and the West on a single state university, often using the powers of a state government to discourage competitors.[22] In Ohio as in New England, nineteenth-century colleges constituted a special kind of foundation: they built up substantial assets—financial, physical, and goodwill—which their boards devoted from time to time to varied and changing purposes—religion; practical skills in reading, writing, mathematics, engineering and business; science; the arts; the cultivation of good citizenship, leadership, and other virtues.[23]

At the beginning of the twentieth century, Ohio boasted more than twenty-five endowed colleges and universities. In the northeastern corner of the state, five had endowments that surpassed $500,000—sufficient at the time to guarantee salaries to at least twenty faculty members (today it would take more than $50 million to underwrite a faculty of that size). These fortunate schools included Oberlin, Western Reserve, and the Case School of Applied Science, as well as Baldwin University (which later merged with neighboring German Wallace), and the Presbyterian College of Wooster. At the time American professional schools generally lacked endowments, but an authoritative account ranked the fund of Western Reserve University's Medical College as the third-largest of the nation's medical schools.[24] A few of the region's large endowments took other forms: in the last two decades of the nineteenth century, telegraph and steel pioneer Jeptha Wade helped create the notable endowed Lake View Cemetery and entrusted seventy-three acres nearby to the city of Cleveland for a park and a site for cultural institutions. Several Cleveland industrialists established the large trusts that eventually combined to create the Cleveland Museum of Art.

Foundations and endowed college funds clearly preceded John D. Rockefeller's decision to create a large general-purpose foundation, devoted not to a particular activity but to "the welfare of mankind" and based in New York—not in Cleveland, where he had launched the Standard Oil Company. Although a few substantial funds appeared in the region during the 1920s and 1930s, large foundations that might be said to follow Rockefeller's example of a general-purpose foundation came later. In northeastern Ohio, several of these were corporate foundations. A study of Cleveland's philanthropic profile prepared for the Filer Commission in the late 1960s counted seven corporate foundations (TRW, Sohio, Lincoln Electric, Cleveland Electric Illuminating Company, Eaton Corporation, and Warner and Swazey) among Cleveland's twenty largest by their donations.[25] To this list we should add corporate funds sponsored by Republic Steel in Cleveland, Nordson in Loraine County, Firestone and Goodyear in Akron, Timken in Canton, and others.

Rockefeller may have exerted his most significant influence on northeastern Ohio foundations through his Cleveland attorney, Frederick H. Goff, who had his Cleveland Trust Company launch the nation's first community foundation in 1914. Under Goff, the Cleveland Foundation emphasized nonsectarian and general charitable purposes. To give the community foundation credibility, and to distinguish it from the then dominant denominational funds, Goff arranged that it would have a distribution committee whose members were designated by leaders of the local chamber of commerce and bar association and by federal judges and university presidents.[26] As Duffus put it in 1928, the community foundation also emphasized control, because it "gives a new significance to the ownership of wealth. Instead of divesting ownership it perpetuates it, and at the same time guarantees proper custody, proper management and proper use of income. It makes the accumulation of wealth respectable by insuring the usefulness of wealth. It makes it honorable for a man to build up a fortune in the community, because it provides the means for the return of that fortune as a whole, or in part, for the permanent service of the community."[27] By the time congressional investigations into foundations reached their height in the 1960s, a few of the region's larger foundations had substantial assets. Some were spending assets down over a couple of decades, and several were corporate foundations handling funds according to the decisions of sponsoring businesses. Our best estimate of the largest foundations by assets in about 1960, based on the available resources, is summarized in table 4.1.

To judge from the unaudited reports submitted to the Foundation Directory for its 1970 edition, the twenty largest foundations by total giving within the Cleveland metropolitan statistical area did not include Hanna, Republic Steel, Timken, Firestone, Brush, Goodrich, or Nord funds; however, it did include Austin Memorial, Sears Family, Ireland,

Table 4.1. Northeastern Ohio Foundations, Reported Assets above $3 million, 1960†[28]

Name	Location	Founding Date	Assets (million $)	Focus
Cleveland Foundation	Cleveland	1914	36	General
George Gund Foundation	Cleveland	1952	30	General
Louis D. Beaumont Foundation	Cleveland	1943	18	General
Elisabeth Severance Prentiss Foundation	Cleveland	1939	15	Medical
Leonard C. Hanna, Jr. Fund	Cleveland	1941	11	Arts
Republic Steel Corp. Ed & Charitable Trust	Cleveland	1950	11	Corporate
Timken Foundation of Canton	Canton	1932	8	Hospitals, Education
Firestone Trust Fund	Cleveland	1954	6	Independent
Firestone Foundation	Akron	1947	6	Family
Brush Foundation	Cleveland	1928	6	Family Planning
Kulas Foundation	Cleveland	1937	5	Music
B.F. Goodrich Trust Fund	Akron	1951	5	Corporate
Thomas H. White Charitable Trust	Cleveland	1913/1939	3	Several Institutions
American Foundation Corporation	Cleveland	1944	3	Natural History
Nord Family/Nordson Foundation	Lorain	1952		General
Martha Holden Jennings Foundation	Cleveland	1954		K-12 Education
John Huntington Fund for Education	Cleveland	1918/1954		Education
Cleveland Development Foundation*	Cleveland	1954		Economic Development

†The last four foundations listed did not declare the size of their assets in 1960, but later reports suggest that they belong here.
*Closely tied to the Cleveland Foundation, which held a $6 million fund for the Cleveland Development Foundation until 1972.

Vernon Stouffer, Roger, and Evan Markas, as well as the other corporate funds noted above.[29]

A full account of the role of foundations in northeastern Ohio before the 1970s would also include several national foundations that engaged with the region in a deep and sustained way. First among these were the Rockefeller Foundation, which was a strong supporter of the Western Reserve University Medical School and University Hospitals; the Russell Sage Foundation, which collaborated with the Cleveland Foundation in the influential 1915 study of the Cleveland Public Schools; the Commonwealth Fund; the Robert Wood Johnson Foundation; and the Kresge Foundation—all important donors to the Western Reserve University Medical School—and later, beginning in the 1960s, the Ford Foundation.

What difference did northeastern Ohio's foundations make through the decades up to the 1970s? According to a 1974 survey, foundation grants accounted for about 3 percent of the income of the region's nonprofits between 1969 and 1973—useful, but far from decisive.[30] In health care, in particular, foundation influence had greatly declined from earlier heights. Health care had once, an informed observer stated, been "the responsibility of the private sector, with capital drives building hospitals, old folks' homes, rehabilitation clinics and out-patient facilities, examples of which are still scattered around the Cleveland area." Such facilities had never met all needs, and after World War II "much of this has changed.... Private subsidy of hospital care is virtually extinct; Washington has 'intruded' ... in hospital additions with Hill-Burton funds; welfare payments comprise a big part of the budgets of after-care facilities; private health agencies such as Heart and Cancer no longer call the shots in research and development."[31]

As in New York City, Rochester, Philadelphia, Pittsburgh, Baltimore, Chicago, and Minneapolis-St. Paul, northeastern Ohio's foundations did much to build their region's philanthropic and charitable infrastructure.[32] Foundations and endowed funds continued to subsidize churches, schools, and seminaries; to promote different religious and secular values and practices; and to aid selected religious and secular missions abroad. Increasingly, they concentrated their giving on the schools and arts organizations in Cleveland's University Circle,[33] and on selected colleges and community and arts organizations in Oberlin, Wooster, Akron, and Canton.[34]

Some funds supported more particular causes. The Brush Foundation (derived from an early fortune in electrical manufacturing) supported the birth control movement—or, as it said, significant "efforts toward betterment of the human stock and toward regulation of the increase of the population."[35] During the 1930s, the smaller Payne Fund sponsored a series of pioneering and sometimes controversial studies on the theoretically corrupting influence that movies and other forms of popular culture had on America's youth.[36] From its start in 1952, Akron's Paul P. Tell Foundation provided substantial funding to Christian evangelism. Some of the connections between Northeastern Ohio funds and institutions were (and remain) very close: between several funds at the Cleveland Foundation and Case and Western Reserve; between the Elisabeth Severance Prentiss Foundation, University Hospitals, and St. Luke's Hospital; between the Beaumont Foundation and Western Reserve's School of Applied Social Sciences and the Cleveland Orchestra; between the Kulas and Reinberger Foundations and music; between the Leonard C. Hanna and the White funds and the Cleveland Museum of Art; and between the Nord Foundation and Loraine County, the Timken Foundation and Canton, and the Knight Foundation and Akron.

Through participation and leadership in the community chest and through priority setting for capital campaigns, foundations helped set the region's agenda for health, education, and welfare. This philanthropic infrastructure promoted cooperation among the region's great religious communities in important ways. Encouraged by a committee of the Cleveland Chamber of Commerce—which was chaired by Jewish community leader Martin Marks and included key representatives of Catholic as well as Protestant interests—from the 1910s onward, northeastern Ohio foundations underwrote coordinating agencies that were both nonsectarian and religious. These included the Welfare Federation, which became the Center for Community Solutions and United Way of Greater Cleveland; the Greater Cleveland Healthcare Association; the Neighborhood Centers Association; the Jewish Community Federation; Catholic Charities; and the Protestant Federation of Churches, which later became the Interchurch Council.[37] During the difficult years of depression and war, the Cleveland Foundation and other funds kept the community chest afloat. Some later observers saw this as a passive activity, but Cleveland's community chest played a much more central role than is now easy to imagine. In 1930, it provided nearly half the income for the city's hospitals and more than half of the income for many of the city's religiously affiliated orphanages.[38]

In its earliest years when it had no resources to speak of, the Cleveland Foundation helped the region gain a reputation for innovative and effective forms of civic cooperation through excellent studies of current issues and through organizing public conversations. Among the results were significant reforms of the city's public school system (with the aid of the Russell Sage Foundation), trial courts (aided by prominent law faculty from Harvard), and the creation of the remarkable "Emerald Necklace" of interconnected parks around Cuyahoga and neighboring counties—which is now known as the Metroparks.[39]

In a similar spirit during the late 1950s, Mrs. William G. Mather persuaded several of the large foundations to join her and other individual donors (who were often working through their smaller family foundations) in creating a master plan for the region's prime cultural and medical center, and then in establishing the University Circle Development Foundation (which later became the University Circle, Inc.) to put the master plan into effect. This work absorbed hundreds of thousands of dollars and was slow to show results. Eventually, University Circle, Inc., with the support of University Hospitals, Case Western Reserve University (CWRU), the Cleveland Museum of Art, and as many as forty other organizations, coordinated land purchases, parking, police protection, and other services for what is now a significant center of employment and economic growth.[40]

By the late 1950s, foundations fit very closely into northeastern Ohio's tightly networked nonprofit sector, providing strong support for the region's white Protestant, Catholic, Jewish, and nonsectarian communities. As the Civil Rights Movement made clear, however, despite some positive elements of the record at Oberlin, Western Reserve University, Karamu House, some funds of the Cleveland Foundation, and several other institutions,[41] the region's nonprofit network did not provide comparable support for the African American population that had grown rapidly since the 1920s. Several of the region's foundations joined efforts to change this pattern, even as they continued to underwrite some of the arrangements that perpetuated it. From 1954, the Cleveland Development Corporation, funded by the Leonard C. Hanna Jr., Fund of the Cleveland Foundation, and other corporate contributions, used a business-led, top-down approach to promote downtown urban renewal and to encourage the private development of low-income housing. Results were disappointing. In an early 1960 invitation to a meeting, the secretary of the Development Fund wrote that "we shall not devote much time to a report of progress in the past year—a year in which big ideas and most imaginative plans have been pilloried by factional bickering and rejected." This venture closed in 1969.[42] As part of a generalized effort to open the region's civic life to African Americans, in 1967 the Greater Cleveland Associated Foundation (which was also closely connected to the Cleveland Foundation) joined the Ford Foundation in giving grants to a Congress of Racial Equality (CORE) voter registration drive in the city's black neighborhoods. Some observers insisted that this drive assured the election of Carl Stokes as the first African American mayor of a major US city. The objections of those who opposed Stokes's election fed into the congressional debates that led to the federal Tax Reform Act of 1969.[43]

Once elected, Stokes won funding from many sources, including from business leader George Steinbrenner and from the Development Fund for the Cleveland Now! special initiative that underwrote some of Stokes's job-training, youth-serving, and community development plans, and encouraged his hope that the federal government would provide the great bulk of an anticipated $177 million initiative. In the highly charged political atmosphere of the day, news that a Cleveland Now! grant had been given to a Glenville neighborhood organization that became militant and used guns in a 1969 battle in which three policemen died reinforced foundation critics' negative attitudes toward it.[44] Key foundation leaders in Cleveland drew the conclusion that, unless it was very carefully handled, innovative and engaged policy work could be overshadowed by controversy that might discourage the very risk-taking that is often cited as an important rationale for publicly subsidized, private social investment.

Since the 1970s

Northeastern Ohio's largest foundations have grown and changed a great deal in the past forty years, as table 4.2 makes clear. The number of foundations whose assets exceed $20 million (which is the current equivalent of $3 million in 1960), has more than tripled. This is true even though corporate foundations have become less prominent; some of the largest firms have merged or moved so that their headquarters are no longer in Cleveland. Sohio is now part of British Petroleum, whose US offices are in Chicago; Republic Steel is now part of Belgium-based Mittal Steel; Firestone is now part of Bridgestone, which is a Japanese firm with US offices in Chicago; B. F. Goodrich moved from Akron to Charlotte, North Carolina; TRW became part of Northrup-Grumman and is now based in southern California; Akron's Knight Foundation (derived from the newspaper chain) moved to Florida; and, in 2012, Eaton Corporation merged with Cooper Industries, formerly based in Houston, Texas, and relocated its corporate headquarters to Dublin, Ireland. Warner and Swazey, and others have closed. A striking feature of the current table is the presence of several very large foundations and supporting foundations set up in recent years by the three Mandel Brothers, whose Cleveland-based Premier Industrial Corporation enjoyed an extraordinary run of success and growth in the sourcing and delivery of the components of complex machines the last four or five decades of the twentieth century.[45]

This is a much longer list of "large" foundations than existed in the early 1960s. In terms of the labor cost of a major project, today, northeastern Ohio's large foundations have about five or six times the aggregate purchasing power

Table 4.2. Northeastern Ohio Foundations, Assets above $20 million, c. 2015[46]

Name	Type	Founded	Location	Assets c. 2015	Grants c. 2015
The Cleveland Foundation	CF	1914	Cleveland	$2,185,366,489	$101,651,046
American Endowment Foundation	CF*[47]	1994	Hudson	1,038,319,893	294,600,121
Mandel Supporting Foundations—Jack N. and Lilyan Mandel Fund	S	1982	Cleveland	787,886,800	14,435,518
Jack, Joseph, and Morton Mandel Foundation	PF	1953	Cleveland	712,288,476	11,428,242
The George Gund Foundation	PF	1953	Mentor	530,341,218	22,425,190
Mandel Supporting Foundations—Morton L. and Barbara Mandel Fund	S	1982	Cleveland	445,936,911	14,435,518
Jewish Federation of Cleveland	S	1952	Cleveland	428,576,710	81,799,930
Mandel Supporting Foundations—Joseph C. & Florence Mandel Fund	S	1982	Cleveland	405,872,531	14,435,518
Timken Foundation of Canton	PF	1938	Canton	377,843,984	15,520,760
Stark Community Foundation, Inc.	CF	1963	Canton	223,113,299	7,885,162
The Morton and Barbara Mandel Family Foundation	PF	1965	Cleveland	219,487,800	5,442,026
Joseph & Florence Mandel Foundation	PF	1965	Cleveland	198,884,388	7,081,201
University of Akron Foundation	S	1966	Akron	190,699,435	11,999,910
Kent State University Foundation	S	1966	Kent	184,423,320	15,623,933
Akron Community Foundation	CF	1960	Akron	182,005,604	7,214,932
David and Inez Myers Foundation	S	1956	Beachwood	174,266,318	5,699,250
Saint Luke's Foundation of Cleveland	PF	1990	Cleveland	171,905,492	8,959,476
The Kelvin and Eleanor Smith Foundation	PF	1957	Cleveland	160,873,474	8,311,391
GAR Foundation	PF	1967	Akron	160,044,516	7,566,664
The Joseph and Florence Mandel Foundation	PF	1965	Cleveland	155,120,453	5,815,198
The Burton D. Morgan Foundation	PF	1968	Hudson	152,371,400	4,752,000
Catholic Diocese of Cleveland Foundation	S	1946	Cleveland	152,038,721	19,410,093

Benjamin Rose Institute	O	1937	Cleveland	139,696,975	0
Mt. Sinai Health Care Foundation	S	1994	Cleveland	136,468,989	6,068,843
McGregor Foundation	O	2003	E. Cleveland	134,247,186	925,463
Veale Foundation	PF	1964	Pepper Pike	129,075,907	9,556,789
The Nord Family Foundation	PF	1988	Amherst	128,554,263	6,291,702
HCS Foundation	PF	1961	Cleveland	82,245,025	4,743,800
John Huntington Art and Polytechnic Trust	S	1935	Cleveland	120,519,791	8,138,203
Community Foundation of Lorain County	CF	1980	Elyria	113,851,274	4,854,237
Albert J. Weatherhead Estate Trust	PF	1971	Beachwood	103,389,822	10,512,568
The Youngstown Foundation	CF	1942	Youngstown	102,818,799	3,576,064
Cleveland State University Foundation, Inc.	S	1969	Cleveland	99,741,703	10,723,076
The William J. and Dorothy K. O'Neill Foundation	PF	1987	Cleveland	95,796,899	2,973,173
Sisters of Charity Foundation of Cleveland	S	1946	Cleveland	90,456,930	1,550,068
Sisters of Charity Foundation of Canton	S	1946	Cleveland	89,088,080	2,283,548
Margaret Clark Morgan Foundation	PF	2001	Hudson	88,451,400	2,541,000
Barberton Community Foundation	S	1997	Barberton	88,161,751	2,538,528
The Elisabeth Severance Prentiss Foundation	PF	1944	Cleveland	86,521,123	3,180,812
Milton and Tamar Maltz Family Foundation	S	1997	Beachwood	82,943,118	3,700,000
Wean (Raymond John) Foundation	PF	1950	Warren	80,400,623	2,165,504
The Fred A. Lennon Charitable Trust	PF	1994	Pepper Pike	79,648,060	3,255,500
The Reinberger Foundation	PF	1966	Cleveland	71,932,914	2,854,765
The Martha Holden Jennings Foundation	PF	1964	Cleveland	70,840,063	3,228,434
Cuyahoga Community College Foundation	S	1973	Cleveland	65,326,750	1,459,906
The Paul and Carol David Foundation	PF	1980	Canton	63,844,121	1,662,234
Leonard C. Rosenberg Foundation	S	1993	Shaker Hts.	61,801,767	1,139,311
Sam J. Frankino Foundation	PF	2005	Cleveland	61,468,508	3,019,049

(continued)

Table 4.2. *(continued)*

Name	Type	Founded	Location	Assets c. 2015	Grants c. 2015
Eva L. and Joseph M. Bruening Foundation	PF	1988	Brooklyn	58,248,208	2,319,700
Case Alumni Foundation	S	2004	Cleveland	58,121,545	2,069,891
Hoover Foundation	PF	1947	North Canton	52,516,205	2,574,610
Greater Wayne County Foundation	CF	1979	Wooster	51,607,267	5,524,924
John P. Murphy Foundation	PF	1962	Cleveland	51,014,926	2,694,000
Anne Kilcawley Christman Foundation	PF	2002	Youngstown	49,828,750	2,079,840
Deaconess Foundation	PF	1993	Brooklyn	49,673,234	1,239,893
Third Federal Foundation	PF	2007	Cleveland	46,629,828	3,584,465
Park Family Foundation	PF	2004	Cleveland	46,275,330	4,553,317
Charles K. King Trust 3 AWMI	PF	1973	Cleveland	44,403,349	0
FirstEnergy Foundation	C	1963	Akron	43,289,743	5,904,445
Paul & Maxine Frohring Foundation	PF	1961	Pennington	42,637,775	2,660,000
Ellen Garretson Wade Memorial Fund	PF	1944	Brooklyn	42,071,769	2,037,481
J. W. Ellsworth Endowment Trust	S	1953	Brooklyn	42,045,839	2,207,054
The Stocker Foundation	PF	1979	Elyria	39,778,389	2,196,211
Robert R. Rhodes Trust	S	1982	Brooklyn	39,687,731	1,491,503
John Edward & Ida Grove Bicknell Memorial Fund	PF	1963	Brooklyn	38,965,905	2,774,177
Helen G. Bicknell					
Kulas Foundation	PF	1938	Cleveland	38,559,238	1,942,700
Robert A. Immerman Family Foundation	PF	2011	Solon	36,763,809	600,000
Howley Family Foundation	PF	2003	Bratenahl	34,748,345	1,333,555
John H. Hord Estate Trust	S	1971	Cleveland	33,611,708	2,199,459
Frederick E. & Julia G. Nonneman Foundation	PF	1999	Westlake	33,362,924	1,770,843
CPB Foundation	PF	2004	Pepper Pike	33,261,685	2,109,192
Robert & Ita Klein Charitable Foundation	PF	2013	Cleveland	33,018,812	6,526,740
John Huntington Fund for Education	PF	1956	Cleveland	30,704,483	2,592,367

The Abington Foundation	PF	1983	Cleveland	29,729,125	1,392,047
Edward M. Wilson Family Foundation	PF	1980	Cleveland	29,554,148	1,487,500
Maltz Family Foundation	S	1997	Beachwood	28,879,970	23,497,000
J.H. Wade Trust for the Cleveland Museum of Art	S	1971	Brooklyn	28,602,530	1,243,499
James And Angela Hambrick Foundation	PF	2012	Pepper Pike	28,479,736	1,562,975
The Jochum-Moll Foundation	PF	1962	Cleveland	27,629,959	1,822,600
William M. And Alyce Cafaro Family Foundation	PF	1998	Youngstown	27,170,313	1,572,435
Edward A. & Catherine L. Lozick Foundation	PF	1983	Pepper Pike	26,987,939	2,312,530
Warmenhoven Family Foundation	PF	2007	Cleveland	26,968,008	1,244,700
Glenna Joyce Testamentary Trust	S	1980	Cleveland	26,460,886	1,030,829
The American Foundation Corporation	PF	1974	Cleveland	26,089,979	1,154,985
Semi J. And Ruth W. Begun Foundation	S	1989	Cleveland	26,063,668	1,630,436
Richard J. Fasenmyer Foundation	PF	1990	Brooklyn	25,594,847	16,305,000
Randolph J. & Estelle M. Dorn Foundation	PF	1971	Sandusky	25,257,964	1,256,091
OMNOVA Solutions Foundation, Inc.	C	2000	Beachwood	25,091,151	1,425,985
Thomas H. White No. 1 Trust	PF	1913	Brooklyn	24,978,510	1,240,750
The Herbert W. Hoover Foundation	PF	1972	Brooklyn	24,278,508	823,453
Nordson Corporation Foundation	C	1988	Westlake	24,096,555	5,605,942
Marion G. Resch Foundation	PF	1998	Youngstown	23,488,800	1,265,271
Murch Foundation	PF	1958	Cleveland	22,545,684	1,542,000
Trzcinski Foundation	PF	1980	North Royalton	22,343,520	1,502
Geoffrey Gund Foundation	PF	1993	Brooklyn	22,329,153	2,366,065
DBJ Foundation	PF	1990	Cleveland	21,922,026	1,077,700
Brentwood Foundation	PF	1994	Cleveland	21,404,649	1,034,463
Kenneth A. Scott Charitable Trust	PF	1996	Cleveland	21,249,979	977,075
The Louise H. and David S. Ingalls Foundation	PF	1955	Shaker Heights	20,012,939	1,775,700
The Erie County Community Foundation	C	1995	Sandusky	19,927,495	696,259
				$13,452,923,910	$929,457,127

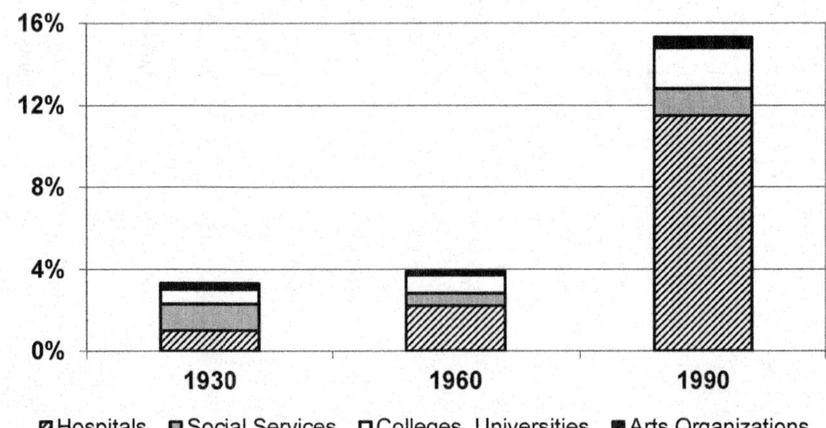

Figure 4.1. Nonprofit Spending as Wage and Salary Share, Cuyahoga County (Cleveland), Ohio, 1930–90

of their earlier counterparts. In comparison to the national economy or to their own region's nonprofits, today's foundations are not quite so much wealthier. If the total assets of the region's large foundations of 1960 amounted to about $200 million, the equivalent gross domestic product share today would be about $3.3 billion. By that reasoning, the region's large foundations have perhaps quadrupled their relative wealth.[48] Total income and expenditures of northeastern Ohio nonprofits grew much faster than foundation assets after 1960, as suggested by figures 4.1 and 4.2, which offer estimates of nonprofit spending as a share of all wages and salaries in four large, nonprofit subsectors, and of the share of total income in Cuyahoga County accounted for by gifts of all kinds (including income from endowments held by operating nonprofits).[49] Nationally in 2013, private contributions from all sources accounted for 11.5 percent of the income of nonreligious nonprofit service organizations. Foundation-giving accounted at most for 3 percent.[50] Thus, in relation to the nonprofit organizations they support, foundations may well have become *less* wealthy, though perhaps not less significant to new initiatives.

However we view their relative size, northeastern Ohio's large foundations support an increasingly diverse array of distinctive purposes. A significant group of the region's foundations now explicitly support religious entities. The Jewish community federations in Cleveland and Akron have attracted numerous supporting foundations for their human services and their religious activities; the Catholic Diocese of Cleveland Foundation

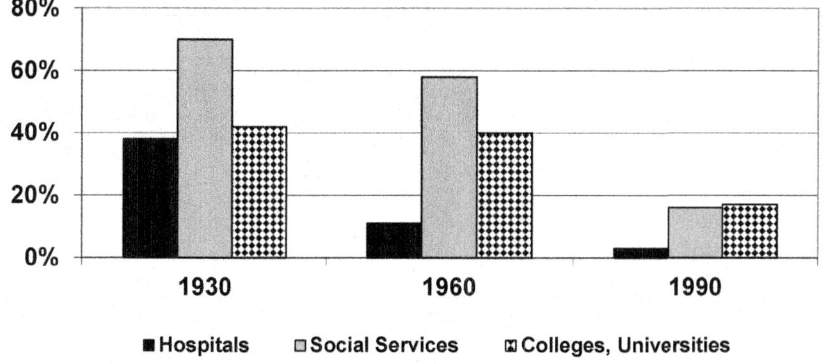

Figure 4.2. Gifts and Endowment Contributions to Income in Three Large Nonprofit Fields, Cuyahoga County, Ohio, 1930–90

has recently made similar arrangements. The Jochum-Moll Foundation has joined Paul P. Tell in funding evangelical Christianity. Beginning in the 1980s, some nonprofit health insurance companies, as well as many nonprofit hospitals (often sponsored by religious communities) began to close. In the course of ending their operations, many of these organizations converted their "charitable assets" (obtained through gifts or tax-exempt operations) into foundations that in most cases devote themselves, in part, to the needs of those communities. This process of converting from a public charity to a private foundation results in what are known as health conversion foundations.[51] The newer health-charity and conversion foundations act in much the same way as community foundations; see table 4.4.[52] Akron's Burton D. Morgan Foundation is devoted to the preservation of the free enterprise system; many grants from the Fred A. Lennon Charitable Trust have a similar purpose.

Northeastern Ohio's foundations have developed an increasingly diverse array of organizational forms. The region's community foundations have grown remarkably (see table 4.3).

It might be said that Northeastern Ohio's legal, financial, and charitable institutions have developed something of a specialty in the creation and management of foundations. Courts have directed that a number of large estates be set up as foundations—and that they then mechanically pay stated shares of income to a list of charities. Foundations that support state universities have acquired significant resources for Cleveland State, Kent State, and the University of Akron (Kent and Akron listed more than $75 million in assets in 2001[53]). At least three large banks headquartered in Cleveland—Key, National City (NCC), and Charter One—developed

Table 4.3. Northeastern Ohio Community Foundations, ca. 2016

	Begun		Assets 2016
Cleveland Foundation	1914	Cleveland	$2,146,075,626
Youngstown Foundation	1918	Youngstown	104,226,258
Akron Community Foundation	1955	Akron	$182,006,000
Stark Community Foundation	1963	Canton	207,057,723
Community Foundation Greater Lorain County	1980	Lorain	117,888,500
Erie County Community Foundation	1995	Sandusky	19,927,495

Table 4.4. Northeastern Ohio Health Conversion Foundations, ca. 2016

	Begun		Assets 2016
Sisters of Charity Foundation of Canton	1946	Canton	89,088,080
St. Ann Foundation	1973	Cleveland	33,600,000
Saint Francis Charitable Trust	1973	Cleveland	21,700,000
Saint Luke's Foundation	1990	Cleveland	171,905,492
Brentwood Foundation	1994	Cleveland	21,404,649
Deaconess Foundation	1994	Cleveland	47,948,038
Mt. Sinai Health Care Foundation	1994	Cleveland	136,468,989
Barberton Community Foundation	1996	Barberton	75,592,031
Sisters of Charity Foundation Cleveland	1996	Cleveland	90,456,930
Community West Foundation	199?	Westlake	99,830,327

substantial foundation and trust management services, with clients in Indiana, Michigan, and Pennsylvania, as well as throughout Ohio (Charter One merged into Citizens Bank of Providence, Rhode Island, in 2004; National City merged into PNC Bank of Pittsburgh in 2010). The American Endowment Foundation (AEF) of Hudson, Ohio, describes itself as seeking "to expand philanthropy in America by making it more attractive and more enjoyable for donors to practice philanthropy;" with assets of more than $1 billion in 2017, it claims to be "the nation's largest independent provider of donor advised funds," giving donors "the freedom to focus on your giving while we take care of all the operational details."[54] Cleveland's Foundation Management Services does not directly hold and invest funds, but provides "personalize[d] grant-making services" for a growing number of private independent and family foundations.[55] For about ten years, the Axios Foundation, whose offices are in Solon (about halfway between Cleveland and Akron), has been raising and sending abroad $1 million or more annually for anti-AIDs campaigns in Africa. And as noted, several national foundations, such as Ford, Joyce, Knight, Kresge, Robert R. McCormick, Rockefeller, and Whitaker, have been giving at least $1 million each year in northeastern Ohio.

Not all moves have bolstered northeastern Ohio's foundation sector. We have noted relocations affecting corporate foundations and banks. Important independent foundations, including especially the John S. and James L. Knight Foundation, formerly of Akron, and the S. Livingston Mather Trust, formerly of Cleveland, have also moved—in these cases, to Miami and to suburban Philadelphia, respectively. The Beaumont and Hanna Foundations closed as intended, as did a number of smaller funds.

In the past forty years, the region's foundations have also worked actively to strengthen the region's nonprofit infrastructure in a wide variety of ways. The Mandel foundations have worked with others to strengthen the leadership of nonprofit and community-development organizations, locally and also in Israel and in other Jewish communities. The George Gund Foundation, the Cleveland Foundation, and many others have helped to diversify the region's philanthropic infrastructure by supporting the creation of organizations in new fields ranging from the Greater Cleveland Roundtable (race relations), Greater Cleveland Community Shares (workplace fundraising for social justice organizations), and the Cleveland Women's Foundation to the Maltz Museum of Jewish Heritage, and the Inventors' Hall of Fame in Akron. After initially responding to the challenges of poverty and racial injustice by funding community organizations and community action in poor neighborhoods, foundations and other donors promoted the creation of strong community economic development organizations, especially in Cleveland. To this end, foundations provided seed money to community development organizations in most Cleveland neighborhoods, funds for special initiatives, and support for central coordinating organizations, especially Neighborhood Progress, Inc., and the Cleveland Housing Network (merged to become Cleveland Neighborhood Progress in 2013).[56]

Although there have been many changes, the pattern of concentrating grants on selected sets of large institutions has continued, as table 4.5 suggests.

We have emphasized large foundations and large grants because they include a substantial majority of the total flow of foundation funds. It is also much easier to gather information on a relatively small number of large foundations and large grants than on the literally thousands of the region's small foundations and tens of thousands of small grants. But our overview would be incomplete if we failed to note the small size of the

Table 4.5. Eighty Northeastern Ohio Recipients of $1 Million or More in Total Foundation Grants, 1999–2003, by Major Institutional Category[57]

University Circle and Allied Organizations[a]	$173.6 M	39%
Other Cuyahoga County Educational and Cultural Organizations[b]	55.0 M	11%
Cuyahoga County Social Service Organizations[c]	47.5 M	11%
Cuyahoga County Educational Initiatives[d]	29.8 M	7%
Cuyahoga County Housing and Economic Development[e]	29.0 M	6%
Cuyahoga County Catholic and Jewish Charitable Federations	14.0 M	3%
Cuyahoga County Commissioners, Courts	9.3 M	2%
Colleges and Universities outside Cuyahoga County[f]	41.6 M	9%
Akron, Canton Social Service, Education[g]	30.8 M	7%
Other Fund Raising and Distributing Entities	21.9 M	5%

[a]Case Western Reserve University
Cleveland Clinic Foundation
University Hospitals of Cleveland
Musical Arts Association
Cleveland Botanical Garden
Cleveland Museum of Art
Western Reserve Historical Society
Cleveland Play House
Free Medical Clinic of Greater Cleveland
Cleveland Orchestra
University Hospitals Health System
Health Museum of Cleveland
Cleveland Institute of Music
Benjamin Rose Institute
Cleveland Museum of Natural History

University Circle, properly considered, is a circumscribed district that does not include the Cleveland Clinic, the Cleveland Play House, the Health Museum of Cleveland, or the Benjamin Rose Institute. But these organizations are closely tied to Case Western Reserve University and are located next to University Circle, so we have included them here. The Cleveland Clinic and University Hospitals have their central administrative, tertiary hospital, and research facilities in or near University Circle, but they own and operate hospitals and clinics throughout the region.

[b]John Carroll University
Ursuline College
Educational TV Association of Metro Cleveland
Great Lakes Museum of Science
University Partnership
Playhouse Square Foundation
Great Lakes Theater Festival
Cuyahoga Community College Foundation
Cleveland State University
Cuyahoga Community College
Cleveland Zoological Society
Cleveland Opera
Notre Dame College of Ohio
Laurel School
Cleveland State University Foundation
Catholic Teachers Endowment Fund
Saint Ignatius High School

[c] United Way
Achievement Center for Children
Greater Cleveland Roundtable
Federation for Community Planning
Vocational Guidance Services
Goodrich-Gannett Neighborhood Center
Fatima Family Center
Cleveland Foodbank
Eliza Bryant Center
Boys and Girls Club of Greater Cleveland
Heather Hill Hospital, Health and Care Center

[d] Cleveland Scholarship Programs
National College Access Network
Cleveland Municipal School District
Learning Communities Network
Cleveland Initiative for Education
Cleveland Education Fund
East Cleveland Public Library

[e] Neighborhood Progress, Inc.
Foundation for Environmental Research

Shorebank Enterprise Group	Northeastern Ohio Regional Economic Development Foundation
Cleveland Tomorrow Program Cleveland Housing Network BioEnterprise Corporation	Cleveland Advanced Manufacturing Greater Cleveland Growth Association
[f]Oberlin College University of Akron College of Wooster	Kent State University Foundation University of Akron Development Foundation
[g]Stark Educational Partnership Wooster City Schools Children's Hospital Foundation of Akron Akron Art Museum Boy Scouts of Akron	YWCA of Canton Canton City Schools United Way of Summit County J. R. Coleman Family Services, Canton

majority of foundation grants, from both large foundations and small ones. Most foundations make few grants of more than $25,000; a look through the Form 990 tax reports on GuideStar reveals that many grants are as small as $10,000 or even $2,500. The small size of most grants, coupled with the sometimes-complex and time-consuming process of applying for them, forces the nonprofit organizations that seek grants to think carefully about whether any particular foundation is worthy. On the other hand, few grant-seekers would favor the imposition of new rules that would discourage donors from setting up new sources of funding.

From the perspective of their donors, the region's foundations provide an institutional way to preserve wealth and allow it to flow to causes, institutions, and purposes they favor, both religious and secular. From the perspective of the region's institution builders, foundation priorities and collaborations have helped determine which pathways of growth and development will win crucial early funding. In this way, northeastern Ohio's foundations have had a significant impact on large organizations. Foundations have also made substantial contributions to the region's philanthropic infrastructure—to the establishment of payroll deduction giving through the Community Chest–United Way movement, of the community foundation, and of the region's unusually strong social service, community development, and religious associations. From the perspective of those who deal in ideas and policies, the region's foundations have underwritten a variety of challenging and sometimes controversial intellectual initiatives—and have not underwritten many others. In the 1910s and 1920s, and again since the 1970s, several foundations have worked with some success to draw attention to important social, educational, and economic challenges in the region, and to promote creative thinking about ways to address challenges through governmental as well as private action. In recent years they have reinforced the region's commitment to scientific and medical research.

But to say all this is not to evaluate the impact of foundation action. On the one hand, foundations have provided only a small and declining share of the resources in any field. On the other, those who direct the region's institutions—as well as those who seek to evaluate them—disagree among themselves as to what, exactly, they are trying to achieve. The fact that funds can flow to foundations as well as directly to operating nonprofit organizations means that operating organizations must devote resources to their dealings with foundations, even as they provide operating nonprofits with a more diverse array of possible funders.

Case Studies

Given the diverse purposes of foundations in northeastern Ohio—and their limited resources—we have decided to focus the second part of our investigation on the way selected groups of large foundations have recently sought to collaborate to make a difference in two fields: regional economic development and K–12 education. Table 4.5 shows that educational initiatives and housing and economic development in Cuyahoga County alone accounted, respectively, for 7 percent and 6 percent of all large grants from large foundations in the region in the years around 2000. Apart from continuing support for the region's nationally noted complex of nonprofit institutions, these purposes attracted the most foundation support.

Economic development and education have long been at the forefront of local conversations about the future of the region. As we've noted, the first major effort of the Cleveland Foundation was to engage experts from New York's Russell Sage Foundation to undertake a very thorough survey of the city's schools. In the 1950s and 1960s, leaders of the Cleveland Foundation and of some substantial corporate foundations sought to jump-start downtown redevelopment and to encourage private investment in low- and moderate-income housing. These early economic development efforts mostly produced frustration, but they did give some business leaders a chance to begin to learn to work effectively with African American and low-income neighborhood leaders. Somewhat more effective efforts continued through the last three decades of the twentieth century, producing some positive results and a good deal of practical experience for the businessmen, lawyers, and nonprofit and community leaders involved. Notable foundation efforts subsidized important efforts to stabilize the City of Cleveland and its neighborhoods. At the beginning of the mayoral administrations of Carl Stokes (1967), George Voinovich (1980), and Frank Jackson (2006), the Cleveland Foundation and others underwrote extensive consulting work designed to help the mayors improve the efficiency and effectiveness of city departments. In 1988, the Cleveland, Gund, and Mandel Foundations moved to create and underwrite Neighborhood Progress, Inc., to coordinate neighborhood, government, and business efforts to stabilize Cleveland's residential neighborhoods. In the late 1980s and in the 1990s, during the mayoral administration of Michael White, these foundations also underwrote some of the work that produced the North Coast Harbor, Rock and Roll Hall of Fame, and the Gateway construction of new homes for the city's professional baseball and basketball teams.[58]

Between 2000 and 2004, the Cleveland *Plain Dealer* and Ideastream, the city's National Public Broadcasting affiliate, collaborated in a series of articles and broadcasts entitled "A Quiet Crisis." How, they asked, could northeastern Ohio build on existing community assets to attract new growth? As *Plain Dealer* reporter Joe Frolik put it, people in the region were concerned about the "downward stuff, the slower than national growth patterns ... the recessions that we went into sooner, went deeper, and came out of later. What people called 'the brain drain'—the loss of talented young people."[59] For decades, Cleveland, Akron, Youngstown, and the other "legacy cities" of the region had seen their steel mills, tire plants, and other industrial factories fall into disrepair as manufacturing moved overseas and technologies transformed the region into a service economy. Many once-vibrant neighborhoods that grew up around industrial areas became dilapidated and depressed as jobs disappeared, population decreased, and the concentration of poverty increased. In the early 2000s, the predatory lending (or subprime mortgage) crisis did further damage, creating a wave of residential foreclosures and consequent tax shortfalls for many municipalities and counties.

Economic Development

The many public discussions of the "quiet crisis" featured representatives of the region's foundations (and their most prominent nonprofit partners). Understanding that their dollars were very limited, northeastern Ohio foundations used the "quiet crisis" and related public discussions to focus attention on economic development and education reform. The foundations encouraged new thinking about local legislation and taxation, funded research and publicized key findings, and encouraged the creation of new regional entities; they also continued to fund specific programs at selected nonprofit organizations. A group of the region's foundations thus promoted the notion that the region must adopt new approaches to economic development and education. In particular, they pressed the region's many local and county governments to collaborate rather than compete with one another to raise the region's educational attainment. They encouraged both governments and business interests to develop more sophisticated understanding of the possibilities for economic growth in the region and to undertake strategic interventions designed to attract and retain people whose education and technical skills would add economic value and help entrepreneurs succeed. The region's leading chambers of commerce—the Greater Cleveland Partnership and the Greater Akron Chamber—shared much of this vision and increased their efforts to work together.[60] Whether the foundations would be more successful in the 2000s than their predecessors had been in the 1950s and 1960s is more difficult to determine.

To pursue this region-wide strategy, northeastern Ohio's foundations had to take up several challenges. As table 4.6 shows, in the five largest metropolitan statistical areas in the region, foundation grant funds are relatively small, amounting to just four-tenths of 1 percent of the total economic activity in the Cleveland statistical area. This is less than two-tenths in Akron, Youngstown, and Canton, and far less in Mansfield.

Nor can foundations easily collaborate across county and municipal boundaries. Northeastern Ohio has a relatively large concentration of private foundations located in the counties that are home to Cleveland, Akron, and Canton: Cuyahoga County (1,954), Summit County (216), and Stark County (89).[63] Cleveland, Akron, Canton, and Youngstown have built dense urban cores over the past 150 years, but parts of these counties, and larger parts of adjacent counties, remain predominantly rural with many small towns. Philanthropic efforts in the region seek to be inclusive, yet substantial disparities in wealth, in the scale and scope of nonprofit networks, in economic activities, and in the diversity of population and educational attainment from place to place can reinforce the determination of local officials and businesses to go their own way.

Variation in local policy priorities tends to reinforce particularism: whereas key stakeholders in Akron suburbs emphasize high-tech manufacturing, Cleveland's leadership may be focused on school reform and Lorain leaders may be focused on a community-based anti-foreclosure campaign. The most prominent foundations' tasks are further complicated by uncertainties about the value of various measures—of access, equal opportunity, or return on investments. And because the staffs of the largest foundations have many different responsibilities, it can be difficult

Table 4.6. Northeastern Ohio Metro Areas: Private Foundation Contributions and GDP

Metropolitan Statistical Area	Total GDP 2011[61]	Total Private Foundation Contributions and Grants Made[62]	Total Private Foundation Contributions and Grants Made as a share of GDP
Cleveland-Lorain-Elyria	108,122,000,000	434,243,226	0.4016%
Akron	28,280,000,000	45,176,786	0.1597%
Youngstown-Warren-Boardman	17,239,000,000	20,712,727	0.1202%
Canton-Massillon	13,234,000,000	21,925,693	0.1657%
Mansfield	3,584,000,000	1,730,026	0.0483%

for them to take the time to reach consensus on possible measures, or on program priorities.[64] Should economic development focus on the creation of affordable housing? Improving public school systems? Attracting new business investment and creating job growth? Improving regional collaboration and institutional infrastructure? Should the foundation focus its limited resources on one of these areas? On all of them?

Moreover, although regional philanthropic leaders share broad agreement that education reform and access to jobs in low-income neighborhoods are critical to general economic development, such concerns are not often integrated into conversations about programs and strategies when foundations, business groups, and leaders of large nonprofit hospitals and universities get together. If the most important metric for economic development is the number of jobs created, does it matter if they are created in the low-income urban cores or the upper-middle class exurbs, or is a job a job? Some even question whether foundations should emphasize economic growth rather than the relief of immediate need. Matthew Rossman, a professor of law at Case Western Reserve University, argues that economic development nonprofits that support for-profit businesses through investment, providing subsidy through business incubation or capacity building "turn the traditional charitable services delivery model on its head by advancing private interests first and betting that benefit to a charitable class will follow."[65]

In northeastern Ohio, foundations including Cleveland, Gund, Knight, GAR, Lennon, and St. Luke's have increased their giving to economic development activities substantially over the decades since 2000, demonstrating a long-term commitment to addressing economic issues. In 2002–2003, the total number of grants related to economic development in the region was 62; by 2004–2005, that number had grown to 126, and by 2009–2010 to 142 grants.[66] Among the leading recipients of economic development foundation grants have been the Fund for Our Economic Future and the former ShoreBank Enterprise Group (SEG): the Fund and SEG each received more than 15 grants of $100,000 or above between 2000 and 2010. In the five years between 2006 and 2010, SEG reported $10.8 million of grant and public support; and the Fund for Our Economic Future reported $19.2 million[67].

Fifty-four foundations across the region set up the Economic Future Fund in 2004 to "strengthen the economic competitiveness of Northeast Ohio through grantmaking, research, and civic engagement."[68] Pursuing a broad regional development strategy designed to expand clusters of firms in such regionally notable fields as advanced manufacturing, technology, and biomedical engineering, the fund directed its efforts to the concerns of business firms of all sizes. It investigated the needs of individual entrepreneurs, midsized firms, and multinational corporations, as well as businesses, nonprofits, and government agencies looking for a new partner to supply a service or specialized component. It has encouraged research into trends and opportunities within the region, the careful evaluation of the region's comparative advantages (and of barriers to enhancing its advantages), the growth of supportive research and teaching at the region's universities, workforce development and training, and a welcoming business climate. In practice, the fund has directed foundation dollars to public and nonprofit business incubators, manufacturing and technology advocates, and capacity-building organizations including JumpStart, Team NEO, BioEnterprise, Magnet, and WIRENet.[69]

The region's foundations have also joined businesses and others to develop new associations for young minority professionals and for highly trained newcomers from abroad, and to attract biomedical device startups. And they have helped underwrite successful efforts to redefine well-placed older (and on a national basis remarkably affordable) neighborhoods—Cleveland's Tremont, Ohio City, Gordon Square, and Collinwood, as well as suburban Lakewood and Cleveland Heights—as places for artists, artisans, music-makers, and other ambitious young people.[70]

Some of the Economic Future Fund's efforts have brought national attention and recognition; analysts have even credited the fund with helping to launch a growing movement to use private economic development initiatives to replace moribund, deadlocked, and ineffective state and federal institutions.[71] Since its founding in 2004, the fund claims to have helped create over 16,500 jobs and to attract over $3 billion in capital investment in the region.[72] While this is an impressive effort, it is spread over a decade and a wide geographic region. When considered on a national scale, these are not big numbers—a single resort or casino in Las Vegas reported injecting $2.3 billion into the local economy by its opening in 2008.[73]

Work in low-income neighborhoods has been especially challenging. ShoreBank Enterprise Group began as the independent nonprofit affiliate of ShoreBank Cleveland, which was a branch of Chicago's ShoreBank, the nation's first economic development bank. ShoreBank paired each of its bank branches outside of Chicago with an independent nonprofit organization to provide services that would support community development.[74] In Cleveland, the nonprofit SEG focused on providing transformational loans to growing small businesses with the capacity to employ local residents in high-poverty neighborhoods. SEG provided intensive capacity-building services—including assistance with accounting, marketing, and workforce development—to these locally owned companies in an effort to support them through the early stages of growth. Loans were provided to companies that would not have been able to secure funding from a traditional bank. The companies were usually at the point when an injection of capital was necessary for the purchase of equipment, technology, or manpower that would drive future growth. SEG also ran a business incubator with a combination of office and industrial space. Its purpose as an organization was to encourage entrepreneurship and homegrown employment in the most underserved neighborhoods on Cleveland's east side.

ShoreBank and the SEG were invited to come to Cleveland in 1994 by the City of Cleveland and by philanthropic and business leaders who wanted to encourage economic development through support of entrepreneurship.[75] Unfortunately, ShoreBank's national headquarters in Chicago suffered substantial losses during the subprime loan crisis, and as a result, the nonprofit split from the bank in 2009. The former SEG reorganized as Cleveland Enterprise and capitalized a new fund in conjunction with the Cleveland Foundation and others: the Evergreen Cooperative Fund.[76] Evergreen Cooperative Fund now underwrites promising small businesses in eight deeply impoverished minority neighborhoods near the University Circle area on Cleveland's east side. Seeking both to add jobs and to encourage firms whose employees are deeply invested in the success of their employer and their neighborhood, Evergreen provides technical assistance, workforce training and placement, and encourages the adoption of a cooperative ownership and management structure. Among its successes to date are a new commercial laundry, an energy assessment and solar power installation firm, and a three-and-a-half-acre greenhouse in a former industrial building.[77]

Another locally targeted economic development organization supported by northeastern Ohio foundations was launched with the aid of Greater Cleveland Community Shares, with small foundation grants. Empowering and Strengthening Ohio's People (ESOP—formerly the East Side Organizing Project) informs homeowners about potentially exploitative mortgages, directs them to subsidies, and helps protect the rights of those who find themselves in foreclosure proceedings. In the wake of the subprime mortgage crisis, ESOP gained substantial funding from lenders that had misled home buyers in Cleveland to provide remediation services.[78]

Foundations have provided significant support to community development organizations including Cleveland Neighborhood Progress and the East Akron Neighborhood Development Corporation. The community development organizations promote and sometimes underwrite residential and commercial real estate development and housing rehabilitation. Or, in the words of the current director of Cleveland Neighborhood Progress, to underwrite "neighborhoods people want to live in around the core of assets that already exist—people, businesses, organizations, and places—and that give the neighborhood its character."[79]

It is difficult to determine the effectiveness of foundation contributions to economic development. Foundations have relatively little money, but money isn't the only important resource. The region's foundations have brought a number of new nonprofit organizations into being, designed to address key economic questions on a regional basis, and supported the growth and development of organizations that have been functioning in this space for decades. These organizations have encouraged collaboration, activism, and entrepreneurship, and have made a difference in the ways people think about northeastern Ohio's economy—and about their own investments in their homes and neighborhoods. And some government and business officials insist that Cleveland's foundation-funded local development efforts have given the region business, legal, nonprofit, and government leaders who are unusually sophisticated about the city's people.[80]

School Reform

Like their counterparts in many other cities, philanthropic foundations have also supported school reform initiatives across northeastern Ohio.[81] In this case study we ask what they have done, and how much difference they have made, in the region's much-heralded charter schools, sometimes supported by vouchers from public school districts. In the 1990s and early 2000s the Walton, Lynde, and Harry Bradley Foundations, and other generally conservative national foundations—but not their Ohio counterparts—underwrote advocacy for the Cleveland school voucher and charter school legislation.[82] Once the US Supreme Court approved the legislation's use of vouchers backed by school district and state taxes, some foundations—again, overwhelmingly national funds committed to the charter school and voucher movements—partnered with school districts and "community" or charter schools to implement the law in various ways. Most recently, local foundations have worked with the Cleveland Public Schools to manage some of the challenges that stem from the law.

Cleveland's charter schools are hybrids—partly private, but mostly reliant on public funds, chiefly taxes raised through local school districts. In Ohio, charter schools obtain authorization from state-approved sponsoring organizations that can be entirely separate from the local school district.[83] Public schools must serve all children in their state-specified geographic districts, must operate under the control of elected school boards, must respect state-defined educational and licensing standards for teachers and administrators, must follow fairly detailed state curricular guidelines and other standards (including equal treatment regardless of race, gender, religion, or national origin), and must accommodate children with physical, emotional, and developmental disabilities. Charter schools are exempt from many of these requirements, including teaching licensure requirements, curriculum guidelines, and geographic and other limitations on the admission of students.[84] They can be operated by private, self-governing nonprofit or profit-seeking corporations. Several of the largest charters are online schools that admit children across the state, and many others accept students from multiple districts.

Like charter schools, Ohio private schools are also exempt from many of the requirements that apply to public schools. Whether they are Catholic, evangelical Protestant, Lutheran, Quaker, or Jewish, schools sponsored by religious groups are private schools; so are independent or unaffiliated schools. Private school exemptions exceed those that apply to charters, which must report to their sponsors, accept greater government oversight, and meet more comprehensive testing. But charters operate almost entirely with government funds. Historically, private schools owe much of their exemption from state teacher qualification, student selection, curricular, and testing requirements to the fact that they depend very heavily on payment of tuition and fees, and on donations.[85]

The US Supreme Court approved the Ohio law directing the use of vouchers backed by tax funds in the case of *Zelman v. Simmons-Harris* in 2002.[86] Walton and some other national foundations quickly partnered with school districts and others to launch community or charter schools. Foundations never underwrote the cost of instruction: the understanding was always that tax-based vouchers, school district buildings made available at below-market-value rents, and other government support would cover essentially all costs. The movement to create charter schools has been driven by the theory that public schools, especially in big cities, were bureaucratic, inflexible, and wasteful, and that if they were forced to compete for resources—for students and the tax dollars and subsidies they bring with them—schools would quickly adopt better practices and improve.[87] Change in the biggest public districts would take time, so the argument went, but charters would allow students trapped in bad schools to move to new schools that would pioneer innovative teaching models and deliver immediate improvements.

The results, however, have been mixed. Many of the charter schools that have opened in the Cleveland School District have been of poor quality, producing worse results than nearby public schools.[88] On average, charters tend to have the same or lower levels of student achievement as their public counterparts, and, controlling for differences among their students, a smaller percentage of high-performing schools than the struggling districts against which they are competing. Advocates for charters argue that over time, students in charter schools do better than their counterparts in public schools. According to the Ohio Department of Education, Ohio's charter schools boast some of the most successful schools in the state, but also the highest proportion of failing schools. In the 2012–2013 school year, 12 percent of charter schools received grades of A or B from the Ohio Department of Education, but 64 percent received grades of D or F.[89]

Moreover the weakening of bureaucratic controls, intended to facilitate innovation, had unfortunate effects the reformers did not anticipate. More than a few unscrupulous promoters proved to be outright thieves; some of northeastern Ohio's charter schools have closed in the wake of financial scandal. Recently, for example, the FBI has opened a criminal investigation into three of the region's charter schools affiliated with a management company in Illinois accused of misspending federal technology grants and of defrauding the federal employee visa program.[90]

Advocates have argued that charter school competition will force public schools to improve, disrupting the unproductive status quo. But disruption can also make things worse. When a corrupt school is forced to close, or when a charter school fails to do even an average job, children from the district suffer educationally and socially. When places must be found at short notice for hundreds of students, and when the funds that come into the district from local taxes and from state aid flow to corrupt and failing charters, a public school district can't follow its plans and children face new uncertainties. Current policies that allow a student—and the funds to pay for the student's education—to shift between public and charter schools at any time further undermine continuity for public schools and for children.

Responding to these challenges, Cleveland mayor Frank Jackson, with considerable support from northeastern Ohio foundations, persuaded the Ohio legislature to pass a special act authorizing the Cleveland Transformation Alliance to improve relations between the city's public school district and its many charter schools. Funded largely by foundations including the Cleveland Foundation, the George Gund Foundation, the Kent H. Smith Charitable Trust, and the Laura and John Arnold Foundation of Texas, the alliance is directed by a board that includes representatives of the Cleveland Municipal School District, the Cleveland Teachers' Union, parents, community social service and religious organizations, and charter school advocates. Cleveland Foundation and George Gund foundation program officers also serve on the board.[91] Regional leaders are already crediting the foundation-supported alliance with playing a noticeable role in the 2014 passage of Cleveland's first successful school levy since 1996.

The Cleveland Transformation Alliance aims to help realize the ambitions of the charter school reform movement by improving the workings of the market for elementary and secondary schooling in the City of Cleveland. In its words, the alliance is "dedicated to providing families with the tools and information they need to make informed education choices for their children."[92] Information is the key: The alliance aims to collect and publicize accurate current information about both charters and public schools, and to make that information easily accessible to families at the time they select schools for their children. The alliance's website provides a map showing the location of every public and charter school in the city and information about each school's programs and the state's A to F ratings of achievement, progress, and graduation rates. The idea is that families will select better performing schools, and that schools will work to improve their ratings so that they can attract more students. This is the consumer side of the Cleveland Metropolitan School District's portfolio strategy: an attempt to strengthen the highest performing schools across the district, regardless of provider, with the goal of tripling the number of students in high-performing schools, and closing failing schools (both district and charter) by the 2018–2019 school year.[93] The website provides the promised information, in easily usable form. Whether families will find the information sufficient—and whether many families will use it—will only be known after time has passed. The website may be more important in influencing policymaker perceptions, but that, too, will only become clear over time.

Conclusion

Northeastern Ohio's daunting economic and educational challenges have many sources. Steeply declining transport costs, technological change, US trade policy, increasing international competition, a long period of regional undercommitment to education, and many other factors brought economic decline. For more than one hundred years the region was central to America's prosperous, progressive manufacturing belt;[94] more recently the larger region has been described as a "rust belt." Many factors have also created pressure for school reform: the historic oppression of African Americans; longstanding tensions between Catholics and Protestants; the region's century-long underinvestment in elementary and secondary education; the nation's continuing determination to leave the details of schooling, and school funding, to states and localities; the sheer difficulty of providing effective education for hundreds of thousands of children from families who belong to a myriad of differing communities, or to no community at all. It is perhaps more remarkable that some foundations are searching for ways to address these challenges than that they are so far having only small success.

Current foundation efforts in northeastern Ohio seek to use very limited dollars to find points of leverage—to coordinate multiple public and private actors, to underwrite useful studies, and to convene discussions of ongoing issues among major players and stakeholders. In education as in economic development, the region's needs are far, far greater than the foundations' resources. In both cases, the region's foundations are seeking to encourage positive change both through direct investments and grantmaking, but also through issue advocacy, creativity, and collaboration. More important is the historic support that foundations and endowments have provided to the region's cultural and social infrastructure—to the houses of worship, schools and colleges, arts organizations, and the institutions that manage conflicts among its social communities. Foundation support has helped all these actors coordinate their activities, survive lean times, and advocate for support from government as well as from individual donors.

ELISE C. HAGESFELD, PhD is a lecturer in history at Case Western Reserve University in Cleveland. She brings over a decade of experience as a development professional in the nonprofit sector to her scholarship.

DAVID C. HAMMACK is the Hiram C. Haydn Professor of History at Case Western Reserve University. His books include *A Versatile American Institution: The Changing Ideals and Realities of Philanthropic Foundations*; *American Foundations, Globalization, Philanthropy, and Civil Society: Projecting Institutional Logics Abroad*; and *Making the Nonprofit Sector in the United States: A Reader.*

NOTES

1. R. L. Duffus, "Cleveland: Paternalism in Excelsis," *The New Republic*, April 4, 1928, 214.

2. As Duffus noted in the same place in 1928, "Here, as elsewhere, it will soon be impossible to take the city itself as a social unit; it is regional Cleveland, not merely urban Cleveland, that must be considered. The dominating figures of the city are as likely as not to live outside its political limits." Northeastern Ohio's business communities are currently seeking to work on an eighteen-county regional basis reaching from Sandusky through Cleveland to Ashtabula and down to Youngstown, Akron, Canton, and beyond; see http://www.clevelandplus.com/teamneo/about-us/partners/ (accessed October 26, 2017).

3. The US Census Bureau estimated the 2016 population of the smaller "combined statistical area" of Cleveland-Akron-Canton as just under 3.5 million, 15th largest in the US and very similar to the comparable populations of the Minneapolis-St. Paul and Denver-Aurora. https://factfinder.census.gov/faces/tableservices/jsf/pages/productview.xhtml?pid=PEP_2016_PEPANNCHG.US41PR&prodType=table (accessed October 28, 2017).

4. Kimberley L. Phillips, *Alabama North: African-American Migrants, Community, and Working-Class Activism, 1915–1945* (Urbana: University of Illinois Press, 1999).

5. Michael S. Fogarty, David C. Hammack, and Gasper S. Garofalo, *Cleveland from Startup to the Present: Innovation and Entrepreneurship* (Report of the Center for Regional Economic Issues, Weatherhead School of Management, Case Western Reserve University, 2003). Available at https://www.researchgate.net/publication/242515897_Cleveland_from_Startup_to_the_Present_Innovation_and_Entrepreneurship_in_the_19th_and_Early_20th_Century (accessed October 28, 2017).

6. Michael J. McTighe, *A Measure of Success: Protestants and Public Culture in Antebellum Cleveland* (Albany: State University of New York Press, 1994), 16–21; for numbers indicating that in 1930, at about 100,000, Cleveland's Jewish community ranked about eleventh largest in the world—between the 128,000 of Kiev and the 86,000 of Moscow—see *American Jewish Yearbook*, vol. 32, 1930 (New York: The American Jewish Committee), 223–24.

7. Phillips, *Alabama North*.

8. To capitalize on its excellent links to the East, the region early built a dense network for internal communication. As early as the 1880s, a professor at Western Reserve University (then located in the town of Hudson in Portage County) consulted with an Akron manufacturer in the morning, took an interurban light rail to a business meeting in downtown Cleveland at noon, and returned in time to supervise students in his laboratory in the afternoon.

9. This is a pervasive topic in the essays included in David C. Hammack, John Grabowski, and Diane Grabowski, eds., *Identity, Cooperation, and Competition: Central European Migrants in*

Cleveland, 1850–1930 (Cleveland: Kent State University Press and the Western Reserve Historical Society, 2003). see, for example, 31–34, 89–90, 262, and the index.

10. Brian Ross, "The New Philanthropy: The Reorganization of Charity in Turn of the Century Cleveland," PhD diss., Case Western Reserve University, 1989.

11. http://www.anisfield-wolf.org/.

12. The Cleveland Orchestra maintains a notable summer season at the Blossom Music Center near Akron as well as its nine-month regular season at Severance Hall in Cleveland (and an extensive residency in Miami, Florida). http://www.clevelandorchestra.com.

13. The diocese and its charities arm embrace eight counties: Ashland, Cuyahoga, Geauga, Lake, Lorain, Medina, Summit, and Wayne. http://www.clevelandcatholiccharities.org/cchhsmap.htm.

14. Lauren B. Raff, *1996 Jewish Population Study of Greater Cleveland* (Cleveland: The Jewish Community Federation of Cleveland, 1998), 11.

15. http://www.thefundneo.org.

16. For the characteristics of nineteenth-century foundations in the United States, see David C. Hammack and Helmut K. Anheier, *A Versatile American Institution: The Changing Ideals and Realities of Philanthropic Foundations* (Washington, DC: Brookings Institution Press, 2013), ch. 2. In her thoughtful study of giving and volunteering in Cleveland between 1880 and 1930, Laura Tuennerman-Kaplan focuses on giving for social welfare, ignores endowments, and stresses the use of independent foundations to increase the influence of very wealthy donors. Laura Tuennerman-Kaplan, *Helping Others, Helping Ourselves: Power, Giving, and Community Identity in Cleveland, Ohio, 1880–1930* (Kent, OH: Kent State University Press, 2001).

17. For the contributions of the American Education Society, of the Society for the Promotion of Collegiate and Theological Education at the West, and of denominational sources to colleges in Ohio, see Donald G. Tewksbury, *The Founding of American Colleges and Universities Before the Civil War* (New York: Teachers College Press, 1932); James Findlay, "Agency, Denominationalisms, and the Western Colleges, 1830–1869: Some Connections Between Evangelicalism and American Higher Education," and Roger L. Geiger, "The Era of Multipurpose Colleges in American Higher Education, 1860–1890," both in *The American College in the Nineteenth Century,* ed. Roger L. Geiger (Nashville, TN: Vanderbilt University Press, 2000). Colin B. Burke, *American Collegiate Populations: A Test of the Traditional View* (New York: New York University Press, 1982), cautions that the American Education Society existed to support students in eastern colleges, and that before the Civil War the Society for the Promotion of Collegiate and Theological Education at the West "raised less than one-third of Harvard's 1860 endowment" (43). The Protestant funders accepted endowment bequests as well as gifts to their annual campaigns as they sent aid to churches, schools, students, and colleges.

18. During a celebration of the history of the Western Reserve (in northeastern Ohio) in 1896, Rabbi Michaelis Machol noted that it had been a legacy from New Orleans merchant and philanthropist Juda Touro that had enabled Congregation Tifereth Israel to build its elegant temple. Cleveland Centennial Commission, *Official Report of the Centennial Celebration of the Founding of the City of Cleveland and the Settlement of the Western Reserve* (1896), 206.

19. George Francis Houck, *The Church in Northern Ohio and in the Diocese of Cleveland from 1749 to September 1887* (Cleveland: Short & Forman, 1889), provides sketches of the lives of priests and others who were educated in France, Austria, Bavaria, and elsewhere in Europe; this book also notes gifts of money from Catholic institutions as well as individuals, especially in France and Austria. Tuennerman-Kaplan, *Helping Others, Helping Ourselves,* emphasizes giving to and through community and parish churches and schools by Catholics, as well as by others.

20. An 1896 celebration of the Western Reserve contained references to endowed or "sinking" of construction funds for several churches, religious printing houses, settlement houses, a WCTU music hall, and homes for orphans, unwed mothers, and the elderly, as well as for colleges and

schools (Cleveland Centennial Commission, 107, 111, 204–5, 211, 213). According to one account, Cleveland Presbyterians had by that date contributed $3 million to their colleges (Cleveland Centennial Commission, 213).

21. According to one account, in the mid-1890s funds of $25,000 or more supported such institutions as the Jewish Orphan Asylum and the Montifiore Kersher Home for the elderly. (Cleveland Centennial Commission, 1896).

22. Burke, *American Collegiate Populations,* details differences in state support and control of colleges in the South, the Northeast, and the Midwest (ch. 1). For an excellent detailed study of Presbyterian and Congregationalist funding for northeastern Ohio churches, schools, and colleges before the 1850s, see Amy DeRogatis, *Moral Geography: Maps, Missionaries, and the American Frontier* (New York: Columbia University Press, 2003); for a more general discussion of small colleges in nineteenth-century Ohio, see Kenneth Wheeler, *Cultivating Regionalism: Higher Education and the Making of the American Midwest* (DeKalb: Northern Illinois University Press, 2011). Frederick Rudolph, *The American College and University* (New York: Knopf, 1962), 54, notes that of the more than twenty colleges founded in Ohio before 1850 one or more had been sponsored by each of thirteen faith communities—Presbyterian, United Presbyterian, Congregationalist, Episcopalian, Methodist, Baptist, Lutheran, Swedenborgian, United Brethren, Reformed, Christian, Disciples of Christ, and Catholic. For Michigan's favoring of the University of Michigan and discouragement of other colleges, see Tewksbury, *Founding of American Colleges,* 199–201. Burke, *American Collegiate Populations,* emphasizes efforts of colleges located in the Midwest to win donations from religious and other donors in Pennsylvania, New York, and New England, but adds that "only the most fortunate institutions found a wealthy benefactor who would provide a large endowment" (42).

23. Hammack and Anheier, *A Versatile American Institution,* ch. 2. Burke, *American Collegiate Populations,* provides the most careful account of the enrollments, teaching programs, and finances of nineteenth century colleges.

24. In a discussion of "American Millionaires and Their Public Gifts" in February, 1893, the *American Review of Reviews* (7: 37, 48–60) noted that Cleveland's donors had "rallied about . . . Western Reserve University." For endowments, see the Annual Report of the United States Commissioner for Education (Washington: US Government Printing Office) for 1899–1900, 1901, 1882, and 1960. Johns Hopkins University had the largest medical school endowment; Harvard had the second-largest. According to the College Board of the Presbyterian Church in the United States, the endowment of the College of Wooster had passed $1.1 million by 1911, and in the 1916–1917 academic year, thirty-six Wooster students—by far the largest number of any Presbyterian college in the United States—received from the board $3,150 in tuition aid (College Board of the Presbyterian Church in the USA [1917]: 32).

25. Human Services Design Laboratory, "A Philanthropic Profile of the Cleveland Metropolitan Area," in *Research Papers Sponsored by the Commission on Private Philanthropy and Public Needs* (Washington, DC: US Department of the Treasury, vol. II, part 1, 1977), 927; this study used 1968 or 1969 grant totals from *The Foundation Directory* (New York: Columbia University Press, 4th ed., 1971). In 1967 Allan S. Austin, a prominent business leader, drew this distinction between corporate and family foundations: corporations should give to "'social welfare' causes—hospitals, research projects, and other activities directly attacking the physical and social ills of mankind." Support for the arts should come "from family rather than corporate funds."

26. For a detailed account of the origins of the Cleveland Foundation, see Diana Tittle, *Rebuilding Cleveland: The Cleveland Foundation and Its Evolving Urban Strategy* (Columbus: Ohio State University Press, 1992), 24–33.

27. Duffus, "Cleveland: Paternalism in Excelsis." David C. Hammack, "Community Foundations: The Delicate Question of Purpose," in *An Agile Servant,* ed. Richard Magat (New York: The Foundation Center, 1989), 23–50.

28. Other northeastern Ohio funds that seem likely to have had assets of more than $3 million (at full market value) in 1960:

Name	Location	Founding Date
Payne Fund	Cleveland	1927
Sisters of Notre Dame Trust	Cleveland	1946
Perkins Charitable Foundation	Cleveland	1950
Sapirstein-Stone-Weiss Foundation	Cleveland	1952
Paul P. Tell Foundation, Inc.	Akron	1952
Britton Fund	Cleveland	1952
Louise H. & David S. Ingalls Foundation, Inc.	Shaker Heights	1953
Kelvin & Eleanor Smith Foundation	Cleveland	1955
Treuhaft Foundation	Cleveland	1955
Akron Community Foundation	Akron	1955
William Bingham Foundation	Rocky River	1955
George Codrington Charitable Foundation	Cleveland	1955
Paul & Maxine Frohring Foundation	Cleveland	1958
Timken International Fund	Canton	1959
H.C.S. Foundation	Cleveland	1959
Lois Sisler McFawn Foundation	Akron	1959
John P. Murphy Foundation	Cleveland	1960

The Human Design Services Laboratory study noted above found the following additional foundations to be among the twenty largest by giving in 1968 or 1969: Austin Memorial, Cleveland Associated, TRW, Sohio, Lincoln Electric, Sears Family, Lubrizol, Ireland, Cleveland Electric Illuminating, Eaton Charitable Fund, Vernon Stouffer, Roger and Evan Markas, and Warner and Swazey.

29. The Foundation Center, *The Foundation Directory* (New York: The Foundation Center, 1971).

30. Human Design Services Laboratory, *Philanthropic Profile*, 909. This survey's very incomplete numbers for organizations in education and the arts suggest somewhat higher shares in those fields (913, 914). Several of northeastern Ohio's largest donations have always gone directly to operating organizations without passing through foundations. From the 1880s through the first third of the twentieth century that was true of gifts to University Circle and its institutions from Jeptha Wade, a founder of the Western Union telegraph company, and from his son, Jeptha Wade II; from railway magnate Amasa Stone; from steelmen Marcus A. Hanna and Samuel Mather; of many gifts from John D. Rockefeller; of gifts from John S. Severance to the Cleveland Orchestra; and of many others.

31. Robert S. Merriman, "Cleveland: Faint Halo Around a Solid Tradition of Giving," in Commission on Private Philanthropy and Public Needs, *Research Papers*, vol. II, Philanthropic Fields Of Interest, part 1, (Washington, DC: US Department of the Treasury, 1977), 986–987. Merriman was the director of the Coordinating Council for Foundations in Hartford, Connecticut.

32. On New York, Baltimore, and Chicago, see the relevant chapters in this volume. For Chicago, see Helen Lefkowitz Horowitz, *Culture & The City: Cultural Philanthropy in Chicago from the 1880's to 1917* (University Press of Kentucky, 1976); Kathleen McCarthy,

Noblesse Oblige: Charity and Cultural Philanthropy in Chicago, 1849–1929 (Chicago: University of Chicago Press, 1982); and William S. McKersie, "*Strategic Philanthropy And Local Public Policy: Lessons From Chicago School Reform, 1987–1993* (University of Chicago Ph.D. Dissertation, 1999).

33. Located in University Circle were Western Reserve University and its medical school, Case Institute of Technology, University Hospitals, the Cleveland Orchestra, the Cleveland Museum of Art, the Cleveland Institutes of Music and of Art, and the Cleveland Museum of Natural History; nearby, the Cleveland Clinic. For a discussion of this infrastructure, see David C. Hammack, "Philanthropy," in *Encyclopedia of Cleveland History*, eds. David D. Van Tassel and John J. Grabowski (Bloomington: Indiana University Press, 2nd ed., 1996), also on the web at http://www:ech.cwru.edu/; and John Grabowski, "Social Reform and Philanthropic Order in Cleveland, 1896–1920," in *Cleveland: A Tradition of Reform*, eds. David D. Van Tassel and John J. Grabowski (Kent, OH: Kent State University Press, 1986). Two very useful Case Western Reserve University history PhD dissertations are Brian Ross, *The New Philanthropy: The Reorganization of Charity in Turn of the Century Cleveland* (1989) and Michael FitzGibbon, *Authority and Community: Charity Organization in Cleveland, 1870–1920* (2004). It would, of course, be a mistake to give foundations too much credit for the development of university and hospital organizations that relied more heavily on federal funding and on payments from students and patients and that also relied on support from industry; for Case Western Reserve University, see Darwin H. Stapleton, "The Faustian Dilemmas of Funded Research at Case Institute and Western Reserve, 1945–1965," *Science, Technology, and Human Values* 18, no. 3 (Summer, 1993), 303–314. Support from northeastern Ohio foundations and the families associated with them can be found throughout histories of CWRU and other University Circle organizations, including Carl Frederick Wittke, *The First Fifty Years: The Cleveland Museum of Art, 1916–1966* (Cleveland: Cleveland Museum of Art, 1966); C. H. Cramer, *Case Western Reserve: A History of the University, 1826–1976* (Boston: Little, Brown, and Co., 1976); C. H. Cramer, *Case Institute of Technology: A Centennial History, 1880–1980* (Cleveland: Case Western Reserve University, 1980); Nancy Coe Wixom, *The Cleveland Institute of Art: the First Hundred Years, 1882–1982* (Cleveland: The Cleveland Institute of Art, 1983); Mark Gottlieb, *The Lives of University Hospitals of Cleveland: The 125-Year Evolution of an Academic Medical Center* (Cleveland: Octavia Press, 1991); Donald Rosenberg, *The Cleveland Orchestra Story: "Second to None"* (Cleveland: Gray & Company, 2000).

34. Oberlin, Baldwin-Wallace, Wooster, Mount Union, Malone, and Hiram Colleges, John Carroll University, the Akron Museum of Art, and several hospitals.

35. For the Brush Foundation see Jimmy Elaine Wilkinson Meyer, *"Any Friend of the Movement": Networking for Birth Control, 1920–1940* (Columbus: Ohio State University Press, 2004), 65.

36. Garth S. Jowett, Ian C. Jarvie, and Kathryn H. Fuller, *Children and the Movies: Media Influence and the Payne Fund Controversy* (New York: Cambridge University Press, 1996).

37. Contributions of the Cleveland and George Gund foundations and the S. Livingston Mather Charitable Trust are emphasized in Robert L. Bond, *Focus on Neighborhoods: A History of Responses by Cleveland's Settlement Houses and Neighborhood Centers to Changing Human Needs* (Cleveland: Greater Cleveland Neighborhood Centers Association, 1990), 98. The Neighborhood Centers Association has long provided central fundraising and technical services to the nation's most comprehensive system of settlement houses.

38. David C. Hammack, "Failure and Resistance: Pushing the Limits in Depression and Wartime," in *Charity, Philanthropy, and Civility in American History*, eds. Lawrence Friedman and Mark McGarvie (New York: Cambridge University Press, 2002), 263–80; Federation for Community Planning Records 1913–1974, MS 3788. "Report on Cleveland Welfare Federation Children's Group, 1924–1931," Western Reserve Historical Society, Cleveland, Ohio.

39. Tittle, *Rebuilding Cleveland*; Edward Michael Miggins, "Businessmen, Pedagogues, and Progressive Reform: The Cleveland Foundation's 1915 School Survey," PhD diss., Case Western Reserve University, 1975.

40. Stuart C. Mendel, *Mediating Organizations, Private Government, and Civil Society: Disinvestment Through the Preservation of Wealth in Cleveland, Ohio, 1950–1990* (Lewiston, NY: Edwin Mellen Press, 2005).

41. Oberlin and Western Reserve had a long record of educating African Americans. For example, Reserve's schools of law and medicine often provided professional education to African Americans from states that maintained segregation in their universities (thus allowing those states to meet the minimum "separate but equal" demands of *Plessy v. Ferguson*; on Karamu House see Elisabeth Lasch-Quinn, *Black Neighbors: Race and the Limits of Reform in the American Settlement House Movement, 1890–1945* (Chapel Hill: University of North Carolina Press, 1993), 29–32; on Rockefeller Foundation funds to rebuild Karamu's theater after World War II, see Errol G. Hill and James V. Hatch, *A History of African American Theatre* (New York: Cambridge University Press, 2003).

42. The most detailed account is William Jenkins, "Cleveland Development Foundation: A Partner in Decline," paper presented at the Voinovich Archives Conference on Public-Private Partnerships, Cleveland State University, August 15, 2014. Also see Tittle, *Rebuilding Cleveland.*

43. Richard Magat, *The Ford Foundation at Work: Philanthropic Choices, Methods, and Styles* (New York: Plenum Press, 1979), 82; Tittle, *Rebuilding Cleveland*, 160–167; Dean E. Robinson, *Black Nationalism in American Politics and Thought* (New York: Cambridge University Press, 2001) 96–101; Jiannbin Lee Shiao, *Identifying Talent, Institutionalizing Diversity: Race and Philanthropy in Post-Civil Rights America* (Durham, NC: Duke University Press, 2005), 91–101, 28.

44. Leonard N. Moore, *Carl B. Stokes and the Rise of Black Political Power* (Urbana: University of Illinois Press, 2003), 74, 90–96, and generally chs. 3 (61–78) and 4 (79–99); For a detailed account of the riots in Glenville, including the run up and the aftermath, see Louis H. Masotti and Jerome R. Corsi, *Shoot-Out in Cleveland* (New York: Bantam Books, 1969).

45. https://case.edu/ech/articles/p/premier-farnell-plc/#d.en.195187.

46. Data from the Foundation Center, GuideStar, and reports of supporting foundations; for 2015 or 2016, viewed Oct 29–30, 2017. Key: CF = community foundation; O = operating foundation; PF = private foundation; S = supporting foundation. Information from the Form 990 tax forms for 2010 or 2011, available on GuideStar.

47. The American Endowment Foundation operates under the rules that apply to community foundations, taking new funds under management from many donors each year and making grants to charitable organizations. But unlike nearly all community foundations it does not have a defined geographic focus, and it puts almost all of its emphasis on providing investment and management service to those who set up donor advised funds. See https://www.aefonline.org/ (accessed November 1, 2017).

48. See https://www.measuringworth.com/uscompare/relativevalue.php (October 26, 2017).

49. Calculated from information in the archives of the Cleveland Federation for Community Planning held at the Western Reserve Historical Society, Cleveland, Ohio.

50. Calculated from data in the Urban Institute's *Nonprofit Sector in Brief* for 2014 and 2015, taking account of private giving to public colleges and universities as reported at https://nces.ed.gov/ipeds/datacenter/Statistics.aspx.

51. "Health Conversion Foundations: How to Make Them Relevant| Nonprofit Quarterly." Non Profit News | Nonprofit Quarterly, June 7, 2016. https://nonprofitquarterly.org/2016/06/07/health-conversion-foundations-how-to-make-them-relevant/.

52. http://foundationcenter.issuelab.org/resources/13611/13611.pdf, and information on particular foundations available on http://www.guidestar.org/search (accessed October 29, 2017).

53. According to their 2001 Form 990 tax forms, the University of Akron Foundation held over $124 million, the Kent State University Foundation held over $75 million, and the Cleveland State University Foundation held over $20 million. These differences, together with the level of support

enjoyed by Case Western Reserve University, point up one of the contrasts between the Cleveland and the Akron-Canton wings of the larger metropolitan area.

54. Quotations from www.guidestar.org/profile/34-1747398 and https://www.aefonline.org/donors, assets from Guidestar Search (accessed October 29, 2017).

55. http://www.fmscleveland.com/, October 29, 2017.

56. W. Dennis Keating, Norman Krumholz, and John Metzger, "Postpopulist Public-Private Partnerships," in *Cleveland: A Metropolitan Reader*, ed. W. Dennis Keating, Norman Krumholz, & David C. Perry (Kent, OH: Kent State University Press, 1995), 332–350; Jordan S. Yin, "The Community Development Industry System: A Case Study of Politics and Institutions in Cleveland, 1967–1997," *Journal of Urban Affairs* 20, no. 2 (1998), 137–157.

57. Information on large grants taken from

58. Personal statements by Hunter Morrison, planning director for the City of Cleveland 1981–2001, and James Mason, former vice president, Eaton Corporation, at the Voinovich Archives Project Conference on Public–Private Partnerships, Cleveland State University, August 15, 2014. Norman Krumholz and Kathryn W. Hexter, "Re-Thinking the Future of Cleveland's Neighborhood Developers: Interim Report," Center for Community Planning and Development, Maxine Goodman Levin College of Urban Affairs, Cleveland State University, March 2012. http://urban.csuohio.edu/publications/center/center_for_community_planning_and_development/Re-thinking_the_Future.pdf.

59. Brian Bull, "10 Years Later, Sounding Off On The 'Quiet Crisis'," *Ideastream*, May 29, 2014. http://www.ideastream.org/news/feature/10-years-later-sounding-off-on-the-quiet-crisis. For an extensive collection of the Cleveland Plain Dealer coverage, see http://www.cleveland.com/quiet-crisis/.

60. See Greater Akron Chamber's 2008–2013 strategic plan, entitled *Advance Akron*. The first two objectives are to "grow Greater Akron by broadening and strengthening innovative economic development efforts to sustain job growth and increase local wealth in the short and long-term, with emphasis on technology-based business sectors" and "invest in human capital. Develop the workforce's ability to meet the needs of business by enhancing the education, training, and workforce development programs of the public school systems, higher education institutions, and other available resources".).

61. Data from the Bureau of Economic Analysis at www.bea.gov (October 23, 2013).

62. Data from the Urban Institute National Center for Charitable Statistics at http://nccs.urban.org/ (October 23, 2013).

63. Data from the Urban Institute National Center for Charitable Statistics at http://nccs.urban.org/ (October 23, 2013). For the Cleveland Foundation's overview, see http://www.clevelandfoundation.org/grants/our-priorities/economic-development/.

64. Comments based on conversations with nonprofit and academic professionals at Cleveland State University, Case Western Reserve University, Neighborhood Progress Inc., and Breakthrough Schools.

65. In Rossman's view, the programs and activities of economic development nonprofits should be required to integrate strategies that will directly benefit individuals, organizations, or communities that have been designated as worthy of charitable support. Currently, regional economic development organizations (REDOs) mostly "hope that the privately-owned, profit-seeking ventures they aid will ultimately help those in need in the form of jobs and a flourishing economy." And while these organizations can be "influential and, in some cases, transformative to cities and regions in economic distress," it is not enough to hope that benefits from these public charitable investments will "trickle down" to those who need them most. Matthew J. Rossman, "Evaluating Trickle Down Charity—A Solution for Determining when Economic Development Aimed at Revitalizing America's Cities and Regions Is Really Charitable," SSRN Scholarly Paper. (Rochester, NY: Social Science Research Network, January 8, 2014). http://papers.ssrn.com/abstract=2376470.

66. Foundation Center Database, accessed July 17, 2013.

67. Ibid.

68. "About Us," Fund for Our Economic Future website, accessed August 14, 2013, www.futurefundneo.org/About.

69. JumpStart provides early stage support for entrepreneurs seeking to start a business, and young or small businesses seeking growth; see www.jumpstartinc.org. Team NEO works on more of a regional level, providing business attraction, regional business development, and regional marketing and research; see www.teamneo.org. BioEnterprise is "a business formation, recruitment, and acceleration initiative designed to grow healthcare companies and commercialize bioscience technology"; see https://www.bioenterprise.com/. Magnet is an acronym for the Manufacturing Advocacy and Growth Network, and focuses on helping new and existing businesses develop and implement advanced manufacturing technologies, workforce development, and strategies for growth; see www.manufacturingsuccess.org. WIRENet also focuses on manufacturing in the northeastern Ohio region, and acts as a consultant for businesses seeking help in connecting to a qualified workforce, clean energy technology, and other manufacturers through networking events and ongoing educational programs; see www.wire-net.org.

70. http://www.thisiscleveland.com/about-cleveland/cleveland-neighborhoods/; http://gordonsquare.org/newsletters/GSAD_ENewsletter_issue4.pdf.; http://www.enterprisecommunity.com/servlet/servlet.FileDownload?file=00P30000008q7LYEAY.

71. Bruce Katz and Jennifer Bradley, *The Metropolitan Revolution: How Cities and Metros Are Fixing Our Broken Politics and Fragile Economy* (Washington, DC: Brookings Institution Press, 2013), 64–87.

72. Fund for Our Economic Future, http://www.thefundneo.org/our-impact/economic-outcomes; Nuareen Khan, "Transforming Trash into Crude Oil," National Journal.com. June 15, 2013, 27.

73. Steve Wynn claimed that his new Encore resort in Las Vegas had cost about $2.3 billion by the time it opened in 2008 (CBS News, July 26, 2009; http://www.cbsnews.com/8301-18560_162-4935567.html).

74. James E. Post and Fiona S. Wilson, "Too Good to Fail," *Stanford Social Innovation Review* (Fall 2011). http://www.ssireview.org/articles/entry/too_good_to_fail.

75. Mark S. Rosentraub, *Reversing Urban Decline: Why and How Sports, Entertainment, and Culture Turn Cities into Major League Winners*, 2nd ed. (Boca Raton, FL: CRC Press, 2014), 259–304.

76. "ShoreBank Enterprise Cleveland Partners with Community Leaders to Establish Evergreen Cooperative Development Fund," accessed October 30, 2017, https://community-wealth.org/content/shorebank-enterprise-cleveland-partners-community-leaders-establish-new-fund-aimed.

77. For the Cleveland Foundation's perspective, see http://www.clevelandfoundation.org/grants/our-priorities/neighborhoods/ and http://www.clevelandfoundation.org/grants/our-priorities/greater-university-circle/ (accessed August 31, 2014). On Evergreen Cooperatives, see http://evergreencooperatives.com/about/.

78. For ESOP's work with lenders and government officials as well as homeowners, see http://esop-cleveland.org/index.php?option=com_content&view=article&id=3&Itemid=8 (accessed August 31, 2014). In 2013 the Ohio state attorney general decided not to allocate to ESOP and similar mortgage and foreclosure-advising agencies funds from a national settlement with mortgage servicers accused of illegalities in foreclosure proceedings on programs that would crack down on mortgage fraud, prevent foreclosures or clean up after the mess left by foreclosures, as suggested in the settlement, but to home demolition and children's education. http://www.cleveland.com/open/index.ssf/2013/10/how_mike_dewine_spent_ohios_mo.html. http://www.cleveland.com/business/index.ssf/2011/08/mark_seifert_of_empowering_and.html; http://www.cleveland.com/opinion/index.ssf/2012/08/underwater_homes_drowning_neig.html.

79. Elise Hagesfeld interview with Joel Ratner, CEO of Cleveland Neighborhood Progress, September 23, 2013.

80. Robert L. Smith. "Biomedical Industry Flourishes in NE Ohio: Companies Employ 33,000, Study Finds," *Cleveland Plain Dealer*, April 13, 2014, A1.

81. During the 1990s and the early 2000s, the Cleveland and George Gund foundations played important, though generally supporting roles in the deliberations that led to the replacement of an elected school board in Cleveland with a board appointed by the mayor and to the arrangements for a major school construction program. For an account of the former, see Wilbur C. Rich and Stefanie Chambers, "Cleveland: Takeovers and Makeovers Are Not the Same," in *Mayors in the Middle: Politics, Race, and Mayoral Control of Urban Schools*, eds. Jeffrey R. Henig & Wilbur C. Rich (Princeton, NJ: Princeton University Press, 2003), 159–90. A Gates Foundation small school within-a-school initiative at suburban Cleveland Heights High School had a very brief life; it was noted in a KnowledgeWorks press release of 2004 (http://www.knowledgeworks.org/knowledgeworks-foundation-collaborates-districts-across-ohio-open-53-new-small-high-schools), but then disappeared. According to one estimate, foundations made no grants to the Cleveland Public Schools in 2005; see Sarah Reckhow, *Follow the Money: How Foundation Dollars Change Public School Politics* (New York: Oxford University Press, 2012), 49.

82. Among the other large donors on the pro-voucher side were the DeMoss, Covenant, Edgar and Elsa Prince, DeVos, and Sarah Scaife foundations. Gregory B. Bodwell, *Grassroots, Inc.: A Sociopolitical History of the Cleveland School Voucher Battle, 1992–2002*, PhD diss., Case Western Reserve University, 2006), 218. Bodwell also shows that Gates, Ford, Annenberg, Mott, Columbus, Wallace, William Penn, and Skirball were among the foundations that gave substantially to groups that opposed the law.

83. Charter schools in Ohio are managed by entities separate from their chartering sponsors. Unclear legislation and lack of regulation has resulted in a multiplication of sponsoring agencies and school management organizations. Patrick O'Donnell. "Ohio is the Wild Wild West of Charter Schools Says National Group Promoting Charter Standards." Cleveland Plain Dealer, July 28, 2014. For a list of sponsoring organizations of charter schools in Ohio, see the Ohio Alliance for Public Charter Schools: http://www.oapcs.org/resources/authorizers-ohio For an estimate that between 2007 and 2009 just a select handful of Ohio charters reported any substantive private revenue, see Bruce D. Baker, Ken Libby, and Kathryn Wiley, "Comparing Charter School and Local Public District Financial Resources in New York, Ohio, And Texas," a report for the National Education Policy Center. http://nepc.colorado.edu/files/rb-charterspending_0.pdf.

84. Greg Mild, "Reality Check: Ohio Charter Schools Are Exempt from over 150 State Education Laws," *Plunderbund*, accessed November 11, 2013, http://www.plunderbund.com/2013/11/10/reality-check-ohio-charter-schools-are-exempt-from-over-150-state-education-laws/.

85. On the importance of private funding to private school autonomy, see, for example, the Thomas B. Fordham Institute policy statement at http://edexcellence.net/publications/public-accountability-private-school-choice. The Ohio legislature is considering a bill that would force private schools to administer all the new Common Core standardized tests that Ohio public school students—including students at charter schools—are required to take beginning fall of 2014. Private schools are rigorously contesting this bill. Scott Looney, the director of Hawken School, argues that "if the state requires ten end-of-course exams, aren't I required to offer those 10 courses? . . . This state is dictating what courses we can teach in high school and if the state dictates curriculum, then we have no control." Patrick O'Donnell, "Ohio's Private Schools Fight to Avoid Common Core Exams," *Cleveland Plain Dealer*, May 15, 2014. http://www.cleveland.com/metro/index.ssf/2014/05/ohios_private_schools_fight_to.html.

86. Zelman v. Simmons-Harris, 536 US 639 (2002).

87. Bodwell, *Grassroots Inc.*, 227–231.

88. "Charter Schools Draw Students and Money from High-Ranking Suburban Districts," *Cleveland Plain Dealer* (Cleveland.com, accessed November 12, 2013). http://blog.cleveland.com/metro/2011/11/charter_schools_draw_students.html; "Charter Schools' Failed Promise," *The*

Columbus Dispatch, September 1, 2013, accessed November 11, 2013, http://www.dispatch.com/content/stories/local/2013/09/01/charter-schools-failed-promise.html. "As a Group, Ohio Urban Charter Schools Deliver Similar Performance for Less Money," StateImpact Ohio, accessed November 12, 2013, http://stateimpact.npr.org/ohio/2011/10/19/as-a-group-ohio-charter-schools-deliver-similar-performance-for-less-money/.

89. Ohio Department of Education, *Annual Report for Ohio Community Schools, 2012–2013* (Columbus: Ohio Department of Education, 2013). http://education.ohio.gov/getattachment/Topics/School-Choice/Community-Schools/Forms-and-Program-Information-for-Community-School/Annual-Reports-on-Ohio-Community-Schools/ODE-2013-Community-Schools-Annual-v4.pdf.aspx. A good recent review of studies of charter school effectiveness is David Osborne, "Improving Charter School Accountability: The Challenge of Closing Failing Schools," available at http://files.eric.ed.gov/fulltext/ED533181.pdf, 9–12.

90. Edith Starzyk, "Three Charter School Treasurers Responsible for More than $1 Million in Questionable Spending, Audits Find," *Cleveland Plain Dealer*, accessed March 31, 2012, http://www.cleveland.com/metro/index.ssf/2012/03/three_charter_school_treasurer.html; Peter Krause, "Charter School Officials Accused of Stealing $2 Million," *Cleveland Plain Dealer*, accessed April 30, 2013, http://www.cleveland.com/metro/index.ssf/2013/04/post_137.html; Doug Livingston, "Cleveland FBI Leads Investigation of Charter School Chain," *Akron Beacon Journal*, accessed June 10, 2014, http://www.ohio.com/news/break-news/cleveland-fbi-leads-investigation-of-charter-school-chain-1.494782.

91. "Cleveland Mayor Frank Jackson Set to Name Transformation Alliance Board," *Cleveland Plain Dealer*, accessed December 7, 2012, http://www.cleveland.com/metro/index.ssf/2012/12/clevland_mayor_frank_jackson_s.html; Patrick O'Donnell, "Cleveland's Mingling of Charter and District Schools Gets a $3 Million Boost," *Cleveland Plain Dealer*, accessed June 18, 2014, http://www.cleveland.com/metro/index.ssf/2014/06/clevelands_mingling_of_charter.html.

92. Cleveland Transformation Alliance website, accessed September 2, 2014, http://www.clevelandta.org/about-us.

93. See Cleveland Transformation Alliance website, http://www.clevelandta.org/about-us.

94. David R. Meyer. "Midwestern Industrialization and the American Manufacturing Belt in the Nineteenth Century," *Journal of Economic History* 49, no. 4 (1989), 921–37.

chapter five

PHILANTHROPIC FOUNDATIONS IN CHICAGO

Heather MacIndoe

THE CITY OF CHICAGO HAS a rich philanthropic history shaped by the generosity of such individuals as John D. Rockefeller, Julius Rosenwald, Marshall Field, and others, whose financial gifts established many of the educational and cultural institutions that are synonymous with the city. These wealthy donors were the predecessors of, and, in some cases, contributed the endowments for modern philanthropic foundations that emerged in Chicago and other American cities after World War I. Philanthropic foundations changed the character of philanthropy, with the interests of individual donors being articulated by a professional staff.[1] This chapter examines Chicago-area foundation philanthropy at the end of the twentieth century, before the global economic downturn which began in late 2007. Several distinctive aspects of foundation giving during this period merit discussion, including a small number of dominant local foundations, prioritization for human service funding, growing national foundation support for Chicago-based nonprofits, and the emergence of a place-based strategic philanthropy that has fundamentally reshaped the philanthropy of one of Chicago's largest foundations.

The lion's share of foundation giving to Chicago's nonprofits is donated by a small number of foundations. Two foundations, the Chicago Community Trust and the John D. and Catherine T. MacArthur Foundation, account for more than 20 percent of total foundation giving to Chicago's nonprofits from 1990 to 2005. Foundation support for Chicago's nonprofits tracks national trends, with grants for human service nonprofits ranking second in Chicago and third nationally. While foundation grantmaking continues to be largely a local phenomenon, giving to Chicago's nonprofits from foundations located outside of Illinois and the Midwest grew steadily during the last decade of the twentieth century. By

2005, foundation dollars flowing to Chicago's nonprofits were evenly split between local (Midwestern) foundations and national (predominantly East Coast) foundations. This may be related to several factors, including the expanding influence of the Donors Forum of Chicago (rebranded in 2015 as "Forefront"), a regional association of grantmakers that provides specialized training in various areas such as grant writing, to Chicago area nonprofits. A further distinctive feature of Chicago's foundation philanthropy is the influence of "strategic philanthropy" in the form of the New Communities Program (NCP), a MacArthur Foundation–led initiative begun in 2005, and ultimately supported by several dozen other Chicago and national foundations. The NCP reshaped MacArthur's Chicago-based philanthropy through a strategic focus on neighborhoods as a mechanism of social change.

Growth in and Concentration of Foundation Giving

From 2001 to 2011, giving by Illinois foundations to Chicago's nonprofits increased 46 percent (adjusted for inflation), from $1.4 billion to $2.6 billion dollars. Figure 5.1 shows growth in the number and giving of Illinois foundations. Illinois foundation giving significantly outpaced growth in giving by US foundations overall, which grew by 26 percent (adjusted for inflation) during this same period.[2] By 2011, the number of foundations located in Illinois exceeded 4,200. Like elsewhere in the United States, most philanthropic foundations in Illinois are modest operations with small grants programs and no full-time staff. Illinois foundations consistently ranked sixth in the nation in total giving during this period, behind foundations in New York, California, New Jersey, Washington, and Texas. Illinois-based foundations are geographically concentrated in the Chicago metropolitan area (Cook County), which is home to more than 3,000 philanthropic foundations.[3]

Giving by the large national foundations tracked in the Foundation Center data indicates that a small number of foundations contributed the majority of dollars to Chicago nonprofits. Table 5.1 shows the distribution of cumulative giving by the top fifteen foundation donors to Chicago's nonprofits from 1990 to 2005. Grantmaking by these foundations accounted for over 50 percent of foundation funding to Chicago recipients (represented in the Foundation Center data) during this period. The top four foundation donors together account for 25 percent of total grantmaking to Chicago nonprofits.

Two foundations, the John D. and Catherine T. MacArthur Foundation (MacArthur Foundation) and the Chicago Community Trust (CCT), stand

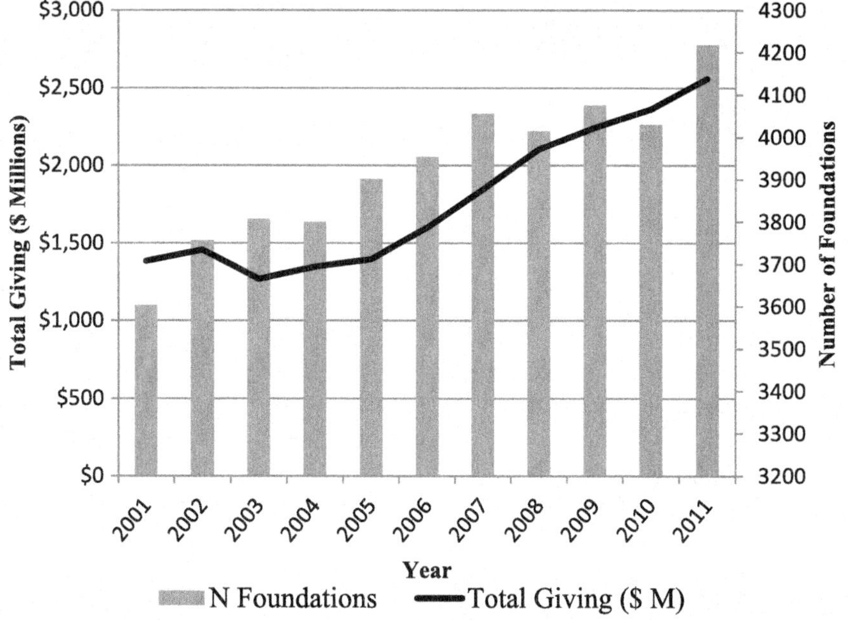

Figure 5.1. Illinois Foundations and Total Giving, 2001–2011. *Source:* The Foundation Center.[4]

out. Together, their grantmaking accounted for about 20 percent of giving to Chicago nonprofits. As of 2005, these foundations were respectively ranked ninth and twenty-first in asset holdings, and tenth and twenty-sixth in giving among the top fifty US foundations. The unique histories of these two foundations shaped their funding priorities.

The MacArthur Foundation

The MacArthur Foundation is particularly notable for its size and for the turmoil of its early history. John D. MacArthur was the founder and owner of Bankers Life and Casualty Company from which he amassed considerable wealth. On his retirement, he and his wife, Catherine, moved to Florida. Foundation scholar, observer, and advisor Waldemar Nielsen wrote: "In the mid-1960s he [MacArthur] and his second wife, Catherine, who had lived in a small house in Chicago, moved into a second-rate hotel he owned in Palm Beach, the Colonnades. His office was a table in the hotel coffee shop . . . where from six in the morning until late in the evening he talked deals with all comers. Much of the time he was picking up parcels of real estate from owners who found themselves in desperate need of money."[6] MacArthur built a substantial and lucrative real estate portfolio in Florida. On his death in January 1978, the board of directors of his

Table 5.1. Top Fifteen Foundation Donors to Chicago Nonprofits, 1990–2005

Foundation	State	Total Grants ($M)	Percent of Total	Cumulative Percent
The Chicago Community Trust and Affiliates	IL	459.3	9.8	9.8
John D. and Catherine T. MacArthur Foundation	IL	453.9	9.7	19.5
Robert R. McCormick Tribune Foundation	IL	257.5	5.5	25.0
Pritzker Foundation	IL	197.8	4.2	29.2
The Robert Wood Johnson Foundation	NJ	163.9	3.5	32.7
Polk Bros. Foundation, Inc.	IL	146.0	3.1	35.9
The Joyce Foundation	IL	143.7	3.1	38.9
Beatrice P. Delany Charitable Trust	IL	96.4	2.1	41.0
The Regenstein Foundation	IL	91.1	1.9	42.9
The Ford Foundation	NY	82.9	1.8	44.7
The Andrew W. Mellon Foundation	NY	78.9	1.7	46.4
Lloyd A. Fry Foundation	IL	73.0	1.6	47.9
BP Foundation, Inc.	TX	72.1	1.5	49.5
Lilly Endowment, Inc.	IN	66.2	1.4	50.9
W. K. Kellogg Foundation	MI	61.1	1.3	52.2
Total		2,443.8	52.2	

Source: The Foundation Center.[5]

foundation included his wife, Catherine, his son, J. Roderick (known as Rod), three senior officers of Bankers Life, and Paul Harvey, a radio commentator whose program had been sponsored by Bankers Life for over twenty-five years. In the first years of the foundation, Rod MacArthur, a self-made millionaire, frequently clashed with other board members as he pushed for the foundation to be on the cutting edge of social change. He conceived, fought for, and initiated the MacArthur Fellows Program. Rod described his concept as grants for "500 to 1,000 of the greatest minds of our time, working on society's greatest problems."[7] The so-called "genius grants" program would become a hallmark of the foundation.

The MacArthur Foundation began making grants in 1979, with most of the internal board squabbles remaining private. Then, in February 1984, Rod MacArthur brought a lawsuit to the Cook County Circuit Court detailing wrongdoing by all but two members of the foundation's board. He demanded that the foundation be placed into receivership or dismantled. Rod's claims stemmed from accusations of poor management by board members, who were still actively involved in the management of Bankers Life. The life insurance company's profits had steadily fallen since the foundation took over ownership. He charged that the dual directors of the foundation and the corporation took extravagant salaries and director's fees. In May 1984, the insurance company sold for $116 million over the sale price the board had previously accepted. Rod vowed to continue his lawsuit against the other board members; however, he was diagnosed with pancreatic cancer and died in December 1984.

In the years since this early turmoil, the MacArthur Foundation established itself as the tenth-largest foundation in the United States in asset holdings and the sixteenth-largest measured by total giving. The foundation has made significant grants to nonprofit organizations in Chicago neighborhoods. Additionally, the MacArthur Foundation ranks in the top five US foundations awarding grants internationally.

Chicago Community Trust (CCT)

The CCT, the second community foundation established in the United States, is another very influential supporter of the Chicago nonprofit sector. Banker Albert W. Harris established CCT in 1915 with an initial endowment of $600,000. CCT's purpose was to create a permanent fund to address civic affairs, education, culture, health, and social services in subsequent generations. Since its founding, CCT has been governed by a volunteer board appointed by outside civic leaders. In 1919, CCT completed its first community assessment, which laid the groundwork for the foundation's ongoing role of identifying and responding to the needs of Chicago residents.

New donor participation and fees from services were provided to individuals and families and boosted CCT's endowment in the 1920s. The endowment continued to grow in the 1930s when much philanthropic attention was focused on war relief funds. By the early 1960s, the Trust's assets exceeded $50 million. In the 1970s, CCT published its first formal guidelines for grant seekers. CCT's permanent endowment topped $100 million by 1977 and exceeded $1 billion by the year 2000. In 2005, CCT ranked thirty-fifth in asset holdings among large US foundations.

Patterns of Foundation Grantmaking: Purpose and Place

The Foundation Center data offer an opportunity to consider grantmaking by the largest US foundations to Chicago nonprofit organizations. The sample of grants analyzed here is not exhaustive, but it is representative of grantmaking by large philanthropic foundations to Chicago's nonprofit recipients. While this data does not capture smaller grants, it provides a picture of the giving patterns of foundations that are arguably best-positioned to impact urban nonprofit organizations and, by extension, the people they serve. The data represents more than 50,000 grants made by 826 foundations to approximately 1,350 nonprofits in the city of Chicago from 1990 to 2005.

Purpose of Foundation Grants

Foundation grantmaking in Chicago encompasses a wide variety of grant purposes described by the National Taxonomy of Exempt Entities (NTEE), the standard classification system for cataloging nonprofit organizations by their primary exempt purpose.[8] Figure 5.2 shows the distribution of foundation grant dollars to Chicago nonprofits by year and grant purpose. Total foundation funding increased 40 percent over the decade, from $210 million in 1990 to $295 million in 2000 (in constant 2005 dollars). Funding for all grant purposes increased from 1990 to 2005. Foundation giving in Chicago tracked national trends emphasizing education, human services, arts and culture, and health. Together, these subject areas account for approximately 62 percent of all grant dollars and 80 percent of all grants from 1990 to 2005. In 2005, the top ranked areas of national foundation support were education, health, human services, and arts and culture. Foundation giving in Chicago focused more on human services.

Geographic Distribution of Foundation Grants

The City of Chicago is partitioned into seventy-seven community areas that each average about thirty-eight thousand in population.[10] Community areas are well known by residents (e.g., Lincoln Park and Hyde Park), widely recognized politically, and often serve as boundaries for service delivery and allocation of resources.[11] Research on the nonprofit sector supports the idea that nonprofit activity is predominantly a local, community-based phenomenon such that nonprofits locate where needs and resources are found and where there are potential members or volunteers.[12]

It is important to note that foundation grants comprise a modest portion of nonprofit revenues.[13] Various researchers have weighed in on the question of whether foundation activities are redistributive, generally concluding they may only be weakly so.[14] Nonetheless, the size of foundation endowments and the unique tax exempt status of these grant-making institutions fuel perennial interest in foundation support for the nonprofit

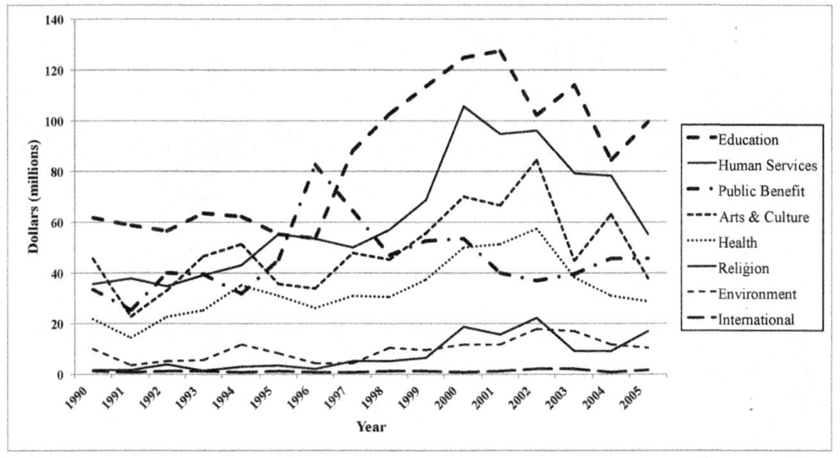

Figure 5.2. All Foundation Grants to Chicago Recipients, 1990–2005. *Source:* The Foundation Center.[9]

sector and in the question of whether foundation grants are going where they are most needed.[15]

Mapping the geographic location of nonprofit grant recipients effectively allocates grant dollars to a given community area. One limitation to this approach is the underlying assumption that the location of a grant recipient is the neighborhood where grant monies are spent. There are undoubtedly spillover effects between neighborhoods, as well as headquarter effects (predominantly in the Loop) where money may be mapped to a headquarter organization (e.g., YMCA of Chicago) but spent at a branch location (e.g., Logan Square YMCA). However, mapping foundation grant dollars across Chicago community areas is suggestive, providing a preliminary view of the distribution of foundation benefits across the city (see fig. 5.3).

Figure 5.3 includes a map of Chicago's seventy-seven community areas alongside a map showing the distribution of aggregate foundation grant dollars. Community areas are shaded by total inflation-adjusted grant dollars with darker areas receiving more foundation support. Total foundation dollars are concentrated in a pattern that radiates outward from the central business district (Loop). There are additional concentrations of funding on the south side of Chicago and north of the Loop. While it is interesting to note the distribution of total funding, it may be more indicative of nonprofit density, rather than a match between foundation dollars and specific needs at the community level. Foundation human service grantmaking has generally been considered to be the most redistributive of foundation

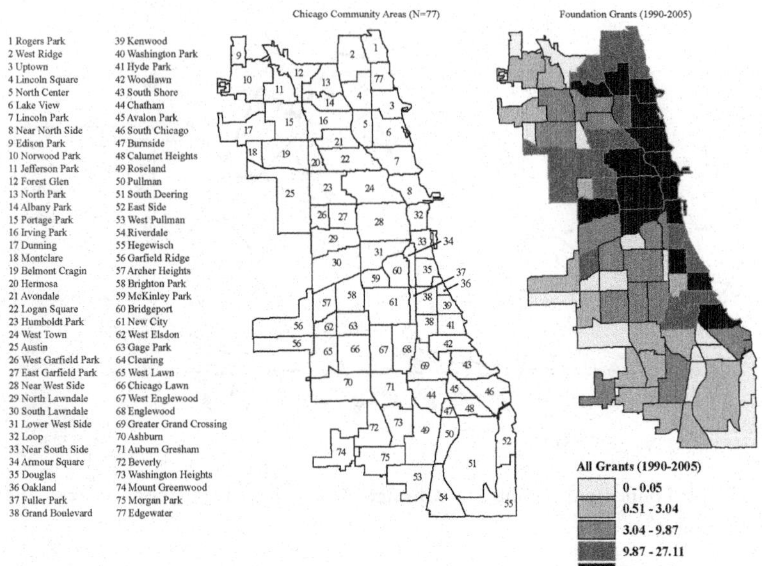

Figure 5.3. Chicago Community Areas and Distribution of Foundation Grant Dollars, 1990–2005[a].

[a]Inflation adjusted 2005 dollars in millions.

activities.[16] In addition, human service nonprofit organizations may be more intrinsically connected with the geographic community in which they are located.

The maps in figure 5.4 compare the percentage of households living in poverty and the distribution of aggregate foundation human service grants in Chicago community areas. The Loop (central business district) and Hyde Park (home to the University of Chicago) are labeled for reference. The darker the shading, the higher the concentration of household poverty (left map) or the greater the amount of foundation grants to human service nonprofits (right map). Three clusters of human service grant dollars are notable and show considerable variation with respect to the distribution of poverty. To the west of the Loop, high concentrations of foundation funding for human services appears to correspond with high levels of household poverty in the same neighborhoods. To the southwest of the Loop, there appears to be a mismatch between poor areas around Hyde Park where foundation support for human services is not as great. Likewise, to the north of the Loop there is a high concentration of human service dollars and a lower concentration of household poverty. Closer examination of individual nonprofits and foundation grants is necessary to understand the apparent mismatch of needs and funds. This examination of where the

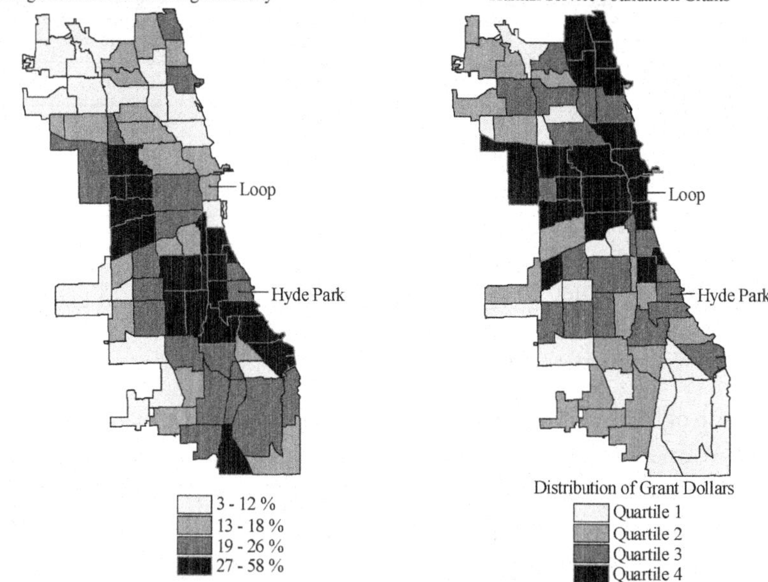

Figure 5.4. Distribution of Households Living in Poverty[a] and Human Service Foundation Grants[b].
[a]US Census, American Community Survey Estimates, 2007-2011
[b]The Foundation Center

money goes raises the question of where foundation dollars originate: in Chicago, Illinois, the Midwest, or elsewhere.

Grantmaking as a Local Phenomenon

According to prior research, foundation grantmaking tends to be concentrated in the local area or region where a foundation is situated.[17] With the exception of foundations with a national reach, such as the MacArthur Foundation, most foundations in Illinois concentrate their grant-making efforts in Cook County.[18] Like foundation giving in other parts of the country, grantmaking to Chicago's nonprofit organizations is overwhelmingly regional and local.[19]

Table 5.2 shows aggregate giving (1990–2005) by foundation donors to Chicago nonprofit recipients according to the geographic location of the foundation. Foundation giving to Chicago nonprofits is dominated by Midwest foundations that contributed 70 percent of all grant dollars and 79 percent of all grants. The next largest group of foundation grantmakers is located in the Northeast (17 percent of dollars and 10 percent of grants), followed by foundations in the South (9 percent of dollars and 9 percent of grants) and the West (0.7 percent of dollars and 4 percent of grants).

Table 5.2. Regional Distribution of Foundation Giving to Chicago Recipients, 1990–2005

	All		Total Grants		Dollars[a]		Mean	
Region	N	%	N	%	N	%	Grant	Median
Northeast	273	33.1	5,011	9.9	817.0	17.4	162,950	45,200
Midwest	263	31.8	39,618	78.6	3,277.4	70.0	82,724	27,500
South	153	18.5	4,455	8.8	403.9	8.6	90,671	28,250
Pacific	107	13.0	971	1.9	152.5	3.3	157,027	31,872
West	30	3.6	334	0.7	31.6	0.7	94,547	25,800
Total	826	100	50,389	100	4,681.9	100	92,915	28,250

[a]Dollars (millions) expressed in inflation-adjusted 2005 dollars.
Source: The Foundation Center.[20]

Interestingly, however, the size of the average grant to Chicago nonprofits from Midwest foundations ($82,724) is lower than the average grant from foundations in other regions. The median grant is also low compared to grants from foundations outside of the Midwest. This suggests that local foundations might be spreading the wealth among local nonprofits, giving smaller average grants to more organizations, while national foundations give larger grants to a smaller number of Chicago nonprofit organizations.

A closer look at the geographic breakdown of foundation giving is even more instructive. Table 5.3 shows the distribution of local versus national funders. Most foundations in the data (87 percent) are national foundations located outside of Illinois. Foundations located in Chicago and Illinois account for 71 percent of grants, comprising 61 percent of all grant dollars during this time period. Only 13 percent of foundations in the sample are headquartered in Illinois. Most of the Illinois-based foundations (68 of 109) are located in Chicago. The review of foundation rankings by total giving (see table 5.1) revealed the dominance of the MacArthur Foundation and the CCT.

The bold type in table 5.3 separates MacArthur and CCT from the other Chicago-based foundations. Giving by these two foundations together accounts for 26 percent of all grants and 36 percent of grant dollars from Chicago foundations. Grants from MacArthur and CCT comprise approximately 20 percent of total grant dollars from all foundations (15 percent of total grants). By comparison, national (non-Illinois) foundations give 30 percent of all grant dollars.

An examination of this aggregate grant-making data supports the contention that foundation giving is local. Is this pattern consistent over the sixteen-year period? An examination of the top fifteen grantmakers to Chicago nonprofits (table 5.1) suggests that the mix of funders may

Table 5.3. Chicago, Midwest, and National Distribution of Foundation Giving, 1990–2005

Location	Foundations	%	No. of Grants	%	Dollars[a]	%
Chicago	68	8.2	29,540	58.6	2,514.0	53.7
Chicago w/o MacArthur & CCT	**66**	**8.0**	**21,806**	**43.3**	**1,600.8**	**34.2**
MacArthur	**1**	**0.1**	**2,607**	**5.2**	**453.9**	**9.7**
CCT	**1**	**0.1**	**5,127**	**10.2**	**459.3**	**9.8**
Illinois (not Chicago)	41	5.0	6,463	12.8	362.4	7.7
Midwest (not Illinois)	154	18.6	3,615	7.2	401	8.6
National	563	68.2	10,771	21.4	1,404.5	30.0
Total	826	100	50,389	100	4,681.9	100

[a]Dollars (millions) expressed in inflation-adjusted 2005 dollars.
Source: The Foundation Center.[21]

be changing. The six national foundations listed in table 5.1 account for 11.2 percent of total giving to Chicago nonprofits. Figure 5.5 shows the percentage of foundation grant dollars distributed by foundation location during this time period. The solid line represents giving by Chicago and Illinois-based foundations, which decreased from 75 percent to 52 percent of total foundation dollars from 1990 to 2005. The dotted line indicates giving by national foundations located outside of Illinois. Total giving by national foundations increased from 25 percent to 48 percent of all foundation grant dollars. By 2005, grant dollars were roughly evenly split between Illinois and Chicago foundations and national foundations.

A variety of factors could contribute to the pattern of increased grant dollars from national foundations flowing to Chicago nonprofits. During this time period, the number of foundations, the value of their assets, and total giving all grew at a fast rate. The field was also becoming more professionalized. The Donors Forum, a regional association of grantmakers established in 1974, significantly expanded its members (foundations) and partners (nonprofits) during this time period. In the mid-1990s, collective action by Chicago foundations, in concert with the Donors Forum, led to the establishment of a Chicago Area Grant Application Form; the purpose of the form was to streamline the funding process, but not all foundations used the application. The creation of the common grant application speaks to the convening power of the Donors Forum as an organization. In 2015, on the retirement of its long-time executive director, the Donors Forum was rebranded as Forefront. The organization continues to provide a variety of professional development opportunities for members of the Chicago nonprofit sector, including networking events with

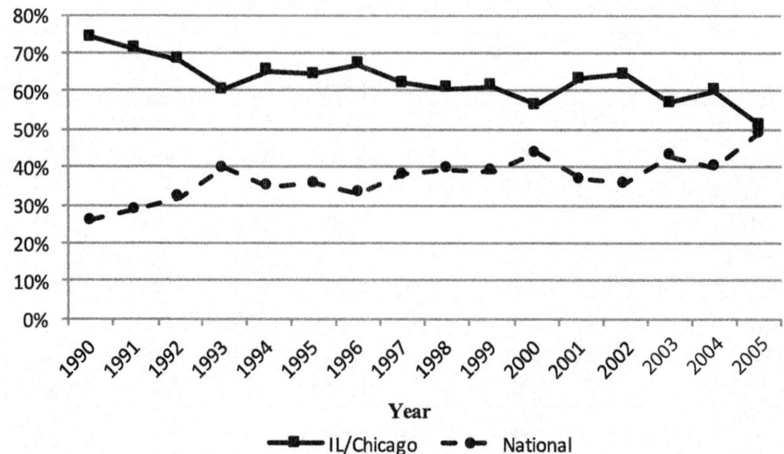

Figure 5.5. Percentage of Grant Dollars, Chicago and National Foundations, 1990–2005. *Source:* The Foundation Center.[22]

nonprofits and funders, grantwriting training, and access to a large library of resources about foundation funding. Approximately 30 percent of Chicago nonprofits represented in the Foundation Center grants data are Forefront nonprofit members. The increase in national foundation dollars could be the result of organizational learning, as nonprofits became more astute in applying for foundation grants and began to apply to a larger pool of foundations across the nations for support.

The pattern of decreasing regional foundation support is also worth attention. Figure 5.6 presents a more fine-grained examination of foundation giving by region. Most of the upward trend in giving by national foundations is accounted for by foundations located in the Northeast (represented by the second line from the top, and the dashed line with solid circles). The top line represents the proportion of dollars granted in a given year by large foundations located in the Midwest. The trend lines for MacArthur and CCT are shown separately. In the case of both foundations, giving (in constant dollars) declined in the 1990s. The decline in Illinois and Chicago foundations' contributions to overall grant dollars is partially attributable to decreases in MacArthur and CCT giving. During this time period, total dollars contributed by Northeast foundations to Chicago nonprofits increased from 9 percent to more than 20 percent. The trend of increasing national, and decreasing regional, foundation funding to Chicago nonprofits (figs. 5.5 and 5.6) could also reflect strategic planning begun in the 1990s by the MacArthur Foundation.

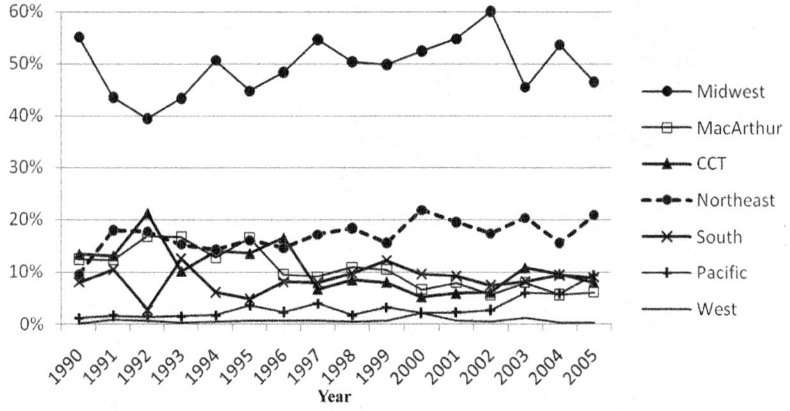

Figure 5.6. Percentage of Grant Dollars by Region with MacArthur and CCT, 1990–2005. *Source:* The Foundation Center.[23]

Reshaping Chicago Grantmaking: The MacArthur Foundation and the New Communities Program (2005–Present)

In the late 1990s, the MacArthur Foundation began planning for a five-year, $17 million investment in specific neighborhoods in Chicago. The foundation partnered with the Local Initiatives Support Corporation of Chicago (LISC/Chicago) and launched the New Communities Program (NCP) in 2005 with an ambitious agenda of neighborhood revitalization.[24] LISC/Chicago, founded in 1980, is an intermediary nonprofit organization that "organizes capital and other resources to support initiatives that will stimulate the comprehensive development of healthy, stable neighborhoods."[25] Since the founding of the NCP in 2005, LISC/Chicago has invested over $120 million in inner-city development.

The MacArthur Foundation is the principal supporter of the NCP, which works in sixteen Chicago neighborhoods: Auburn Gresham, Chicago Lawn, Douglas, Grand Boulevard, North Kenwood-Oakland, East Garfield, Englewood, Humboldt Park, Little Village (South Lawndale), Logan Square, North Lawndale, Pilsen (Lower West Side), South Chicago, Washington Park, West Haven (Near West Side), and Woodlawn. The neighborhoods were primarily selected on the basis of demographic information such as poverty levels and racial composition, the presence of community-based nonprofits, and preexisting community relationships. Other Chicago-based foundation partners in the NCP include Bank One (Chase), the Joyce Foundation, Polk Brothers Foundation, and the State Farm Insurance Companies Foundation.

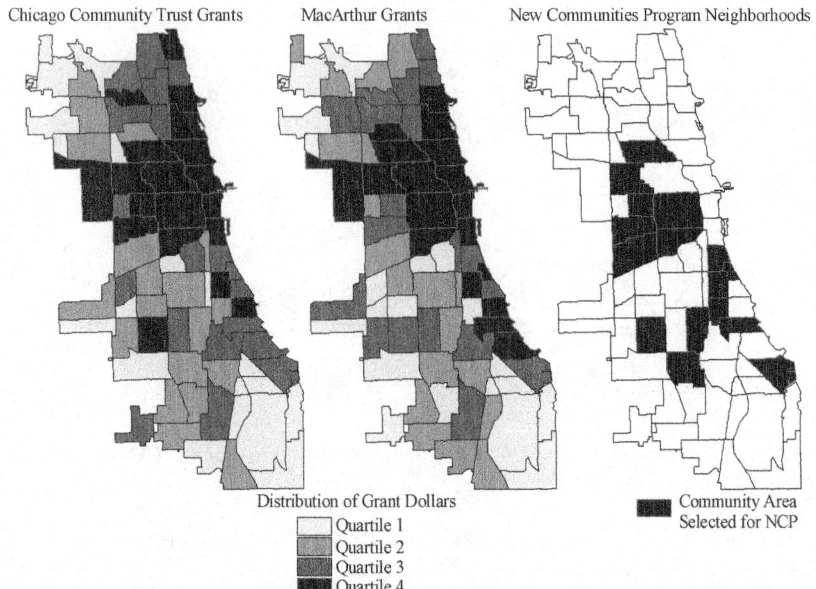

Figure 5.7. Chicago Community Trust and MacArthur Grants (1990–2005)[(a)], and the New Communities Program[(b)].

[a]Total 2005 inflation adjusted grant dollars given by Chicago Community Trust and the MacArthur Foundation, 1990–2005.

[b]Sixteen Chicago community areas selected for the New Communities Program.

The NCP reflects the growing interest in strategic philanthropy and the desire for foundations to leverage their investments in specific communities by attracting additional grant dollars to these areas. NCP identified lead nonprofit agencies in each neighborhood to help coordinate programs among local nonprofits. LISC/Chicago successfully leveraged MacArthur's initial investment, raising millions from dozens of other funders along with city, state, and federal agencies.[26] NCP is part of a larger field of foundation-supported community redevelopment efforts.[27] It has been widely heralded as a success.[28] Building on work in Chicago and ten other communities nationwide, LISC has expanded this model to other urban and rural sustainable community sites across the United States.[29]

Figure 5.7 includes three maps of Chicago community areas shaded by total grant dollars from the CCT (left), total grant dollars from the MacArthur Foundation (middle), and the location of the NCP neighborhoods. As illustrated in figure 5.7, the NCP has seriously restricted the geographic range of grantmaking by the MacArthur Foundation, one of the largest local foundation donors. In the decade and a half prior to the inception of the NCP, the MacArthur Foundation funded nonprofits in fifty-seven Chicago community areas, comparable to the fifty-five community areas supported by the CCT. With NCP, the majority of MacArthur's Chicago grantmaking is focused in sixteen neighborhoods.

Conclusion

Foundation giving in Chicago is highly concentrated, with a small number of large foundations accounting for the majority of the giving. Gradually, the sources of foundation support for Chicago's nonprofits have shifted to grants from national foundations, predominantly located in the Northeast. Recent changes in the grant-making strategy of the MacArthur Foundation may impact the shape of future foundation giving. This discussion of foundation grantmaking to Chicago-based nonprofits raises several questions: Will the trend of increased dollars from national foundations continue? How could this shape the local character of institutional philanthropy in the city? What are the longer term implications of place-based strategies like the NCP?

Heather MacIndoe is Associate Professor and Director of the Doctoral Program in the Department of Public Policy and Public Affairs at the McCormack Graduate School for Policy and Global Studies at the University of Massachusetts–Boston.

Notes

1. Peter Frumkin, "Philanthropy," in *The Encyclopedia of Chicago*, eds. James R. Grossman, Ann Durkin Keating, and Janice L. Reiff (Chicago: University of Chicago Press, 2004), 604–6.
2. Foundation Center and Donors Forum, *Giving in Illinois* (New York: Foundation Center, 2013), 1–12; Foundation Center, "Distribution of Grants from FC 1000 Foundations to US Recipients, by Subject Area, 2005" (New York: Foundation Center, 2014), http://data.foundationcenter.org/#/fc1000/subject:all/nationwide/total/list/2005.
3. Indiana University Lilly Family School of Philanthropy, *Giving in Chicago*. Accessed at http://www.givinginchicago.com. Accessed 19 October 2016.
4. For additional discussion of the Foundation Center data set, see Anheier and Hammack (2010), Appendix A, 403–4.
5. For additional discussion of the Foundation Center data set, see Anheier and Hammack (2010), Appendix A, 403–4.
6. Waldemar A. Nielsen, *The Golden Donors: A New Anatomy of the Great Foundations* (New York: E. P. Dutton, 2002 [1985]), 102.
7. Nielsen, *The Golden Donors*, 104.
8. David R. Stevenson, *The National Taxonomy of Exempt Entities Manual* (Washington, DC: National Center for Charitable Statistics and Foundation Center, 1997).

9. For additional discussion of the Foundation Center data set, see Anheier and Hammack (2010), Appendix A, 403–4.

10. Amanda Seligman, "Community Areas," in *The Encyclopedia of Chicago* (Chicago: The Newberry Library, 2004), 190–91.

11. Gerald Suttles, *The Man-Made City: The Land-Use Confidence Game in Chicago* (Chicago: University of Chicago Press, 1990).

12. Nicole Marwell, "Privatizing the Welfare State: Nonprofit Community-Based Organizations as Political Actors," *American Journal of Sociology* 69 (2004): 265–91; Jennifer R. Wolch and R. K. Geiger, "The Distribution of Voluntary Resources: An Exploratory Analysis," *Environment and Planning* 15 (1983): 1067–82; Julian Wolpert, *Patterns of Generosity in America: Who's Holding the Safety Net?* (New York: The Twentieth Century Fund, 1993); Miller McPherson 1983, "An Ecology of Affiliation," *American Sociological Review* 48 (1983): 519–32.

13. Elizabeth Boris and Julian Wolpert, "The Role of Philanthropic Foundations: Lessons from America's Experience with Private Foundations," in *Third Sector Policy at the Crossroads: An International Nonprofit Analysis*, eds. Helmut Anheier and Jeremy Kendall (New York: Routledge, 2001), 69–90; James Ferris and Nicholas Williams, "Foundation Strategy for Social Impact: A System Change Perspective," *Nonprofit Policy Forum* 1 (2010): 1–24; David Hammack and Helmut Anheier, "American Foundations: Their Roles and Contributions to Society," in *American Foundations: Roles and Contributions*, eds. Helmut Anheier and David Hammack (Washington, DC: Brookings Institution Press, 2010), 3–28; Julian Wolpert, "Communities, Networks, and the Future of Philanthropy," in *Philanthropy and the Nonprofit Sector in a Changing America*, eds. Charles T. Clotfelter and Thomas Ehrlich (Bloomington: Indiana University Press, 1999), 247.

14. See, for example, Julian Wolpert, "Redistributional Effects of America's Private Foundations," in *The Legitimacy of Philanthropic Foundations: United States and European Perspectives*, eds. Kenneth Prewitt, Mattei Dogan, Steven Heydemann, and Stefan Toepler (New York: Russell Sage Foundation, 2006), 123–49.

15. See, for example, Mark Dowie, *American Foundations: An Investigative History* (Cambridge, MA: MIT Press, 2001); Kenneth Prewitt, "Foundations," in *The Nonprofit Sector: A Research Handbook*, eds. Walter Powell and Richard Steinberg (New Haven, CT: Yale University Press, 2006), 355–77.

16. Robert A. Margo, "Foundations," in *Who Benefits from the Nonprofit Sector?*, ed. Charles T. Clotfelter (Chicago: University of Chicago Press, 1992), 207–34; Julian Wolpert, "The Distributional Impacts of Nonprofits and Philanthropy," in *Measuring the Impact of the Nonprofit Sector*, eds. Patricia Flynn and Virginia Hodgkinson (New York: Kluwer Academic, 2001), 123–36; Julian Wolpert, "Redistributional Effects of America's Private Foundations," in *The Legitimacy of Philanthropic Foundations: United States and European Perspectives*, eds. Kenneth Prewitt, Mattei Dogan, Steven Heydemann, and Stefan Toepler (New York: Russell Sage Foundation, 2006), 123–49.

17. Kevin Bolduc, Phil Buchanan, and Judy Huang, *Listening to Grantees: What Nonprofits Value in Their Foundation Funders* (Boston: Center for Effective Philanthropy, 2004); Elizabeth Boris, Philanthropic Foundations in the United States (New York: Council On Foundations, 2000); Heather MacIndoe. "Public Goods and Public Claims: Foundation Philanthropy in Chicago (1990–2000)." (PhD diss. University of Chicago, 2007). *Dissertation Abstracts International*, 68, 751; William McKersie, "Local Philanthropy Matters: Pressing Issues for Research and Practice," in *Philanthropic Foundations: New Scholarship, New Possibilities*, ed. Ellen Condliffe Lagemann (Bloomington: Indiana University Press, 1999), 329–58; Wolpert, "Redistributional Effects of America's Private Foundations."

18. Foundation Center, *Aggregate Fiscal Data of Foundations in Illinois, 2011* (New York: Foundation Center, 2013), accessed at http://data.foundationcenter.org/#/foundations/all /state:IL/total/list/2011; Indiana University Lilly Family School, *Giving in Chicago*.

19. Wolpert, *Patterns of Generosity*; "Communities, Networks, and the Future of Philanthropy."

20. For additional discussion of the Foundation Center data set, see Anheier and Hammack (2010), Appendix A, 403–4.

21. For additional discussion of the Foundation Center data set, see Anheier and Hammack (2010), Appendix A, 403–4.

22. For additional discussion of the Foundation Center data set, see Anheier and Hammack (2010), Appendix A, 403–4.

23. For additional discussion of the Foundation Center data set, see Anheier and Hammack (2010), Appendix A, 403–4.

24. Christopher Walker, Sarah Rankin, and Francisca Winston, "New Approaches to Comprehensive Neighborhood Change: Replicating and Adapting LISC's Building Sustainable Communities Program" (Washington DC: Local Initiatives Support Coporation, 2010).

25. LISC/Chicago, *New Communities Program: Quality-of-Life Plan Summaries, Chicago Neighborhood Plans* (Chicago: LISC/Chicago, May 2005, http://www.newcommunities.org /CMAdocs/NCPChicagoPlans.pdf.

26. Christopher Walker, Sarah Rankin, and Francisca Winston, "New Approaches to Comprehensive Neighborhood Change: Replicating and Adapting LISC's Building Sustainable Communities Program" (Washington DC: Local Initiatives Support Coporation, 2010).

27. http://www.macfound.org; Karen Mossberger, *From Gray Areas to New Communities: Lessons and Issues from Comprehensive US Neighborhood Initiatives*, GCI Working Paper-10-02 (Chicago: The Great Cities Institute at the University of Illinois at Chicago, 2010), https:// greatcities.uic.edu/wp-content/uploads/2013/08/Mossberger_Karen_5.09.pdf.

28. David Greenberg, Nandita Verma, Keri-Nicole Dillman, and Robert Chaskin, "Creating a Platform for Sustained Neighborhood Improvement: Interim Findings from Chicago's New Communities Program" (Chicago: Chapin Hall at the University of Chicago, February 2010). https://www.mdrc.org/sites/default/files/full_68.pdf.

29. Walker, Rankin, and Winston, "New Approaches to Comprehensive Neighborhood Change."

chapter six

THE RISE OF GRANT-MAKING FOUNDATIONS IN THE SOUTH*

Martin Lehfeldt and Jamil Zainaldin

It is doubtful that any section of our nation honors its particularity with more fervor than the South. Intertwined with the roots of jazz, gospel, the blues, country music, and rock 'n' roll are culinary and literary traditions, a rural past, and a pace of life that clearly distinguishes this region from other parts of the country. The South cherishes history, and much of its life draws on deep pools of memory. For that reason, as activists and historians working in the region, we consider a broad historical perspective to be essential to an understanding of philanthropy in this unique setting.

Because "foundation" has no legal definition, any not-for-profit or even for-profit organization may claim the name. We have chosen to make our references, and most of our generalizations, to grant-making foundations whose primary purpose is to provide support to other not-for-profit institutions. These foundations are part of a distinctly American form of social organization and democracy that occupies an essential middle ground between citizens and government. They protect the interests of people whose needs are not met by the government, and they enhance the services that government does provide.[1]

The style of their grantmaking varies. It may focus on the relief of suffering, the improvement of living standards, social reform, or civic engagement.[2] From our perspective, foundations are at their best when contributing to the solution of social problems, the building of community, and, to paraphrase Maimonides in his "Eight Levels of Charitable Giving," helping people move from dependency to independence.[3]

In recent years, foundations have secured a steadily increasing influence in southern life. Unimaginable as it would have been even ninety years ago, today the South is home to more than fourteen thousand foundations that manage $80.4 billion in charitable capital—sufficient growth to merit the placement of a Foundation Center regional library in Atlanta. Their numbers include independent foundations with large endowments, nearly two hundred community foundations, operating foundations, corporate foundations, and thousands of family foundations (see table 6.1).[4]

During the years before the Great Depression, however, the indigenous foundations of the region essentially included only the Duke Endowment in North Carolina, several small community foundations, and a few scores of locally focused family foundations. Had we titled this chapter "The History of Southern Foundations," the abbreviated manuscript would have covered less than a century. However, other foundations (most of them based in the North) appeared much earlier and influenced the course of the region's history. They are an essential part of our story.[5]

* * *

A visitor traveling through the South in 1790 might easily have inferred that slavery was nearing extinction. Soil depletion and erosion from plantation-style agriculture made slave ownership a financial drain.

Economic salvation came from an unlikely source. While a guest at Mulberry Grove Plantation near Savannah in 1793, the Yale University graduate Eli Whitney designed a device to separate the fiber of short-staple cotton from the seed. His invention of the cotton engine (the "gin") revolutionized the harvesting of that crop. Large-scale cotton plantations worked by slaves using gins that were manufactured in New Haven, Connecticut, reinvigorated the institution of slavery and changed the course of southern history.[6]

The South's economy, albeit controlled by a small percentage of the population, began to match the strength of the industrial North.[7] With territorial expansion west into the Louisiana Purchase lands, by the 1830s southern cotton production became the raw fuel that sustained New England textile mills, financed Northern railroad and turnpike development, and promoted international trade. By 1850, the South had become a critical link in America's burgeoning market system. Its harvested cotton accounted for 41 percent of the world's supply and 55 percent of the nation's international exports. Measured in slaveholding and land, all twelve of the wealthiest counties in the US in 1860 were in the South. Put another way, more than half of the richest 1 percent of the US population on the eve of the Civil War lived in the southern states.[8]

Table 6.1. Foundations in the South (2013)

State	No.	Assets
AL	930	$ 2,804,783,000
AR	307	4,680,821,000
FL	5,144	20,199,912,000
GA	1,530	13,197,233,000
KY	529	2,432,847,000
LA	526	3,528,639,000
MS	257	1,204,438,000
NC	2,267	15,383,069,000
SC	518	2,149,082,000
TN	820	6,309,522,000
VA	1,555	8,539,558,000
	14,383	$80,429,904,000

Source: Foundation Center, 2015.

A portion of this enormous cache of wealth flowed into the channels of generosity as a white minority funded religious, educational, and cultural institutions for themselves, their families, and those closest to them. To illustrate the magnitude of the wealth (and the charitable behavior of its owners), consider the partial listing presented in table 6.2 of southern private higher learning institutions started before the Civil War that these individuals and families helped to establish and support.

Growing wealth throughout the North and the South begat growing interest in charitably inspired reforms, including efforts to expand the electoral franchise to those without property, improvements in child welfare, and prison reform.[9] Especially far-reaching were the feminist sentiments that found a voice at the 1848 Seneca Falls, New York, convention, and the push to establish universal compulsory education. In the South, however, these laudable impulses stopped short at the boundary line of slavery. The heavy investment required to suppress one-third of the region's population and to rationalize that suppression did not encourage the extension of progressive activity. Southern charity steadily contracted into forms of benevolence that did not disturb the foundations of society. Similarly, the religious revivalism in the South tended to emphasize personal rather than social or societal salvation, and that liberating message of evangelical Protestantism became a keystone in the defense of slavery.[10]

A widening crack in the region's different understandings of "charity" surfaced in 1836 when Congress debated the legality of the federal government

Table 6.2. Antebellum Institutions of Higher Learning: Recipients of Southern Charity

Year Founded	Name of Institution	State
1749	Washington and Lee	VA
1770	College of Charleston	SC
1772	Salem	NC
1775	Hampden-Sydney	VA
1780	Transylvania	KY
1794	Tusculum	TN
1819	Centre	KY
1825	Centenary	LA
1826	Furman	SC
1830	Randolph-Macon	VA
1830	Spring Hill	AL
1833	Mercer	GA
1835	Oglethorpe	GA
1836	Emory	GA
1837	Davidson	NC
1848	Rhodes (started as Southwestern)	TN
1854	Wofford	SC
1855	Berea	KY
1855	Huntingdon	AL
1857	University of the South	TN

accepting the bequest of James Smithson to found an institution for the "increase and diffusion of knowledge."[11] Senator John C. Calhoun of South Carolina vigorously opposed it in the Senate; Representative John Quincy Adams of Massachusetts defended it in the House. To Adams, the Smithson bequest was a model of private benevolence fused with governance for the good of all. Calhoun saw *any* formal and private monetary linkage between philanthropy and government—especially national government—as an unconstitutional empowerment of a private interest.[12] Indeed, for Calhoun, the Smithson bequest was the very opposite of benevolence, which he saw as personal and private. (It took a decade for the legislation to pass.)

Though regional differences can be overstated, Calhoun was acutely aware and defensive about a changing national sentiment, particularly the rising clamor for slavery's abolition after 1830. He came to slavery's defense in 1837 in an address on the Senate floor.[13] The institution was not, as his southern predecessors had conceded, a necessary evil (said Jefferson, "we have the wolf by the ear, and we can neither hold him or safely let him go") but a positive good.[14] His brush painted the "peculiar institution" as an element of family where mutual ties of obligation and affection drew masters and "servants" together. To slavery's defenders, southern hierarchy symbolized Christian charity overseen by the household head, the plantation owner, and the master—usually one and the same. Unlike the "wage slavery" and alienation of a capitalistic and urbanizing North, southerners took care of their own.[15]

To the candid observer, Calhoun's slavery apologetic was beside the point. The business of cotton was *business*, part of a thoroughgoing national and international market system involving massive transfers of goods and capital.[16] For southerners especially, a divided understanding of themselves and their world enabled them to embrace liberty and hierarchy, as well as Old World values of family, honor, chivalry, and Christian charity, even as some became merchant princes of the new capitalism.[17]

Ultimately, the nation's sectional differences became so great that most slave-holding states, despite pockets of antisecession feeling, elected to leave the Union in the months after Lincoln's 1860 electoral victory. Five years later, the same southern states that had become vital economic partners in the nation's expansion for the first six decades of the nineteenth century found themselves utterly devastated by an enemy that waged total war. By the time Lee signed the surrender documents at Appomattox, the South was in psychological, emotional, and physical ruin.[18]

* * *

A victorious North set in motion a movement that culminated in Radical Reconstruction. The participants included a coalition of federal and private interests, the Freedman's Bureau, Northern activists, religious denominations, educators, private philanthropists, and a limited number of native southerners as well as transplants from the North who served as advisors and members of governing boards. Their ultimate goal was to rebuild the defeated region in the image of the free northern states as the new freedmen became integrated into the civil life of the former Confederate states. They would live and work side by side with whites and govern in a democracy mandated by the newly adopted Thirteenth, Fourteenth, and Fifteenth Amendments to the US Constitution.[19]

In one important respect, however, post–Civil War benevolence differed dramatically from its predecessors in the region. Northern industrialists who had prospered because of the war constituted a new breed of philanthropists. Although they came from states that had been hotbeds of abolitionism, for them philanthropy was not simply an affair of the heart. It was also a calculated investment. They approached giving as an exercise in problem-solving—much as they had instituted "scientific" managerial principles in their plants and factories to supply the North's successful war effort.

They understood that the challenge of working in a shattered South was unprecedented. Guided by a strong belief in strategic management, they created funds to improve literacy and offer instruction not only to the freed slaves and their children but also to poor whites, to build libraries and schools, to support informal networks of mutual aid, and to address public health deficiencies. These new problem-solvers further recognized that their philanthropy could not by itself reclaim the South. Rather, they assumed that the practical knowledge gained from their admittedly experimental endeavors would prompt the new southern state governments to build on these efforts. A private response to a public problem supplemented by federal support might stimulate recovery and usher in a new civil order.

One of the most influential of the new philanthropists was George Peabody, a Massachusetts native and international investment banker who divided his time between London and the United States. Repulsed by the horror of massive destruction he witnessed during a visit to the "stricken South" but simultaneously energized by the possibility of a new beginning, in 1867 he gave $2 million to create the Peabody Education Fund. His intention, in his own words, was to "encourage the intellectual, moral, and industrial education of the destitute children of the Southern and Southwestern States of our union; my purpose being that the benefits intended shall be distributed among the entire population, without other distinction than their needs and opportunities of usefulness to them."[20] Well before Andrew Carnegie, his example spoke volumes about the civic responsibility of the newly rich.[21]

For a decade, this new coalition of federal and private interests—driven by motives that embraced both altruism and self-interest and sustained by the Lincolnian vision of a "new nation conceived in liberty"—gave promise of working. Seven southern states put laws on the books that granted blacks equal access to all public places. Louisiana and South Carolina enacted legislation that assured integrated schools. Black elected officials sat in the region's state legislatures and occupied local political offices. And in the North, the trend decidedly was in the direction of implementing the 1875 Civil Rights Act that removed barriers to discrimination in public accommodations.

* * *

The North's political will, however, was weaker than the spirit of George Peabody and other benefactors of the time. In the hotly disputed presidential election of 1876, the Republican Party betrayed its promise to the 3.9 million freed slaves. In return for a pledge of support from white southern congressmen that put Rutherford Hayes in the White House, the party agreed to end federal occupation of the South. White Democratic Party southerners returned to power as the region's "redeemers" and brought Congressional-dictated Reconstruction and the prospects of civil rights for one-third of the region's population to an end.

Henry Grady, the entrepreneurial newspaperman from bustling, business-hungry Atlanta, and other publicists campaigned hard to fashion a new identity for the South. They promoted the image of a region marked by robust economic resurgence, North–South financial cooperation, and racial harmony. However, this last descriptor was contradicted by the facts. Southern states in the 1880s and 1890s began passing laws that gradually drew, and then extended a color line of separation—first to streetcars, then to drinking fountains, restrooms, public accommodations and services, and entrances to buildings. Booker T. Washington, the nation's most influential African American, had little choice but to offer a tacit endorsement of the gospel of the "New South" during his now-famous speech at the Cotton States and International Exposition in 1895.[22]

In 1896, the US Supreme Court drew the final curtain on the possibility of a transformed South in the *Plessy v. Ferguson* case when it ordained the "separate but equal" doctrine.[23] The new public order, dubbed "Jim Crow," not only established a rigid separation of the races in every aspect of public life, but also ensured compliance through legally sanctioned reprisals as well as unpunished vigilante terrorism.

As this ugly charade of democracy evolved, a parallel historical invention surfaced that became known as the "Lost Cause"—a new euphemism for the war between the states. Nurtured and promoted by many white southern women and members of the clergy, the Lost Cause movement rapidly became a cultural "religion" proclaiming the age-old, knightly virtues of southern honor and valor as the war's true and lasting legacies. According to this popular rendition of history (which quickly found its way into southern school textbooks), northern aggression—not slavery—was the cause of the war, and the antebellum years had been marked by racial concord and opulence. This mythology reached its largest audience in 1939 when the film version of *Gone with the Wind* valorized the Old South as a place of "cavaliers and cotton fields" where gallantry "took its last bow."[24]

Because Jim Crow laws were state-based, southern state governments again became invested in states' rights as a way to defend and police the status quo. A reactionary, race-baiting form of politics took hold in southern states after 1900 that not only warned of "rule by negroes," but also lashed out against a "lower class of whites" whose populist, biracial reform agendas threatened an emergent Democratic Party power structure.

Outside the South, the progressive era was bringing about incremental change as government addressed issues of workplace safety, wages, and monopoly. Strategy-oriented "organized charity" promoted the reform of child labor, education, working conditions and wages, electoral corruption in government, and women's suffrage. To be sure, in the South progressivism did have some influence on railroad regulation, education, and child labor, but public policy generally bowed to the demands of white supremacy. It was a difficult and dangerous time to ally oneself with positive social change.[25]

* * *

Nonetheless, in 1882, John F. Slater, inspired by his Christian beliefs, established a $1 million fund that would bear his name to support public and higher education for southern African Americans. A native of Rhode Island whose family owned and operated textile mills in New England, Slater incorporated his fund in New York State and called for it to be managed by a ten-person board. Its members included a former US president (Rutherford B. Hayes), a chief justice of the United States Supreme Court (Morrison Waite), a prominent and wealthy abolitionist, an Episcopal bishop, a financier who also helped found the YMCA, and the presidents of Columbia and Cornell Universities.[26]

In 1902, John D. Rockefeller Sr. funded the General Education Board (GEB), strongly influenced by the report from his son, John Jr., about a tour of Negro schools in the South the previous year. Rockefeller had begun giving away his fortune years earlier. As the "funding father" of the University of Chicago in 1891, he ranked research and education high on his list of priorities.

The GEB's aim was to strengthen public education for southern children by providing salary support to state agents for white and Negro schools. The Rockefellers recruited George Foster Peabody (no relation to the founder of the Peabody Fund) to serve on the GEB. A native of Columbus, Georgia, Peabody was a talented man who had built a lucrative career in railroads and banking in pre-war Pennsylvania. In addition to his work with the GEB, he went on to become an important philanthropist in his own right as a benefactor of the Penn Normal Industrial and Agricultural School in

South Carolina; the Hampton Institute in Hampton, Virginia; and the Tuskegee Institute in Alabama. He also advocated successfully for the creation of Episcopal Church schools for African Americans in the South.[27]

The Rockefeller family's philanthropic support of education also led it into health-related endeavors. The discovery that the virtual epidemic incidence of hookworm (often contracted through bare feet) was keeping significant numbers of southern children away from school prompted the launching and funding of a massive and successful public health program to eradicate this disease.[28]

In 1905, Anna Jeanes, a Quaker benefactress from Philadelphia, created a trust to be administered by the GEB to assist rural schools for blacks in southern states. Its primary thrust was the employment of so-called "Jeanes teachers," African American industrial supervision instructors who emphasized vocational education and school improvement. These Jeanes teachers were the inspiration for some of the southern region's first indigenous grantmaking when these black teachers themselves established the Virginia Randolph Fund (named in honor of the first supervisor supported by the Anna Jeanes Fund).[29]

The Russell Sage Foundation, created in 1907, adopted the informed and scientific approach to philanthropy that had been pioneered in the Peabody, Slater, and Rockefeller initiatives. Its early investigations involved slum conditions in northern cities. The foundation branched out to the South under the guidance of John C. Campbell, a North Carolinian who sought to improve the prospects for children of Appalachia through educational reforms. He approached the foundation in 1908 with a proposal to support a comprehensive survey of church-based and public education in that mountainous region. In 1913, the foundation opened its Southern Highlands Division in Asheville, North Carolina.[30]

The steel magnate Andrew Carnegie brought his entrepreneurial and managerial skills to the field of scientific philanthropy. Putting into practice his "gospel of wealth," he created endowment funds and foundations and challenged the wealthy to follow his model. Because public libraries were a rarity, the largely self-educated but impressively literate Carnegie embarked on a campaign that brought 1,689 "Carnegie libraries" to communities in the United States, 178 of them in the South.[31]

Two years later, the Phelps Stokes Fund, created in 1911, issued an historic study documenting racial disparities in the funding of southern education. In 1917, the head of the fund, Thomas Jesse Jones, published *Negro Education: A Study of the Private and Higher Schools for Colored People in the United States* as a guide for northern philanthropy.[32]

From 1913 to 1932, during an era when most black schools operated in one-room buildings or church structures, the Julius Rosenwald Fund (established by the former chairman of Sears, Roebuck & Co. in 1917) followed the now-established corporate management model driven by a change-oriented mission. Turning for advice to influential educators like Booker T. Washington, the fund contributed to the construction of more than five thousand schools for blacks in fifteen states and was instrumental in the development of Dillard University in New Orleans as a regional black liberal arts college.[33]

A year after the great flood of 1927 devastated the Mississippi Delta, the Rockefeller Foundation used challenge grants to establish eighty city, county, and state health departments around the region.[34] During the same period the Commonwealth Fund helped to build rural hospitals.[35] Throughout this decades-long period of post-Civil War recovery and racial segregation, the American Missionary Association, northern white denominations, and national black denominations continued to found schools and colleges for African Americans, including a medical school and schools of nursing.[36]

Black generosity in support of black education, as a percentage of both assets and income, surpassed all other philanthropy. Tuskegee Institute's *Negro Yearbook* in 1915 noted that African Americans, during the fifty years after the Civil War, contributed more than $25 million (approximately $500 million in current value) to build and sustain educational institutions.[37] Indeed, in evidence since the Colonial era are traditions of black community building, intramural support, and education despite seemingly insurmountable obstacles.[38]

A few institution-specific operating foundations and institutional endowments came earlier, but the first grant-making foundation to be established in the South by southerners appears to be the Feild Co-Operative Association, organized in 1912. Its primary interest was in education with a focus on individual scholarships. In 1925, the foundation's directors established a self-perpetuating, revolving educational loan fund.[39] It was a rare philanthropic claim to fame for Mississippi; in 1890 the state legislature had banned married people from leaving more than one-third of their estates to charity. The move was a heavy-handed reaction to spurious deathbed "conversions" by which some unscrupulous clergymen had robbed presumed heirs of anticipated property.[40]

Although Frederick H. Goff had conceived and established the first US community foundation in Cleveland in 1914 (a concept soon replicated in other industrialized northern cities), the movement made little headway in the South.[41] The region launched its first community foundation in Winston-Salem, North Carolina, in 1919 with a $1,000 endowment gift from Francis Fries, a banker and railroader, and much of whose wealth derived from his textile mill in Grayson County, Virginia.[42] Hard times capped by the Great Depression years delayed the formation of the second community foundation until 1943, when Walter Scott Montgomery's leadership and initial gift of $10,000 created the Spartanburg County Foundation in South Carolina.[43]

It was during this era that the first truly major foundation in the South was created by James Buchanan ("Buck") Duke, who established the Duke Endowment with $40 million in December 1924. After the war, Buck's father—who had served as a Confederate soldier—his brother, Benjamin, and his sister, Mary Duke Lyon, had slowly built their family tobacco business. Their decision in 1884 to begin the mechanized mass production of cigarettes proved to be highly successful; it led to the acquisition of other companies that evolved into the American Tobacco Company. Even the Wilson Administration's successful antitrust prosecution against this enormous and complex corporation did not dissipate the family fortune; the Dukes had also invested in both the textile industry and hydroelectric power, and had formed the Duke Power Company in 1925.

As they personally prospered, the Dukes also demonstrated an instinct for generosity through their support of Trinity College (forerunner of Duke University), affiliated with the Methodist Church, as well as hospitals and orphanages. After the death of their father and sister, the two brothers systematized their giving in North and South Carolina. In 1924, Duke established the endowment. Its remarkable indenture of trust specifically names Duke University, Davidson College, and Furman University as perpetual beneficiaries, but it also includes an African American institution founded in 1867 that would become Johnson C. Smith University. It further prescribes support for not-for-profit hospitals and children's homes in the Carolinas, rural Methodist churches in North Carolina, retired pastors, and their surviving families. When Duke died less than a year after the foundation's formation, his will left an additional $67 million to bolster the initial gift of $40 million.

Offsetting the paucity of philanthropic institutions in the poverty-stricken South was a generosity of spirit and concern for broad civic improvement that sprang from the ranks of southern Jewish merchants.[44] These families, many of whom would later form private foundations, were in the forefront of contributing to municipal hospitals, parks, cultural facilities, and "the pursuit of equality in education and civil rights."[45]

An early example of this commitment was Rabbi Judah Wechsler, of Meridian, Mississippi, who led a movement to establish schools for African Americans in the 1880s. Jewish donors also were benefactors of the historically black colleges and universities started by and for the freedmen during the latter decades of the nineteenth century. These donors were white southerners (many of them or their forbears had fought for the Confederacy), and some were undoubtedly segregationists. Nonetheless, the theological concepts of *tikkum olam* ("repairing the world"), *chesed* ("loving-kindness"), and *tzedakah* ("righteous duty") were deeply instilled and reinforced by their often-progressive rabbis.[46]

* * *

The single enduring demographic characteristic of the South for nearly a century after 1865 was out-migration. African Americans began leaving the region as soon as they could during and after Reconstruction. In 1910 about 450,000 blacks lived outside the South. During WWI to 1920 their numbers grew to about 800,000 (a 75% increase)—a trend that continued through the next two decades. About 1.5 million blacks were living outside the South by the onset of the Second World War. [47]

Whites too were fleeing the region, spurred by the hopelessness of sharecropping and a steady rise in farm foreclosures. Between 1900 and 1930, 3.3 million whites, many of whom had subsisted on the region's hundreds of thousands of square miles of poor farms and pulpwood forests, made their way to the North and westward. The rate of out-migration doubled (to 20 percent) in the decade of 1940s.[48]

This enormous exodus of human talent drained the South of much of its creative leadership and labor force, and nobody rushed in to fill the vacuum. The national waves of immigration that had swept through the country in the 1880s and 1920s skirted the South, because the region still lacked the allure to attract outside investors or in-migrants.

A singular positive exception to these trends was the emergence of textile manufacturing, which became to the post-1900 South what the growing of cotton had been to the nineteenth century. Though southern mills predated the Civil War, it was not until after 1880 that the industry began its rise, surpassing New England's output by 1900 and becoming the region's single largest industrial employer. Sprouting along the rivers and rail lines of the Piedmont that ran through Virginia, the Carolinas, portions of Tennessee, north Georgia, and Alabama, spinning mills drew on a vast labor force of unemployed white families who had been forced off their land by foreclosures and sharecropping.[49]

No portion of the United States was more crushed by the Great Depression than the South, much of which was still recovering from the ravages of the Civil War and whose population in 1930 was almost 65.9% percent rural (compared to 43.9% for the nation as a whole).[50] The collapse was no respecter of the color line; both poor whites and blacks suffered. Much more than economic, poverty was physical, psychological, and spiritual. Writing for *American Mercury* in 1927, Wilbur J. Cash dissected the effects, cruelties, and constricted world views that were born of poverty, racism, lack of education, and lives bound to the soil and the mill.[51]

A special commission appointed by President Franklin D. Roosevelt in 1938 issued its *Report to the President on the Economic Conditions in the South.* The document labeled the entire region as "the nation's No.1 economic problem."[52] The region was not without visionary white and black leaders and writers who promoted a social science of reform, but popular journalists and commentators, most notably H. L. Mencken, were quick to describe this part of the country as "the Sahara of the Bozart," an educational disaster and a cultural wasteland.[53]

Yet in retrospect, the Great Depression also set in motion the first steps of a true reconstruction that helped set the stage for the modern foundation's rise in the South. Roosevelt did not need a special commission to tell him about rural poverty or economic distress. He had seen it with his own eyes on dozens of extended-stay trips to Warm Springs, Georgia, for hydrotherapy and rest. For Roosevelt, the rural poor had faces and names. Under his presidential direction, federal funds now poured into the region to respond to its need for rural electrification, public works and transportation projects, agricultural improvements, supports for farmers and their families, and minimum hours and wages for textile industry workers. Not unimportantly, a simultaneous rise to powerful leadership positions in Congress by southern Democrats—whatever their social views—gave new political leverage to the region and a corresponding rise in national stature.[54]

However, northern philanthropy had never really left the South, often still making compromises with Jim Crow. But in the 1930s some of these earlier foundations began to promote social change. One such philanthropic investment came through the New World Foundation that helped to establish the Highlander Folk School in eastern Tennessee in 1932, intended to train labor organizers in the South. It later broadened its curriculum to include the training of civil rights leaders like Rosa Parks and coaching African Americans to overcome the barriers of literacy tests at the polls.[55] Beginning in 1937, the Peabody, Slater, Jeanes, and Randolph funds became consolidated to form the Southern Education Foundation (SEF). Originally based in Washington, DC (four US presidents served on its board), it subsequently relocated to Atlanta, where it built its own facility in order to conduct its uniquely (for those times) biracial board meetings. SEF's move also reflected a renewed commitment to attacking some of the region's fundamental equity issues in education—though again there were practical limits to what could be done.[56]

Hard on the heels of the New Deal-financed infrastructure programs, World War II brought naval shipyards and ports, military bases, training facilities for the US Army's infantry and aviation cadets, and the production of steel, synthetic rubber, and tin. The South was in the throes of a major change that was perhaps more important than the Civil War itself.[57]

With new windows open to the rest of the world, a few southerners also began to create capital of their own. Led by the marketing genius of Robert W. Woodruff, the Atlanta-based Coca-Cola Company spawned a network of bottlers in southern states as it began its national and international expansion. Bottling franchises in Chattanooga, Columbus, Mobile, New Orleans, and other southern cities became sources of local philanthropy.[58] Woodruff created his own philanthropy—the Trebor (Robert spelled backward) Foundation in 1937.[59] A year later the Emily and Ernest Woodruff Foundation, named for his parents, came into being. For four decades, until liquidated, it had an enormous charitable impact on both the white and black educational, medical, cultural, religious, and recreational institutions of Atlanta. That tradition of philanthropy has been continued by the Robert W. Woodruff Foundation and several related foundations until the present day.[60]

As was the case with Coca-Cola, the organized southern philanthropy that existed during the 1940s and 1950s was tightly bound to the fortunes of that small number of families who profited from distinctively southern businesses. One was the Reynolds family of North Carolina, who, like the Duke family, had built its initial wealth from tobacco. From that wealth sprang the Z. Smith Reynolds Foundation, the Kate B. Reynolds Charitable Trust, the Sapelo Foundation, and the Mary Reynolds Babcock Foundation.

Any reference to the creation of structured philanthropy in the South during the 1940s and 1950s demands special mention of the wealth from textile manufacturing on which it drew and from the powerful impact this giving had on many parts of the region. The first such significant textile-based foundation was the Gregg-Graniteville Foundation, established in South Carolina in 1941, with roots stretching back to 1845, when William Gregg, a Virginia native known as the father of southern cotton manufacturing, received a charter for the Graniteville Company. A visionary who carefully studied the cotton goods industries of England and New England to seek greater efficiency, he relied on local people to build the mill as well as operate it, and offered wages that were at the same level as those paid to northern mill workers. Somewhat of a utopian for his day, and the practitioner of an enlightened brand of paternalism, he also provided quality housing for his workers, as well as a church and a small library.[61]

In 1942, James C. Self, founder of what would become Greenwood Mills in the South Carolina town of that name, incorporated the Self Family Foundation. Its initial and primary purpose was building a hospital for the people of the county. Although there were decided tax advantages associated with foundation formation, when the hospital opened Self described his contribution as a "debt of gratitude to the community that has been so good to me." Also in 1942, the colorful World War I flying ace Colonel Elliott Springs, another textile tycoon, created the Springs Foundation in Fort Mill, South Carolina. A year later, Charles A. Cannon established the Cannon Foundation in Concord, North Carolina, and the Callaway Foundation came into being in LaGrange, Georgia.

Although the South continued to be the recipient of northern philanthropy and federal relief, a handful of not-for-profit organizations could now look to a slowly growing number of new southern family foundations for support. Some churches, which received the bulk of individual southern charity, in turn created orphanages, homes for unwed mothers, and shelters for the homeless. As in the North, the South's white middle class women organized volunteer clubs that advocated for improvement of schools and city beautification. The burgeoning African American middle class financially supported its college fraternities and sororities (many of which focused on the professional advancement of their members) and other organizations like Jack and Jill of America, established in 1938 in Philadelphia to provide "cultural, social, civic, and recreational activities that stimulate and expand the mind to enhance life" for children.[62]

The new wealth made possible the strengthening of more southern not-for-profit institutions. Successful white business leaders and family members contributed to the formation and sustenance of symphony orchestras, opera companies, and museums. Organized white southern philanthropy and the grantmaking of northern foundations during the post–World War II years funded separate black hospitals, educational institutions, and other helping agencies. The generosity of African Americans themselves tended toward support of their churches and the schools and colleges established for African Americans.

A few northern philanthropic institutions built on earlier strategic approaches and elected not simply to alleviate the effects of racial discrimination but instead to support studies that documented its crippling impact. The Carnegie Corporation underwrote the 1944 publication of Gunnar Myrdal's *An American Dilemma: The Negro Problem and American Democracy,* which would be cited in the Supreme Court's *Brown v. Board of Education* decision a decade later. Within a week of that ruling, the Ford Foundation–funded book, Harry S. Ashmore's *The Negro and the Schools,* provided a comprehensive study of racial inequity among public schools in the South.[63]

Still, the emerging southern wealth of the postwar years did not begin to approach the vast national and international corporate assets that manufacturing and commercial establishments in the northern, Midwestern, and Pacific states generated. It was those assets that helped to support state and local government services, vigorous institutions of higher education, and organized philanthropy elsewhere in the country. In the South, it was not only the relative scarcity of indigenous capital (public and private) that stifled true progress; a large factor was the determination of many white citizens to retain a stratified society that turned on race, social class, hierarchy, and paternalism. By the mid-1950s the "new" South still looked sadly familiar. Clearly, the social dynamics of the South would have to change radically before many more of its people (more than one-third of whom continued to live in poverty) could share in the prosperity being enjoyed by much of the rest of the nation. Some funders were quietly seeding the possibilities for change, but most philanthropy helped to perpetuate racial segregation by benignly operating within the strictures of traditional white southern society.

* * *

The South's true watershed period is the Civil Rights Movement. In December 1955, a black boycott of the city bus system in Montgomery, Alabama, set in motion an unstoppable tide of events. Again it was northern philanthropy—The Field Foundation, Ford Foundation, New World Foundation, Stern Family Foundation and Taconic Foundation—that provided the financial support for initiatives like the Voter Education Project, the Highlander Folk School, the Legal Defense and Educational Fund, and the Southern Regional Commission.[64] The Ford Foundation also supported the Southern Education Reporting Service, which provided coverage about the battle over segregated schools that many politically conservative southern newspapers would not print.[65]

During the 1960s, the Ford and Cummins Engine Foundations made early investments in the Delta Corporation, a new private enterprise mechanism for addressing poverty in the Mississippi Delta. Drawing on the services of loaned Cummins executives, the new not-for-profit enterprise created the Fine Vines blue jeans company and Mid-South Stamping, which for a time were the region's largest black-owned companies. These same foundations also funded the nation's first catfish farms in Mississippi to provide jobs for low-income, rural African Americans.

Forced by journalists like Ralph McGill, courageous clergy, and other leaders to look at itself in the mirror, the South began its pilgrimage to rejoin the nation. These moral beacons stood in the tradition of a small coterie of intellectuals, writers, and journalists who declined to remain mute in the "silent South." Working quietly and in league with black leaders through organizations like the Commission on Interracial Cooperation, which had been founded in 1919 (later the Southern Regional Council), they sought solutions to the region's deepest problem.

The overthrow of the South's official social system opened the floodgates for other long-delayed changes. The pathbreaking scholarship of native son historian C. Vann Woodward and that of his friend and fellow-historian John Hope Franklin, along with social commentators such as Lillian Smith, found new audiences and reopened mythical southern history, culture, and literature to intellectual reexamination.[66] Perhaps most important, though, was the economic transformation that followed the eradication of legalized segregation. Investors who had long been hesitant to enter a region characterized by poor race relations now began to feel more comfortable about coming south. Both large and small white-owned businesses discovered what for them had been the invisible purchasing power of African Americans. Rising employment opportunities for all citizens led to greater investment in higher education to provide the training for a new workforce.

A most telling sign that the reformation of the South was indeed real was the beginning of a return migration into the region by African Americans, many of them children and grandchildren of those who had fled the South during the Reconstruction and Jim Crow eras. Today, the South is home to 45 percent of the nation's African American population (which is 12.6 percent nationwide).[67]

Portions of the newly created capital found its way into charitable endowments and a steadily growing number of private foundations came into being by the mid-1970s. The annual rate of foundation creation in the southeastern United States began to exceed the national rate in 1977 and accelerated into the late 1980s.

Without the presence of wealth, there can be no philanthropic endowments. However, without the presence of not-for-profit organizations (those "voluntary associations" that so impressed de Tocqueville), philanthropy is the sound of one hand clapping. They are essential partners for the translation of the charitable impulse into social action, and ultimately for philanthropy's legitimacy.

The Civil Rights Movement also inspired or strengthened alternative civic associations in the region. These grassroots activist associations signaled not only the first stages of true democratization in the South, but also the formation of a biracial, progressive civic spirit and political will that harkened back to the agrarian populism of the early 1890s.

During the mid-1960s, a handful of populist and sometimes politically motivated congressmen (some still acutely mindful of foundation support of the Civil Rights Movement) sought to force foundations out of existence or, at the very least, to prohibit their right to exist in perpetuity. The most draconian features of the proposed legislation never materialized, but foundations now found themselves more tightly regulated. In response, William C. Archie, executive of the Mary Reynolds Babcock Foundation, and a handful of other leaders in the South (primarily from North Carolina and Georgia) gathered and established the Southeastern Council of Foundations (SECF) to serve members in the contiguous states of Alabama, Florida, Georgia, Louisiana, Mississippi, North Carolina, South Carolina, Tennessee, and Virginia. This later expanded to include Arkansas, Kentucky and, for a short while, West Virginia. Since its founding it has been the region's premier convener of philanthropic institutions to promote wise and imaginative grantmaking, legal compliance, public accountability, exemplary governance and management, and sound financial investment practices.

Although the South was becoming far wealthier than it had been for many years, few individuals had been able to amass the kinds of charitable reserves associated with James B. Duke or Robert W. Woodruff. With a few notable exceptions, many of the new foundations formed in the South during the 1970s and 1980s were relatively small family philanthropies with assets of less than $10 million.[68] (The "intergenerational transfer of wealth" publicized by Boston College's Paul G. Schervish and John J. Havens had not yet surfaced.)[69]

In 1994, President Robert Hull and the board of the SECF determined that any future expansion of philanthropic resources in the region would depend on the formation and strengthening of community foundations. From 1994 to 1998, a new Community Foundation Initiative, aided by booming markets and favorable changes in the tax laws, contributed to increased numbers of community foundations throughout the region. As elsewhere in the country, charitably inclined individuals with discretionary assets who did not wish to establish private foundations discovered that community foundations are remarkably efficient and convenient vehicles for their generosity.

Today, 118 of these foundations in the South constitute about 15 percent of the nation's total of 763 and also about 15 percent ($9.8 billion) of the national total of $64.9 billion.[70] None has reached the asset size of the Silicon Valley Community Foundation ($4.7 billion) or the Tulsa Community Foundation ($3.7 billion), but two of them are among the twenty-five largest in the country.[71] Many have become not just simply convenient vehicles for personal philanthropy; they are also initiators of far-reaching ventures to serve community-wide needs.

One other major catalyst has fueled the expansion of charitable capital in the South during the past twenty years: the creation of so-called "health conversion" or "health legacy" foundations with proceeds from the sale of not-for-profit hospitals and health plans to for-profit companies. Today, of the 300-plus of these foundations nationally, approximately 130 are in the South.[72] These foundations (a barely measurable percentage of the region's foundations) hold an estimated $8.2 billion in assets, slightly more than 10 percent of the South's philanthropic capital. The majority are based in small towns and cities where they have emerged as the principal philanthropic institutions for their service areas. Four elected to become community foundations, but the rest are private foundations. They tend to regard the promotion and provision of health as central to their missions, but many interpret health in very broad fashion. As a result, unfettered by tradition and precedent, they have elected to fund programs in areas like adult literacy, economic development, early childhood development, public safety, and government accountability as strategies that promote broad community health.

Most indicators suggest that the South's philanthropic assets will continue to grow as the celebrated intergenerational transfer of wealth continues for perhaps another two decades. The Affordable Care Act of 2010 and ACA's prospects (whatever form it may take in a new administration) are likely to stimulate the formation of additional health legacy foundations; community foundations grow steadily, as does corporate grantmaking, and the support of the Ford, Kellogg, Mott, Gates,

Table 6.3. Southern Community Foundations, 2013

State	Number	Total Assets
AL	9	$ 337,380,278
AR	3	$ 190,142,269
FL	26	$1,619,836,366
GA	14	$1,210,753,271
KY	6	$ 445,693,579
LA	5	$ 983,658,868
MS	8	$ 154,009,396
NC	17	$2,339,651,698
SC	9	$ 494,944,081
TN	4	$ 962,612,115
VA	17	$1,070,251,960
	118	$9,808,347,881

Annie E. Casey Foundations, as well as other national foundations, continues to provide vital resources for the region's nonprofit organizations and programs. Especially fortunate will be those portions of the region that can count on the continued generosity of the Woodruff-source foundations, the Duke Endowment, the Walton Family Foundation, and the John S. and James L. Knight Foundation (which continues to be philanthropically active in ten southern communities that are or were the home of Knight-Ridder newspaper publications).

Nevertheless, it is instructive to place this growth in context. Although philanthropic resources are growing, they still constitute only about 15 percent of the national total. Moreover, although the South has taken large strides to disassociate itself from the shadow of its past, the legacy of difficult times lingers in the forms of higher-than-average incidents of heart disease, cancer, diabetes, infant death, low birth weight, and the lowest school graduation rates in the nation. Like other American cities, the South's metropolitan areas are plagued by residential and commercial sprawl, automobile congestion and pollution, and underfunded public transit. Problems of economic stagnation and population outflow plague many of the region's smaller municipalities.

As is the case throughout the United States, the focus of most southern grant-making foundations remains highly localized. Only a few of them give internationally or even nationally; a very small number of them give regionally, and relatively few choose to give on a statewide basis. The majority of southern foundations (like most grantmakers in the United States) also are not rocking the boat with their philanthropy.

Although they continue to be supportive of churches and temples, private preparatory schools, independent colleges and universities, health centers, performing arts venues and museums, and well-established social service agencies, remarkably few support not-for-profit organizations that are engaged in advocacy to change public policy that blocks the advancement of the region's most marginalized citizens.

Nonetheless, growing numbers are directing their assets and energies to address the root causes of social dysfunction. The Winthrop Rockefeller Foundation, named for its donor, the late governor of Arkansas, focuses its attention on economic development, education, and economic, racial, and social justice. The Woodruff-source funds in Atlanta recently invested heavily in a new "Achieve Atlanta" program in collaboration with the Community Foundation for Greater Atlanta and others to increase significantly the number of high school graduates by 2025. Two other exemplars of transformational philanthropy are the Z. Smith Reynolds Foundation in Winston-Salem, North Carolina, and its younger "cousin," the Mary Reynolds Babcock Foundation. The current vision of Z. Smith Reynolds is "to promote social, economic and environmental justice, to strengthen democracy, through an educated and informed populace, to encourage innovation and excellence in a dynamic nonprofit sector, to support progressive public policy and social change, to foster cooperation and respect among all racial, ethnic, and socio-economic groups, to build strong, vibrant, economically sound, and peaceful communities."[73] The Mary Reynolds Babcock Foundation states even more simply: "We seek to help people and places move out of poverty and achieve greater social and economic justice."[74] It also argues for the importance of involving youth and young adults in the work of philanthropy and is one of the few southern foundations that actively supports social justice advocacy by its not-for-profit grant recipients.

Another indicator of health in the South's philanthropy sector is the diversity of the staffs and boards of the region's foundations as women and people of color assume positions of leadership in a field that was for many years a white male-dominated sector. Midway through the second decade of the twenty-first century, the nation commemorated the fiftieth anniversaries of the 1964 and 1965 Civil Rights and Voting Rights Acts. Transformational in scope and a culmination of a long freedom movement that reaches back to the Colonial era, it is here that the South's true reconstruction begins and, with it, philanthropy's next episode. Like all foundations, those of the South retain a great deal of freedom. In a region rich with expanding promise and possibility, it is to be hoped they choose to exercise their growing wealth and influence to advance the hard-won gains that remain vital to all our futures.

MARTIN LEHFELDT, a writer and speaker, is a former foundation program officer; college administrator; consultant to local, regional, and national not-for-profit organizations; and President of the Southeastern Council of Foundations.

JAMIL ZAINALDIN is a historian, educator, and humanities advocate. President of Georgia Humanities since 1997, he works with communities, foundations, state government, educators, the National Endowment for the Humanities, and the nonprofit sector.

Acknowledgments: The authors express their appreciation to David Hammack and Stephen Smith for reading and suggesting improvements to the original version of this essay. We also acknowledge the helpful comments from John Inscoe and Stanley Katz. Any errors or omissions that remain are entirely our own, of course. Thank you also to the Fox Center for Humanistic Inquiry of Emory University, the Foundation Center, the Southeastern Council of Foundations, and Georgia Humanities for their contributions and encouragement.

NOTES

* This document is a highly condensed version of a full-length book manuscript, *The Promise: Grant-making Foundations and the Building of Civil Society in the South*, on which the authors continue to work.

1. See Thomas Adam, ed., *Philanthropy, Patronage, and Civil Society: Experiences from Germany, Great Britain, and North America* (Bloomington: Indiana University Press, 2004).

2. Adam Davis and Elizabeth Lynn, eds., *The Civically Engaged Reader* (Chicago: Great Books Foundation, 2006). This reflective reader on the diverse meanings of "civic" draws from literature, history, philosophy, commentary, and Biblical sources with chapters delineating "Associating," "Serving," "Giving," and "Leading."

3. It is always helpful as we approach a third decade of a new century to remember Maimonides and his reflections from a very distant past. See Maxwell King, "Maimonides and Me: Lessons from up and down the ladder of giving," in *Philanthropy Magazine* (May/June 2004), retrieved 10/21/17 at: http://www.philanthropyroundtable.org/magazine/may_june_2004. Maimonides' "Eight Levels of Tzedakah" appears in Amy A. Kass, ed. *Doing Well, Doing Good: Readings for Thoughtful Philanthropists* (Bloomington: Indiana University Press, 2008), 95–96.

4. Source: Foundation Center, 2015. For the purpose of this essay, "the South" includes the eleven-state region served by the Southeastern Council on Foundations.

5. Southern philanthropy also includes so-called "Christian foundations," denominational foundations, and Jewish federations—some of which are quite large—established to support the building of churches and synagogues, the work of seminaries and colleges, and other more specifically focused ecclesiastical activities such as evangelism and mission work. Many of them, like

community foundations, function as vehicles for personal giving. Space limitations do not permit a more extensive discussion of their role.

6. Ironically, Whitney's advocacy for the use of interchangeable parts in manufacturing later contributed greatly to the North's production capabilities and thereby to its victory in the Civil War. http://www.georgiaencyclopedia.org/articles/history-archaeology/eli-whitney-georgia (accessed October 21, 2017).

7. Slave ownership extended to between 20 percent and 25 percent of white families with significant distributional disparity (half of all slave owners owned five or fewer slaves; one in ten owned twenty or more).

8. Adam Rothman, "The Slave Power in the United States, 1783–1865," in Steve Fraser and Gary Gerstle, eds., *Ruling America: A History of Wealth and Power in a Democracy* (Harvard University Press, 2005), 72. See also Harold D. Woodman, *King Cotton and His Retainers: Financing and Marketing the Cotton Crop of the South, 1800–1925* (Lexington: University of Kentucky Press, 1968); Stephen Yafa, *Big Cotton: How A Humble Fiber Created Fortunes, Wrecked Civilizations, and Put America on the Map* (New York: Penguin, 2005).

9. Timothy James Lockley, *Welfare and Charity in the Antebellum South* (Gainesville: University Press of Florida, 2007), 3, 6, 114, 216. What Lockley has uniquely added to our perspective of regional charity is the overlapping similarities between North and South (especially commonalities of the role of women and "Republican Motherhood") as well as distinctive differences. On the significance of this perspective—essentially a claim for recognizing also a dynamism in Southern philanthropy that is generally associated with the antebellum North—see Philip N. Mulder, *The American Historical Review*, vol. 113, no. 5, 1 December 2008, 1539–40. See also note 15.

10. By 1830, both proslavery advocates in the South and abolitionists in the North were employing biblical citations to defend their positions, a pattern each side brought to the Civil War that imbued their causes with spiritual significance. Harry S. Stout, *Upon the Altar of the Nation: A Moral History of the Civil War* (New York: Viking, 2006). In his Second Inaugural Address President Lincoln wove his own message into these conflicting verities of belief: "It may seem strange that any men should dare to ask a just God's assistance in wringing their bread from the sweat of other men's faces, but let us judge not, that we be not judged. The prayers of both could not be answered. That of neither has been answered fully. The Almighty has His own purposes. 'Woe unto the world because of offenses; for it must needs be that offenses come, but woe to that man by whom the offense cometh.'" http://avalon.law.yale.edu/19th_century/lincoln2.asp (accessed October 21, 2017).

11. Smithson, an Englishman, was attracted to the United States because of its revolutionary commitment to liberty. A highly regarded scientist in his time, Smithson, who was no friend of slavery, proclaimed himself part of a scientific movement in Europe whose members saw themselves as "citizens of the globe and pledged allegiance first of all to truth and reason. Their highest aspiration was to be a benefactor of all mankind." Heather Ewing, *The Lost World of James Smithson* (New York: Bloomsbury, 2007), quoted in *Inside Smithsonian Research* no. 16 (Spring 2007): 15.

12. For perhaps the same reasons, and the confusion of mingling private funds with national governance, Congress had earlier declined to act on President George Washington's call for the creation of a national university. George Thomas, *The Founders and the Idea for a National University* (Cambridge: Cambridge University Press, 2014), 46–50.

13. John C. Calhoun, "On the Reception of Abolition Petitions," Feb. 6, 1837, *The Senate, 1789–1989, vol. 3, Classic Speeches, 1830–1993* (Washington, DC: Government Printing Office, 1995), 175.

14. Library of Congress, Exhibition, "Thomas Jefferson: The West," letter to John Holmes, Monticello, April 22, 1820; accessed 10/22/2017 at https://www.loc.gov/exhibits/jefferson/jeffwest.html#159.

15. On North–South charity distinctions, see Althea K. Nagai et al., *Giving for Social Change: Foundations, Public Policy, and the American Political Agenda* (Westport, CT: Praeger, 1994), 10; Kathleen D. McCarthy, *American Creed: Philanthropy and the Rise of Civil Society, 1700–1865* (Chicago: University of Chicago Press, 2003), 176–79. For an exception, though one that still points to regional differences, see Suzanne Lebsock, *Women Together: Organizations in Antebellum Petersburg, Virginia* (New York, 1984), excerpted in David C. Hammack, ed., *Making the Nonprofit Sector in the United States: A Reader* (Bloomington: Indiana University Press, 1998), 224–47. See also note 9.

16. In his now-classic overview, Edward Pessen concludes that "Northern acquiescence in southern slavery does not erase this crucial difference between the sections, but it does argue for the complementarity and economic interdependence of North and South." Edward Pessen, "How Different from Each Other Were Antebellum North and South?," *American Historical Review* 85, no. 5 (1980): 1123.

17. Bertram Wyatt-Brown, *Southern Honor: Ethics and Behavior in the Old South* (New York: Oxford University Press, 1982), 1–24. In this classic work, Wyatt-Brown utilizes Hawthorne's short story, "My Kinsman, Major Molineux," as a northern foil that encapsulates a New England conception of the role and place of honor during the era of the American Revolution that many Southerners shared in the 19th century. Wyatt-Brown suggests that ethics and, therefore, charity in the South be judged on its own terms and not (at least, exclusively) on its relationship with the institution of slavery.

18. Stig Forster and Jorg Nagler, eds., *On the Road to Total War: The American Civil War and the German Wars of Unification, 1861–71* (Cambridge, UK: Cambridge University Press, 1997).

19. Eric Foner, *Reconstruction: America's Unfinished Revolution, 1863–77* (New York: Harper & Row, 1988).

20. The "stricken South" and the fund's purpose appear in the appendix to the *Washington Congressional Globe* (February 13, 1867), 122.

21. Franklin Parker, *George Peabody: A Biography* (Nashville, TN: Vanderbilt University Press, 1971); Earle H. West, "The Peabody Fund and Negro Education, 1867–80," *History of Education Quarterly* (Summer, 1966): 3–21. The Peabody Fund anticipated the legal model for focused philanthropy. Barry D. Karl and Stanley N. Katz, "The American Philanthropic Foundation and the Public Sphere, 1890–1930," *Minerva* (Summer, 1981): 236–70.

22. Derrick P. Alridge, "Atlanta Compromise Speech," *New Georgia Encyclopedia*, accessed July 25, 2015 from http://www.georgiaencyclopedia.org. The construction of a "New South Creed," woven into a public relations appeal for Northern investment, is described in Paul M. Gaston, *The New South Creed: A Study in Southern Mythmaking* (Baton Rouge: Louisiana State University Press, 1976).

23. 163 US 537 (1896).

24. Charles R. Wilson, *Baptized in the Blood: The Religion of the Lost Cause, 1865–1920* (Athens: University of Georgia Press, 1980); Hugh Ruppersburg, "Gone With the Wind (Film)," *New Georgia Encyclopedia*, accessed July 25, 2015 from http://www.georgiaencyclopedia.org. One of the earliest mass fundraising appeals was that of the United Daughters of the Confederacy, founded in 1895. Their efforts supported the construction of thousands of monuments, cemeteries, and memorials—paid for with private donations—to Confederate veterans and war dead.

25. Dewey W. Grantham, *Southern Progressivism: The Reconciliation of Progress and Tradition* (Knoxville: University of Tennessee Press, 1983).

26. Leslie H. Fishel, Jr., "The John F. Slater Fund," *Hayes Historical Journal* (Fall, 1988): 47–51.

27. The GEB is assessed in Eric Anderson and Alfred A. Moss, Jr., *Dangerous Donations: Northern Philanthropy and Southern Black Education, 1902–30* (Columbia: University of Missouri Press, 1999), and John H. Stanfield II, "Private Foundations and Black Education and Intellectual Talent Development," in *Philanthropic Giving: Studies in Varieties and Goals*, ed. Richard Magat (New York: Oxford University Press, 1989), 340.

28. The Rockefeller Foundation created the Rockefeller Sanitary Commission in 1901 to eradicate the Hookworm Disease, thought to infect 40% of the region's population: Rockefeller Sanitary Commission for the Eradication of Hookworm Disease, *Annual Report* (Washington, D.C.: Offices of the Commission, 1911–15). See also John Ettling, *The Germ of Laziness: Rockefeller Philanthropy and Public Health in the New South* (Cambridge, MA: Harvard University Press, 1981).

29. Arthur D. Wright, *The Negro Rural School Fund, Inc.—Anna T. Jeanes Foundation, 1907–1933* (Washington, DC: Negro Rural School Fund, Inc., 1933); Lance G. E. Jones, *The Jeanes Teacher in the United States, 1908–33* (Chapel Hill: University of North Carolina Press, 1937).

30. Campbell became secretary of the North Carolina office; from there he traveled throughout the region, collecting data and documenting his findings. In 1921, the Russell Sage Foundation published (posthumously) Campbell's classic opus, *The Southern Highlander and His Homeland.* Also see David C. Hammack and Stanton Wheeler, *Social Science in the Making: Essays on the Russell Sage Foundation, 1907–47* (New York: Russell Sage Foundation, 1994), 1–33. The Foundation fostered institution building that combined research and political action.

31. Andrew Carnegie, "The Best Fields for Philanthropy," in *The North American Review* 149, no. 397 (December, 1889); Michael Lorenzen, "Deconstructing the Carnegie Libraries," accessed March 1, 2015 from http://www.lib.niu.edu/ipo/1999/il990275.html; Theodore Jones, *Carnegie Libraries across America: A Public Legacy* (Hoboken, NJ: Preservation Press, 1997).

32. Historians are divided in their interpretation of Northern philanthropy in the South. James D. Anderson writes, "Northern philanthropists were undoubtedly motivated by a mixture of sentimentalism, humanitarianism, and sociopolitical interests . . . designed primarily to develop an economically efficient and politically stable southern agricultural economy by training efficient and contented black laborers while leaving the southern racial hierarchy intact." "Northern Foundations and the Shaping of Southern Black Rural Education, 1902–35," *History of Education Quarterly* 18, no. 4 (Winter 1978):371–96. But it is also the case that some proponents as well as critics of philanthropy have adopted a view of blacks as passive, if not helpless objects of charity, when the reality is that blacks themselves were substantial donors as an exercise in self-help. See J. M. Stephen Peeps, "Northern Philanthropy and the Emergence of Black Higher Education: Do-Gooders, Compromisers, or Co-Conspirators?," *Journal of Negro Education* 50 (1981): 251–69. A more recent critique of Julius Rosenwald and his partnership with Booker T. Washington is "Booker T. Washington: The Great American Philanthropist Who Decided What Blacks Should Teach," *The Journal of Blacks in Higher Education*, No. 24 (Summer, 1999), 52–55. For a parallel analysis in the North, see David C. Hammack, "Patronage and the Great Institutions of the Cities of the United States: Questions and Evidence, 1800–2000," in Adam, *Philanthropy, Patronage, and Civil Society*, 79–100.

33. Alfred Perkins, *Edwin Rogers Embree: The Julius Rosenwald Fund Foundation Philanthropy and American Race Relations* (Bloomington: Indiana University Press, 2011), 95–132; James D. Anderson, *The Education of Blacks in the South, 1860–1935* (Chapel Hill: University of North Carolina Press, 1988), 238–78. Mary Hoffschwelle's study, *The Rosenwald Schools of the American South* (Gainesville: University Press of Florida, 2006), documents the number of schools constructed with Rosenwald support (5,358) as well as their distribution in fifteen southern states. The close working relationship between Rosenwald and Booker T. Washington is the focus of Stephanie Deutsch's study, *You Need a Schoolhouse: Booker T. Washington, Julius Rosenwald, and the Building of Schools for the Segregated South* (Evanston: Northwestern University Press, 2015).

34. John M. Barry, *Rising Tide: The Great Mississippi Flood of 1927 and How It Changed America* (New York: Simon & Schuster, 1997), 331; Robert H. Bremner, *American Philanthropy* (Chicago: University of Chicago Press, 1988), 129–30.

35. K. Clements, *The Life of Herbert Hoover: Imperfect Visionary, 1918–1928* (New York: Palgrave MacMillan, 2010), 371–94; The Commonwealth Fund, *Annual Report* (New York: Harkness

House, 1932); "History of Fund Work" at http://www.commonwealthfund.org/about-us/foundation-history (accessed October 21, 2017).

36. On the role of missionaries in the South and their impact on education in South Carolina and Georgia, see generally Elizabeth Jacoway, *Yankee Missionaries in the South: The Penn School Experiment* (Baton Rouge: Louisiana State University Press, 1980), 23–61 and Jacqueline Jones, *Soldiers of Light and Love: Northern Teachers and Georgia Blacks, 1865–1873* (Chapel Hill: University of North Carolina Press, 1980), 109–39. On the role of the AMA in the development of black schools and colleges, see Joe M. Richardson, *Christian Reconstruction: The American Missionary Association and Southern Blacks, 1861–1890* (Tuscaloosa: University of Alabama Press: 2009), 1–14, 35–54; Leon Litwack, *Been in the Storm So Long: The Aftermath of Slavery* (New York: Alfred A. Knopf, 1979), 450–501.

37. Adam Faircloth, *Teaching Equality: Black Schools in the Age of Jim Crow* (Athens: University of Georgia Press, 2001), 1–19; Emmett D. Carson, "The Evolution of Black Philanthropy: Patterns of Giving and Voluntarism" in Magat, *Philanthropic Giving*, 92–102; John H. Stanfield II, *Historical Foundations of Black Reflective Sociology* (Routledge, London and New York, 2016), 59–82; John H. Donohue III, James J. Heckman, and Petra E. Todd, "The Schooling of Southern Blacks: The Roles of Legal Activism and Private Philanthropy, 1910–1960," *Quarterly Journal of Economics*, February, 2002, 225–68.

38. The New Englander William Lloyd Garrison is commonly credited as the founder of the abolitionist movement. In fact, it began in 1817 with "3,000 African Americans gathered in Philadelphia to protest colonization." Wendy Gamber, "Antebellum Reform: Salvation, Social Control, and Social Transformation," in *Charity, Philanthropy, and Civility in American History*, eds. Lawrence J. Friedman and Mark D. McGarvie (New York: Cambridge University Press, 2004), 148. During the Great Migration, blacks formed nonprofit associations like the National Association for the Advancement of Colored People (NAACP), the National Urban League, the African American branches of the YMCA and YWCA, and Marcus Garvey's Universal Negro Improvement Association (UNIA). Claude A. Clegg III, "Philanthropy, the Civil Rights Movement, and the Politics of Racial Reform," in Friedman and McGarvie, *Charity, Philanthropy, and Civility*, 344. W. E. B. DuBois's scholarship documented the initiatives and improvement efforts of blacks to buttress his argument that it was racism, and not lack of ability, that made bleak the prospects of African Americans in the South and the United States. W. E. B. DuBois, *Economic Cooperation among Negro Americans* (Atlanta, 1907), excerpted in Hammack, *Making the Nonprofit Sector*, 265–80.

39. http://www.feildstudentloans.org/ (accessed October 21, 2017).

40. Mississippi, like other southern states, had a long, strong history of individual charitable giving. However, this law stunted the establishment and growth of private foundations as well as university endowments for nearly a century (it was not repealed until the 1987–88 legislative session).

41. David C. Hammack, "Community Foundations: The Delicate Question of Purpose," in *An Agile Servant: Community Leadership by Community Foundations*, ed. Richard Magat (New York: The Foundation Center, 1989), 23–50.

42. http://docsouth.unc.edu/bios/pn0000547_bio.html:http://www.wsfoundation.org/about.html (accessed October 21, 2017).

43. "Spartanburg County Foundation: Your Community Foundation" at http://spcf.org/about-us/our-history/ (accessed October 25, 2017).

44. For example, the Rich family in Atlanta, the Godchaux family in New Orleans, the Thalhimers in Richmond, the Goldsmiths in Memphis, the Hesses in Birmingham.

45. Stuart Rockoff, "Community Engagement: A Southern Jewish Legacy," accessed October 21, 2017, from www.isjl.org/history.html.

46. Julie Adkins, Laurie Occhipinti, and Tara Hefferan, eds., *Not by Faith Alone: Social Services, Social Justice, and Faith-Based Organizations in the United States* (New York: Rowman & Littlefield,

2010), 1–32, 165–86; Gary A. Tobin, *The Transition of Communal Values and Behavior in Jewish Philanthropy* (San Francisco: Institute for Jewish and Community Research, 2001) 14–17. On *Tzedakah* (philanthropy and social justice) as a tenet of American "Civil Judaism," see Jonathan Woocher, *Sacred Survival: The Civil Religion of American Jews* (Bloomington: Indiana University Press, 1986), 87–89.

47. J. Trent Alexander, "Demographic Patterns of the Great Black Migration," in Steven A. Reich, *The Great Black Migration: A Historical Encyclopedia of the American Mosaic* (Santa Barbara, Denver, Oxford: ABC-Clio), 96–98.

48. Neil Fligstein, *Going North: Migration of Blacks and Whites from the South, 1900–1950* (New York: Academic Press, 1981), 93–106.

49. For the story of an urban mill community dependent upon rural in-migration, see Douglass Flamming, *Creating the Modern South: Millhands and Managers in Dalton, Georgia, 1884–1984* (Chapel Hill: University of North Carolina Press, 1992), 79–119.

50. US Census Bureau, "Urban and Rural Population 1900–1990," released Oct. 1995.

51. W. J. Cash, "The Mind of the South," *The American Mercury*, Oct. 1929, 185–192. A readable PDF of the article can be accessed at www.unz.org/Pub/AmMercury-1929oct-00185?View=PDF (accessed October 21, 2017). Cash expanded his essay twelve years later into a classic statement that influenced a rising generation of Southern intellectuals, writers, and historians. His treatment of the region was a frontal assault on the mythology of the Old South, whose tradition of violence and racism seemed to him to constitute a social pathology. Alfred A. Knopf, Inc. published the first edition of the book, *The Mind of the South*, 1941.

52. In Roosevelt's "Message to the Conference on Economic Conditions of the South," July 4, 1938, he writes: "It is my conviction that the South presents right now the nation's No. 1 economic problem-the nation's problem, not merely the South's. For we have an economic unbalance in the nation as a whole, due to this very condition of the South." Gerhard Peters and John T. Woolley, *The American Presidency Project*. http://www.presidency.ucsb.edu/ws/?pid=15670 (accessed October 21, 2017).

53. Huntington Cairns, ed., *The American Scene: A Reader* (New York: Knopf, 1977), 157–68.

54. "[W]hen Democrats gained control of the House in 1931, southerners wielded the chairman's gavel on 29 of 47 committees—including virtually all the most influential panels: Ways and Means (James W Collier of Mississippi), Rules (Edward W. Pou of North Carolina), Rivers and Harbors (Joseph J. Mansfield of Texas), Naval Affairs (Carl Vinson of Georgia), Military Affairs (Percy Quin of Mississippi), Judiciary (Hatton Sumners of Texas), Interstate and Foreign Commerce (Sam Rayburn of Texas), Banking and Currency (Henry B. Steagall of Alabama), Appropriations (Joseph W. Byrns of Tennessee), and Agriculture (John Marvin Jones of Texas). Of the 10 most attractive committees, southerners chaired nine (J. Charles Linthicum of Maryland, a border state, chaired the Foreign Affairs Committee). Southerners also held two of the top three positions in House leadership: John Nance Garner of Texas served as Speaker, and John McDuffie of Alabama was the Majority Whip." In "Power of the Southern Bloc in Congress," History, Art, and Archives: United States House of Representatives, accessed October 21, 2017, http://history.house.gov/Exhibitions-and-Publications/BAIC/Historical-Essays/Temporary-Farewell/Southern-Bloc/.

Regarding their "social views" which extended as well to state and local domains, the classic statement is V.O. Key's: "the predominant consideration in the architecture of southern political institutions has been to assure locally a subordination of the Negro population and, externally, to block threatened interferences from the outside with these local arrangements." *Southern Politics in State and Nation* (reprinted by University of Tennessee Press, 1984), 665.

55. John M. Glen, *Highlander: No Ordinary School* (Knoxville: University of Tennessee Press, 1996), 9–26, 154–84.

56. A brief history of the SEF appears in "150 Years," at: http://www.southerneducation.org/150-Menu-Test/150-Years-of-SEF-2.aspx (accessed October 21, 2017). The question of how to assess the effectiveness of Northern philanthropy on the eve of World War II (in terms of objectives, impact, and degree of complicity with the Southern status quo) is examined in Roy E. Finkenbine, "Law, Reconstruction, and African American Education in the Post-Emancipation South," in Friedman and McGarvie, *Charity, Philanthropy, and Civility*, 161–78. Finkenbine points out that for all the compromises made with institutionalized racism, Northern-supported colleges for blacks in the South "provided meaningful training in the liberal arts" for those "who challenged the existing racial prejudices and worked fervently for a more egalitarian future."

57. Morton Sosna, "More Important than the Civil War? The Impact of World War II on the South," *Perspectives on the American South: An Annual Review of Society, Politics and Culture* 4 (1987): 145–58.

58. Mike Cheatham, *Your Friendly Neighbor: The Story of Georgia's Coca-Cola Bottling Families* (Macon, GA: Mercer University Press, 1999), 1–24. Bottling rights included a negotiated agreement with an independent franchise that enjoyed exclusive access to Coca-Cola syrup. By 1930, bottle sales of Coca-Cola for the first time exceeded fountain sales, making small (and here and there, large) fortunes for dozens of owners in communities throughout the South like Columbus, Birmingham, Hattiesburg, New Orleans, Chattanooga, and Tallahassee. Setting an example for local bottlers who adopted "Your Friendly Neighbor" as their community motto, Robert Woodruff, the company's CEO, gave generously and always anonymously, though few were fooled.

59. See "Robert Woodruff," at http://www.georgiaencyclopedia.org/articles/business-economy/robert-w-woodruff-1889-1985 (accessed 10/25/2017). Through his foundation's gifts, Woodruff did more to establish Atlanta as the capital of the new South than any other individual. Among the lesser-known stories are his behind-the-scenes role in establishing the institution known today as the Centers for Disease Control and Prevention. After Woodruff's death in 1985, the board changed the foundation's name to the Robert W. Woodruff Foundation. The foundation shares office and staff with the Joseph B. Whitehead, Lettie Pate Evans, and Lettie Pate Whitehead Foundations, though each is governed by its own board and charter. This arrangement came about through the friendship and business relationship between Woodruff and Lettie Pate Whitehead Evans, the wife of one of the original Coca-Cola bottlers and the first woman to serve on the Coca-Cola Company's board of directors.

60. The proceeds from that liquidation included a one-time gift of $105 million to Emory University.

61. www.anygreenplace.com/jones/WilliamGregg.pdf (accessed October 21, 2017).

62. http://www.blacknews.com/directory/black_african_american_organizations.shtml (accessed October 21, 2017).

63. Harry S. Ashmore, *The Negro and the Schools* (Chapel Hill: University of North Carolina Press, 1954).

64. http://resourcegeneration.org/2014/07/50-years-after-the-civil-rights-act-the-four-key-foundations-who-funded-the-movement/ (accessed October 21, 2017); J. Craig Jenkins, "Social Movement Philanthropy and American Democracy," in Magat, *Philanthropic Giving*, 293–314; Clegg, "Philanthropy, the Civil Rights Movement, and the Politics of Racial Reform," 341–61.

65. Gene Roberts and Hank Klibanoff, *The Race Beat* (New York: Knopf, 2006), 12–23.

66. Lillian E. Smith, *Killers of the Dream* (New York: W.W. Norton, 1949); "Lillian E. Smith," http://www.georgiaencyclopedia.org/articles/arts-culture/lillian-smith-1897-1966 (accessed October 21, 2017).

67. This percentage is for the eleven states included in this study. Source: 2010 US Census.

68. The National Center for Family Philanthropy reports that of *all* family foundations created since 1990, 78 percent have less than $10 million in assets. https://www.ncfp.org/blog/2015/nov-ten-biggest-trends-in-family-philanthropy (accessed October 21, 2017).

69. https://www.bc.edu/content/dam/files/research_sites/cwp/pdf/41trillionreview1.pdf (accessed October 21, 2017).

70. Source: Foundation Center, 2015.

71. Foundation for the Carolinas in Charlotte ($1.8+ billion) and the Community Foundation for Greater Atlanta ($900+ million).

72. Sabrina Jones Niggel and William P. Brandon, "Health Legacy Foundations: A New Census," *Health Affairs* 33, no. 1 (2014): 172–77.

73. https://www.grantforward.com/sponsor/detail/z-smith-reynolds-foundation-2213 (accessed October 21, 2017).

74. https://www.mrbf.org/about (accessed October 21, 2017).

chapter seven

THE FOUNDATIONS OF TEXAS

Peter Frumkin and Heather MacIndoe

EVERYTHING IN TEXAS IS BIGGER, even its philanthropic foundations. From its history in the oil and cattle industries to its distinctive politics and talk of independence, Texas has always been something of an outlier. Its large philanthropic sector is varied and distinctive and its practices reflect the state's culture and pride. Today, there are over six thousand private foundations in the state, controlling over $24 billion in assets. More than half of these philanthropic assets are held by a group of 146 large foundations, each with endowments of more than $25 million (see table 7.1). The three thousand small Texas foundations with endowments under $1 million control collectively less than $1 billion of the state's philanthropic wealth. Thus, while big foundations flourish in Texas, just like other regions in the country, there is still room for the smaller institutions. Compared to other states, Texas ranks high in terms of its representation on the list of the hundred largest foundations in the United States. On this list of the hundred largest foundations ranked by assets, Texas appears seven times, behind only New York and California.

What is distinctive about Texas philanthropy? What is special about the regulatory environment in the state? Who benefits from Texas philanthropy? How are foundation grants geographically distributed in this large state? These are some of the questions we try to answer in this chapter. We review the landscape and history of Texas foundations, then turn to an analysis of current giving, focusing on the movement of philanthropic funds across the regions of the state.

DISTINCTIVE REGULATORY TREATMENT

The philanthropic landscape of Texas is shaped at least in part by a distinctive regulatory and policy history. Aimed at keeping philanthropic funds at home, Texas has over the years experimented with ways of

Table 7.1. Distribution of Texas Foundations by Assets

Total Asset Level	Number	Number Filing with IRS	Total Revenue	Total Assets
Under $1 million	3,206	2,928	469,356,512	994,403,613
$1–10 million	3,078	1,187	946,816,494	4,090,151,022
$10–25 million	174	174	696,643,575	2,997,613,975
More than $25 million	146	146	2,023,097,983	16,910,152,886
Total	6,604	4,435	4,135,914,564	24,992,321,496

Source: Internal Revenue Service (IRS) Business Master File (01/2007), National Center for Charitable Statistics.

ensuring that wealth that is created in Texas stays in Texas. In addition, the landscape and shape of the Texas foundation field has been affected by developments in the broader area.

The most transparent attempt to keep Texas money in the state can be found in the state's laws related to inheritance taxes. Under Articles 7119 and 7122 of Chapter V, Revised Civil Statutes of 1925, the Texas law on inheritance taxes allowed property passing to or for the use of any religious, educational, or charitable organization within the state of Texas to be eligible for a significantly lower tax rate.[1] However, transferring or using the property *outside* of Texas would result in an inheritance tax of up to 20 percent, depending on the size of the estate. Table 7.2 provides a comparison of tax rates on inherited property within Texas and outside of Texas.

This pro-Texas bias was in place for some forty years. In 1965, the law was changed to excuse bequests to tax-exempt foundations from this inheritance tax even if they are located or have previously supported organizations outside Texas. However, this old tax break may explain why so many of the foundations created between 1925 and 1965 focus their giving exclusively in Texas.

The legacy of legislating geographic restrictions on Texas foundation giving extends to the present day. In 2009, Texas adopted a new law to ensure that orphan trusts, or trusts under the stewardship of lawyers or banks after their founders have died, continue to comply with the founders' wishes. The law requires trustees to notify the state attorney general's office and to secure court approval before moving a trust or foundation out of Texas.[3] The courts are directed to determine whether moving a trust out of Texas would interfere with the trustee's ability to comply with the donor's intentions. This situation arises when the local banks originally selected as trustees are acquired by multinational financial institutions

Table 7.2. Tax Rates on Inherited Property in Texas, 1925

Taxable Value	Inheritance Tax Rates (1925)	
	Within Texas	Outside Texas
$0–$500	0%	0%
$501–$10,000	0%	5%
$10,001–$25,000	0%	6%
$25,001–$50,000	1%	8%
$50,001–$100,000	2%	10%
$100,001–$200,000	3%	12%
$200,001–$500,000	4%	12%
$500,001–$1,000,000	5%	15%
$1,000,000+	6%	20%

Source: Texas Revised Civil Statutes of 1925.[2]

based outside Texas. The law intends to prevent nonfamily trustees, such as banks and lawyers, from using the foundation's assets to serve interests other than the founders' because family trustees are no longer around to encourage compliance. Like the older inheritance law, the underlying intent of this measure is to ensure that that the interests of donors and recipients in Texas be protected.

Beyond these regulatory quirks, Texas foundations also confront broader more universal regulations that have shaped the entire field. For example, the Tax Reform Act of 1969 (TRA 1969) set forth the federal definition of a private foundation that is still in use today. Foundations are subject to the mandatory distributions regulation (section 4942) that requires private foundations to make minimum annual distributions for their charitable purposes equal to the greater of their net annual income and a fixed percent of the fair market value of its assets held for investment.[4]

In addition, all private foundations must abide by the restrictions on excess business holdings (section 4943 of TRA 1969), which prohibits a private foundation and its disqualified persons from together holding more than a 20 percent interest in any donor-controlled business enterprise.[5] One example of this provision's impact on private foundations is illustrated in the case of the Houston Endowment. Under this provision, the foundation had to sell its controlling interest in the *Houston Chronicle* by a statutory deadline of 1989. In 1983, the foundation was able to muster enough political clout to persuade twenty-three members of the Texas delegation to the US House of Representatives to sponsor a special bill that would exempt the foundation from the excess business holdings provision, allowing it to retain its ownership of the newspaper. The bill failed, and the Houston Endowment sold its interest in the *Chronicle* to the Hearst Corporation in 1987, two years before the final divestiture deadline.

The Big Foundations of Texas

In her historical review of private philanthropic foundations in Texas (1920–1950), Mary Kelley identifies George W. Brackenridge as the first Texas entrepreneur whose wealth was contributed to form a private foundation.[6] In 1925, five years after his death, the trustees of Breckenridge's estate established a foundation to support the education of black and white students. Kelley characterizes 1930 to 1945 as a period of strong growth for Texas foundations. Some of the foundations established during this period (e.g., Moody Foundation, Houston Endowment, Brown Foundation) remain among the largest in the state today.

The Moody Foundation was created in 1942 with the diverse assets of William L. Moody, which included the American National Insurance Company, the Moody National Bank of Galveston, three newspapers, a hotel chain, vast ranchland, and many oil and mineral properties. The foundation's website states that it was created to fulfill the mission of benefiting "in perpetuity present and future generations of Texans," but Waldemar Nielsen reports that Moody's main concerns in creating the foundation were to ensure that his family retained control over his properties and to avoid taxes.[7] Moody stipulated that the corpus of the trust was to be kept intact and its income applied to religious, charitable, scientific, and educational purposes within Texas. According to Texas law at the time, using the property to benefit these issues within the state allowed the foundation to significantly decrease its inheritance taxes.

After Moody's death in 1954, the foundation became embroiled in a series of family legal disputes that divided its four family trustees into two rival factions. As a result of a lawsuit filed by the Texas attorney general alleging that the foundation could not operate for the benefit of the people of Texas under its current conditions, the family made several compromises and added three nonfamily members to the board of trustees. These independent trustees worked to activate the foundation while combating new legal, financial, and managerial problems.

The foundation's early gifts were mostly to local charities, but after 1960 it began funding programs throughout Texas. Large contributions to colleges, hospitals, and welfare organizations to build new facilities and support to children's health projects, libraries, and historic preservation were characteristic of this period. In the 1970s and 1980s, the Moody

Foundation initiated several large projects, including the restoration of a train depot as a railroad museum and offices for local nonprofits, the construction of Galveston Island Musical Theater and the Transitional Learning Center, and the preliminary development of the Moody Gardens complex. During this time, the foundation also began to focus on people-oriented programs, supporting educational scholarship and loan programs, social welfare agencies, and arts organizations. The Moody Foundation's giving is still heavily focused on Galveston, but with the establishment of another office, it is making efforts to expand coordination of grantmaking in North Texas. Its presence in Austin and Dallas is particularly in the areas of children's issues, environmental projects, social services, and arts education.

The Houston Endowment was incorporated in 1937 by Jesse H. Jones, who made his fortune as a builder and real estate operator. Like Moody, Jones also acquired assets in a variety of fields including life insurance, banking, ranchland, and urban real estate. After his death, the Houston Endowment received controlling shares in twenty-six separate corporations in addition to various urban and rural properties and mineral rights. This made it necessary for the foundation board to devote substantial efforts to direct business management, such as the acquisition the rival newspaper *Houston Press* by the endowment-owned *Houston Chronicle* in 1964.[8]

By the mid-1950s, the Houston Endowment's properties included many prominent buildings and businesses in Houston, Fort Worth, and New York City. Its general investment strategy has been to upgrade and ensure the profitability of its properties, and then to convert them into a diversified portfolio of government and corporate securities. In response to the excess business holdings portion of the US Tax Reform Act of 1969, the foundation began selling its businesses and buildings and investing the proceeds in securities. The sale of the *Houston Chronicle* to the Hearst Corporation in 1987 completed this process.[9]

Much like the Moody Foundation, the Houston Endowment was created with the mission of supporting any charitable, educational, or religious undertaking. Early grants were primarily used to construct facilities, such as a performing arts center, hospital facilities for the Texas Medical Center, and the Houston Museum of Fine Arts. However, the foundation's philanthropic efforts have slowly shifted away from facility construction and more towards social and quality-of-life issues. Following Jones's wishes, the endowment had a philanthropic focus on education from the beginning, creating a scholarship program for high school seniors in 1958 that continues today. Jones also had a personal interest in the development of higher education for blacks, which is reflected in a number of grants to black colleges. Historically, the Houston Endowment has had an excellent legacy in prudent asset management in order to provide good health-care facilities, promote educational opportunity for students of all classes and backgrounds, and support the development of the performing arts in Houston and southeastern Texas.

Herman Brown was another construction magnate, a cofounder of the Brown and Root engineering and construction firm that is now one of the world's largest building companies. He and his brother, George, formed the Brown Foundation in 1951 to "distribute funds for public charitable purposes, principally for support, encouragement and assistance to education, the arts and community service."[10] Its focus on the arts is probably a result of Herman Brown's wife, Margarett Root Brown's, interest in art, ballet, literature, and music. Margarett Brown served on the boards of various arts organizations and encouraged Herman, who was more of a businessman than a philanthropist, to serve on several civic boards as well. Herman Brown's civic record, which includes both philanthropy and business practices, is not without some controversy, particularly in the area of labor relations.[11]

Before 1970, the Brown Foundation had no full-time professional staff and operated out of offices at Brown and Root. After the US 1969 Tax Reform Act was passed, the foundation opened several separate offices and appointed a financial officer from Brown and Root as its executive head. The foundation's board still consists predominantly of family members. Since its inception, the foundation has disbursed more than $1 billion to supporting the arts and humanities, education, medicine and science, and civic and public affairs. Approximately 80 percent of foundation funds have been awarded within Texas, with a special emphasis on the Houston area. Many of its earlier grants were used for land, buildings, and endowments to Texas colleges, hospitals, and museums. The Brown Foundation makes grants to fund other organizations and does not have any philanthropic projects of its own. During their lifetimes, Herman and George Brown made it clear that they disliked publicity and preferred their donations to remain anonymous. Reflecting these wishes, as of 1970, the Brown Foundation did not issue public reports; instead, it permitted its grantees to release information only when necessary.[12]

Sid W. Richardson made his fortune in the oil booms of the American Southwest after the 1930s. Although he began donating to local charities and student scholarships after becoming affluent, he set up the

Sid W. Richardson Foundation in 1947 to broaden his philanthropic horizons at the urging of friend and civic leader Amon Carter. After his death in 1959, most of his properties were transferred to the foundation, including land, oil leases, operating companies, and a portfolio of stocks and bonds. In 1961, the foundation had to take out loans to pay back the complicated tax liabilities associated with Richardson's estate. Thus it had to devote much of its income for the next decade to pay off loans. Much of its efforts also focused on managing its properties, collecting revenues, and settling obligations and claims. The Richardson Foundation's board has always been small, with four or five trustees, including family members and executives of Richardson businesses. Except for the Richardson Collection of Western Art, the Richardson Foundation is primarily a grant-making entity that does not have other philanthropic projects of its own. Most of its grants go toward physical facilities and general support of education, healthcare, human services, and the arts.

Like Richardson, Algur H. Meadows became wealthy through his success in the oil business. He built the General American Oil Company of Texas into one of the most prosperous independent oil and gas production companies in the nation. In 1948, he established the Meadows Foundation with his first wife, Virginia, to support the people and institutions of Texas. During their lifetimes, the foundation enabled the Meadows to establish programs throughout Texas in health, education, arts and culture, human and social services, and civic development. For example, Meadows donated his extensive Spanish art collection to Southern Methodist University (SMU) to form a museum in the memory of his first wife. He also gave SMU a collection of contemporary Italian sculpture to honor his second wife, and much of his Impressionist collection was donated to the Dallas Museum of Art after his death. Within its five general areas of giving, the foundation currently supports three initiatives in particular: improving public education, protecting the environment, and reducing mental illness. Its current grant strategy is to prioritize the provision of essential human services and to focus otherwise on the above three issue areas.

Texas foundation philanthropy was shaped by the formation of one of the first regional associations of grantmakers in 1948. This group, now known as the Council of Southwest Foundations (CSF), hosted the first Conference of Texas Foundations and Trusts in 1949.[13] The organization became a clearinghouse for information about establishing and maintaining philanthropic foundations. They published the first directory of Texas foundations in 1954 and began offering a quarterly newsletter in

1957. In 2008, the CSF hosted a sixtieth anniversary celebration in Austin. Today, the council has over two hundred foundation members from seven southwestern states and continues its work to help foundations better fulfill their charitable missions. The fact that the council has a regional focus and not an explicitly Texas focus has opened the way for numerous smaller city and state groups of grantmakers to flourish over time. These groups satisfy the needs of Texas foundations in cities like Houston and Dallas and allow them to meet and discuss local issues and concerns.

The many large Texas foundations ultimately share a few features, no matter the differences in their origins and operation. Philanthropy in the large foundations has long been understood as giving back to Texas out of pride in the state. Unlike the way donors might think about giving in other parts of the country—where a city might be the locus of loyalty—many of the large foundations of Texas were set up by donors with large personalities who believed in the special status and exceptionalism of Texas. These ideas and feelings have a long history, reaching all the way back to questions of whether Texas deserved to be a republic unto itself.

Geographical and Subject Focus

Almost all twenty of the largest Texas foundations still primarily, if not exclusively, direct their giving within the state. Twelve foundations specifically restrict their grants to programs located within Texas and only consider out-of-state initiatives that will directly benefit Texans, such as creating a Texas chapter of a national organization that is headquartered in another state. The remaining foundations do not require as stringent an affiliation with Texas for their grantees, but they still predominantly focus on specific regions of the state. However, this giving pattern may be slowly changing in some foundations, such as the Burnett Foundation. Although it donates a substantial portion of its grants to the Fort Worth area, the Burnett Foundation has also recently supported relatively unaffiliated out-of-state initiatives, such as various art museums in Santa Fe, New Mexico, a cancer center in New York, and Oregon Public Broadcasting.

The Dell Foundation is a more extreme example of this shift toward greater geographic inclusiveness. After its creation in 1999, Dell's initial grants were primarily used to improve education and children's health in Austin and central Texas. However, in just ten years, it has expanded its giving to a national and international scope, with particular attention to India and Africa.[14] It is the only foundation of the group that supports international projects, which may be related to several factors that further distinguish it from the other foundations. The Dell Foundation is not only

the most recently established foundation; it is also especially si
that it was founded during a period of increasing cultural an
globalization, using assets derived from technological advances tha
drove and benefited from such interconnectedness.

This contrasts with the other foundations' funding sources, which were generally derived from local natural resources such as oil, minerals, ranchland, lumber, or services targeted towards a regional customer base such as newspapers, hotels, or banking. Outsourcing labor, customer service, supply provision, and manufacturing to other countries, and interacting with foreign markets and competitors in the course of his business dealings, undoubtedly made founder Michael Dell more personally connected to, and concerned with, conditions in foreign countries than other Texas foundation donors, who were not nearly as affected by international contact in their lifetimes. Although those donors had strong allegiances to Texas and their specific regions, the convergence of these factors makes the Dells much more globally conscious and may explain the unique position of their foundation as the only one that awards grants worldwide.

There is a substantial amount of overlap in the issues funded by the large Texas foundations. All of the foundations described above focus on one of the following common areas of philanthropic interest: education, arts, medicine and health, human and social services, and community development. Public safety, religion, and wildlife preservation are some of the issues that these large foundations address. Across these areas, the big foundations of Texas have generally not shied away from giving grants for constructing facilities or other capital expenditures, such as building schools, hospitals, parks, and cultural centers, especially early on in their giving. In *The Golden Donors,* Waldemar Nielsen describes this phenomenon as a tendency for Texan foundations to monumentalize the donors through their philanthropy.[15] Many of the donors' wives have steered their philanthropy toward developing the arts in Texas, thus helping to meet the state's need for social infrastructure. However, Texas foundations have not made much impact in addressing social problems such as racism or poverty. Compared to their long-standing support for educational scholarship programs or various arts initiatives, Texas foundations have only recently begun to focus more on funding social and human services. Environmental sustainability is another overlooked field, possibly because many foundations are funded by oil money or hold interests in oil-related enterprises. The Meadows Foundation is one of the few foundations in the group focusing on environmental issues. It has recently adopted green building guidelines and gives preference to grantees whose construction

or renovation funding requests follow these recommendations to help meet its goals for reducing water and energy consumption.

In sum, the foundation field in Texas is large, but it is populated by a small group of institutions that control the preponderance of philanthropic funds. The distinctive regional identity of Texas foundations can be found in an element of the broader culture of the state: a pride in Texas and a desire to advance the interests of its residents and communities. While some of the new money that was created by the technology boom is beginning to broaden horizons, changes in philanthropy—and in Texas—tend to be slow and incremental.

Texas Foundation Grantmaking in Recent Decades

In order to provide an overview of recent Texas grantmaking, we analyze cross-sectional data from the Foundation Center. Although the Foundation Center grant data is not an exact census of US grantmaking, it arguably presents the best available data set of the most influential foundation giving, offering a sample of the largest US foundations. The data include grants made by Texas foundations to recipients located outside of Texas (non-Texas grants). The grants data is supplemented with foundation information (foundation age, assets, type, location) from the Foundation Center's *Foundation Directory Online*.[16]

Table 7.3 provides an overview of the Texas grant data. The Texas grant data describe 20,206 grants made by 653 foundations, 112 of which are headquartered in Texas, to approximately five thousand Texas nonprofits. The number of grants and the total dollar amount of the grants doubled from 1990 to 2003. These fourteen years of grantmaking describe $2.4 billion in grants made to Texas nonprofits by foundations in Texas and other parts of the United States.

One distinctive pattern in the Texas grant data is that the majority of foundation grants made to Texas nonprofits were made by Texas foundations. Figure 7.1 shows the distribution of grant dollars to Texas nonprofits according to foundation location. The shaded portion of each bar indicates the proportion of grant dollars donated by Texas foundations (79.3 percent on average). Texas nonprofits also won grants from foundations located outside of the state. Thirty percent of national foundation givers to Texas nonprofits are located in the Midwest, 29 percent in the Northeast, 25 percent in the South, 14 percent in the Pacific Northwest, and 2 percent in the West. Prior research on foundation philanthropy has established that the majority of foundation grantmaking is concentrated in the local area or region where the foundation is located.[17]

Table 7.3. Foundation Grants to Texas Nonprofit Organizations[a]

Year	No. of Grants	%	Total Dollars (millions)	%
1990	3,166	15.7	$385.0	16.1
1995	4,413	21.8	$445.7	18.7
2000	6,360	31.5	$774.6	32.4
2003	6,267	31.0	$784.3	32.8
Total	20,206	100	$2,389.6	100

[a]Grants from Texas and national foundations.
Source: Foundation Center.

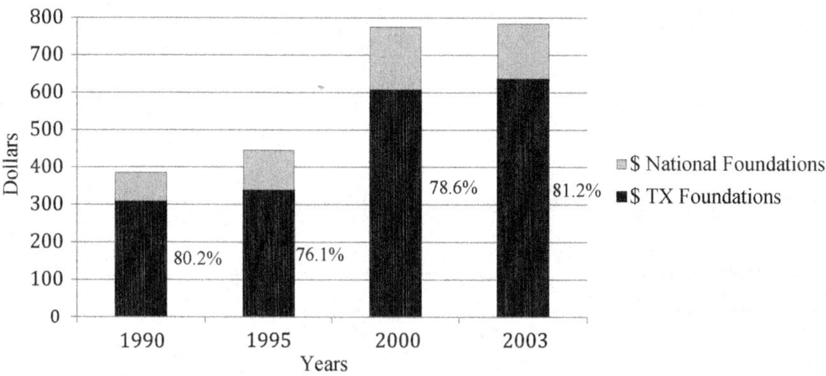

Figure 7.1. Distribution of Grant Dollars (millions) by Foundation Location
Source: Foundation Center.

Table 7.4 identifies the top ten Texas foundation donors in the data. With one exception, the Communities Foundation of Texas (a community foundation), all of the top Texas donors in the decade around the turn of the millennium are independent foundations. The Houston Endowment, the largest Texas foundation donor, accounts for 11 percent of grant dollars from Texas foundations during this period. Giving is highly concentrated among the top ten Texas foundations, which together account for 51 percent of grant dollars from Texas foundations to Texas nonprofits. Giving by the top ten national foundations is concentrated, but to a lesser degree than giving by the top ten Texas foundations. Together these foundations account for 39 percent of grant dollars from national foundations to Texas nonprofits.

The next section examines variation in foundation giving by type, age, and asset distribution.

[…]. Top Texas Foundation Donors to Texas Nonprofits

	Foundation	No. of Grants	% All Grants	Dollars (millions)	% All Dollars
1	Houston Endowment, Inc.	1,043	7.0	210.4	11.1
2	The Moody Foundation	99	0.7	184.5	9.7
3	The Brown Foundation, Inc.	618	4.1	128.9	6.8
4	Communities Foundation of Texas, Inc.	1,007	6.8	103.5	5.5
5	The Robert A. Welch Foundation	477	3.2	75.3	4.0
6	The Cullen Foundation	183	1.2	57.1	3.0
7	T. L. L. Temple Foundation	363	2.4	55.7	2.9
8	Amon G. Carter Foundation	327	2.2	53.1	2.8
9	The Meadows Foundation, Inc.	392	2.6	53.0	2.8
10	The Burnett Foundation	208	1.4	47.1	2.5
	Total from Texas Foundations	14,905		1,893.8	

Source: Foundation Center.

Foundation Characteristics: Type, Age, and Assets

The Texas grants data describe grants made by 653 foundations, only 112 of which are located in Texas. Table 7.5 shows the distribution of grant dollars by foundation type. The largest group of foundations in the data is composed of independent and corporate foundations. Almost 84 percent of dollars granted by Texas foundations are made by independent foundations, followed by 8 percent from corporate foundations. Dollars from national foundations are more broadly distributed, with 72 percent from independent foundations and 23 percent from corporate foundations. Texas foundations contributed just over 79 percent of all grant dollars in the data, with national foundations contributing just over 20 percent. The average foundation has been in operation for just under forty-five years.

With one exception (independent foundation grants), the average grant from Texas foundations was larger than that of national foundations (located outside of Texas). Interestingly, the mean grant (see table 7.5) from Texas independent foundations is about 50 percent smaller than the mean grant from national independent foundations. However, mean grants from Texas corporate foundations are approximately 40 percent *larger* than grants from national corporate foundations. Likewise, grants from Texas community foundations are, on average, twice as large as grants from national community foundations.

Table 7.5. Percent Total Grant Dollars (Millions) and Mean Grant Size by Foundation Type

			% Dollars		Median Grant		
Foundation Type	Number	Age (years)	TX	National	All	TX	National
Independent	409	47.9	83.9	71.8	150,685	90,467	170,668
Corporate	194	34.3	8.2	22.7	49,506	62,697	38,357
Community	34	53.8	7.0	1.8	89,461	146,833	76,950
Operating	16	46.9	0.9	3.7	117,754	121,950	113,898
Total	653	44.7	100	100	118,263	127,060	93,530

Source: Foundation Center.

The foundations in the data also evidence a distinct relationship between foundation asset size, total grants, total dollars, and mean grant size. Table 7.6 shows the distribution of foundations by asset size and location. Because the Foundation Center data is based on a sample of large US foundations, we expect the data to be biased in favor of larger foundations. The Texas grant data contains information on grantmaking by about half of the largest Texas foundations (compare table 7.1). Whereas most foundations are on the smaller end of the asset distribution (table 7.1), it is this percentage of large foundations that is responsible for the lion's share of grantmaking. This is confirmed in table 7.6, which shows the distribution of grant dollars by foundation assets. The largest foundations by asset size gave 84 percent of the grants and 90 percent of the grant dollars in the data. In addition, the mean grant given by the largest foundations is approximately 60 percent larger than the average grant given by foundations with less than $1 million in assets.

As previously discussed, Texas inheritance tax laws prior to 1965 encouraged Texas foundations to concentrate their grant-making efforts within the state. Table 7.7 shows the distribution of grant dollars to Texas nonprofits by period of foundation establishment and location of foundation. The first row in table 7.7 provides statistics for the older cohort of foundations that were established prior to the 1965 change in the inheritance tax laws. The last two columns of the table indicate that these foundations spent almost 88 percent of their grant dollars within Texas. Although foundations established after the 1965 law change still spent a majority of their grant dollars (about 70 percent) within Texas, considerably more grantmaking (18 percent) by these younger foundations was concentrated

Table 7.6. Foundation Assets, Grants, Dollars, and Mean Grant Size

Foundation Assets	Percentage of Foundations	Percentage of Grants	Percentage of Dollars	Mean Grant
Under $1M	17.5	10.0	6.6	77,817
$1–$10M	8.4	2.5	1.3	62,709
$10–$25M	8.7	3.8	2.2	68,493
More than $25M	65.4	83.7	89.9	127,023
Total	100.0	100.0	100.0	118,263

Source: Foundation Center.

Table 7.7. Foundation Giving by TX Foundations Only by Period of Establishment

Foundation Created	Total Grant Dollars (Millions)	% Total Dollars	Total Grant Dollars to TX Recipients	Total Grant Dollars to non-TX Recipients	% Dollars to TX Recipients	% Dollars to Non-TX Recipients
1925–1965	1,699.1	74.1	1,492	207.1	87.8	12.2
After 1965	593.8	25.9	401.8	192.1	67.7	32.3
Total	2,292.9	100	1,893.8	399.2	—	—

Source: Foundation Center.

outside the state. While this could be the result of shifting priorities on the part of Texas foundations, or the general increase in assets and giving of foundations nationally during this period, it is likely also related to the liberalization of Texas inheritance laws in 1965 which no longer penalized giving outside of Texas.

Grant Purposes

Foundation grantmaking to Texas nonprofits is directed toward a variety of areas. Figure 7.2 shows the distribution of total grant dollars by year and grant purpose. The typology used to characterize grant purposes comes from the National Taxonomy of Exempt Entities (NTEE), the standard classification system for cataloging nonprofit organizations by their primary exempt purpose.[18] The NTEE was created in 1985 through a collaborative effort of the National Center for Charitable Statistics at the Urban Institute, the Foundation Center, and the independent sector.[19] The basic divisions of the NTEE shown in figure 7.2 are as follows:

- Arts, Culture, and Humanities (e.g., museums and performing arts)
- Education (e.g., schools and libraries)

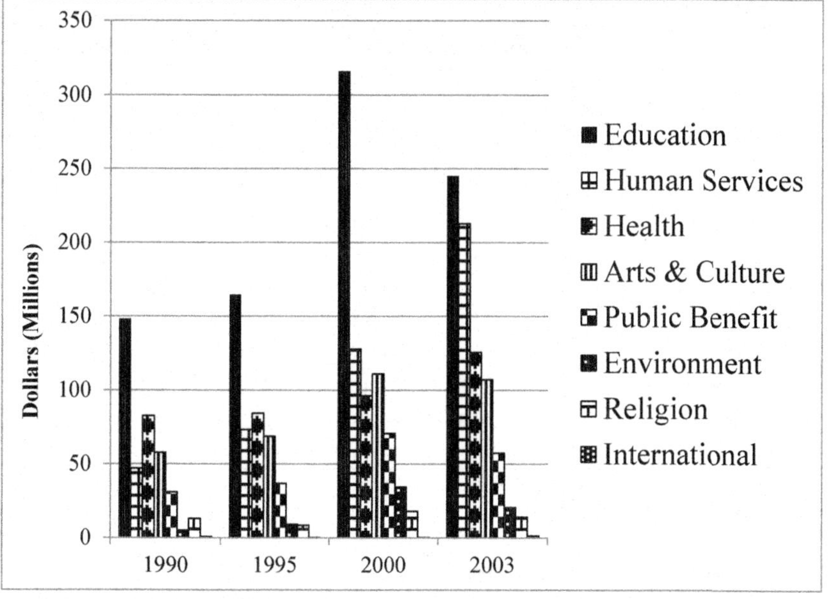

Figure 7.2. Distribution of Dollars by Grant Purpose. *Source:* Foundation Center.

- Environment and Animals (e.g., pollution control, animal protection)
- Health (e.g., hospitals, medical research)
- Human Services (e.g., food, housing, employment)
- International (e.g., foreign policy research)
- Public Benefit (e.g., voter education, consumer rights, public safety)
- Religion-related (e.g., congregations and other religious groups)

Grants for educational purposes consistently comprise the largest percentage of foundation giving, between 31 and 41 percent of total grant dollars. Human service grants are the next-largest category of giving, increasing more than twofold from 12 percent in 1990 to 27 percent in 2003. These are followed by grants for health-related purposes, which accounted for 12 to 21 percent of total grant dollars. Grants for art and cultural purposes are ranked next, averaging 15 percent of grantmaking across the four years.

Most, but not all, of foundation grant dollars come from Texas foundations. It is possible that foundations headquartered in Texas have different grant-making priorities than non-Texas foundations that support Texas nonprofits. Table 7.8 compares giving by Texas and national foundations. In all cases, except giving for international purposes, the median grant from Texas foundations is larger than that of national foundations. For ble 7.8. Comparison of Grant Purposes by Foundation Location

	National Foundations			**Texas Foundations**		
Grant Purpose	Total Dollars (millions)	%	Mean Grant	Total Dollars (millions)	%	Mean Grant
Education	215.2	43.4	128,236	658.3	34.8	152,954
Human Services	72.0	14.5	62,403	388.9	20.5	101,437
Health	66.7	13.5	117,255	322.3	17.0	147,849
Arts and Culture	47.6	9.6	66,679	296.7	15.7	121,837
Public Benefit	73.7	14.9	88,516	122.2	6.5	110,114
Environment	8.5	1.7	65,752	60.9	3.2	123,812
Religion	10.5	2.1	53,319	43.3	2.3	83,831
International	1.6	0.3	57,482	1.1	0.1	34,450
	495.8		93,530	1,893.8		127,060

Source: Foundation Center.

both Texas and national foundations, more than 50 percent of grant dollars are accounted for in two grant categories: education and human services. Overall, the distribution of grants from Texas and national foundations is very similar.

Geographic Distribution of Texas Foundation Giving

Approximately 80 percent of grant dollars given by US foundations to Texas nonprofits are given by Texas-based foundations. In part, this may be related to inheritance tax laws favoring in-state giving. We know less about the distribution of grant dollars across the state of Texas. Do certain cities or regions of the state disproportionately benefit from foundation grants? In a related question, do certain geographic areas of the state send more foundation grants to other regions in Texas? This section examines two aspects of the geographic distribution of grant dollars to Texas nonprofits: (1) the distribution of grant dollars across and between Texas cities, and (2) the distribution of grant dollars between the eleven Health and Human Service regions designated by the Texas Health and Human Services Commission.

The Texas grant data describes foundation giving to nonprofits located in 410 cities throughout the state of Texas. Most of these cities (387) are exclusively receivers of foundation grants: nonprofits in the

Table 7.9. Comparison of Grant Dollars Received and Sent from Texas Cities

	% of Grant Dollars		2000 Population Rank[(a)]
Texas City	Sent	Received	
Houston*	39.9	34.3	1
Dallas*	17.5	17.3	3
Fort Worth*	11.4	10.1	6
Galveston	9.8	11.8	42
San Antonio*	7.6	6.9	2
Lufkin*	2.9	1.1	71
Austin	2.1	8.6	4
Midland*	1.4	1.4	24
Abilene	1.1	1.2	19
Irving*	1.1	0.4	12
Plano*	1.0	0.1	9
Amarillo*	0.7	0.8	22
Wichita Falls*	0.6	0.5	21
Laredo	0.6	0.7	13
Lubbock	0.5	1.4	11
Corpus Christi	0.4	0.8	8
Richmond*	0.3	0.2	178
Temple*	0.3	0.2	44
Kerrville*	0.2	0.2	108
Waco	0.2	1.3	18
Victoria*	0.1	0.1	37
Seminole*	0.1	0.0	256
Tyler	0.1	0.5	28
	100	88.5	

*Cities are net senders of foundation grants.
[(a)]US Census, Texas Population Estimates, 2000, https://factfinder.census.gov/
Source: Foundation Center.

cities receive foundation grants, but there are no foundations in those cities that send grants to other areas of the state. In fact, only twenty-three Texas cities were both receivers and senders of foundation grants. Table 7.9 lists these cities, sorted by the percentage of foundation grant dollars sent from the city to other areas of Texas (column 2). Interestingly, three large cities (Houston, Dallas, and Fort Worth) give and receive relatively equal shares of foundation grant dollars and account for the lion's share of grant dollars. Note that the percentage of grant dollars received totals 88.5 percent because the table does not include the 387 Texas cities that received, but did not send, grant dollars. Cities that are net senders of foundation grants are marked with an asterisk. For example, as shown in table 7.9, Houston nonprofits received approximately 34 percent of all grant dollars in the data. Foundations located in Houston donated almost 40 percent of the total grant dollars in the data, making Houston a net sender of foundation grants. Table 7.9 includes seven of the top ten Texas cities by population. Galveston and Austin are the top net receivers of foundation grants.

This analysis indicates that grantmaking in Texas is highly concentrated. Foundations located in two cites, Houston and Dallas, account for almost 60 percent of all foundation grant dollars. Likewise, nonprofits in these two cities received approximately 52 percent of all grant dollars. When the city of Fort Worth is considered, these three cities account for approximately 70 percent of all grant dollars sent, and about 62 percent of all grant dollars received, respectively. Figure 7.3 provides another way to conceptualize these senders and receivers.

Figure 7.3 plots the combination of dollars sent and received for the twenty-three Texas cities listed in table 7.9. The dotted line in figure 7.3 represents the breakeven point. Cities on this line send and receive equal amounts of foundation grant dollars. Cities above the dotted line are net senders of foundation grants; foundations in these cities sent more grant dollars to other areas of Texas than nonprofits in these cities received. Cities located below the dotted line in figure 7.3 are net receivers of foundation dollars.

While examining the distribution of foundation dollars across Texas cites is one approach to describing the geographic distribution of Texas grant dollars, the vast size of the state suggests a need to look beyond these urban centers. Texas is the second-largest US state in both area (behind Alaska) and population (behind California). Approximately 7.8 percent of the US population lives in Texas. Texas is as large as all of New England, New York, Pennsylvania, Ohio, and North Carolina combined. In an effort to organize the delivery of services in this large state, the Texas Health and Human Services Commission grouped the state's 255 counties into eleven regions. These Health and Human Services Regions (HHS regions) offer a chance to assess the regional distribution of grant dollars in the state of Texas.

Figure 7.4 shows the eleven HHS regions along with major Texas cities. Four HHS regions together account for the majority of grant dollars sent by Texas foundations and received by Texas nonprofits. These four regions are shaded in figure 7.4 and described in greater detail in

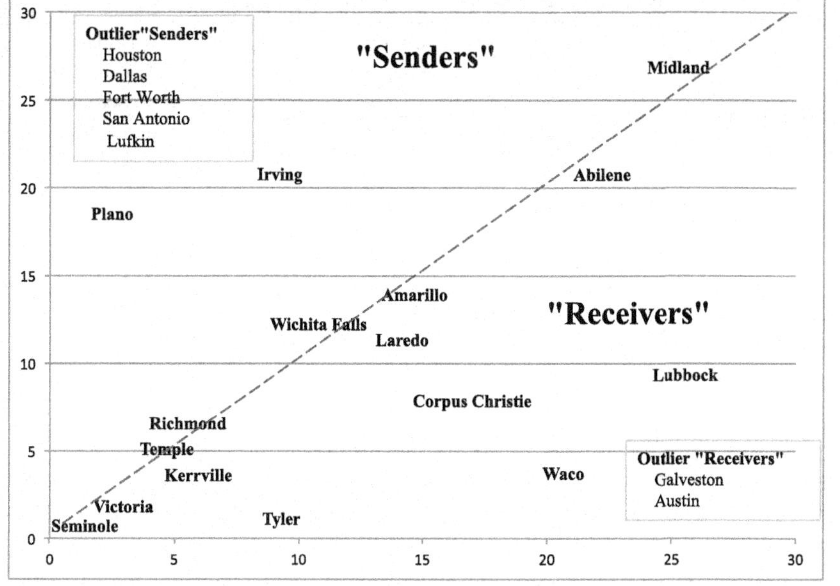

Figure 7.3. Comparison of Texas Cities "Sending" and "Receiving" Foundation Grants

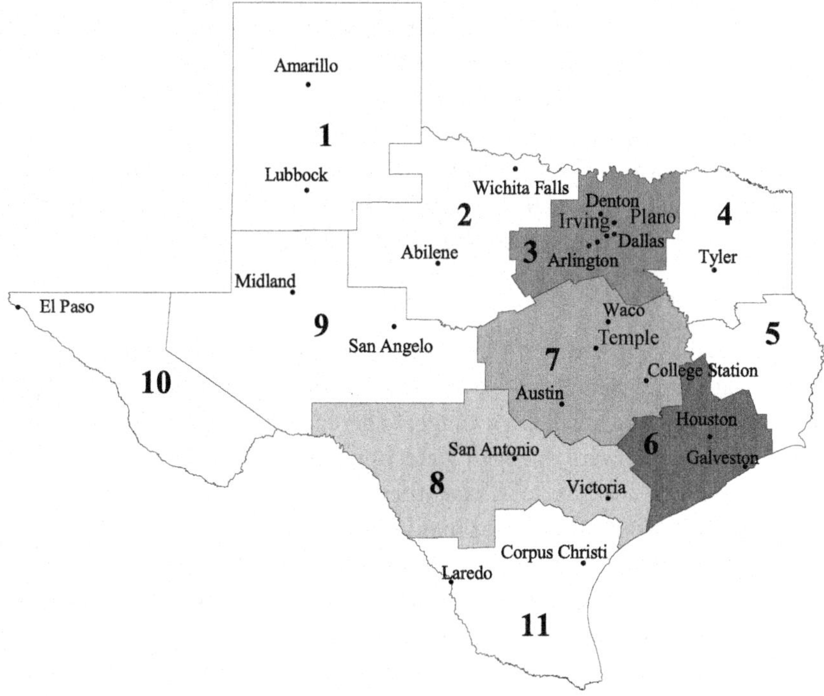

Figure 7.4. Texas HHS Regions and Major Cities

Table 7.10. Distribution of Grant Dollars by Texas HHS Regions

		% of Grant Dollars, Texas Foundations		% Dollars Received from National Foundations
HHS Region	Major Cities	Sent	Received	
6	Houston, Galveston	50.1	42.9	28.1
3	Dallas, Fort Worth	30.9	26.7	23.5
7	Austin	2.6	11.8	23.5
8	San Antonio	8.0	7.0	11.9
		91.6	88.4	87.0

Source: Foundation Center.

table 7.10. Foundations located in HHS regions 3 and 6 gave over 80 percent of grant dollars in the data. Nonprofits in these regions were also the largest recipients of grant dollars, receiving almost 70 percent of all grant dollars. The seven unshaded HHS regions in figure 7.4 each account for less than 3 percent of grant dollars sent or received in the state of Texas.

While Texas foundation giving is highly concentrated, is the distribution of grants to Texas nonprofits from National foundations similarly distributed? The last column of table 7.10 shows the distribution of grant dollars from non-Texas foundations to the selected HHS regions. Nonprofits in these four regions receive 87 percent of grant dollars from national foundations. Similar to the distribution of dollars from Texas foundations, regions 3 and 6, the locations of Dallas and Houston, together receive almost 70 percent of non-Texas grant dollars.

Texas, My Texas

As one considers the mix of Texas and non-Texas giving by foundations in the state, it is clear that—over time—Texas foundations have kept much of their giving local. On average, 83 percent of the grant dollars from Texas foundations were spent in-state (see table 7.11). When the philanthropic funds do leak out of Texas, they stay concentrated in the South (see table 7.12). Roughly twice as many grants and twice as much funding went to nonprofits in the South compared to the Northeast. Other areas like the West and Pacific regions fared even worse than the Northeast in terms of attracting Texas philanthropic funds.

When we look at which cities were the most generous in terms of sending funds out of state, San Antonio emerges ahead of larger cities like Dallas and Houston. As shown in table 7.13, over 90 percent of all Texas

Table 7.11. Texas Foundation Grants by Location of Recipient[(a)]

	Texas Recipients		Non-Texas Recipients	
Year	Total Dollars (millions)	% Total Giving	Total Dollars (millions)	% Total Giving
1990	308.9	80.1	76.7	19.9
1995	339.2	82.5	71.7	17.5
2000	608.5	82.6	128.6	17.4
2003	637.2	84.6	115.6	15.4

[(a)]The total dollar amount in this table differs from that in table 7.3 which includes grants from foundations outside of Texas, as well as Texas foundation grants.
Source: Foundation Center.

Table 7.12. Texas Foundation Grants to Non-Texas Recipients by Region

Region	N Grants	%	Total Dollars (millions)	%
South	2,231	34.7	142.2	36.2
Midwest	1,563	24.3	89.5	22.8
Northeast	1,178	18.3	69.2	17.6
Pacific	1,004	15.6	53.8	13.7
West	455	7.1	37.8	9.6
Total	6,431	100.0	392.5	100.0

Source: Foundation Center.

Table 7.13. Giving Outside of Texas by Region

Region	No. of Grants	%	Total Dollars (millions)	%
San Antonio	1,590	24.7	110.5	28.1
Houston	1,759	27.4	109.2	27.8
Irving	1,664	25.9	74.9	19.1
Dallas	670	10.4	39.7	10.1
Fort Worth	411	6.4	36.6	9.3
Austin	146	2.3	6.8	1.7
Plano	77	1.2	5.6	1.4
Lufkin	16	0.2	3.2	0.8
Waco	33	0.5	2.3	0.6
Wichita Falls	13	0.2	1.4	0.4
Amarillo	1	0	0.7	0.2
Abilene	20	0.3	0.6	0.2
Midland	17	0.3	0.6	0.1
Seminole	6	0.1	0.2	0.1
Tyler	3	0	0.1	0
Galveston	4	0.1	0.1	0
Lubbock	1	0	0	0
Total	6,431	100	392.5	100

Source: Foundation Center.

foundation giving reaching beyond the state's border comes from the five largest metropolitan areas (San Antonio, Houston, Irving, Dallas, and Fort Worth).

Conclusion

Texas foundation philanthropy has a flavor as distinctive as the local barbecue. Starting with early laws aimed at limiting foundation giving to Texas charities, the Texas foundation landscape is decidedly focused inward, even if the early restrictions on out-of-state giving have long been removed from the books. Texas philanthropy follows the state's broader identity as a nation unto itself, neither part of the deep South nor part of the desert West, although it overlaps with both regions. The culture of philanthropy in the state may be shifting with the arrival of new high-tech wealth, but change is likely to be slow and take years to work itself out.

When looking at the foundation organizational landscape in Texas, several features stand out. Giving in Texas is still largely dominated by independent foundations, and the community and corporate foundation fields are small given the sheer size, diversity, and wealth of the state. Our analysis suggests that levels and forms of foundation giving are related to foundation characteristics such as age and asset size. When it comes to the focus of Texas foundations, there is a relatively close match to the national trends with education, human service, and health representing the largest areas of concentration.

The data on the geographical dispersion of foundations and the flow of grant funds confirm that Texas is a state with a high level of concentration of philanthropic assets in major cities, particularly Dallas and Houston. These cities, where early fortunes were made in cattle and oil, remain critical forces driving the flow of philanthropic funds across the state. There are great disparities in philanthropic resources when one compares east and west Texas to the central and southern areas where the major urban areas are located.

With no estate tax and no state income tax, Texas has recently attracted large numbers of wealthy residents from other states, particularly California. As the fiscal crisis in many states continues to stress wealth holders, Texas's relatively robust economy and pro-business policies bode well for the health of Texas philanthropy. With a sound set of philanthropic institutions in the major cities and young wealth related to the information technology boom still years away from finding its home in foundations, the presence of Texas on the national philanthropic stage is likely to increase—that is, assuming that Texas neither experiences a major fiscal reversal, nor secedes from the union.

PETER FRUMKIN is the Mindy and Andrew Heyer Chair in Social Policy, Director of the Master's in Nonprofit Leadership Program, and Faculty Director of the Center for Social Impact Strategy, all at the University of Pennsylvania. He is author of *On Being Nonprofit* and *Strategic Giving*, and co-author of *Serving Country and Community and Building for the Arts.*

HEATHER MACINDOE is Associate Professor and Director of the Doctoral Program in the Department of Public Policy and Public Affairs at the McCormack Graduate School for Policy and Global Studies at the University of Massachusetts Boston.

NOTES

1. Texas State Law Library, "Texas Historical Statutes Project 1925 Constitution of the United States and Texas," 2062, 2061. Accessed at www.sll.texas.gov/assets/pdf/historical-statutes/1925/1925-2-revised-civil-statutes-of-the-state-of-texas.pdf.
2. Texas State Law Library, "Texas Historical Statutes Project 1925 Constitution of the United States and Texas," 2061. Accessed at www.sll.texas.gov/assets/pdf/historical-statutes/1925/1925-2-revised-civil-statutes-of-the-state-of-texas.pdf.
3. Stephanie Strom, "Texas Adopts Law on Stewardship of Trusts after Founders Die," *New York Times* (June 28, 2009), A16.
4. Peter Frumkin, "The long recoil from regulation: Private philanthropic foundations and the Tax Reform Act of 1969," *The American Review of Public Administration* 28 (1998): 266–286.
5. John M. Strefeler and Leslie T. Miller, "Exempt Organizations: A Study of Their Nature and the Applicability of the Unrelated Business Income Tax," *Akron Tax J.* 12 (1996): 223.
6. Mary L. Kelley, *The Foundations of Texan Philanthropy* (College Station: Texas A&M University Press, 2004), 12.
7. Waldemar A. Nielsen, *The Golden Donors: A New Anatomy of the Great Foundations* (New York: E. P. Dutton, 2002 [1985]); "Moody Foundation," www.moodyf.org.
8. www.houstonendowment.org/about/history/.
9. www.houstonendowment.org/about/history/.
10. www.brownfoundation.org/background.
11. Richard Magat, *Unlikely Partners: Philanthropic Foundations and Labor Unions* (Ithaca, NY: Cornell University Press, 1998), 1–242.
12. Magat, *Unlikely Partners.*
13. Kelley, *Foundations of Texan Philanthropy.*
14. www.msdf.org/india/; www.msdf.org/south-africa/.
15. Nielsen, *The Golden Donors.*
16. www.fconline.foundationcenter.org.
17. Elizabeth Boris, *Philanthropic Foundations in the United States* (New York: Council On Foundations, 2000); Kevin Bolduc, Phil Buchanan, and Judy Huang, *Listening to Grantees: What Nonprofits Value in Their Foundation Funders* (Boston: Center for Effective Philanthropy, 2004);

William McKersie, "Local Philanthropy Matters: Pressing Issues for Research and Practice," in *Philanthropic Foundations: New Scholarship, New Possibilities*, ed. Ellen Condliffe Lagemann (Bloomington: Indiana University Press, 1999), 329–58; Julian Wolpert, "Communities, Networks, and the Future of Philanthropy," in *Philanthropy and the Nonprofit Sector in a Changing America*, eds. Charles T. Clotfelter and Thomas Ehrlich (Bloomington: Indiana University Press, 1999), 247.

18. David R. Stevenson, *The National Taxonomy of Exempt Entities Manual* (Washington, DC: National Center for Charitable Statistics and Foundation Center, 1997).

19. Russy D. Sumariwalla, "Toward a national taxonomy of exempt entities," *Washington, DC: Aspen Institute and United Way of America* (1986).

chapter eight

FOUNDATIONS IN LOS ANGELES

David B. Howard and Helmut K. Anheier[1]

"Men and women have learned that there is no greater satisfaction than that of leaving a portion of their wealth to the lasting benefit of posterity."

—The Los Angeles Community Trust, May 21, 1929

Introduction

Modern foundations arrived in the Los Angeles region after they first developed on the East Coast and in the Midwest where they had ushered in a new era of philanthropy. An antidote to both old-world noblesse oblige and conventional charity, American philanthropy took bold steps in a society of minimal state powers and devolved governance.[2] The major innovations that took place in American philanthropy between 1890 and 1920, especially the general-purpose grant-making foundation dedicated to solving social problems of many kinds, came to the western parts of the country decades later. Unlike in New York or Chicago, the nexus between industrial fortunes and philanthropic engagement had no need to carve out new ground, at least initially. Los Angeles, like other cities in the West, could benefit from the complex and lengthy political, legislative, and legal battles East Coast foundations had won in Washington, DC, and state capitals like Albany. At first, foundations in Los Angeles seemed to follow templates modeled on the large East Coast foundations, but for decades to come, they remained at a smaller scale—and none could rival the size and import of the larger East Coast foundations, such as the Rockefeller Foundation.

Benefiting from East Coast institutional innovations, yet functioning in an economy, society, and culture that were and were becoming increasingly different, what patterns and roles did foundations in Los Angeles develop? The social, economic, and political concerns of the rising, growing metropolitan area of Los Angeles were and are unlike those of the eastern United States. They are also different from the California Bay Area or Washington State, which developed in rather distinct patterns.[3] Did foundations emerge along lines similar to what has been observed for other parts of the country, or do we see a distinct profile? Could we expect Los Angeles foundations to either be or become more like their brethren elsewhere, or might they point to something different, something new?

Foundations have grown in scale and scope in the Los Angeles region, and they did so more than in the United States as whole, beginning after World War II and especially since the 1990s. This growth pattern shifted the geographic fulcrum of institutional philanthropic activity away from a concentration on the East Coast, especially New York. Yet unlike the situation there, foundations in Los Angeles have been much less studied. Fewer historical accounts and empirical portraits have been made. This chapter offers an assessment of foundations in Los Angeles against the background of their historical development, current roles, and likely future trajectories. Specifically, we ask: What differences have foundations made over time, and what contributions are they currently making? We also explore whether these patterns are distinct from the rest of the country, and, if so, what the implications are for our understanding of the role of foundations in America.

Going beyond earlier studies of foundational activity in Los Angeles,[4] this chapter first provides an overview of the history, scope, and role of foundations in the Los Angeles metropolitan area.[5] It then explores the extent to which the emergence of foundations in the region mirrors that of their counterparts outside the region.[6] Post–War World II affluence—spurred by federal investments in aerospace and defense, the emergence of the Hollywood motion picture and other industries, the attractiveness of the climate, and the development of upscale communities—helps to explain the growing presence of wealth in the region during the second half of the twentieth century. Today, the philanthropic community of Los Angeles is one of the largest in the country, with greater foundation numbers, assets, and grant dollars than most states.

We will then study the present and find that, despite the growth and absolute size of the local foundation sector, per capita foundation activity in Los Angeles ranks in the middle of the country's largest metro areas and foundation giving has failed to keep pace with gross metropolitan product growth going back more than a decade. We highlight the contributions foundations have made and are making today to generate a clearer understanding of the roles they perform, as well as how these might be different from other parts of the country.

Los Angeles

Adjectives commonly used to describe Los Angeles include "dynamic," "diverse," "sprawled," "decentralized," and "unbalanced." A tremendous economic force and a leader in social and cultural trends, Los Angeles is a key international commercial hub, home to a strong industrial base, and the center of the US entertainment industry.[7] The Los Angeles economy is the seventeenth-largest in the world, second only to New York among local US economies.[8] Los Angeles County—which includes the City of Los Angeles, eighty-seven other cities, and numerous unincorporated areas—is by far the most populous county in the United States, with almost ten million residents. Los Angeles County is also one of the most diverse counties in the country, and boasts the largest population of minority residents among counties.[9]

In addition to the expansive geography, large population, and vast economy, the nature of the local social sector and political fragmentation make the Los Angeles region an illustrative case for exploring the role of foundations and philanthropic efforts writ large. Los Angeles is one the most economically segregated regions in the country, and philanthropy could play an important role in addressing critical issues related to the divide between poor and affluent neighborhoods.[10] Income and wage disparity in the region conjures allegorical reference to the Dickensian dichotomy of the haves and have-nots—indeed a tale of two cities (or counties, as it were).[11]

The local nonprofit economy or sector, which represents about 6 percent of GMP, plays a critical role in providing an array of public goods and services, and many nonprofits—particularly larger agencies and institutions—rely on foundation grantmaking.[12] The high demand for health and human services, education and schools, and arts and cultural offerings creates widespread opportunities for foundations to have an impact through supporting service delivery, advocacy and policy change, stakeholder convenings, and promoting innovation. This chapter will highlight several examples where foundations have spawned and continue to spearhead community-based initiatives, help build prominent institutions, fight for reform efforts, and provide critical financial support during times of economic downturn and government cutbacks. We will also point out that Los Angeles foundations could have done more in the past, and that they are now in a process of searching for new modes to increase their contributions and impact.

Scholars like John Mollenkopf and Raphael J. Sonenshein have pointed to the fragmented political and administrative governance of the region, including a county jurisdiction that overlaps with multiple city governments and special entities, like the Los Angeles Unified School District, which are neither part of city nor county government but form largely independent systems.[13] This pattern is replicated in financial resource capacities, where the county takes on expenditure responsibilities for health and social services that in metropolitan areas like New York would be lodged with the municipal government. Like Mollenkopf and Sonenshein, Jennifer Wolch links this fragmented governance pattern to the poor coordination that has long characterized the region, leading in part to impeded implementation of effective solutions to pressing social issues (e.g., homelessness, transportation, pollution, and education).[14]

The fragmentation of governance that characterizes the Los Angeles area makes the emergence of public-private partnerships difficult. Such collaborations between public agencies and private nonprofit organizations—and between government and foundations in particular—have been sparse.[15] Well into the early twenty-first century, and despite the growing importance of nonprofit organizations in higher education, health, and the arts, no overall pattern of nonprofit-government cooperation developed in a sustained and forward-looking way.[16] However, there are indications that this institutional weakness is being addressed, and various initiatives suggest that changes are afoot in this respect. In 2006, then Los Angeles Mayor Antonio Villaraigosa appointed the first cabinet-level liaison to philanthropy. More recently, the Mayor's Office of Strategic Partnerships (OSP), funded by three local foundations, began working with a variety of entities to address issues related to transportation, housing, and job training, all with the intention of creating long-term change, and County level initiatives followed.[17] The OSP attracted private dollars (including support from the California Community Foundation) to expand programs like Summer Night Lights, a successful citywide anti-gang initiative.

Los Angeles also continues to feel the effects of Proposition 13, a 1978 state ballot initiative that restructured property tax laws and subsequently reduced state tax revenues.[18] The resultant atrophy of funding for state institutions and public services for low-income communities, funding that was further eroded by welfare reform legislation in the 1990s at the state and federal levels, led to increased pressures on the nonprofit and private philanthropic sectors to fill the gaps.[19] In the wake of Proposition 13, funding for K–12 public education was particularly impacted, as California fell well behind national averages in revenues and expenditures per pupil.[20] During the Great Recession (2008–2011), the region's fiscal challenges were exacerbated by lower amounts of city revenue coming from property taxes.[21]

Amidst a complex government structure, the Los Angeles region does have a large charitable sector—the largest nonprofit sector (in total numbers) outside of the New York metropolitan area, with nearly thirty-two thousand nonprofits. It is a sector facing considerable challenges with respect to diversity, service capacity, and access.[22] Indeed, the Los Angeles region's nonprofit sector in per capita terms is lower than the national figures—only slightly below the number of nonprofits per ten thousand population, but 27 percent lower than the nonprofit expenditures per capita. Furthermore, many local high-need areas also have the weakest nonprofit infrastructure in terms of numbers and expenditures per capita.[23] This combination of high needs and low capacity creates challenges for funders.

Private foundations have been an important source of revenue for nonprofits in the arts and culture.[24] State funding of the arts has played a lesser role throughout, and stark cuts to the arts and arts education in the early 2000s created another gap that private foundations attempted to fill.[25] With per capita state spending on the arts in California among the lowest in the country,[26] private foundations have nonetheless helped Los Angeles become home to many major arts and cultural institutions, including the J. Paul Getty Museum, the Music Center and Walt Disney Concert Hall in Downtown, and the Norton Simon Museum in Pasadena.[27] However, foundation support of the independent scene of small nonprofit arts groups, including many small theaters and community arts centers, remains low.

In light of these distinctive traits, and as institutional philanthropy continues to evolve in the region, what trends have emerged and what role have foundations played in the social and political development of Los Angeles? And how do these trends and roles compare to other regions in the country?

A Brief History of Foundations in Los Angeles

Los Angeles is home to one of the largest pools of foundation assets in the country—but it did not start out that way. Over time, the distribution of American foundations has spread out from a heavy concentration in the East (New York City, in particular), and the West Coast has slowly increased its share of philanthropic institutions and activity. In Los Angeles, the post–World War II economic boom and subsequent population growth occurred several decades after the East Coast financial and industrial coming of age, and the emerging role of private foundations in Los Angeles closely followed that pattern. Industrial development, the establishment of the motion picture industry, oil discovery, aircraft production, and other factors—most notably as a result of Cold War–era federal defense investments in the region—paved the way for prominent individuals to leave their mark through institutional philanthropic endeavors.

Data from the Foundation Center's first edition of the *Foundation Directory*, which was published in 1960, show that New York City foundations represented nearly one-quarter of all foundations at the time and controlled 62 percent of total assets and over half (53 percent) of all grant dollars.[28] In contrast, Los Angeles County had 3.1 percent of the nation's foundations, representing less than 1 percent of all assets and 1.5 percent of grants. The foundation community in Los Angeles in 1960 was still, however, one of the largest in the country.[29] At the time, fewer than ten states had more foundations or more total grant dollars than Los Angeles.

Over the next fifty years, Los Angeles foundations increased their share of the nationwide philanthropic sector, albeit modestly. By 2011, Los Angeles foundations' national share had grown, in terms of numbers, assets, and total giving, to 4 percent, 7 percent, and 4 percent, respectively.[30] The East Coast is still home to many of the best-known foundations in the United States. But while names like Broad, Keck, Ahmanson, and Weingart may not resonate with the national public the way Gates, Ford, Rockefeller, and Carnegie do, a number of LA-based foundations have been and remain influential actors in areas including the development of institutions of higher education and arts and culture, and promoting reform efforts in health and education.[31]

To be sure, the most-studied of the twentieth century foundations reside in the Northeast, although several prominent foundations are located on the West Coast. In 2011, four out of the top ten foundations in the United States (in terms of assets) were on the West Coast (of which three are in California). But just one of the three—the J. Paul Getty Trust—is based in Los Angeles.[32] Because the largest foundations in Los Angeles tend to invest grant dollars locally, and few of them engage in significant international grantmaking, local funders have not developed nationwide recognition.

Examining the trajectory of private foundation establishment in the region highlights two distinct periods in which the largest foundations—those with current assets in excess of $100 million—were formed: the 1950s and the 1990s. As is the case nationally, the majority of foundations currently operating in Los Angeles—more than three-quarters (77 percent)—were established after 1990. The 1990s technology-driven economic boom allowed for an increased accumulation of wealth and accompanying incentives to form charitable foundations. Yet unlike in Silicon Valley and the Bay Area, the new growth industries (information technology) in Los Angeles were much less concentrated. They were also less characterized by an entrepreneurial renaissance to carry over from the world of start-up businesses to philanthropy. Thus, the region saw minimal formation of new types of philanthropic vehicles in the past two decades.

Whereas the first half of the twentieth century is generally regarded as the major formative era for American foundations, this period—billed as the classic institution-building era by Hammack and Anheier—was far more productive in the East Coast regions. Late nineteenth-century industrialization generated exorbitant pockets of wealth through which Rockefeller, Carnegie, and others formed some of the most influential foundations in modern times.[33] Major institutions in Los Angeles were yet to be established.

In the early twentieth century, a number of foundations were created in the San Francisco Bay area (e.g., the Lux Foundation [1908], the Avery-Fuller Children's Center [1914], and Oakland's Latham Foundation [1918]), but Los Angeles's establishments were scarce prior to the 1920s.[34] One exception was the Los Angeles Community Foundation (formed in 1915 and later renamed the California Community Foundation), which was one of the nation's earliest community foundations.[35] In a May 21, 1929, letter to readers published in *The Los Angeles Times*, the Foundation was described as a "public trust, patterned after the similar community trusts . . . [that] provides a medium through which anyone may make large or small donations, endowments or bequests."[36] By the 1940s, the California Community Foundation was one of the nation's most active—ranking fifth in giving and tenth in total assets out of seventy-three community foundations surveyed in the United States, Canada, and Hawaii.[37]

Independent private foundations, although not in great numbers, emerged in the first half of the twentieth century in Los Angeles. The John Randolph Haynes and Dora Haynes Foundation was created in 1926 and is the oldest independent general purpose foundation in Los Angeles—and one of the earliest in California.[38] After moving to Los Angeles from Philadelphia in 1887, the Hayneses made their wealth in real estate and banking. A physician by trade and a major progressive reform figure, John Randolph Haynes became a prominent advocate for workers' protections, direct legislation, and social justice for Native Americans.[39] Others, like George Pepperdine, pursued more conservative objectives, and would leave their own indelible impacts on the region.

The southern California oil industry created pockets of wealth that fueled significant philanthropic investments. G. Allan Hancock funneled his earnings from petroleum production into the Allan Hancock Foundation for Marine Research (now the Hancock Institute for Marine Studies) at the University of Southern California (USC), and also donated a vast amount of land (including the La Brea tar pits) for public use.[40] George Pepperdine, who made millions in auto part sales, established the George Pepperdine Foundation in 1931, and in 1937 the foundation funded the construction, endowment, and operating costs of Pepperdine College—now Pepperdine University.[41]

The Pepperdine Foundation also represents a faction of substantial religious-based philanthropies that have created an impact in Los Angeles. A lifelong member of the Churches of Christ, Pepperdine founded his namesake university in part to place adequate emphasis and greater stress on religious teaching and Christian character.[42] Conrad N. Hilton, the international hotel magnate and a devout Catholic, established his namesake trust in 1944 (later becoming a foundation in 1950) with a mandate to relieve the suffering, the distressed, and the destitute. Over the decades, the Hilton Foundation has remained committed to, among other causes, supporting the Catholic Sisters, a group that had profoundly influenced him since childhood. In 1949, Carrie Estelle Doheny established her namesake foundation after she and her husband, oil tycoon Edward Doheny, commissioned and funded the construction of St. Vincent de Paul Church in Los Angeles. The Doheny Foundation continues to be one of the region's largest supporters of religious causes. The Dan Murphy Foundation, incorporated in 1957, has been one of the largest supporters of the Roman Catholic Diocese and Archbishop over the years. In addition, Jewish philanthropy has produced prominent contributions to the region. The Jewish Community Foundation was founded in 1954 and has become one of the region's largest foundations with assets of more than $1 billion.

The entertainment industry has also played a large philanthropic role in Los Angeles, even if Hollywood's foundation giving has been less than commensurate with the industry's revenue generation. The Entertainment Industry Foundation (EIF), founded in 1942 by Samuel Goldwyn and other influential Hollywood figures as the Permanent Charities Committee of the Motion Picture Industry, illustrates an early philanthropic effort of the entertainment studios and industry to help maximize Hollywood's generosity during the Second World War.[43] In 2012, EIF contributed more than $33 million in grant funding to a range of charitable causes. Hollywood's impact on private foundation grantmaking is discussed later in the chapter.

Postwar affluence and industrial expansion led in part to the formation of many of the nation's best-known foundations.[44] According to Foundation Center (1960) records, there was also a vast increase in the number of company-sponsored foundations during the 1950s. This was a pivotal era for foundation establishments in Los Angeles as well. A host of industrialists and financiers who made their fortunes in southern California or chose to reside in the area, created some of the largest and most influential foundations to date during this time. Following the rapid growth of the philanthropic sector in the 1950s, foundations became the target of widespread scrutiny from government and the public alike. Foundation leaders in southern California established the Los Angeles Inter-Foundation Center (now known as Southern California Grantmakers) in response to the growing demand for regulation and scrutiny of private foundations in the 1960s and 1970s.[45]

Consistent with nationwide trends, Los Angeles foundations experienced tremendous growth—including a proliferation of foundation establishments—during the 1990s. The health of the economy and the dot-com boom helps account for the philanthropic expansion in the region, but other trends played a part in the growth as well. Beginning in the late 1970s, a nationwide series of conversions of Blue Cross healthcare companies to for-profit corporations spawned a number of new private foundations over the next two decades. The two largest foundations to emerge from the conversions are located in the Los Angeles area and serve the state of California. In 1992, after Health Net's nonprofit-to-for-profit conversion, the company was required to endow more than $300 million into a foundation—the California Wellness Foundation. Since that time, California Wellness has awarded more than fifty-seven hundred grants, totaling more than $719 million, in support of health promotion, wellness education, and disease prevention. In 2011, its assets were valued at nearly $800 million.

When Blue Cross of California created WellPoint Health Networks, a for-profit corporation, the California Endowment was created. The Endowment's assets represent 46 percent of the aggregated assets of the top twenty-five new health foundations in the United States.[46] In 2006, the endowment opened a new facility in Downtown Los Angeles—the Center for Healthy Communities—which provides a state-of-the-art meeting space for nonprofit-related events and houses several prominent local nonprofit and philanthropic organizations (e.g., Southern California Grantmakers, the Center for Nonprofit Management, and Community Partners). The endowment's assets were valued at close to $3.7 billion in 2011, making it by far the largest of the new health foundations in the nation and the largest independent private foundation (in terms of both assets and giving) in Los Angeles.[47]

Although the two health conversation foundations in Los Angeles represent the bulk of the region's sectoral growth in the 1990s, several other prominent foundations emerged during the decade. Michael Eisner—former CEO of the Walt Disney Company—formed the Eisner Foundation in 1996 with his wife, Jane Leonard I. Green, a pioneer in the development of the leveraged buyout industry, established the Green Foundation in 1994. Globally, Los Angeles is best known for being one of the world's entertainment capitals—with Hollywood at the epicenter of the entertainment industry. The presence of Hollywood certainly has implications for local philanthropy, and even if the industry hasn't produced the largest local foundations, substantial grant-making foundations have become philanthropic vehicles for many successful artists, producers, and the like. Examples include the Wasserman Foundation (founded by Lew Wasserman, a prominent Hollywood agent with Music Corporation for America [MCA], and his wife, Edie, with assets greater than $180 million), the John W. Carson Foundation (created by former *Tonight Show* host Johnny Carson, with assets greater than $160 million), and the David Geffen Foundation (with assets greater than $90 million).

The motion picture industry represents just one piece of a vibrant cultural scene and arts economy in Los Angeles. Private foundations, as philanthropic vehicles for wealthy Los Angeles residents, have provided key funding streams for many of the city's most beloved cultural centers: the Dorothy Chandler Pavilion, Mark S. Taper Forum, Ahmanson Theatre, Walt Disney Concert Hall, the Skirball Cultural Center, the Norton Simon Museum, the Broad Contemporary Art Museum, and others.

The historical development of foundations in Los Angeles displays some key differences and some parallels to the broader national patterns. Because of the relatively late economic and industrial development of Los Angeles, the late nineteenth-century and early twentieth-century eras of particular-purpose, sectarian grantmaking and classic institution building were experienced on a smaller scale there.[48] The increase in foundation activity in the 1950s marked a pivotal era of philanthropic growth in the region; while foundations in other regions were redefining their roles during this time, many of the largest foundations in Los Angeles were defining their missions and purpose for the first time. Unlike other foundation capitals of the country such as New York (e.g., Rockefeller Foundation), Cleveland (e.g., Community Foundation), or the Bay Area (with its venture philanthropy), Los Angeles does not seem to have yet made its innovative mark on the development of American philanthropy—a point to which we will return after taking a look at the empirical contours of foundations in Los Angeles.

The Scale and Scope of Foundations in Los Angeles

The history of independent grant-making foundations in Los Angeles dates back nearly a century, and the evolution of institutional philanthropic scope in the region has very much been a product of social and economic climate change. The emergence of the very large, well-known Los Angeles–based foundations largely followed national trends in the postwar 1950s and the growing economy of the 1990s. This section charts the current scale and scope of foundations in Los Angeles, using data from the Foundation Center's Statistical Information Service and Grants Sample Database.

The Los Angeles metropolitan area's foundation community makes a strong case for consideration as the country's second-largest behind that of the New York metropolitan area.[49] While New York ranks highest—by far—in terms of the number of foundations, total assets, and total giving, Los Angeles ranks fourth, second, and fifth in each respective category. Table 8.1 shows that Los Angeles, Chicago, and San Francisco run fairly close behind New York in most categories. Due to the Gates Foundation, Seattle ranks high in both assets and giving.

The overall number of foundations—inclusive of independent private, operating, corporate, and community foundations—in the Los Angeles metropolitan area more than doubled between 1997 and 2011. Independent private foundations (126 percent) and community foundations (125 percent) more than doubled, while corporate foundations (71 percent) grew more modestly in terms of numbers. The number of operating foundations nearly tripled (169 percent). Overall, the number of Los Angeles foundations grew at a similar rate as that in the San Francisco metropolitan area (127 percent), and at a faster rate than the state (113 percent) and the

Table 8.1. Top Ten US Metropolitan Areas: Total Number of Foundations, Total Foundation Assets, and Total Foundation Giving, 2011

	Total Number of Foundations			Total Foundation Assets			Total Foundation Giving	
1	New York	9,775	1	New York	110,281,729,114	1	New York	10,302,577,629
2	Chicago	3,541	2	**Los Angeles**	**44,294,554,972**	2	Seattle	3,673,284,558
3	Philadelphia	3,460	3	Seattle	43,193,199,363	3	San Francisco	2,549,044,171
4	**Los Angeles**	**3,112**	4	San Francisco	29,532,585,488	4	Chicago	2,383,152,894
5	Boston	2,511	5	Chicago	26,828,549,246	**5**	**Los Angeles**	**2,167,199,523**
6	Pittsburgh	1,895	6	Philadelphia	21,700,960,358	6	Boston	1,260,986,550
7	San Francisco	1,842	7	Boston	17,196,308,760	7	Philadelphia	1,139,158,736
8	Miami	1,727	8	Minneapolis	14,224,700,783	8	Minneapolis	979,461,819
9	Dallas	1,706	9	Washington, DC	13,396,638,733	9	Houston	971,510,034
10	Washington, DC	1,610	10	Dallas	12,655,839,818	10	Washington, DC	927,309,679

Source: The Foundation Center, 2013. The search set includes all active private and community grant-making foundations located in the state. Only grant-making operating foundations are included. Metropolitan areas are as designated by the US Office of Management and Budget (OMB). Total giving includes grants, scholarships, and employee matching gifts.

United States (85 percent). Figure 8.1 shows that in 2011 there were more than 3,100 foundations in the Los Angeles area. In terms of annual growth rates, the most considerable growth occurred between 1999 and 2001—the heart of the dot-com boom. During the Great Recession (2008–2011), growth rates remained stagnant before a slight uptick in 2011. While Los Angeles foundations are impressive in absolute terms, on a per capita basis, however, they appear less prominent nationally. In terms of the number of foundations per 10,000 population, assets per capita, and giving per capita, Los Angeles ranks twentieth, tenth, and fourteenth, respectively.

Between 1997 and 2011, total foundation assets in the Los Angeles metropolitan area grew by 48 percent, adjusted for inflation (see fig. 8.2). Despite greater relative growth in the number of foundations, asset growth among Los Angeles foundations was higher than nationwide growth (37 percent) and on a par with statewide growth (51 percent), but lower than growth among San Francisco Bay area funders (82 percent).

Foundation assets experienced a precipitous decline when the dot-com bubble burst in 2000. Assets dropped 17 percent between 2000 and 2002, but experienced a steady increase between 2002 and 2007 (average

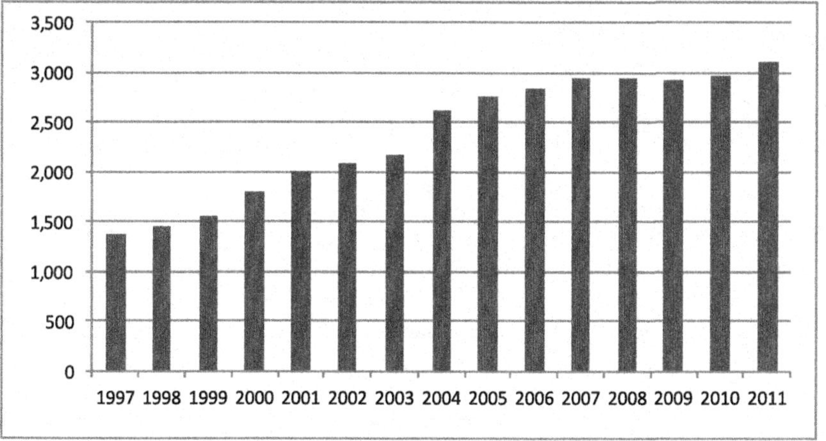

Figure 8.1. Total Number of Foundations, Los Angeles Metropolitan Area, 1997–2011. *Source:* The Foundation Center, 1999–2013.

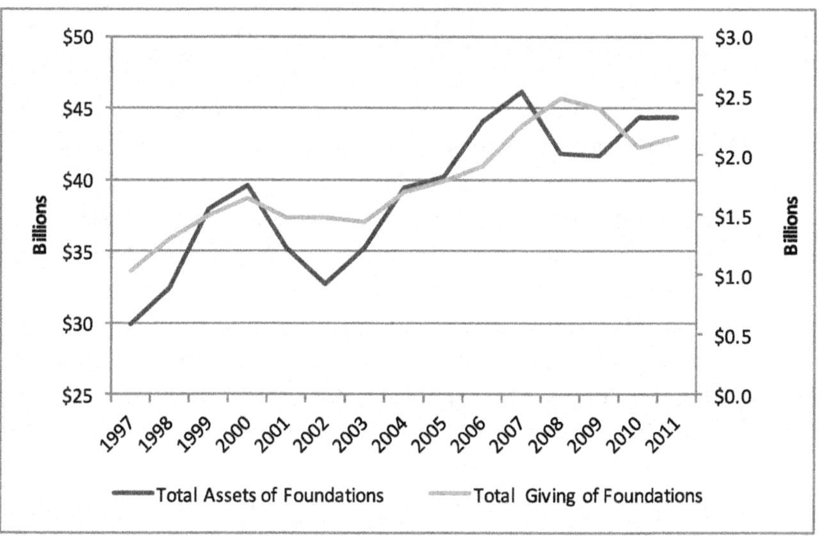

Figure 8.2. Total Foundation Assets and Giving, Los Angeles Metropolitan Area, 1997–2011. *Source:* The Foundation Center, 1999–2013; FC Stats: The Foundation Center's Statistical Information Service (foundationcenter.org/findfunders/statistics/).

annual growth was over 8 percent during that time). However, assets dropped again—by 9 percent—during the economic downturn in 2008 and 2009, and only rose slightly from 2009 to 2011.

Total giving by Los Angeles foundations more than doubled from 1997 to 2011, closely following asset growth patterns over time (figure 8.2). During both economic downturns reflected in figure 8.2, giving levels

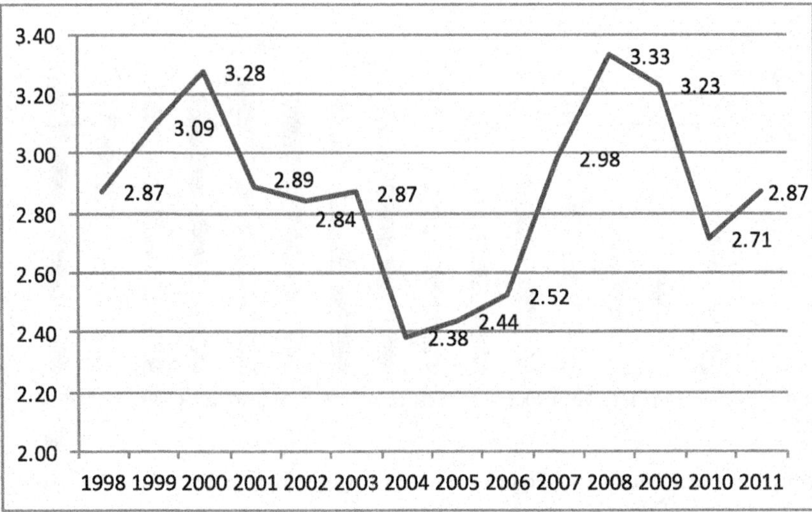

Figure 8.3. Los Angeles Foundation Grants per $1,000 Gross Metropolitan Product (GMP)[50] 1998–2011. *Source:* The Foundation Center; FCStats; US Conference of Mayors.

proved steadier than assets. In 2008, while assets dropped by 9 percent, giving actually rose by 11 percent, before experiencing a decline.

Despite overall growth of the sector since 1998, the value of foundation grants has struggled to keep pace with economic growth in the Los Angeles metropolitan area. As shown in figure 8.3, growth in foundation grant dollars has fluctuated in terms of its share of GMP in recent years. Between 2006 and 2008, foundation grant share of GMP rose by 32 percent, but 2009–2010 witnessed a steep drop in share of GMP. So while the importance of foundations relative to government overcame a steady decline in the years preceding the great recession, the share of GMP had reverted back to 1998 levels by 2011.

Despite the economic downturn, notable local philanthropists like Edythe and Eli Broad and Michael and Lori Milken (both couples who have signed onto the Giving Pledge inspired by Warren Buffet and Bill and Melinda Gates) have used foundations as vehicles to maintain and even quicken the rates at which they make large gifts to a variety of institutions.

Community Foundations

Although Los Angeles was one of the first cities in the United States to establish a formal community foundation, Los Angeles community foundation assets trail those of several other major US metropolitan areas. In 2011, Los Angeles ranked sixth in the United States in terms of community

Table 8.2. Number of Community Foundations, Total Community Foundation Assets, and Total Community Foundation Given, US Metropolitan Areas with Community Foundation Assets of $1 Billion or More, 2011

Metro Area	Number of Community Foundations	Total Community Foundation Assets	Total Community Foundation Giving	Total Community Foundation Assets Per Capita	Total Community Foundation Giving Per Capita
1 San Francisco	4	$2,806,081,323	$209,133,739	$639	$48
2 New York	5	$2,189,340,537	$166,705,528	$188	$14
3 Cleveland	4	$1,897,216,028	$82,640,075	$917	$40
4 Chicago	14	$1,860,706,299	$117,775,177	$196	$12
5 Minneapolis	9	$1,492,338,050	$115,379,381	$455	$35
6 Los Angeles	**9**	**$1,366,337,020**	**$158,385,855**	**$106**	**$12**
7 Portland, OR	2	$1,242,896,303	$67,698,508	$562	$31
8 Kansas City, MO	2	$1,190,121,242	$220,815,373	$589	$109
9 Dallas	3	$1,080,632,405	$97,908,802	$166	$15
Total		$14,045,036,802	$1,138,533,636	$45	$4
% United States		24%	26%		

Source: Foundation Center, 2013; FC Stats: The Foundation Center's Statistical Information Service (foundationcenter.org/findfunders/statistics/); US Census Bureau, 2011 American Community Survey.

foundation assets (table 8.2). Los Angeles does rank fourth, however, in total community foundation giving (due to the California Community Foundation). Los Angeles community foundation assets, assets per capita, and giving per capita lag behind other regions.

Grant Analysis

The following foundation grant data were compiled from the Foundation Center's grants sample database.[51] These analyses help to characterize the Los Angeles foundation funding environment in terms of grant size, grantee characteristics, and relation to the broader local nonprofit sector. These data, though not inclusive of an extended history, provide a useful overview for gauging the nature and breadth of foundation support in Los Angeles.

In order to compare Los Angeles grant size data to state and national levels, 2005 Foundation Center grants sample data were analyzed. It should be noted that this analysis includes only grants above $10,000. Table 8.3 shows national, state, and local grant size data by National Taxonomy of Exempt Entity (NTEE) major group categories. In 2005,

Table 8.3. Mean and Median Grant Size, by NTEE Major Groups, United States, California, and Los Angeles, 2005

	United States		**California**		**Los Angeles**	
NTEE Major Groups	Mean	Median	Mean	Median	Mean	Median
Arts and Culture	$110,099	$25,000	$85,524	$25,000	$95,836	$25,000
Education	$177,298	$35,000	$151,529	$30,000	$149,718	$40,000
Environment	$124,989	$30,000	$149,853	$30,000	$66,582	$30,000
Health	$144,494	$30,000	$115,859	$25,000	$157,017	$50,000
Human Services	$67,030	$25,000	$56,487	$22,724	$76,802	$25,000
International, Foreign Affairs and National Security	$191,584	$40,000	$99,527	$35,000	$94,523	$45,000
Public/Societal Benefit	$132,452	$35,000	$132,671	$30,000	$127,904	$50,000
Religion	$78,249	$24,250	$115,207	$25,000	$179,409	$31,223
Mutual and Membership Benefit	$227,721	$17,500	$50,000	$40,000	$100,000	$100,000
Unknown	$49,965	$20,000	$33,333	$32,500	$50,000	$50,000
Total	$124,127	$25,620	$109,008	$25,000	$119,457	$35,000

Source: Foundation Center Grants Sample Database, circa 2005.

the average Los Angeles grant included in the Foundation Center 2005 sample was 4 percent lower than the national average and 9 percent higher than the state average.[52] Average and median grant sizes for health, human services, and religion were higher than both the national and state averages. Education grants were smaller than the national and state averages, although the median education grant size in Los Angeles was larger than that in the country and the state. Environment and international, foreign affairs, and national security were below state and national levels. Arts and culture grants were larger than the state average, but below the national average.

With the exception of grants to support health-related nonprofits, giving by Los Angeles foundations closely resembles national trends in terms of share of grant dollars by subfield (see table 8.4). Whereas 13 percent of foundation grant dollars support health in the United States, 26 percent of Los Angeles foundation grant dollars support health. This trend is explained in part by the presence of two large health foundations, the California Endowment and the California Wellness Foundation. Grants to support education (32 percent) rank first in the share of grant

Table 8.4. Share of Grant Dollars, by Subfield, US and Los Angeles Foundations, 2005

	Los Angeles Foundations to All Recipients			**US Foundations to All Recipients**		
Subfield	Amount ($)	%	Rank	Amount ($)	%	Rank
Education	220,833,246	32%	1st	5,531,119,288	34%	1st
Health	176,016,504	26%	2nd	2,200,298,908	13%	4th
Human Services	115,432,658	17%	3rd	2,206,803,338	13%	3rd
Arts and Culture	63,539,096	9%	4th	1,981,647,630	12%	5th
Public Affairs/ Society Benefit	61,649,770	9%	5th	2,595,439,863	16%	2nd
Environment and Animals	18,909,155	3%	6th	911,746,695	6%	6th
Religion	20,452,599	3%	7th	361,590,574	2%	8th
International Affairs, Development, and Peace	10,492,102	2%	8th	630,907,376	4%	7th
Mutual and Membership	100,000	0%	9th	5,038,909	0%	9th
Unknown	50,000	0%	10th	3,422,788	0%	10th
Total Grant Dollars	687,475,130	100%		16,428,015,369	100%	

Source: Foundation Center Grants Sample Database, circa 2005.

dollars among Los Angeles foundations, while health (26 percent), human services (17 percent) and arts and culture (9 percent) are ranked second, third, and fourth, respectively.

Table 8.4 shows the differences in the share of grant dollars given to nonprofit subfields between Los Angeles foundation grants to local and nonlocal recipients. Nearly 24 percent of grant dollars to non–Los Angeles recipients are health-related, compared to 27 percent of Los Angeles foundation grants to local organizations. These data again highlight the influence of the health conversion foundations in Los Angeles and the extent to which their giving skews the data. Los Angeles foundations give a relatively low share of grant dollars (6 percent) to fund arts and culture organizations outside of Los Angeles, reinforcing the local emphasis of arts funding in the region.

Table 8.4 also shows the distribution of grants by subfield for gifts from nonlocal funders to Los Angeles–based recipients. Compared to the national averages, Los Angeles receives a lower share of health and human service grant dollars from non–Los Angeles foundations, whereas

Table 8.5. Share of Grant Dollars, by Subfield, US and Los Angeles Foundations (Los Angeles vs. Non–Los Angeles Comparisons), 2005

	Los Angeles Foundations to Los Angeles Recipients		**Los Angeles Foundations to Non–Los Angeles Recipients**		**Non–Los Angeles Foundations to All Recipients**		**Non–Los Angeles Foundations to Los Angeles Recipients**	
Subfield	Amount ($)	%	Amount ($)	%	Amount ($)	%	Amount ($)	%
Arts and Culture	43,645,371	13%	19,893,725	6%	1,918,108,534	12%	67,404,583	18%
Education	98,135,808	29%	122,697,438	36%	5,310,286,042	34%	167,342,654	45%
Environment and Animals	3,883,139	1%	15,026,016	4%	892,837,540	6%	6,217,006	2%
Health	94,446,821	27%	81,569,683	24%	2,024,282,404	13%	41,502,986	11%
Human Services	66,161,659	19%	49,270,999	14%	2,091,370,680	13%	31,559,856	9%
International Affairs, Development, and Peace	3,122,464	1%	7,369,638	2%	620,415,274	4%	4,216,055	1%
Mutual and Membership	0	0%	100,000	0%	4,938,909	0%	0	0%
Public Affairs/Society Benefit	23,797,927	7%	37,851,843	11%	2,533,790,093	16%	43,180,044	12%
Religion	10,401,288	3%	10,051,311	3%	341,137,975	2%	7,572,138	2%
Unknown	0	0%	50,000	0%	3,372,788	0%	50,000	0%
Total Grant Dollars	343,594,477	100%	343,880,653	100%	15,740,540,239	100%	369,045,322	100%

Source: Foundation Center, 2005.

nonlocal funders grant a higher than average share of dollars for arts and culture and science and technology in Los Angeles. This pattern might indicate that funding for health and human services tends to be more locally focused among non–Los Angeles grantees. In terms of the arts and sciences, Los Angeles has several large cultural institutions (e.g., Walt Disney Concert Hall in Downtown Los Angeles) and scientific hubs (e.g., California Institute of Technology [Caltech]) which have garnered large shares of support (including major capital investments) from foundations outside of Los Angeles.

Table 8.5 compares how much Los Angeles foundations engage in grantmaking outside of the region versus how much they give to local recipients, demonstrating that Los Angeles foundation grant dollars are evenly split. When examining grant dollars received by Los Angeles–based recipients, slightly more than half (52 percent) came from non–Los Angeles–based foundations.

Top Recipients

As is the case in most areas of high philanthropic investment, the top recipients of foundation grants year-to-year tend to be universities (table 8.6). From 2009 to 2011, the top four Los Angeles grant recipients (and eight of the top twenty) were universities. The University of Southern California (USC) received the highest amount of total grant dollars in 2011 (more than $218 million)—the fourth highest total in the United States. Also reflected on the list are several arts and culture institutions and two prominent private hospitals.

This section provided a quantitative analysis meant to illustrate how the Los Angeles foundation community compares nationally. While Los Angeles boasts a large foundation sector in absolute terms, on a per capita basis and based on growth relative to GMP, the sector is less impressive. Giving trends reflect patterns of asset growth in relation to economic conditions, although there is evidence that giving levels tend to sustain themselves even as assets experience declines (this trend is consistent with national patterns as well). Overall, the results of the grants database reveal that Los Angeles foundations do not differ significantly from the national pattern and that, with some notable exceptions such as health and human services, foundation grantmaking is basically comparable to that of the nation. In the next section, we examine more closely the role of foundations in Los Angeles, and provide some qualitative support and explanation of the quantitative analysis.

Table 8.6. Top Twenty Los Angeles–based Foundation Grant Recipients, 2009–2011

Recipient Organization	City	Total Dollars Awarded ($)	Number of Grants
University of Southern California	Los Angeles	374,252,356	438
California Institute of Technology	Pasadena	173,734,421	203
University of California	Los Angeles	143,146,237	371
UCLA Foundation	Los Angeles	83,727,642	196
Los Angeles County Museum of Art	Los Angeles	61,780,592	85
College-Ready Promise	Los Angeles	60,135,000	3
California State Polytechnic University	Pomona	42,000,000	1
University of California	Irvine	38,021,760	86
Childrens Hospital Los Angeles	Los Angeles	35,438,698	93
Skirball Cultural Center	Los Angeles	35,087,022	49
Claremont McKenna College	Claremont	34,737,256	73
Foundation for Global Sports Development	Los Angeles	30,000,000	1
California Charter Schools Association	Los Angeles	24,785,971	41
City of Hope	Duarte	23,968,957	30
Colburn School of the Performing Arts	Los Angeles	22,871,000	17
Green Dot Education Project	Los Angeles	16,707,384	20
Broad Center for the Management of School Systems	Los Angeles	16,412,517	4
Cedars-Sinai Medical Center	Los Angeles	15,906,433	37
Museum of Contemporary Art	Los Angeles	15,222,030	26
K C E T Community Television of Southern California	Los Angeles	14,738,604	41

Source: The Foundation Center, 2009–2011.
Based on all grants of $10,000 or more awarded by a national sample of 1,339 larger US foundations (including 800 of the 1,000 largest ranked by total giving). For community foundations, only discretionary grants are included. Grants to individuals are not included in the file. The search set includes only larger US foundations awarding grants in the metropolitan area. Grants by smaller local foundations are not represented. Metropolitan areas are as designated by the US Office of Management and Budget (OMB).

Foundation Roles

One important way to assess how Los Angeles foundations differ from those in other regions of the country, in the aggregate, is to look at their roles or contributions. Anheier and Hammack proposed a classification of foundation roles.[53] This section explores how Los Angeles foundations fall into a variety of role categories. In general terms, this chapter examines illustrative examples of charitable relief efforts—foundation initiatives that largely complement or supplement government spending—and philanthropic efforts that spur innovation, pursue systemic change, and promote social justice and equality.

Immediate Relief

One of the largest areas of foundation activity in Los Angeles—particularly in the human services—occurs through relief efforts focused on the immediate needs of various marginalized populations. Through these initiatives, some of which are described below, foundations tend to supplement government funding or services. While the philanthropic contributions in dollar amount terms do not measure up to the government support of programs that address issues such as homelessness and healthcare, foundation-funded efforts have spearheaded programs that have later attracted more public dollars.

For example, the Conrad N. Hilton Foundation has granted approximately $42 million over the past twenty years to support local solutions to long-term homelessness. The grants have largely supported permanent supportive housing initiatives that have complemented funding efforts by local government.[54] While certainly a generous contribution, the $42 million multiyear commitment reflects just a fraction of the annual Los Angeles funding from the US Department of Housing and Urban Development (about $90 million) and the region's estimated $875 million in public spending on homelessness.[55] But the support has also included cost-benefit research that has influenced greater public investment in solving the problem (e.g., Los Angeles County's Project 50, which led to a $105 million commitment from the county).

Building Out Institutions

Particularly in the fields of higher education and the arts, Los Angeles foundations have provided substantial support for expanding local institutions. As mentioned earlier, local universities are the largest recipients of foundation grant dollars. An analysis of the largest grants ($1 million or more) made to Los Angeles–based recipients over the past decade shows that both Caltech and USC have received close to $500 million each from foundation grants of that size. The W. M. Keck Foundation alone has donated nearly $300 million to USC.

As mentioned, foundations play an important role in the Los Angeles arts and culture sector—the second largest arts economy in the country (behind New York). Foundations in the region have stepped in to supplement reduced government spending on the arts, particularly in the area of arts education. Arts and culture organizations in Los Angeles are more dependent on foundation dollars than arts organizations nationally. Private foundation grants make up about 2 percent of the Los Angeles County nonprofit sector's overall revenue, and foundation support accounts for 12 percent of arts and culture nonprofit revenue (compared to 8 percent for the country as a whole).[56] When the California Arts Council budget was virtually eliminated in 2003, exacerbating previous cuts to public arts education funding, a number of private foundations offered significant support as a way to make up for lost public investment.[57] In 2005, while Los Angeles County arts nonprofits received less than $250,000 in grant support from the California Arts Council, Los Angeles–based foundations gave more than $40 million in local arts grants. Nearly twenty Los Angeles–based foundations alone exceeded California Arts Council funding to local organizations.[58] In 2006, the Jewish Community Foundation and the Los Angeles County Arts Commission jointly funded over 150 arts residency programs in local public schools. The James Irvine Foundation—headquartered in San Francisco but with an affiliate office in Los Angeles—has also heavily invested in local arts initiatives.

Los Angeles foundations have made substantial investments in the region's cultural institutions, helping to build out the arts economy. From 2003 to 2013, local foundations have awarded the Los Angeles County Museum of Art, the largest art museum in the western United States, more than $150 million. In the late 1980s, Lillian Disney donated $50 million toward what would become the Frank Gehry–designed Walt Disney Concert Hall, home of the Los Angeles Philharmonic and a critical ingredient in the redevelopment of Downtown Los Angeles.[59] Between 2003 and 2011, the Walt and Lilly Disney Foundation granted nearly $25 million to the Los Angeles Philharmonic.

Policy Reform and Advocacy

Despite limitations on lobbying and political activities for nonprofit organizations writ large, private foundations have increasingly become involved with public policy in recent years. As a way to leverage philanthropic assets and in attempt to create longstanding "system change," foundations have increasingly focused "on ambitions for transforming systems and producing substantial improvements in outcomes."[60]

Foundation watchdog groups like the National Committee for Responsive Philanthropy (NCRP) have called on funders to direct more resources towards advocacy work and policy change. In 2010 NCRP released a report on foundation support for advocacy, organizing, and civic engagement in LA.[61] Major foundations, including the California Endowment and the California Community Foundation, have embraced the idea of funding advocacy efforts. The Endowment requires such activity among all grantees.

In the wake of the No Child Left Behind Act of 2001, and as charter schools continue to emerge in Los Angeles, foundations have given more than $250 million to school reform and charter school efforts in Los Angeles. The Broad Foundation has donated more than $70 million to these efforts. In 2010, the Los Angeles Unified School District had more charter schools than any other district in the nation, with 183 schools serving 78,000 students.[62]

Healthcare reform, particularly in relation to the rollout of the Affordable Care Act, has also garnered substantial support and involvement from the local health-focused foundations in Los Angeles. The big health foundations—including the California Endowment (TCE) and the California Wellness Foundation (TCWF)—regularly support initiatives focused on prevention of unwanted pregnancy, community violence reduction, promoting healthy aging, and other issues that address the needs of underserved populations and supplement government programs operated by the County Departments of Public Health and Mental Health. TCE and TCWF provide close to $200 million annually to local nonprofits and coalitions working to improve access to quality healthcare, particularly among underserved populations, with a focus on public awareness campaigns, policy reform, and equitable healthcare. TCE has launched a partnership with the White House to ensure that the fifteen million Latinos in California has sufficient access to and education about the new healthcare laws.

Social justice change is another area where several Los Angeles–based funders have become increasingly involved. Whether in terms of ethnicity, income, national origin, or geography, high rates of diversity help define the Los Angeles region. Four funders—the California Community Foundation, TCE, TCWF, and the Liberty Hill Foundation, which is a grant-making 501(c)(3) public charity—have been particularly active in social justice funding. These funders have routinely offered support to local social justice organizations, including LAANE, Strategic Alliance for a Just Economy (SAJE), and ACORN (now the Alliance of Californians for Community Empowerment). The local health foundations have made recent investments in policy reform agendas that address local criminal recidivism and uninsured children.[63] Issues related to advocacy and diversity are discussed further in the next section.

Increased calls for foundation transparency and accountability have crossed over into the realm of diversity—diversity with respect to foundation leadership, the organizations that foundations support, and the communities that benefit from foundation giving. Groups like the Greenlining Institute and Diversity in Philanthropy have called for more support of minority-led nonprofits and for foundations to keep better track of diversity data.[64] Greenlining, a public policy research and advocacy institute based in Berkeley, California, which receives funding from prominent foundations like Ford, California Wellness, and James Irvine, began releasing a series of reports in 2005 that analyzed numerous issues related to diversity and philanthropy. The initial report showed that of the top fifty independent foundations and the top twenty-five community foundations, only 3 percent awarded grant dollars to minority-led organizations.[65] Interestingly, the report stated that corporate foundations, including the Wells Fargo Foundation, the Verizon Foundation, and the Washington Mutual Foundation, awarded more than 40 percent of their total grant dollars to minority-led organizations.

The reports issued by Greenlining led to a 2006 legislative hearing before the California Black, Latino, and Asian Pacific Islander Legislative Caucuses. Shared perspectives of foundation, nonprofit, and corporate leadership led in part to the introduction of Assembly Bill 624 by California State Assembly member Joe Coto (a member of the California Latino Legislative Caucus) in 2007. The bill sought to monitor diversity-related philanthropic activities, prompting a number of local foundations to band together in opposition of the legislation. The legislation was eventually withdrawn when a coalition of nine foundations agreed to give at least $30 million over three years to support minority-led nonprofits in addition to adopting a more strategic approach to building nonprofit leadership capacity among minority-led community-based groups.[66] The coalition includes some of the largest funders in Los Angeles, including TCE, California Wellness, the Ralph M. Parsons Foundation, the Annenberg Foundation, the Ahmanson Foundation, and the Weingart Foundation.[67]

The Funders Collaborative for Strong Latino Communities is another example of a philanthropic effort to reach a minority target population. Administered by Hispanics in Philanthropy, in 2004 the Collaborative awarded $1 million to thirteen southern California–based Latino nonprofits, including the East Los Angeles Classic Theater in Monterey Park and Los Angeles–based Homies Unidos, to help build their organizational capacity and leadership.[68]

A Place-Based Approach

Following the innovative models set forth by the Annie E. Casey Foundation and other prominent funders that have implemented place-based funding approaches, several Los Angeles–based foundations have begun to focus more on specific geographies. Perhaps one of the most poignant examples of a place-based strategy came about in the aftermath of the 1992 riots in South Los Angeles—the worst local episode of civil unrest since the 1965 Watts riots. The Los Angeles Urban Funders (LAUF), a coalition of eighteen foundations that included the philanthropies of three major banks, invested $30 million into three low-income Los Angeles neighborhoods—Pacoima, Vermont/Manchester, and Hyde Park.[69] LAUF partners included the California Community Foundation, TCE, the James Irvine Foundation, Liberty Hill Foundation, the Prudential Foundation, the Rockefeller Foundation, the Jewish Community Foundation, and Sony Pictures Entertainment. The LAUF model has been touted as an exemplar in collaborative funding, in particular due to its focus on community planning and resident involvement.[70]

Place-based initiatives have become more commonplace over time. The California Endowment and California Community Foundation have adopted, to varying extents, placed-based funding approaches. The Endowment has focused its grantmaking on fourteen communities throughout the state (three of which are in Los Angeles County). The Endowment's Building Healthy Communities Initiative is investing $1 billion over ten years into fourteen selected communities. The California Community Foundation employed an extensive community selection process, which involved stakeholder engagement and community demographic and indicator research. The funding will benefit a range of challenged areas, including larger metropolitan areas like Sacramento and Long Beach in addition to smaller rural communities throughout the state.

In 2007, the California Community Foundation launched its Community Building Initiative (CBI) in El Monte, an underserved area of eastern Los Angeles County. The Foundation engaged the community in an assessment and planning initiative, which helped craft a strategic plan to focus on youth and school support, health, and asset building. In addition to traditional grantmaking, CBI's goals include engagement with local government and leveraging further support from the private sector.

As placed-based approaches have become more attractive to funders, other grant-making entities have followed suit. Notably, First 5 Los Angeles (F5LA), a public commission funded by local tax dollars, focused on child advocacy, has adopted a place-based approach for its most recent strategic plan. Though not a private foundation, F5LA has invested nearly $700 million in local community.

Conclusion and Thoughts on Future Developments

Foundations in Los Angeles have played a number of roles over the past sixty years, helping to build out the region's largest cultural centers and universities, making substantial investments in healthcare access and policy reform, and strengthening the capacity of an over-burdened nonprofit sector, particularly in the human services. Mainly serving in a complementary role to government, although coming close to a substitute for public investment in some examples (e.g., arts education), foundations have helped promote and preserve higher education and arts and culture institutions, have sought strategic approaches by influencing public policy, have experimented with placed-based approaches, and have provided key investments in building the nonprofit sector's capacity.

The Los Angeles foundation sector's development has shown similarities and differences compared to broader national patterns. The pioneering era for philanthropy in southern California occurred during a time of postwar affluence and industrial expansion. The economic boom of the 1990s, fueled in part by West Coast innovation, led to another surge in Los Angeles foundation activity and formation. Yet it was, and largely remains, a history of growing scale but not necessarily also growing importance, with two exceptions: first, healthcare and higher education, both fields with high concentrations on few recipient organizations, and second, a stronger emphasis on advocacy.

Of course, private foundations have impacted a broad spectrum of institutions in Los Angeles. Although the larger foundations in the area were not established until after World War II, many of the region's major institutions, particularly those of higher education, were primarily the products of philanthropy. The data presented here highlights the substantial foundation support of local universities as well as large cultural institutions—and increasingly so over time.

Many of the region's largest foundations don the façades of significant cultural centers, schools, and social service facilities (e.g., the Broad

Contemporary Art Museum, Disney Hall, the Weingart Center, the S. Mark Taper Amphitheatre, the Getty Museum, and USC's Keck School of Medicine and Annenberg School of Communications), yet such support has by and large remained rather conventional, and followed philanthropic trends from other regions (e.g., place-based approaches). And while foundations have played important roles in response to crises (e.g., the 1992 civil unrest, state cuts to arts education, and the Great Recession), they have yet to appear at the forefront of developments in philanthropy, with some exceptions (e.g., TCE), than other regions on the West Coast, especially the Bay area.

Ferris makes the point that the youth of Los Angeles foundations provides opportunity to shape the philanthropic agenda as it were, as these funders will "come of age" in the coming decades.[71] However, the vast literature on organizations suggests that newness rather than maturity aligns with innovation. Why indeed would we expect Los Angeles foundations to adopt imaginative and creative approaches once they have been established for decades, when they too often have not done so when entering fields much less institutionalized and with much less inertia than their peers on the East Coast? Should we not expect innovative impulses to emerge from Los Angeles philanthropy today, populated as it is by numerous foundations of recent origin?

In terms of innovation, and particularly in relation to the question posed at the beginning of this chapter—that is, whether a distinct pattern of Los Angeles philanthropy has emerged—it is important to recall aspects of the regional context in which foundations exist: the largest unsheltered homeless population in the country, a growing number of Latinos (who nearly outnumber non-Latinos at the city and county level) seeking more voice and opportunities to escape poverty and precarious jobs, perennial struggles to improve performance in local schools, environmental degradation, continued budget strains, and so on. Against this background, one conclusion is simply this: However large in numbers and assets foundations may become in the future, their individual as well as collective contributions and impact cannot be at a scale relative to the size of the many social, economic, educational, and cultural challenges confronting Los Angeles. Of course, they will make many worthwhile and important contributions, and numerous current and future examples of philanthropic engagement of wealthy individuals will stand out—be it in the arts (e.g., the Broad art museum next to Disney Hall), a new research institute at one of the region's universities, or building nonprofit capacity. But will such contributions be enough?

Perhaps the question of what distinct and innovative grant-making pattern seems to emerge in Los Angeles requires a shift in focus: above, we emphasized the track record of Los Angeles foundations in place-based philanthropy and the experience of foundations working together, be it in response to the 1992 riots or in the fields of arts education, mental health, or social justice. These initiatives seem to have set the course for what could in future become a pattern for philanthropy in Los Angeles, and perhaps become its hallmark: foundations lead partnerships that involve government agencies as well as nonprofits and even businesses that are focused on particular fields or places.

The new collaborations go well beyond the liaison office established by the mayor in the 2000s; they also go beyond the creations of the Los Angeles Mayor's Fund and the Philanthropy Office at the County level since then. They typically involve cross-sector partnerships in which foundations do more than initiate a process in the hope of passing it on to government, as the following examples reveal:

- An early example, the Home for Good campaign developed by United Way of Greater Los Angeles, was launched in 2010 through a grant from the Conrad N. Hilton Foundation. In 2012, the project announced $105 million of public and private support to alleviate homelessness in Los Angeles.
- "LA in Synch" seeks to establish a coordinated approach for local nonprofits and government agencies in response to federal funding proposals. Rather than having organizations compete against each other, the project, led by the Annenberg Foundation, builds constellations among local agencies capable of competing at the national level.
- Another is "Pacific Standard Time," spearheaded by the Getty Trust and supported by other foundations to support local museums through a coordinated effort that brought larger and smaller museums together.
- In the social services field, ten foundations cooperated with the County government on a "Blue Ribbon Commission" on child welfare, leading to the establishment of the Office of Child Protection.
- The Nonprofit Sustainability Initiative, funded by ten local foundations including the Weingart and Parsons foundations, seeks to increase the efficiency of nonprofit providers by building scale and scope capacities, including mergers and other ways of close cooperation.
- The civic engagement project LA 2050, launched by the Goldhirsh Foundation, involves thousands of citizens in hundreds of nonprofit organizations and businesses next to government representatives in developing a positive vision of a future Los Angeles.

Until the Great Recession, a somewhat curious conclusion we could have drawn about the role of philanthropy in the Los Angeles region was that it is much less daring, more conventional, less the innovator, and more the adaptor than the ever-changing, dynamic society of the region's millions of inhabitants would suggest. We would have asked whether Los Angeles foundations would, in the future, be able to deploy the creativity and innovative potential they undoubtedly harbored, and whether they would in the end be able to make the contributions society rightly expected of them.

Nearly a decade later, Los Angeles foundations have made much headway in these respects. The fragmentation of local government, persistent budget pressures, mounting social, economic, and other problems seemingly too big for private foundations to address, and many related factors—they have long been seen as a weakness and indeed, as an impediment, toward achieving sustained philanthropic impact. These frustrating circumstances ultimately invited innovative responses among local foundation leaders, with the regional umbrella organization Southern California Grantmakers[72] and university-led seminar series[73] supporting their gestation. These responses resulted in a still-emerging pattern that could perhaps be best described as the coalition model of philanthropy to leverage impact. It involves concerted efforts, spearheaded by foundations as well as others founders, and diverse coalitions of implementing agencies—be they public or private, for-profit, or nonprofit. Ideally, they contain elements of crowd-funded and crowd-supported approaches to address a local need in view of some policy change. But foundations do not harbor the expectation that government will necessarily step in after some initial period and see to the longer term sustainability of whatever such coalitions seek to achieve.

Whether Los Angeles foundations will be able to live up to the promise of the coalition model, and indeed see it through its fuller development, remains an open question. But what the findings suggest is that the coalition model may well be the pattern that makes southern California philanthropy distinct from giving in New York and the Bay area.

David B. Howard is Senior Vice President of Research, Evaluation and Learning at Covenant House International and Adjunct Lecturer at the New York University Silver School of Social Work. He has published on the nonprofit sectors of New York and Los Angeles.

Helmut K. Anheier is President, Dean, and Professor of Sociology at the Hertie School of Governance. He also holds a chair of sociology at Heidelberg University and serves as Academic Director of the Centre for Social Investment. He is author of *Nonprofit Organizations: Theory, Management, Policy.*

Notes

1. The authors acknowledge those who have contributed to various iterations of this work, especially Eve Garrow, Jennifer Mosley, Marcus Lam, and Jocelyn Guihama. The work reported here was funded, in part, by a grant of the Aspen Institute. We are also grateful for the comments received by the editors of this volume, and for input on current developments from James Ferris, Wendy Garen, and Claire Peeps.

2. David C. Hammack and Helmut K. Anheier, *A Versatile American Institution: The Changing Ideals and Realities of Philanthropic Foundations* (Washington, DC: Brookings Institution Press, 2013), chaps. 2 and 3.

3. See chap. 9 of this volume, "Foundations in San Francisco and Silicon Valley," by Carol J. Silverman and Arleda Martinez.

4. Tom Sitton, *The Haynes Foundation and Urban Reform Philanthropy in Los Angeles: A History of the John Randolph Haynes and Dora Haynes Foundation* (Los Angeles: The Historical Society of Southern California,1999); James M. Ferris, Rachel Potter, and Michael Tuerpe, *Foundations for Los Angeles? An Analysis of the Scale, Scope and Reach of Foundation Philanthropy in Los Angeles County* (Los Angeles: The Center on Philanthropy and Public Policy. University of Southern California, 2005); James M. Ferris, "Philanthropy in Southern California," in *Looking Ahead: The Changing Landscape of Philanthropy*, ed. Sushma Raman (Los Angeles: Southern California Grantmakers, 2010), 4–5.

5. Philanthropy in Los Angeles remains rather understudied, and, unlike in New York and in other major centers of foundation activities, the philanthropic community has made few investments in creating a local research infrastructure.

6. Within the context of this chapter, Los Angeles refers to the Los Angeles-Long Beach-Santa Ana Metropolitan Statistical Area (MSA), which includes Los Angeles and Orange Counties. Unless otherwise indicated, foundation and nonprofit data are aggregated at the MSA level. In some instances, references are made to Los Angeles County or the city of Los Angeles.

7. David L. Gladstone and Susan S. Fainstein, "The New York and Los Angeles Economies from Boom to Crisis," in *New York and Los Angeles: The Uncertain Future*, eds. David Halle and Andrew A. Beveridge (New York: Oxford University Press, 2013), 79–102.

8. United States Conference of Mayors, *US Metro Economies. GMP and Employment Report: 2015–2017* (Lexington, MA: HIS Global Insight [USA], 2016), 26, http://uscm.wpengine.com/wp-content/uploads/2017/02/201606-metroeconomies.pdf, viewed Oct. 30, 2017.

9. US Census Bureau, *American Community Survey* (Washington, DC: US Census Bureau, 2011). According to the Census Bureau, Los Angeles County has the thirteenth-largest percentage of nonwhite residents among cities in the continental United States.

10. Gladstone and Fainstein, "New York and Los Angeles Economies."

11. United Way of Greater Los Angeles, 2010. *L.A. County 10 Years Later: A Tale of Two Cities. One Future.* Los Angeles, CA.

12. Helmut K. Anheier, Marcus Lam, and David B. Howard, "The Nonprofit Sector in Los Angeles and New York City," in *New York and Los Angeles: The Uncertain Future*, eds. David Halle and Andrew A. Beveridge (New York: Oxford University Press, 2013), 513–32; Hyeon Jong Kil and David B. Howard, *Hard Times: Impacts, Actions, Prospects. The State of the Nonprofit Sector in Los Angeles 2010* (Los Angeles: UCLA Center for Civil Society, 2010).

13. John Mollenkopf and Raphael J. Sonenshein, "New York City and Los Angeles: Government and Political Influence," in *New York and Los Angeles: The Uncertain Future*, eds. David Halle and Andrew A. Beveridge (New York: Oxford University Press, 2013), 137–53.

14. Jennifer Wolch, *Places to Play: Environmental Justice and the Distribution of Urban Parks and Recreation in Los Angeles* (Sacramento: The American Institute of Architects, California Council, 2013). Available at http://www.aiacc.org/tag/jennifer-wolch/.

15. Torie Osborn, "Generating Creative Public-Private Partnerships in an Era of Change," in *Looking Ahead: The Changing Landscape of Philanthropy*, Southern California Grantmakers (Los Angeles: Southern California Grantmakers, 2010).

16. Anheier, Lam, and Howard, "Nonprofit Sector."

17. James M. Ferris and Nicholas P. O. Williams, *Philanthropy and Government Working Together: The Role of Offices of Strategic Partnerships in Public Problem Solving* (Los Angeles: The Center on Philanthropy and Public Policy, University of Southern California, 2012); Osborn, "Generating Creative Public-Private Partnerships in an Era of Change."

18. George Sweeting and Andrea Dinneen, "New York City and Los Angeles: Taxes, Budgets, and Managing the Financial Crisis," in *New York and Los Angeles: The Uncertain Future*, ed. David Halle and Andrew A. Beveridge (New York: Oxford University Press, 2013), 193–217.

19. Sushma Raman, "Focusing on Advocacy," *Stanford Social Innovation Review*, Fall 2011.

20. California Budget Project 2011, "A Decade of Disinvestment: California Education Spending Nears the Bottom" (Sacramento: California Budget Project); Julia Wrigley, "Los Angeles and New York City Schools" in *New York and Los Angeles: The Uncertain Future*, eds. David Halle and Andrew A. Beveridge (New York: Oxford University Press, 2013), 263–85.

21. Sweeting and Dinneen, "New York City and Los Angeles."

22. Yeheskel "Zeke" Hasenfeld, Mindy Chen, Eve Garrow, Bill Parent, and Jocelyn Guihama, *Spread Thin: Human Services Organizations in Poor Neighborhoods* (The State of the Nonprofit Sector in Los Angeles Report) (Los Angeles: UCLA Center for Civil Society, 2013).

23. Helmut K. Anheier, Hyeon Jong Kil, David B. Howard, Eve Garrow, and Marcus Lam. Local Patterns and Dynamics (The State of the Nonprofit Sector in Los Angeles 2008) (Los Angeles: UCLA Center for Civil Society, 2008); Hasenfeld et al., *Spread Thin*.

24. Helmut K. Anheier, David B. Howard, Hyeon Jong Kil, and Jocelyn Guihama. Arts in the Balance. Arts Funding in Los Angeles County:1998–2008 (Los Angeles: UCLA Center for Civil Society, 2009).

25. Anheier, Howard et al. Arts in the Balance.

26. National Agency of State Arts Agencies, 2013. State Arts Agency Legislative Appropriations Preview Fiscal Year 2014. Available at http://www.nasaa-arts.org/Research/Funding/State-Budget-Center/FY2014-Leg-Approp-Preview.pdf.

27. Andrew Deener, Steven P. Erie, Vladimir Kogan, and Forrest Stuart, "Planning Los Angeles: The Changing Politics of Neighborhood and Downtown Development," in *New York and Los Angeles: The Uncertain Future*, ed. David Halle and Andrew A. Beveridge (New York: Oxford University Press, 2013), 385–412; Anheier et al. 2008.

28. Data contained in *The Foundation Directory* (Edition One, 1960) has some notable limitations and should be interpreted with some caution. The directory excludes "very small" foundations, defined as those foundations that neither possessed assets of $50,000 nor had made grants of at least $10,000 in the latest year of record. Foundations in the center records totaled approximately 12,000 in 1960, but the directory includes only 5,202 of these. Furthermore, some suggest that because Form 990 data was at times difficult to collect, particularly in the Southern and Western regions, there may be a large portion of organizations unaccounted for in these data.

29. Foundation Center., Foundation Library Center., & Russell Sage Foundation. (1960). The Foundation directory. New York: Foundation Center; distributed by Columbia University Press.

30. Foundation Center, *FCStats*. Available at http://foundationcenter.org.

31. The individuals referenced here were the eventual benefactors of the Eli and Edythe Broad Foundation, the W.M. Keck Foundation, the Ahmanson Foundation, and the Weingart Foundation.

32. It should be pointed out that Getty is an operating foundation that funnels grant dollars into the Getty Center and Getty Villa—two of the city's most celebrated arts and culture centers—as opposed to a wider pool of grantees.

33. Helmut K. Anheier and David C. Hammack, eds., *American Foundations: Roles and Contributions* (Washington, DC: Brookings Institution Press, 2010).

34. Sitton, *Haynes Foundation and Urban Reform.*

35. Sitton, *Haynes Foundation and Urban Reform.*

36. *Los Angeles Times*, Display Ad 8—No Title, May 21, 1929 (*Los Angeles Times, 1923–Current File*, 7). Retrieved November 5, 2010, from ProQuest Historical Newspapers, *Los Angeles Times* (1881–1987) (Document ID: 378961251).

37. *Los Angeles Times*, "Local Foundation Given High Rank," August 28, 1941 (*Los Angeles Times, 1923–Current File*, 28). (Retrieved November 5, 2010, from ProQuest Historical Newspapers, *Los Angeles Times* (1881–1987) (Document ID: 413800421).

38. Sitton, *Haynes Foundation and Urban Reform*, 39–44.

39. Sitton, *Haynes Foundation and Urban Reform*, 22–37.

40. Abraham Hoffman, *Needs and Opportunities in Los Angeles Biography: Part Two: 1900–1940* (Long Beach: Historical Society of Southern California, 2001).

41. Steven S. Lemley, "A Long and Deep Past: Excerpted from an Address Delivered at the Pepperdine University Bible Lectures, May 5, 2010," *Pepperdine Magazine* 2, no. 1 (Summer 2010). Retrieved from http://magazine.pepperdine.edu/index.php/2010/08/a-long-deep-past/.

42. http://www.pepperdine.edu/about/our-story/history/.

43. Richard N. Aft and Mary Lu Aft, *Grassroots Initiatives Shape an International Movement: United Ways Since 1876* (United States: Philanthropic Leadership, 2004) 89; Ferris, "Philanthropy in Southern California."

44. Ferris, "Philanthropy in Southern California," 4–5.

45. Sushma Raman, "Looking Ahead: The Changing Landscape of Philanthropy," in *Looking Ahead: The Changing Landscape of Philanthropy*, Southern California Grantmakers (Los Angeles: Southern California Grantmakers, 2010), 3.

46. Grantmakers in Health, A Profile of Foundations Created from Health Care Conversions, 2009. Available at http://www.gih.org/files/usrdoc/2009_Conversion_Report.pdf.

47. Foundation Center, *FCStats*. Available at http://data.foundationcenter.org/#/foundations/all/nationwide/top:assets/list/2011.

48. Hammack and Anheier, *A Versatile American Institution*, 43–48.

49. Prior to 2004, the Los Angeles metropolitan area, as designated by the US Office of Management and Budget (OMB), included both Los Angeles County and Kern County. In 2004, the Los Angeles metropolitan area was modified to include Orange County and no longer included Kern. The significance here is that Orange County has a much more robust philanthropic sector than Kern County (a sparsely populated and highly mountainous region of the state). In 2004, sixty-four Kern County private foundations filed a 990-PF whereas Orange County had 714 filers.

50. GMP data are reflected for the Los Angeles–Long Beach metropolitan area for years 1998–2003 and Los Angeles–Long Beach–Santa Ana metropolitan area for years 2004–2007 (this coincides with the Foundation Center's GMP definitions). Analysis excludes grants less than $10,000, grants made directly to individuals, expenditures for foundation-administered projects, community foundation grants from restricted or donor-designated funds, and grants awarded by private or community foundation to another US foundation.

51. The Foundation Center data is from the Foundation Center's 2005 grants sample, which includes all grants of $10,000 or more awarded to organizations by a sample of larger foundations. For community foundations, only discretionary and donor-advised grants are included. Grants to individuals are not included in the file. The data contain detailed information on

all grants awarded in 2005. For additional discussion of the Foundation Center data set, see Anheier and Hammack (2010), Appendix A, 403–4. In 2017 the Foundation Center website describes its data on grants as consisting of information from "1,000 of the largest US … independent, corporate, and grant-making operating foundations, as well as unrestricted and donor-advised fund grants (when available) for community foundations." It reports information about "domestic and international giving" of this group of 1000 foundations "to organizations by issue, population, and geographic focus." This data set omits "all of the grants" under $10,000. According to the Foundation Center, "[g]iving by these foundations together accounts for more than half of overall US foundation giving each year." The foundation center data set includes information about "the full authorized value of the grant in the year the grant was made, if this information was provided by the foundation," or "the amount paid in the year it was reported." Information about the purposes of grants, the geographic area in which the organizations that received grants were located, and the population for which the grant was intended, come not from independent analysis, but "from direct reporting of grant-level data to the Foundation Center by foundations, foundation web sites and other public reporting, and from the IRS information returns filed annually by all US foundations." http://data.foundationcenter.org/about.html (accessed October 28, 2017).

52. Foundation Center Grants Sample Database, 2005.

53. Helmut K. Anheier and David C. Hammack, *American Foundations: Roles and Contributions* (Washington, DC: Brookings Institution Press, 2010), 9–14.

54. Abt Associates. Evaluation of the Conrad N. Hilton Foundation Chronic Homelessness Initiative 2014 Report. Available at https://hilton-production.s3.amazonaws.com/documents/8/attachments/Evaluation_of_the_Conrad_N._Hilton_Foundation_Chronic_Homelessness_Initiative_2014_Report_Abt_Associates_Inc._October_2014.pdf?1439473929.

55. Los Angeles Area Chamber of Commerce and United Way of Greater Los Angeles. Home for Good. The Action Plan to End Chronic and Veteran Homelessness by 2016. 2010, 4. Available at http://homeforgoodla.org/wp-content/uploads/2015/01/2010-Action-Plan.pdf.

56. Helmut K. Anheier, David B. Howard, Hyeon Jong Kil, and Jocelyn Guihama. Arts in the Balance. Arts Funding in Los Angeles County: 1998–2008. (Los Angeles: UCLA Center for Civil Society), 2009.

57. Facing a $38 billion budget deficit in 2003–04, the California Legislature enacted a number of deep cuts in spending. As a result, General Fund support for the California Arts Council was reduced from $18 million to $1 million (a 94 percent reduction from the 2001–02 funding levels).

58. Helmut K. Anheier, Eve Garrow, Marcus Lam, David B. Howard, and Jocelyn Guihama. Arts in the Balance: Arts Funding in Los Angeles County. 1998–2005. (Los Angeles: UCLA Center for Civil Society, 2006), 26.

59. Deener et al., "Planning Los Angeles."

60. James M. Ferris, *Foundations and Public Policy Making* (Los Angeles: Center on Philanthropy and Public Policy, University of Southern California, 2003); James M. Ferris and Nicholas P. O. Williams, *Foundation Strategy for Social Impact; A System Change Perspective* (Los Angeles: Center on Philanthropy and Public Policy, University of Southern California, 2009), 11.

61. Lisa Ranghelli and Julia Craig, *Strengthening Democracy, Increasing Opportunities: Impacts of Advocacy, Organizing and Civic Engagement in Los Angeles* (Washington, DC: National Committee for Responsive Philanthropy, 2010).

62. Wrigley, "Los Angeles and New York City Schools."

63. Sushma Raman, "Focusing on Advocacy." Stanford Social Innovation Review, Fall 2011, 26.

64. Christian González-Rivera, Courtney Donnell, Adam Briones, and Sasha Werblin, *Funding the New Majority: Philanthropic Investment in Minority-Led Nonprofits* (Berkeley, CA: Greenlining Institute, 2008).; Orson Aguilar, Tomasa Duenas, Brenda Flores, Lupe Godinez, Hilary Joy, and

Isabel Zavala. Fairness in Philanthropy Part I: Foundation Giving to Minority-led Nonprofits. (Berkeley, CA: Greenling Institute, 2005). According to the Greenlining Institute's methodology, a minority-led organization is "one whose staff is 50 percent or more minority; whose board of directors is 50 percent or more minority; and whose mission statement and charitable programs aim to predominantly serve and empower minority communities or populations."

65. Aguilar et al. (2005) "Fairness in Philanthropy".

66. Ian Wilhelm, "Calif. Foundations Pledge $30 Million to Help Minorities," *The Chronicle of Philanthropy,* December 28, 2008. Available at http://philanthropy.com/article/Calif-Foundations-Pledge/62983/.

67. Foundation Coalition, "Strengthening Nonprofit Minority Leadership and the Capacity of Minority-Led and Other Grassroots Community-Based Organizations" (December 22, 2008). Available at https://www.issuelab.org/resource/strengthening-nonprofit-minority-leadership-and-the-capacity-of-minority-led-and-other-grassroots-community-based-organizations.html.

68. Thomas E. Backer and Miyoko Oshima, The State of Nonprofit Capacity Building in Los Angeles 2004 (Los Angeles, CA: Southern California Grantmakers), 3. Available at https://www.csun.edu/sites/default/files/Statec-b%20LA-state2004.pdf.

69. Michael Anft, "A New Way to Curb Poverty," *Chronicle of Philanthropy,* April 15, 2004. Available at http://philanthropy.com/premium/articles/v16/i13/13000601.htm.

70. Thomas E. Backer, "Strengthening Nonprofits: Foundation Initiatives for Nonprofit Organizations," in *Building Capacity in Nonprofit Organizations,* eds. Carol J. De Vita and Cory Fleming (Washington, DC: Urban Institute, 2001), 54–55. Available at http://www.urban.org/UploadedPDF/building_capacity.pdf; Lucy Bernholz, *Creating Philanthropic Capital Markets: The Deliberate Evolution* (Hoboken, NJ: John Wiley & Sons, 2004); Mary Ellen S. Capek and Molly Mead, *Effective Philanthropy: Organizational Success Through Deep Diversity and Gender Equality* (Cambridge, MA: MIT Press, 2007).

71. Ferris, "Philanthropy in Southern California."

72. Membership of SCG has doubled over the past five years, and the participation of member organizations in SCG events has increased significantly.

73. For example, Professor James Ferris at the Center for Philanthropy and Public Policy at the University of Southern California has, for over a decade, convened leadership seminars for foundation representatives. Similarly, the annual state-of-the-nonprofit-sector reports by the UCLA Center for Civil Society provided some of the empirical foundation for philanthropic leaders to develop and test their grant-making strategies.

References

Anheier, Helmut K., Eve Garrow, Marcus Lam, David B. Howard, and Joceyn Guihama. *Arts in the Balance: A Survey of Arts Funding in Los Angeles County: 1998–2005*. Los Angeles: UCLA Center for Civil Society, 2006.

Anheier, Helmut K., Marcus Lam, Jennifer Mosley, Eve Garrow, and Jocelyn Guihama. *New Horizons: The State of the Nonprofit Sector in Los Angeles 2006.* Los Angeles: UCLA Center for Civil Society, 2006. Available at http://civilsociety.ucla.edu/practitioners/publications/reports.

Chang, Curtis. "Los Angeles Shines in Collaboration for Capacity Building," on Stanford Social Innovation Review website. Last modified February 17, 2012.

Christie, Les. "The Nation's Most Ethnically Diverse Counties." Accessed March 8, 2010, http://money.cnn.com/2007/08/08/real_estate/most_diverse_counties/index.htm.

Howard, David B. "Getty, J. Paul" in *International Encyclopedia of Civil Society,* eds. Helmut K. Anheier and Stefan Toepler. New York: Springer Science + Business Media, 2009.

Howard, David B. "Parsons, Ralph Monroe," in *International Encyclopedia of Civil Society*, eds. H. K. Anheier and S. Toepler. New York: Springer Science + Business Media, 2009.

Howard, David B., Hyeon Jong Kil, Jocelyn Guihama, and William Parent. *Resilience and Vulnerability: The State of the Nonprofit Sector in Los Angeles 2010*. UCLA Center for Civil Society. Available at http://civilsociety.ucla.edu/practitioners/publications/reports, 2009.

Linnell, Deborah S., and Timothy Wolfred. "Creative Disruption. Sabbaticals for Capacity Building and Leadership Development in the Nonprofit Sector. Third Sector New England and CompassPoint Nonprofit Services." 2009. Available at https://www.issuelab.org/resource/creative-disruption-sabbaticals-for-capacity-building-and-leadership-development-in-the-nonprofit-sector.html.

McCombs, Jennifer Sloan, and Stephen J. Carroll. "Ultimate Test: Who Is Accountable for Education If Everybody Fails?" Santa Monica, CA: Rand, 2005. Available at https://www.issuelab.org/resource/creative-disruption-sabbaticals-for-capacity-building-and-leadership-development-in-the-nonprofit-sector.html.

Sample, Steven B. "Los Angeles: The Capital of the Pacific Rim. An Address to the Los Angeles World Affairs Council on November 10, 2008." Last accessed March 15, 2010, https://about.usc.edu/presidentemeritus/speeches/address-to-the-los-angeles-world_affairs_council/.

TCC Group. *Fortifying LA's Nonprofit Organizations: Capacity-Building Needs and Services in Los Angeles County*, 2010. Available at http://www.weingartfnd.org/files/Capacity-Report-Final.pdf.

chapter nine

FOUNDATIONS IN SAN FRANCISCO AND SILICON VALLEY

Carol J. Silverman and Arleda Martinez

San Francisco and Silicon Valley are two adjacent regions with unique histories, foundation infrastructures, and cultural ideals, connected by geography and economic interdependence. San Francisco's is more mature, defined by generations of experience. With its culture of technological innovation and venture capital, Silicon Valley (considered here as San Mateo and Santa Clara Counties) is in the process of developing a new foundation infrastructure, whose full impact is yet to be felt.

The story of giving in the two regions is the story of dramatic shifts in wealth, desire for comforts and culture in a growing metropolis, and the development of moral perspectives after building successful businesses. It is also a story that continues to unfold as restless innovation shifts the geographic boundaries of wealth and need. The Bay Area generated its first great wave of wealth during the Gold Rush in the 1850s. How that wealth not only incubated but also grew a mature San Francisco foundation community is an important part of the story of Bay Area foundations. The next great wave of wealth washing over the Bay Area began in Silicon Valley, although San Francisco plays an increasing role in the story. This new infusion is inspiring and reinvigorating the practice of philanthropy in the San Francisco Bay Area in surprising ways.

In this essay, we discuss how the great wealth of both regions created robust philanthropic infrastructures. We base our analysis in part on writings about philanthropy and in part in existing financial data gathered by the Foundation Center and the National Center for Charitable Statistics. The story revealed by the history and by the numbers shows that foundations reflect the culture and concerns of the two regions while suggesting a future of interdependence.

After the Rush: Building a Sound Society

California's Gold Rush, which transformed San Francisco from a small settlement into a bustling center of trade and commerce, left a lasting legacy in its foundations. Gold Rush wealth and Gold Rush population growth transformed San Francisco in ways that still affect the city and the region. From a settlement of two hundred souls in 1846, San Francisco grew into a boomtown of thirty-six thousand by 1852. By 1870, it was the largest city west of the Mississippi (a distinction the city held until the 1906 earthquake).[1]

Boomtown San Francisco was a difficult and dangerous place, and throughout the late 1800s San Francisco was a by-word for lawlessness and loose living. By 1849, over fifty thousand gold-hungry miners seeking wealth in the northern part of the state had landed in San Francisco. But for all the gold pulled out of the rivers of California by treasure hunters from around the world, the most significant fortunes were made by those who served the gold miners, furnishing provisions, clothing, and other goods. The tradesmen, developers, and bankers of San Francisco settled in the city, and these families became increasingly distressed by the difficulties faced by so many in the city and as well as those who were looking for the comforts of civilization.[2]

The wealthy families of San Francisco set about carving civilization out of the boomtown wilderness with great energy and innovation. One early example is found in the life and work of Mary Crocker, wife of Charles Crocker, one of the "big four" railroad investors responsible for the western portion of the First Transcontinental Railroad and the creation of the Pacific Railroad. Mary Crocker was noted for her devotion to charity; she and other wealthy San Franciscans established settlement houses including the San Francisco Ladies Protective and the Relief Society. Founded in 1853, the Relief Society is still operating today as a private foundation that provides retirement housing. Perhaps more importantly, these families impressed on their children the importance of philanthropy. On her death in 1889, Mary Crocker's four surviving children established a trust in her name. The oldest family foundation west of the Mississippi, the Mary A. Crocker Trust continues to fund projects in the Bay Area; the trustees are all descendants of Mary Crocker.

Foundations Reflect the Growing City

By 1900, San Francisco was the undisputed capital of commerce and culture in the US West, and then disaster struck: half the city was destroyed in the earthquake and fire of 1906. The people of San Francisco did not abandon their city; they rebuilt and the idea of organized philanthropic action began to take root. In 1926, a Boston newspaper reported that "A Combine of Twelve Kindly Millionaires" in San Francisco would donate large sums to establish a community foundation. The twelve included a who's who of San Francisco's elite families: Charles Merrill, Charles Crocker, and Aaron Fleishhacker were merely three of whom worked to establish San Francisco's first community chest in the early 1920s. After the Boston newspaper story, over seventy people sent letters requesting funds for such things as a study of criminal justice procedures for indigent prisoners and a crusade for better wages for mother labor. The son of one of the kindly millionaires, Mortimer Fleishhacker, later observed that, whereas the twelve were interested in using their financial and business expertise in service of San Francisco's general welfare, the plan for a community foundation was not firm at that time.[3]

The idea of a foundation responsive to changing community needs was expressed in 1936 with the establishment of the Rosenberg Foundation and then the Columbia Foundation in 1940. Columbia, in turn, made the first grant to the fledgling San Francisco Foundation, a community foundation established in 1948 to "create pride and unity and improve quality of life," according to a recent Foundation CEO Sandra R. Hernández, MD in a post on their website when she occupied the role. The San Francisco Foundation has since become one of the nation's largest community foundations, awarding grants totaling more than $800 million in the first decade of the 2000s.

Family Foundations and the Legacy of Levi Strauss[4]

The Mary A. Crocker Trust, the first family foundation in San Francisco, is representative of the pattern of foundation development in the city and area. San Francisco's wealthy families established family foundations and handed the idea of philanthropy on to their children. Perhaps the most famous and certainly the most widely known of the great San Francisco businesses is Levi Strauss and Company, founded by Levi Strauss to outfit the gold seekers pouring into San Francisco. The wealth generated by the company and shepherded by Strauss's descendants continues to resonate in San Francisco foundations.

During his lifetime, Strauss endowed the first scholarships to the University of California at Berkeley (ensuring that half were set aside for women), and, on his death in 1902, he left bequests to a number of charities such as the Pacific Hebrew Orphan Asylum and the Roman Catholic Orphan Asylum. At the time, Strauss's fortune was estimated to be around $6 million, that is, about $158 million in 2012 dollars. Unmarried, Strauss left the company to his nephews, the sons of his sister, Fanny

Table 9.1. Levi Strauss Company Legacy: Descendent Funds in 2010

Name	Grants Given	Total Assets	Founded
Evelyn and Walter Haas Jr. Trust	26,481,167	484,856,814	1952
Richard and Rhoda Goldman Fund	39,848,325	286,842,100	1951
Walter and Elise Haas Fund	12,654,962	229,082,013	1952
Mimi and Peter Haas Fund	8,136,414	197,819,957	1983
Joanne and Peter Haas Jr. Fund	4,691,168	118,720,833	2006
Columbia Foundation	2,264,708	81,532,388	1940
Levi Strauss Foundation	8,000,211	67,918,540	1952
Goldman Environmental Foundation	1,090,812	60,447,109	
Margaret E. Haas Fund	1,640,197	39,574,046	2006
Levi Legacy TOTAL	104,807,964	1,566,793,800	
James Irvine Foundation	59,311,064	1,589,353,533	

Source: Author's calculations based on National Center for Charitable Statistics PF data.

(Vogele) Stern. Even in death, Strauss provided largesse to the growing city of San Francisco. Although he directed this philanthropy primarily to the small Jewish community—providing bequests to the Pacific Hebrew Orphan Asylum, the Emanu-El Sisterhood, and the Home for Aged Israelites—he also gave money to the Roman Catholic and Protestant Orphan Asylums.

The scope of the Levi Strauss Company legacy is evident when the philanthropic efforts of the Haas family, descendants of Strauss's sister, are tracked. The Haas family established important family foundations whose impact on the city is felt to this day. Table 9.1 lists the Levi Strauss Company legacy foundations and shows that, if taken together, these foundations would constitute the second-largest foundation in San Francisco, accounting for nearly twice as many grants as those of the James Irvine Foundation (San Francisco's largest foundation as of 2010).

Diverse Wealth Creation

The Levi Strauss legacy is important, but San Francisco generated its wealth in many sectors and established several important foundations because of it.

The Irvine and Ben Joseph fortunes were made in real estate, that of Elbridge Stewart in food, the Koret and the Camp Foundations in apparel, Bowes in venture capital, and Bechtel in construction. Table 9.2 summarizes the largest foundations by assets in 2010.

In contrast to San Francisco, where foundations are created on diverse sources of wealth (one would have to look to the eleventh-largest

Table 9.2. Largest San Francisco Foundations, 2010

	Grants Given	Total Assets
James Irvine Foundation	59,311,064	1,589,353,533
Shimon Ben Joseph Foundation	65,494,873	837,220,914
Evelyn and Walter Haas Jr. Trust	26,481,167	484,856,814
Elbridge Stuart Foundation	19,424,135	463,272,990
Koret Foundation	15,276,231	444,724,401
Richard and Rhoda Goldman Fund	39,848,325	286,842,100
William K. Bowes Jr. Foundation	53,294,592	273,512,333
S. D. Bechtel Jr. Foundation	34,633,729	270,196,380
Camp Foundation	0	260,982,102
Walter and Elise Haas Fund	12,654,962	229,082,013

Source: Author's calculations based on National Center for Charitable Statistics PF data.

foundation in 2011—the Yellow Chair Foundation—to find one with roots in the technology sector), Silicon Valley foundations are marked from the beginning by close ties to technology.

The Shift of Economic Power to Silicon Valley

While people often view Silicon Valley as a relative newcomer both as an economic center and as a center of wealth, it has a long and rich history. San Jose, established in 1777, was the first town founded in California and the first state capital when California gained statehood in 1850. By the early twentieth century, the region was known as the Valley of the Heart's Delight because of the astonishingly fertile soil, artesian water, and the resulting rich agricultural produce. However, the wealth of Silicon Valley and its intense identification with technology can be traced to the railroad, and in particular to Leland Stanford. Stanford was a railroad baron who served as governor of California and used his wealth to endow not a foundation, but Stanford University. Stanford University, in turn, served as a hub for technological development. In the early 1950s, Stanford University created the Stanford Industrial Park (later renamed the Stanford Research Park) as a home for light industry. Tenants were given access to take Stanford University courses, and Stanford faculty were given one day a week where they could consult for companies at the park. By the 1980s, the park housed a large number of companies, including Ampex, Hewlett-Packard, and Lockheed Space. An infusion of government research dollars further cemented the region's leading role in the technology sector.[5]

The Hewlett-Packard Company (HP) was founded in 1939 by Stanford University classmates William Hewlett and David Packard. At the time, there was no notion of Silicon Valley. Hewlett and Packard were simply at work in their now-famous garage in a sleepy Bay Area town called Palo Alto. The company they founded would shift the economic dynamics in the San Francisco Bay Area and thus play an important role in Bay Area's foundations.

William Hewlett established what has become the largest foundation in the Bay Area in 1967—the William and Flora Hewlett Foundation, which is also the twelfth-wealthiest foundation in the world. A few years earlier, David Packard had founded the David and Lucile Packard Foundation, the second-largest Bay Area foundation as of 2010, and the sixteenth-largest in the world. Since its inception, the Hewlett Foundation has made grants of over $4.5 billion to thousands of organizations in the San Francisco Bay Area, across the United States, and around the world. Early grants were made to organizations in education, population, and the arts, as well as environment, health, and vital services to support the needy in the Bay Area. In 2010, the Packard Foundation held over $6 billion in assets. Between 1993 and 2006, Packard gave over $1.6 million in grants through its conservation and science program. Still true to its founders' vision, it funds work to address population growth, promote positive reproductive health, and support programs for women, children, and communities. Lucile Packard was the chair of the board of the Children's Health Council, and she worked closely with the Stanford Convalescent Home, which later evolved into the Lucile Packard Children's Hospital.[6] Second- and third-generation family members still play an active role in both foundations today, and because of this, these family foundations show their kinship with the established foundations in San Francisco. Just as the San Francisco–based family foundations worked to build the quality of life in San Francisco, these two Silicon Valley family foundations have played an almost incalculable role in giving back to and enhancing the quality of life of Silicon Valley.

Although these two important foundations are identified as Silicon Valley foundations, they follow more closely the patterns of San Francisco-based foundations. It would take another generation before Silicon Valley began to develop its own philanthropic identity.

The Rise of the Silicon Valley–Based Foundations

The history of Silicon Valley is often traced to the HP garage and to the important role Stanford University played in fostering research and development in the technology industries. As home to many of the world's largest technology corporations as well as thousands of small startups, the wealth in Silicon Valley is enormous. The San Jose-Sunnyvale-Santa Clara Metropolitan Statistical Area has the most millionaires and the most billionaires per capita in the United States, largely a result of the high-technology sector.[7] For a number of years, however, it seemed as if the new millionaires and billionaires of the Valley eschewed philanthropy, and were often compared to the robber barons of the past. In their defense, Silicon Valley entrepreneurs have claimed the rigors of running significant businesses and developing new technologies. As William Hewlett put it, "You forget that Dave [Packard] and I didn't start giving away our fortune until we were fifty years old. Before that, we were too busy running our company. Just wait: they'll [younger Silicon Valley executives] come around, too."[8]

William Hewlett has been proven correct in his prediction. As shown in table 9.3, Silicon Valley wealth generated a flurry of philanthropy starting in 1999 when Jeffrey Skoll, the co-founder of eBay, established the Skoll Foundation. The Skoll Foundation was followed in rapid succession by the Gordon and Betty Moore Foundation (Intel), the Crankstart Foundation (Sequoia Venture Capital—derived from funding in Google, Yahoo!, PayPal, YouTube, and Zappos, among others), the Omidyar Network Fund (eBay), the Tosa Foundation (Cisco Systems), and the Carl Victor Page Memorial Foundation (Google).

Do these new Silicon Valley foundations differ from the established foundations in San Francisco? If they do differ, in what ways? In 2011, Emmett Carson, the influential CEO of the Silicon Valley Community Foundation, proclaimed the community foundation model to be "broken."[9] The Silicon Valley Community Foundation, at that time, was the twenty-seventh–largest community foundation in the United States, with more than 1,500 philanthropic funds and $2 billion in assets under management (it now is the largest). It was formed in 2006 as a merger of the Peninsula Community Foundation and Community Foundation Silicon Valley to create one united foundation capable of creating positive regional change on a larger scale. It was officially launched on January 3, 2007. So what alarmed Carson? During a meeting of 1,400 community foundation leaders, Carson discussed the rise of new providers of donor-advised funds and the emergence of a competitive philanthropic marketplace. For-profit firms now compete with public foundations for donor dollars.[10] Carson's comments come from the heart of Silicon Valley, where new models of philanthropy are being incubated, and where established community foundation practices (as typified in the San Francisco Foundation and in the Silicon Valley Community Foundation) are being challenged by investment firms.

Table 9.3. Ten Largest Silicon Valley Foundations by Founding Date, 2012

Name	Grants Given	Assets	Year
Henry J. Kaiser Family Foundation	573,389	576,659,804	1948
David and Lucile Packard Foundation (7/16)	234,075,887	6,100,637,478	1964
William and Flora Hewlett Foundation (6/12)	219,102,012	7,377,220,546	1966
Packard Humanities Institute	12,119,528	732,975,558	1987
Skoll Foundation	13,019,308	512,811,241	1999
Gordon E. and Betty I. Moore Foundation (9)	226,688,561	5,585,288,763	2000
Crankstart Foundation	465,000	342,540,850	2002
Omidyar Network Fund, Inc.	23,416,480	271,603,906	2004
Tosa Foundation	65,826,351	549,604,936	2004
Carl Victor Page Memorial Foundation	6,270,000	253,770,261	2006

Note: The numbers in parentheses represent ranking among the largest foundations in the United States/World.

Bringing Local Innovation to Worldwide Issues

By 2012, *The Wall Street Journal* was reporting on a veritable philanthropic storm from Silicon Valley: six partners of the venture capital firm Andreessen Horowitz (backer of Instagram and Zynga) announced that they will give away half their earnings; high-tech executives, including PayPal founder Elon Musk and Facebook cofounder Dustin Muskovitz, signed onto Warren Buffet's Giving Pledge (an interesting echo and update of San Francisco's twelve kindly millionaires of a century ago); Facebook cofounder Mark Zuckerberg gave $100 million to Newark's public schools; Google's Sergey Brin and his wife, Anne Wojcicki, promised $1 million to a local antipoverty charity (if it is matched by other Silicon Valley tech leaders).[11]

To what extent does the philanthropy emerging in Silicon Valley reflect a distinct culture—a culture that has been fostered by the larger culture of the Bay Area, but has, like any child, developed its own personality? People have said that entrepreneurship is a form of entertainment in Silicon Valley. More seriously, Silicon Valley's culture is "supported by a social fabric that maintains constant, ongoing conversations through which you can test and develop your thoughts, find folks to work with, and turn ideas into action."[12] Certainly, the foundations that have been established in Silicon Valley since 2000 reflect the way that philanthropy there has been influenced by the culture of experimentation with traditional philanthropic forms. There are several examples of this, notably the Skoll Foundation with its emphasis on supporting "social entrepreneurs" and the Omidyar Network, which describes itself as a philanthropic venture firm. The "evangelist" of the Silicon Valley way of philanthropy during the first decade of the 2000s has been Laura Arrillaga-Andreessen.

Arrillaga-Andreessen first appeared on the scene in 1998, when she founded the Silicon Valley Social Venture Fund (SV2). The stated aim of SV2 is not only to provide funds, but also to "leverage the intellectual, human and network capital of ... donors to support ... Grantees," by presenting a "diverse menu of events and opportunities to engage one another, our Grantees, and the community."[13] Although the idea of venture philanthropy has been around for some years now (John D. Rockefeller III coined the term in 1969), Arrillaga-Andreessen has worked tirelessly to relate the idea to Silicon Valley and its younger leaders in particular. Mark Zuckerberg, the young founder of Facebook, credits her with sharing a context for giving that he could relate to, citing in particular her engineering approach to philanthropy. Arrillaga-Andreessen believes that the "tech entrepreneurs [of Silicon Valley] are looking to marry their professional and philanthropy activity in a way that previous generations did not." She argues that the donors should use the same strategic thinking, including research and evaluation, to determine how to philanthropically invest their dollars. Technology can be used to link donors and nonprofits, where donors can not only invest but also donate their time and expertise. She is attempting to create models and mechanisms to help them do that.[14]

Economic Interdependence, Different Philanthropic Trajectories

Although San Francisco and Silicon Valley have strong ties of economic interdependence—San Francisco is itself a hub of technological innovation, particularly of Web 2.0 companies such as Twitter, Zygna, and Salesforce, and many who work in Silicon Valley commute from San Francisco (using a network of private buses that transport workers who live in San Francisco to technology centers in Silicon Valley)—their philanthropic cultures are on different trajectories and reflect different values. San Francisco foundations represent a mature orientation, one characterized by longstanding, diverse institutions, representing generations of accumulated experience. Silicon Valley foundations, on the other hand, are much younger, reflective of a culture of experimentation and innovation, and expressing intense interest in new models.[15]

Bradford K. Smith of the Foundation Center said that "Silicon Valley has become the epicenter of philanthropy in the US, if not the world."[16] His observation is trenchant, not just in terms of philanthropy dollars raised in Silicon Valley, but in the scope of Silicon Valley's ambition. After decades of being accused of being misers or of giving away their money anonymously (Steve Jobs), Silicon Valley's entrepreneurial philanthropists are now pursuing their dreams of changing the world for the better with the same vigor that their companies changed the world through technological innovation. Smith also notes that he anticipates the new wealth of Silicon Valley will continue its philanthropy throughout the lives of its entrepreneurial leaders.

San Francisco's longstanding and self-reflective foundations, on the other hand, are now engaged in a wide-reaching discussion about their future. The venerable Columbia Foundation and the Richard and Rhoda Goldman Fund have decided to cease operations. The Columbia Foundation has given approximately $85 million since 1940, including the first start-up grant to the San Francisco Foundation. The Richard and Rhoda Goldman Fund has given almost $700 million to twenty-six hundred nonprofits, including the San Francisco Symphony, the University of California Berkeley, the San Francisco Food Bank, and projects to combat rural malnutrition. On the announcement of the closing of the Richard and Rhoda Goldman Fund, John Goldman observed, "My dad didn't believe in the perpetuity of foundations. He always told us he thought it was important to have foundations recognize what was happening in a contemporary setting, with contemporary people."[17] By the end of 2013, both foundations had distributed their remaining assets among successor family foundations run by descendants. This was consistent with the way that the Strauss family kept its philanthropic dollars within family foundations, where the legacy grew with the generations. The tradition of philanthropy remains strong as a generation passes, and a new generation takes up the responsibility.

Comparing San Francisco and Silicon Valley: What the Numbers Tell Us

Our question is how, if at all, these two cultures are reflected in the hard numbers. A qualitative analysis presents a more nuanced picture of two different philanthropic cultures. When we move beyond the cultural analysis to what and where foundations actually give, we find important distinctions and a few similarities.

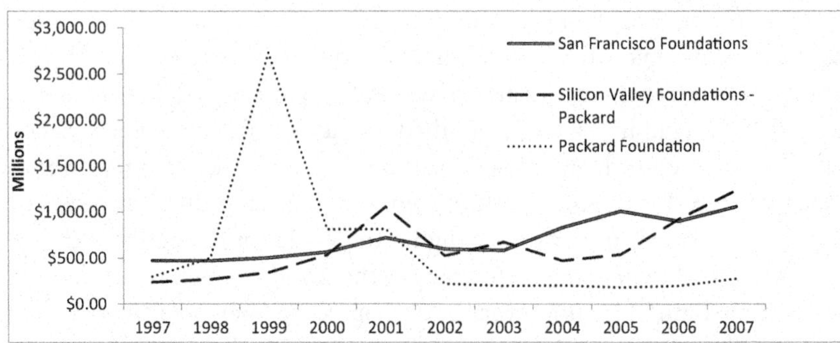

Figure 9.1. Total Grants and Contributions. Silicon Valley foundation assets are affected by tech sector economics.

The Importance of Sources of Wealth

As already documented, the largest Silicon Valley foundations are endowed by wealth created in the technology sector, and the largest San Francisco foundations by wealth from a diversity of sectors. Thus, Silicon Valley foundations have been more affected by the ups and downs of their sector of origin. Figure 9.1 shows how much the so-called burst of the technology bubble during late 1990s affected foundations. The Packard Foundation, which had not diversified its assets, drove the change in grants and has been separated from Silicon Valley foundations for clarity. Even accounting for Packard, the effect of the downturn in the technology sector on Silicon Valley foundations can be clearly seen. San Francisco foundations, in contrast, were only marginally affected. This shows the great importance of a single industry to Silicon Valley, and the extent to which philanthropic giving can be affected by economic setbacks in that industry.

The Basics: How Many and How Large?

Both San Francisco and Silicon Valley are populous. According to the 2012 Census estimates, San Francisco housed 802,863 residents, while Silicon Valley was home to over to 2.5 million (San Mateo County reported 739,311 people and Santa Clara County 1,837,504).[18]

In 2011, according to the National Center for Charitable Statistics, there were 932 foundations in San Francisco, making a total of $1,135,925,655 in grants and holding $11,820,641,144 in total assets. In Silicon Valley, there were 1,942 registered private foundations making a total of $1,866,747,178 dollars in grants and holding $28,092,469,514 in total assets.[19] By absolute numbers, Silicon Valley possesses a large foundation infrastructure, but it is also a larger region. Another way to look

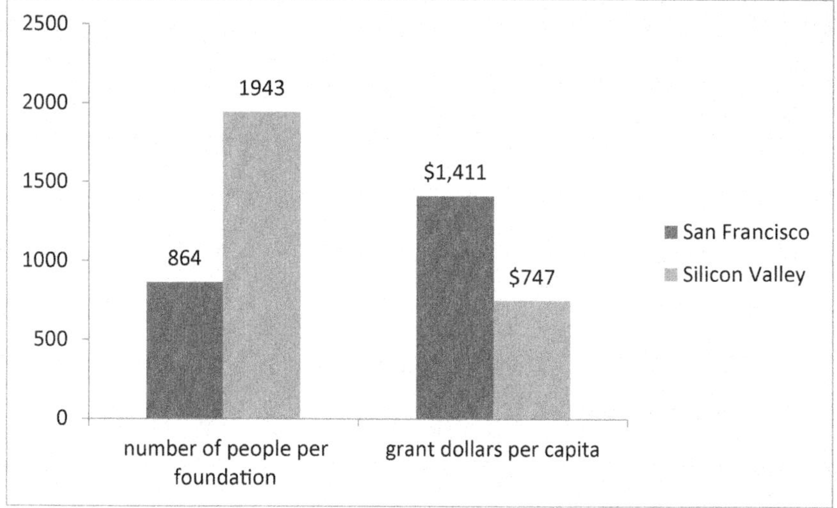

Figure 9.2. Relative Presence of Foundations. San Francisco has a much larger foundation sector relative to its population. *Source:* 2011 data, National Center for Charitable Statistics.

at these numbers is to examine the relative presence of the foundations, compared to the population.

The graph in figure 9.2 simply divides the number of foundations by the population of the respective regions. It shows that, relative to the population, San Francisco has over twice as many foundations as does Silicon Valley. The same is true for grant dollars—San Francisco "spends" $1,411 dollars per capita while Silicon Valley spends approximately half as much. It should be noted that this comparison is presented only to show the relative presence of the foundations—they do not expend all grant dollars in their counties. This will be discussed in more depth shortly.

Age of Foundations

As previously discussed, San Francisco's foundations are older than those in Silicon Valley. Figure 9.3 shows the age of the foundation as indicated by the date of the IRS ruling (the founding date may be earlier than the date of the IRS designation). The graph shows the dramatic growth rate of Silicon Valley foundations since the 1990s. Forty percent of Silicon Valley foundations currently in operation were given their IRS ruling in the past thirteen years, whereas only 25 percent of San Francisco foundations were given a ruling in the same time period. In contrast, 45 percent of San Francisco foundations were founded before 1990, compared to only 20 percent of those in Silicon Valley.

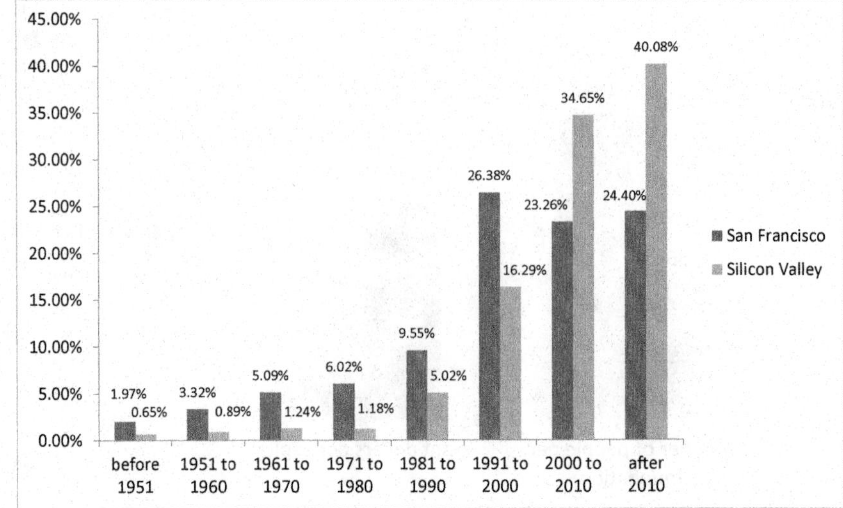

Figure 9.3. Age of Foundations. Silicon Valley is rapidly forming new foundations, whereas San Francisco has an older foundation sector. *Source:* National Center for Charitable Statistics, 2013 BMF.

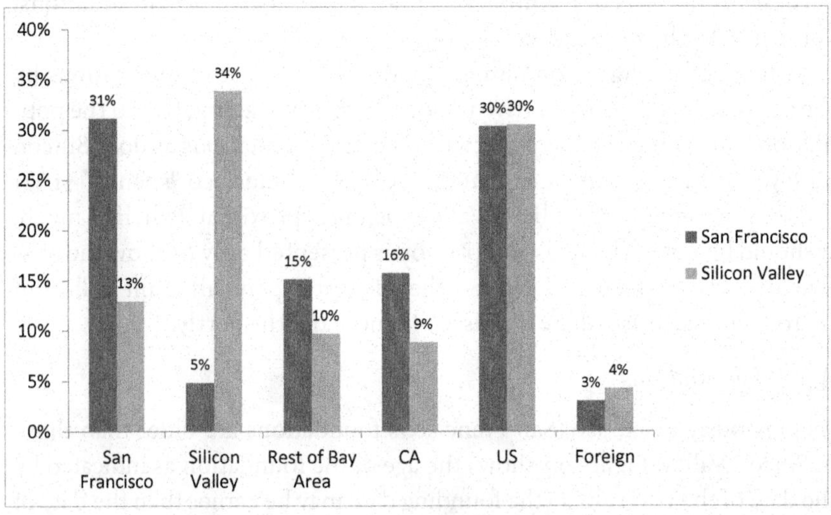

Figure 9.4. Percentage of Grants Going to Different Regions. Approximately one third of grants go to the region where the foundation is located. *Source:* Foundation Center 2005 grants database.

Where Foundations Give[20]

As shown in figure 9.4, both regions direct approximately one-third of their grants to nonprofits located in their respective regions. Silicon Valley foundations are more than twice as likely to fund nonprofits in

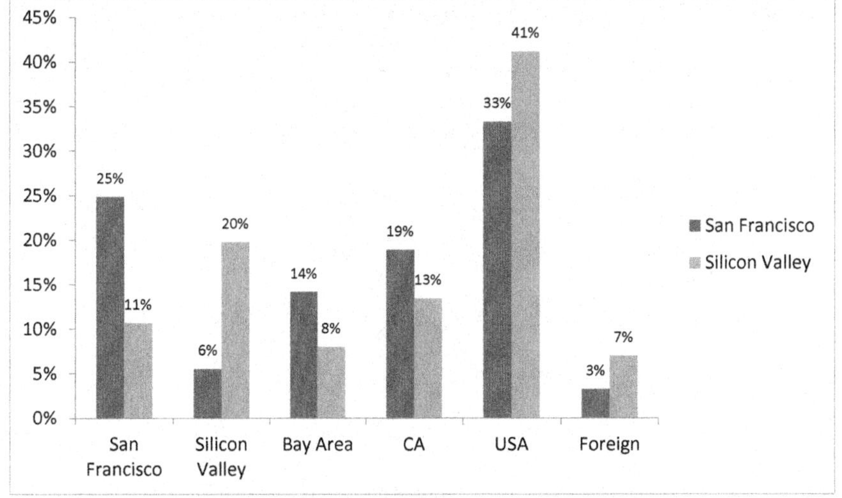

Figure 9.5. Percentage of Grant Dollars Going to Different Regions. Grant dollars track the same basic pattern as grants. *Source:* Foundation Center 2005 grants data.

San Francisco as are San Francisco foundations to fund in Silicon Valley. However, San Francisco foundations are more likely to fund nonprofits elsewhere in California.

Figure 9.5 shows the percentage of dollars expended in different regions. Although there are minor percentage difference between this figure and the aforementioned one, the general pattern is similar. Both regions are more likely to fund within their own region, with San Francisco foundations funding throughout California and Silicon Valley foundations funding in other parts of the United States.

Several knowledgeable observers have suggested that Silicon Valley foundations are more likely to fund overseas because of the area's large, educated population of individuals who have relocated from other countries to work in its technology sector. The grants data, at least as of 2005, does not bear this out. Only a small percentage of grants and grant dollars go to countries other than the United States, and there are not large differences between Silicon Valley and San Francisco in this respect. It may be that donor-advised funds would show a different picture, but we are not able to capture these funds with our data.

What Foundations Support

An analysis of the percentage of grants (figure 9.6) going to different substantive causes shows that San Francisco foundations are more likely to fund in the areas of the arts, culture and humanities, and in human ser-

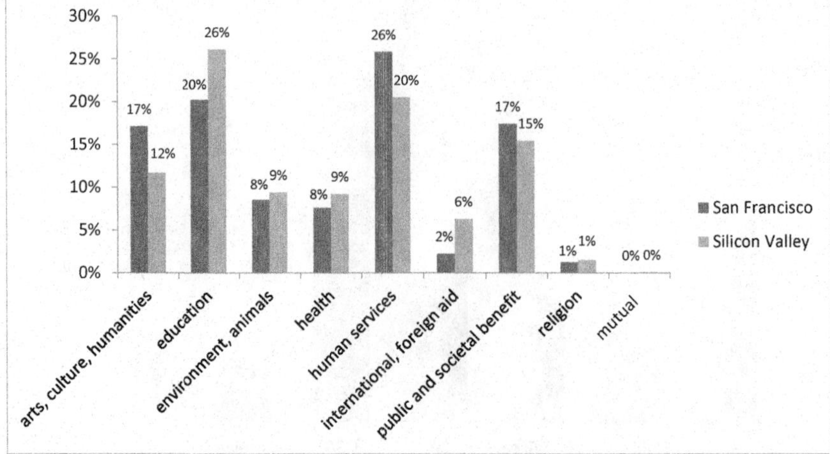

Figure 9.6. Percentage of Grants by Major Grant Areas. San Francisco foundations are more likely to fund the arts, humanities, and human services and Silicon Valley to fund education. *Source:* Foundation Center 2005 grants data.

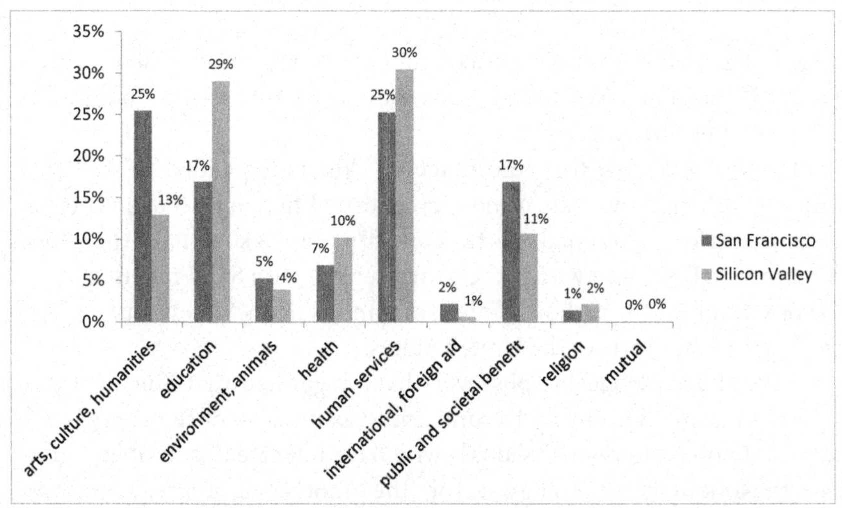

Figure 9.7. Percentage of Grants by Major Grant Areas, made to nonprofits in own region. San Francisco foundations are almost twice as likely to give grants for local arts, humanities, and cultural purposes, whereas Silicon Valley foundations are more likely to give grants in education. *Source:* Foundation Center 2005 grants data.

vices. Silicon Valley foundations are more likely to fund education. If we turn to the percentage of grants made to local nonprofits, the pattern is even clearer. As shown in figure 9.7, a far greater percentage of grants are made to local arts, culture, and humanities organizations in San Francisco,

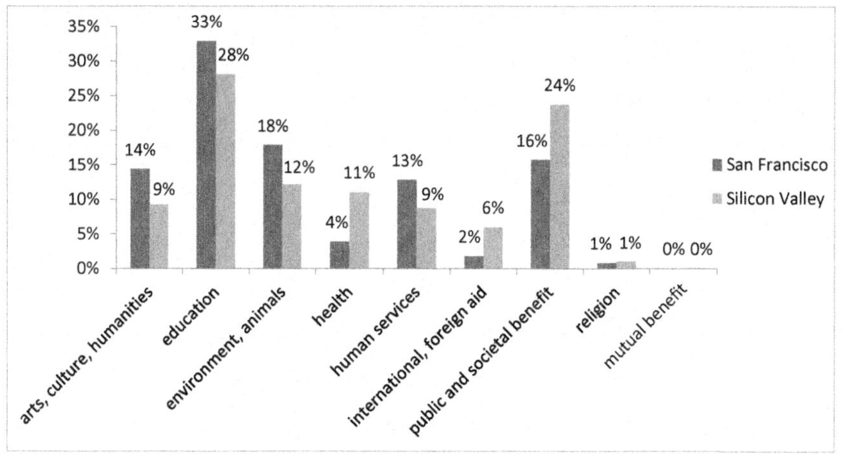

Figure 9.8. Percent Dollars by Major Grant Areas. San Francisco foundations devote a higher percentage of their grant dollars to arts, culture and humanities, and environment, whereas Silicon Valley Foundations are more likely to fund health and public/societal benefit organizations.

whereas Silicon Valley foundations are more likely to fund local education nonprofits.

These findings also support earlier conclusions. It is often said that the new wealth of Silicon Valley is often directed towards international causes, reflecting the interests of the owners and employees of the technology firms. These graphs show that Silicon Valley foundations are more likely to support international causes than is the case for San Francisco foundations, but that the actual amount directed internationally is small; only slightly more than 6 percent of all funding from foundations goes to support international causes (and potentially to US nonprofits doing international work).

Foundation Center Grants Data

These tables show that San Francisco foundations are more likely to support arts, culture, and humanities in general, and particularly more likely to support them locally. Silicon Valley foundations are more likely to support education, particularly within Silicon Valley, and much more likely to support local health nonprofits. Neither region supports religious causes.

These findings become more understandable when the recipient of the funding is identified. Eleven percent of all grants made by Silicon Valley foundations to Silicon Valley nonprofits go to support Stanford University and its hospital. Twenty percent of all dollars granted locally

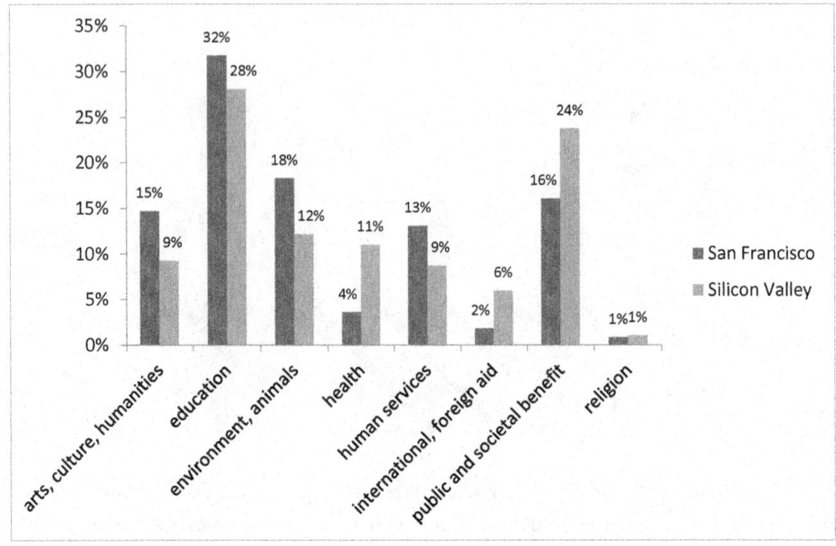

Figure 9.9. Percent of Dollars to Local Foundations, Grants to Stanford and University of California Institutions Removed. San Francisco devotes a slightly higher percent of funds to education. *Source:* Foundation Center 2005 grants data.

similarly go to Stanford. The comparison figure for San Francisco is that 2 percent of all grants go to the University of California, San Francisco, and University of California, Hastings College of the Law, both part of the University of California system, and 9 percent of all dollars goes to support these institutions. It should be noted that these dollars do not include donor-advised funds, which are often used to support educational institutions. As a result, the percent of philanthropic dollars going to Stanford may well be higher.

As shown in figure 9.9, the educational disparity largely disappears when grants by Silicon Valley foundations to Stanford and to University of California institutions by San Francisco foundations are removed. Silicon Valley foundations are still more likely to grant a higher percent of their dollars to health organizations.

Conclusion

The findings here paint two pictures. Although the culture of philanthropy may be different in Silicon Valley, and it certainly is much younger and faster growing, this area is about as likely as San Francisco to fund grants locally; it devotes only a small percentage of its grant dollars internationally; and it does not differ from San Francisco in the substantive areas where it directs its grant dollars. The two major differences between the areas are that San Francisco foundations invest more heavily in arts, culture, and humanities, and Silicon Valley foundations invest more heavily in Stanford University. However, 40 percent of Silicon Valley foundations have been founded in the past thirteen years; accordingly, their contributions are not as easily found in the numbers, in part because the grant data is from the mid-2000s, and also because the largest foundations are older and their contributions overshadow the younger and smaller ones. Thus, for example, the grants analyzed include only twenty-three grants made by the Omidyar Foundation and none by the Tosa or Crankstart Foundation—three of the largest Silicon Valley foundations established since 2000. Our guess is that, as long as wealth continues to be created by the technology sector, and that sector remains headquartered in Silicon Valley, we will see an increasing presence of foundations in that region.

How this will change the funding pattern of Silicon Valley is unknown. Will the newly created foundations mature to less entrepreneurial grant-making, and come to resemble their older and larger peers? Will Silicon Valley foundations diversify their grants as founders, who may have been new to the region when the foundation was established, develop deeper roots in their home community?

Equally unknown is how the increasingly large technology sector in San Francisco, along with the population that lives in San Francisco and commutes to technology jobs in Silicon Valley, will affect the culture of philanthropy in San Francisco. It may well be that this report documents a period in which the two regions could be distinguished from each other, but that those distinctions will become increasingly irrelevant over time.

Carol J. Silverman is Director of Program Evaluation for Telecare, a mental health service provider. She has authored numerous texts documenting the role of nonprofits and philanthropy in California as a research director at the Institute for Nonprofit Management at the University of San Francisco, and the Thelton E. Henderson Center for Social Justice at the University of California, Berkeley, School of Law.

Arleda Martinez is Administrative Manager at the YWCA of Greater Portland in Oregon. While with the Institute of Nonprofit Management at the University of San Francisco, she contributed to the studies *San Francisco's Nonprofit Sector* and to *The Inland Empire Nonprofit Sector.*

Notes

1. United States Census Bureau, "Population of the 100 Largest Urban Places, Tables 10–13." http://www.census.gov/population/www/documentation/twps0027/tab13.txt; http://www.census.gov/history/www/through_the_decades/fast_facts/1870_fast_facts.html.

2. http://www.sanfrancisco.com/history/.

3. John Rickard May, *Bay Area Foundation History, Vol. 1: Building a Community Foundation* (Berkeley: University of California, Berkeley, The Bancroft Library Regional Oral History Office, 1976). http://bancroft.berkeley.edu/ROHO/collections/subjectarea/ics_movements/philanthropy.html.

4. Fanny Stern was the daughter of Jacob Stern, the second president of the Levi Strauss Company. William Haas Sr.'s nephew, Walter, married Elise Stern, daughter of Sigmund Stern and Fanny Stern's first cousin (Charles's wife). Control of Levi Strauss passed from Jacob Stern to his brother, Sigmund, then to Sigmund's son-in-law, Walter Haas Sr. His son, Walter Haas Jr., served as CEO and president from 1958 to 1971 and chairman of the board from 1971 to 1976. Walter Haas Jr. was Abraham Haas's grandson and William Haas Sr.'s grandnephew. http://www.sfheritage.org/haas-lilienthal-house/haas-lilienthal-house-history/.

5. John Sandelin, "The Story of the Stanford Industrial/Research Park." Paper prepared for the International Forum of University Park Science, China (2004). Available at http://otl.stanford.edu/documents/JSstanfordpark.pdf.

6. http://www.lpch.org.

7. Elisabeth Eaves, "America's Greediest Cities," *Forbes*, December 3, 2007. https://www.forbes.com/2007/11/30/greediest-cities-billionaires-forbeslife-cx_ee_1203greed.html.

8. Michael S. Malone, "Silicon Insider: High-Tech Philanthropy," *ABC News*, November 19, 2012.

9. Sarah Duxbury, "Emmett Carson: Community Foundation Model 'Broken,' at Risk," *San Francisco Business Times*, September 20, 2011. http://www.bizjournals.com/sanfrancisco/blog/2011/09/community-foundation-model-at-risk.html.

10. Ellie Buteau, Mark Chaffin, and Phil Buchanan, "What Donors Value: How Community Foundations Can Increase Donor Satisfaction, Referrals and Future Giving," Center for Effective Philanthropy, 2014. http://www.effectivephilanthropy.org/wp-content/uploads/2014/04/CEP-Research_What-Community-Foundation-Donors-Value.pdf.

11. Holly Finn, "Young, Rich and Charitable," *The Wall Street Journal*, May 4, 2012. https://www.wsj.com/articles/SB10001424052702304746604577380452583348994.

12. Martin Kenney, ed., *Understanding Silicon Valley: The Anatomy of an Entrepreneurial Region* (Stanford, CA: Stanford University Press, 2000).

13. "About SV2," Silicon Valley Social Venture Fund website, accessed October 25, 2012, http://www.sv2.org/page/about-us.

14. Claire Cain Miller, "Could Silicon Valley Rethink Philanthropy?" *The New York Times*, December 18, 2011. http://bits.blogs.nytimes.com/2011/12/18/could-silicon-valley-rethink-philanthropy/?ref=.

15. For a discussion of the "Silicon Valley view", see Paul Brest, "Smart Money," *Stanford Social Innovation Review* 1, no. 3 (2003): 44–53.

16. Claire Cain Miller, "Rebooting Philanthropy in Silicon Valley," *The New York Times*, December 11, 201, http://www.nytimes.com/2011/12/18/business/a-philanthropy-reboot-in-silicon-valley.html.

17. Kevin Fagan, "Richard and Rhoda Goldman Fund Gets Split 3 Ways," *The San Francisco Chronicle*, January 19, 2011, http://www.sfgate.com/bayarea/article/Richard-and-Rhoda-Goldman-Fund-gets-split-3-ways-2478863.php.

18. www.census.gov.

19. http://nccs-data.urban.org/showDD.php?ds=core.

20. This analysis is based on grants data furnished by the Foundation Center for 2005.

chapter ten

WASHINGTON STATE'S FOUNDATIONS

Steven Rathgeb Smith, Beth L. Lovelady,
Natalie C. Alm, and Kate Anderson

Introduction

In the past seventeen years, the foundations of Washington State have gone from relative insignificance to holding a prominent place in nationally and globally organized philanthropy, due to the establishment and growth of the Bill & Melinda Gates Foundation.[1] The extraordinary size of the Gates Foundation, together with its high-profile support for a wide range of important contemporary policy priorities including educational reform, international health care improvement, and outcome evaluation have quite understandably attracted enormous attention. Indeed, the Gates Foundation seems to embody many of the emergent and widely discussed trends in organized philanthropy, especially the concern with outcomes and policy impact, but in a very outsized fashion.[2] Further, the Gates Foundation has often successfully attracted other donors and partners in support of its own policy goals. Washington State is also home to many other wealthy high-tech individuals who have created their own family foundations in recent years and who contributed to the growth of local community foundations, including the Seattle Foundation.

This chapter examines the foundation universe in Washington State through the use of national and local data sources. Particular attention is devoted to overall asset levels, giving patterns, and the relationship between foundations in the state and local nonprofits, especially as these key indicators compare to other states and national averages. As will be demonstrated in subsequent pages, the Washington State foundations, excluding the Gates Foundation, have grown at a faster rate than foundations nationwide. However, giving patterns remain quite consistent with national averages.[3] Throughout the chapter, the analysis of Washington State foundations will also strive to isolate the influence of the Gates Foundation on aggregate giving and asset patterns as well as place foundations in the state within the overall context of the state's institutional history and economic development. The outsized profile of the Gates Foundation also tends to mask the more traditional pattern of grant giving among most Washington State foundations.

Washington State: A Brief History

The geography of the state has profoundly affected its growth and development, which in turn has affected the development of foundations in the state. The Cascade Mountains separate the western region of Washington from the eastern part of the state. The latter is largely agricultural, with relatively sparse population compared with western Washington. Indeed, more than 50 percent of the state's population resides in King (home to Seattle), Pierce, and Snohomish Counties.[4] The state officially achieved statehood in 1889, and at the time, the economy relied heavily on agriculture in eastern Washington and on natural resources like lumber and wood products, fishing and whaling, and the fur trade in western Washington.

In 1900, Frederick Weyerhaeuser purchased 900,000 acres of Washington State timberland from the Northern Pacific Railway to start the Weyerhaeuser Company.[5] The company's headquarters were housed in Tacoma, and its presence solidified Washington State as a major source of lumber for the nation. During the twentieth century, Weyerhaeuser, the only major Washington State firm based in the lumber industry, grew into a large multinational corporation with extensive timber holdings throughout the world. The Weyerhaeuser Foundation, founded in 1948, was one of the leading in-state foundations for most of the mid- to late twentieth century. The largest out-of-state foundation in Washington was the Northwest Area Foundation (originally founded in 1934 as the Louis W. and Maud Hill Foundation), based in Minneapolis but supporting programs in the eight states of the Northwest region.[6]

Nonetheless, the vast areas of the state controlled by the federal government, including the US Forest Service, greatly limited the development of major private employers. Consequently, diversification of the economy away from natural resources and agriculture was slow. During World War I, the Boeing Company, headquartered in the Seattle area until 2001, began manufacturing airplanes for the US Armed Forces, the US Mail Service, and finally passenger planes in 1928.[7] After World War II, it grew to be a world leader in aviation technology.[8]

By the 1970s, the economy still depended heavily on natural resources and agriculture (and the military through a number of large army and navy bases), despite the large economic contribution of Boeing. Indeed, when Boeing experienced difficulties in the early 1970s, Seattle experienced a deep decline in home values and high unemployment. It was not until the early 1980s that the economy of Seattle and Washington State began to fundamentally change and diversify. China was emerging as a major economic power, and trade with China and other Pacific Rim nations was increasing sharply; Seattle was a natural hub for the growing import and export trade. Also, changes in communication helped reduce the cost of doing business with Washington State–based firms.

Certainly, an important catalyst for the economic diversification of the Seattle/Puget Sound region was the formal founding of Microsoft in 1981. By 1986, the company's stock had gone public at $21 per share. Within one year, the stock value rose to $85 per share, making Bill Gates a billionaire at the age of thirty-one.[9] Microsoft's rapid growth led to the formation of a "tech boom" in Washington during the early 1990s. Former Microsoft programmers left the company to form start-ups such as RealNetworks. Paul Allen, one of the original Microsoft founders, left the company to establish Vulcan Enterprises, which has invested in a wide variety of companies and has played a central role in the development of downtown Seattle and its South Lake Union district. Allen also established the Paul G. Allen Family Foundation to channel his philanthropic donations. Organizationally, the Allen Foundation functions as a philanthropic arm of Allen's company, Vulcan.

In addition to start-ups by former Microsoft employees, other entrepreneurs such as Jeff Bezos (Amazon.com), Howard Schultz (Starbucks), Jeff Brotman (Costco), Paul Brainard (Aldus/Pagemaker), Rob Glaser (RealNetworks), and Jed Smith (Drugstore.com) found the Seattle area rife with opportunity for internet businesses in the late 1990s. Unfortunately, the technology or "dot-com" bubble burst in March 2000, and many start-ups failed. However, the technology industry continues to be strong today in western Washington, and leading companies such as Starbucks and RealNetworks have established their own corporate foundations. Many high-tech entrepreneurs such as Bezos, Glaser, Brainard, and Jeff Raikes and Steve Balmer of Microsoft have also established their own family foundations.

Thus, Washington State's economy today is quite different from the Northern Pacific, Great Northern, Weyerhaeuser, and Boeing days of the mid-twentieth century. Indeed, in 2010, there were seven Fortune

500 companies headquartered in Washington State: Costco Wholesale Corporation, ranked at number 25, followed by Microsoft, Amazon.com, Starbucks Corporation, Nordstrom, Inc., Paccar, Inc., and Weyerhaeuser.[10] All seven of these companies are headquartered in the Seattle metropolitan area. Washington ranked thirteenth in the nation in personal income per capita ($42,857 in 2008) and tenth in median household income ($58,078 in 2008).[11] These prominent Fortune 500 companies and the overall wealth of the Seattle/Puget Sound region are major factors in the growth of organizations such as Social Venture Partners and the proliferations of foundations such as the Paul G. Allen Family Foundation and the Starbucks Foundation. Outside the three-county Puget Sound region, the Washington State economy continues to rely heavily on agriculture and a declining timber market. The agricultural market is very large and is also very export-oriented, especially to Pacific Rim countries. Some of the export industry for agricultural products also flows through the Portland area, because the Columbia River is a key transport vehicle for grain and other products.

According to national statistics, Washington State also appears to have a significant culture of giving and volunteering. For instance, the state ranks tenth in the nation in percentage of citizens who volunteer, with an average of 42.9 volunteer hours per capita each year.[12] Seattle ranks fourth in the percentage of citizens who volunteer among all large US cities.[13]

A Brief History of Washington Foundations

The relative youth of Washington State compared to the eastern and midwestern United States is evident in the historical development of foundations in the state. In 1889, Washington State was the forty-second state to join the Union, so it is not surprising that there were no foundations registered in Washington prior to 1900. During the next several decades, the growth in foundations was incremental, due largely to the slow growth of the economy and the population in the twentieth century until the 1980s. After the high-tech explosion of the 1980s and thereafter, the number of foundations grew sharply. Thus, in 2007, only 9 percent of registered foundations in Washington had been established before 1980, compared to 26 percent of larger foundations (assets of $1 million or more) nationwide.[14]

As evident in table 10.1, the evolution of foundations in Washington State can be divided into two distinct phases. In the 1940s and 1950s, the number of foundations increased by 92 percent, with a 99 percent increase in assets. During this period, the Seattle Foundation (a local community

Table 10.1. Number and Assets of Washington Foundations by Decade of Establishment

Decade Established	Number	Assets
1900–1909	1	$6,900,832
1910–1919	1	1,757,070
1920–1929	1	1,318,289
1930–1939	2	12,611,510
1940–1949	13	876,935,400
1950–1959	25	874,820,047
1960–1969	31	2,901,166,166
1970–1979	22	1,242,771,565
1980–1989	122	797,625,363
1990–1999	473	41,089,596,913
2000–2007[67]	413	2,102,762,085
Data not available	307	316,554,261
Total	1,411	$50,224,819,501

Source: The Foundation Center, 2009. http://foundationcenter.org/gain-knowledge/foundation-data.

foundation), the Medina Foundation (started by a descendent of Matthew G. Norton, founder of the Weyerhaeuser Company), and the Norcliffe Foundation were established in 1946, 1947, and 1952, respectively. The Annie E. Casey Foundation was founded in Seattle in 1947 by Jim Casey (the founder of United Parcel Service) and his siblings. The Seattle Foundation and the Norcliffe Foundations have remained among the largest foundations in Washington State and were among in the top ten foundations in Washington by assets in 2010.

Subsequently, incremental growth occurred in the number of foundations in the 1950s and 1960s. Casey Family Programs was created in 1973 as an operating foundation by Jim Casey after the United Parcel Service moved its headquarters to New York City. This foundation has been dedicated to improving child welfare throughout the country. In 2001, the Marguerite Casey Foundation was created by Casey Family Programs with a mission of improving the situation of low-income children and their families. Both foundations placed in the top ten foundations in terms of assets in 2010.

In the 1970s, however, the number of new foundations dropped by 29 percent, with a corresponding 57 percent drop in assets of the new foundations (due to a Boeing "bust" and serious problems with the state economy).[15] Another factor was the congressional passage of the Tax Reform Act of 1969, which significantly increased foundation regulations. The notable exception to this overall decline in foundation formation was Tektronix cofounder Jack Murdock's establishment of the M. J. Murdock Charitable Trust in 1975, with a focus on grant-making in the five-state area of Oregon, Washington, Idaho, Montana, and Alaska. Although Murdock's company was located in Beaverton, Oregon, he located the foundation headquarters where he lived in Vancouver, Washington. The M. J. Murdock Charitable Trust has grown to be one of the largest foundations in Washington State and was ranked third in terms of assets and giving in 2010.

The second major growth period for foundations in Washington State occurred during the dot-com boom of the 1980s and 1990s. During this period, the number of foundations grew by 86 percent with an increase of 97 percent in assets. Four of the top ten foundations in Washington State by assets in 2010 were founded during this more recent growth spurt: The Samis Foundation (1987), the Paul G. Allen Family Foundation (1989), the Bill & Melinda Gates Foundation (1994), and the Russell Family Foundation (1994).[16] As cofounders of Microsoft, Paul Allen and Bill Gates represent some of the greatest successes of the high-tech industry boom, which with the establishment of the Gates Foundation brought a drastic change to organized philanthropy in Washington.

Boeing Company Charitable Trust

Boeing did not establish a conventional corporate foundation as it grew in the twentieth century. Instead, the company created the Boeing Company Charitable Trust to channel its philanthropic giving program. Boeing provides substantial funding to nonprofits through its marketing and business donation program. It also has a matching gifts program for employees. The company has had a policy of paying the salaries of professional employees who were "loaned" to local social service agencies to help them with important management tasks. Additionally, Boeing was crucial in creating the Corporate Council for the Arts (now called ArtsFund), a philanthropic funding organization dedicated to supporting the arts in King and Pierce Counties. Overall, the company organizes its current philanthropic efforts under the umbrella of its Global Corporate Citizenship program, which includes donations made through the Charitable Trust; thus, it still is not a conventional private foundation, although it remains a very important source of philanthropic funding for community organizations.[17]

The Seattle Foundation

The Seattle Foundation was established in 1946 with an initial endowment of $289,000. It grew slowly during its initial decades, but it then benefited greatly from the high-tech boom beginning in the 1980s. The foundation's endowment was over $788 million in 2013.[18] A substantial portion of its endowment is comprised of donor-advised funds; typically, these funds are given to the foundation with specific instructions from the donor on the purposes of the grant, including the policy field (such as child welfare) or geographic location for the grant. Essentially, donor-advised funds are an alternative to creating a private foundation for wealthy donors. Many community foundations, including the Seattle Foundation, have a large percentage of their assets in these funds. The unrestricted component of its endowment–like many community foundations–is much smaller than the restricted component represented by these donor-advised funds. From 2009 to 2013, former Seattle mayor Norm Rice served as the CEO of the Seattle Foundation. Rice wanted to expand the Seattle Foundation's reach to younger donors using social networking and other online tools.[19] To that end, the Seattle Foundation launched the GiveBIG initiative in 2011. A one-day event to encourage philanthropy and bring new donors to local nonprofits, GiveBIG is modeled after similar events in other cities. In 2012, the event raised $4.1 million and more than doubled that amount the following year, when it raised $8.8 million.[20] Rice has also emphasized education-related grantgiving and collaborated with other foundations, including the Gates Foundation, in support of local initiatives in such areas as early childhood education.

The Bill & Melinda Gates Foundation

The Gates Foundation dates its formal origins to the incorporation of the William H. Gates Foundation in December 1994 with assets of about $94 million in Microsoft stock. In 1997, the Gates Library Foundation was incorporated to provide internet access to all libraries in the United States.[21] The Gates Library Foundation was reorganized in 1999 as the Gates Learning Foundation, incorporating both library and education initiatives and including a gift of $1.1 billion in Microsoft stock from Bill and Melinda Gates. At this time, an additional $2.2 billion was donated to the William H. Gates Foundation, putting these Gates-affiliated foundations in the top thirty and top ten US foundations by assets, respectively. These combined gifts were also the largest charitable donation ever made.[22]

In 2000, the William H. Gates Foundation and the Gates Library Foundation merged and became the Bill & Melinda Gates Foundation, with assets totaling $21.1 billion.[23] The goal of the merger was to "increase efficiency and communication between four main initiatives: Global Health, Education, Libraries, and Pacific Northwest Community Grants."[24] The Foundation was immediately the largest foundation in the country and embarked on a series of highly visible initiatives, including public school reform and the fight against AIDS.

The next major changes in the organization and assets of the Gates Foundation came in 2006. The work of the foundation was reorganized into three programs: Global Development, Global Health, and the United States.[25] Of even greater note, Warren Buffet pledged the majority of his wealth—ten million shares of Berkshire Hathaway stock, valued at $31 billion in June 2006—to the Gates Foundation, to be distributed by Buffet's estate as long as either Bill or Melinda Gates is a trustee.[26] Warren Buffet's gift replaced the Gates's 1999 gift as the largest charitable donation ever made. As a condition of Buffett's gift, the Gates Foundation is required to spend the full dollar amount of Buffet's gift annually in addition to the regular Gates Foundation grant distribution. At the time of the donation, it was speculated that, depending on the future value of Berkshire Hathaway stock, this gift had the potential to double the Gates Foundation's annual distributions.[27] In fact, the Gates Foundation's annual giving increased from $1.6 billion in 2006 to $2.5 billion in 2010.

It is particularly noteworthy that the Gates Foundation intends to expend all of its resources during the twenty-first century. According to the foundation, "because Bill, Melinda, and Warren believe the right approach is to focus the foundation's work in the twenty-first century, we will spend all of our resources within fifty years after Bill's and Melinda's deaths. In addition, Warren has stipulated that the proceeds from the Berkshire Hathaway shares he still owns on his death are to be used for philanthropic purposes within ten years after his estate has been settled."[28]

In order to better manage the large infusion of wealth and disbursement requirements, the Gates Foundation also created a two-entity structure in October 2006. The Bill & Melinda Gates Foundation distributes money to grantees and the Bill & Melinda Gates Foundation Asset Trust manages the endowment assets.[29] This enables the Gates Foundation to separate program work from the investment of assets. It also reduces conflicts of interest, because Buffet has no involvement in the Foundation Asset Trust and therefore does not affect decisions regarding Berkshire Hathaway stock.[30] In 2010, the trust reported assets of $36.8 billion and the foundation reported assets of $37.4 billion.[31]

Washington Foundations in National Perspective

In 2010, Washington State foundations represented 1.7 percent of the total number of US foundations, held 7.4 percent of the nation's foundation assets, and distributed 6.5 percent of the total giving,[32] ranking Washington fourth in the nation for total giving behind New York, California, and New Jersey. According to the National Center for Charitable Statistics (NCCS), Washington State had 2,021 registered private foundations and 24,639 registered public charities in 2010. In other words, Washington had 12.2 public charities for every private foundation (compared with 9 nationally).[33] In addition, Washington was ranked first in the nation in foundation giving in 2010 as a percentage of the gross state product. In 2010, foundation giving accounted for 0.87 percent of the gross state product, meaning that for every $100 in economic output there was close to $1 in foundation giving. Although Washington is ranked thirteenth in the nation in population, foundation giving per capita in 2010 was $442, making Washington the third-largest state for per capita foundation giving.[34] In contrast, foundation giving accounts for an average of 0.32 percent of gross state product nationally and per capita foundation giving is $148.

These national rankings highlight two important characteristics of Washington State foundations. First, the universe of foundations in Washington is relatively small. Many of the newer foundations are the product of the high-tech boom and thus are connected to high-tech entrepreneurs and their families. Second, the Gates Foundation drastically changed the position of Washington State's foundations within a comparative national perspective. In 1998, prior to the dramatic escalation of the philanthropic giving of Bill and Melinda Gates and the concomitant consolidation of the Gates family giving into Gates Foundation, Washington ranked eighteenth in total giving, twenty-fourth in percent of gross state product, and twentieth in giving per capita.[35]

Overall, the majority of private foundations in Washington in 2010 were independent (88.3 percent), followed by operating (7.4 percent), corporate (2.9 percent), and community (1.4 percent), which mirrors the national proportions for foundation types (89 percent, 6.5 percent, 3.5 percent, and 1 percent, respectively). Accordingly, as noted in figure 10.1, independent foundations held 92.8 percent of the assets (66 percent, or $6.6 billion, excluding the Gates Foundation) and gave 95.9 percent of the grants (75.3 percent, or nearly $370 million, excluding the Gates Foundation) in 2010. Operating foundations in Washington were second in terms of assets, holding $2.1 billion and 4.5 percent (21.1 percent,

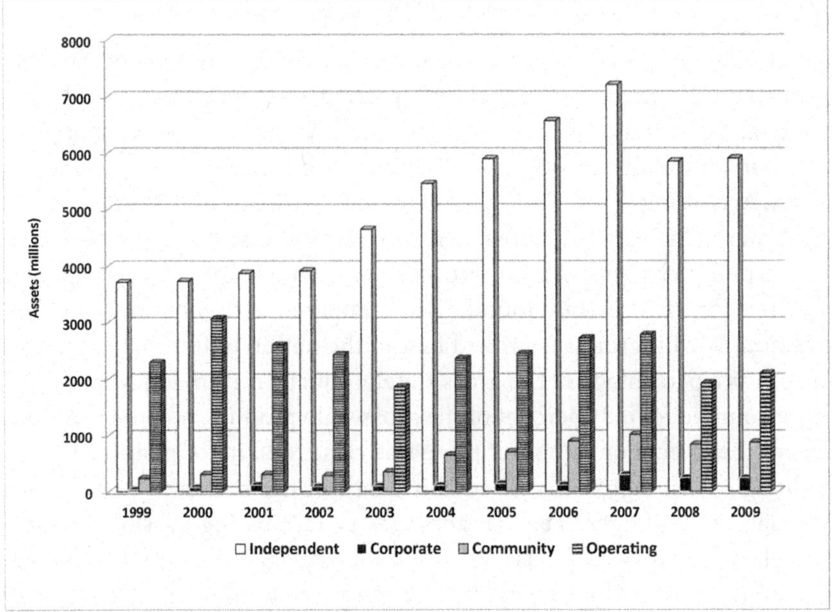

Figure 10.1. Assets by Foundation Type, 1999–2009 (Excluding Gates Foundation) (Foundation Center, FC Stats, excludes Bill & Melinda Gates Foundation)

excluding the Gates Foundation) but only gave 0.3 percent of the funding (1.5 percent, excluding the Gates Foundation), compared to 6.1 percent assets and 9.3 percent giving nationally. In 2009, the majority of those operating foundation assets (92.2 percent) were held by Casey Family Programs, which is the second-largest operating foundation by total asset size in the nation behind the J. Paul Getty Trust. Casey Family Programs has emerged as one of the largest and most visible funders of social and community development programs in the United States. As noted in table 10.2, Casey Family Programs' assets were worth more than $1.9 billion in 2010.

One other noteworthy operating foundation in Washington State is the Frye Museum, located in Seattle. The museum was formally created in 1952 to house the art collection of a wealthy Seattle family. The stipulations of the original gift required free admission and the support of the museum activities by the foundation itself. Its assets in 2011 were approximately $52 million.[36]

Corporate foundation giving in Washington was $251 million and 1 percent of total giving in 2010 (5.8 percent, excluding the Gates Foundation), which was much lower than the national average of 10.7 percent (figure 10.2). In terms of giving, the Safeco Insurance Foundation

Table 10.2. Top Ten Washington Foundations by Assets, 2010

Foundation Name	Foundation Type	Total Giving
1. Bill & Melinda Gates Foundation	Independent	$37,430,150,458
2. Casey Family Programs	Operating	1,935,207,121
3. M. J. Murdock Charitable Trust	Independent	795,007,236
4. The Seattle Foundation	Community	663,201,900
5. Marguerite Casey Foundation	Independent	598,485,474
6. The Norcliffe Foundation	Independent	394,286,595
7. Gary E. Milgard Family Foundation	Independent	234,751,675
8. Washington Research Foundation	Independent	166,004,322
9. The Russell Family Foundation	Independent	130,939,740
10. Samis Foundation	Independent	118,747,565

Note: Includes grants, scholarships, and employee matching gifts; excludes set-asides, loans, program-related investments (PRIs,) and program expenses.
Source: The Foundation Center, 2010.
http://data.foundationcenter.org/?_ga=1.1700785.1275628255.1477281855.

was the largest corporate foundation until recently (2009), ranking thirteenth in the state and giving more than $7 million and possessing more than $60 million in assets.[37] However, Safeco has largely disappeared from the corporate landscape, having been absorbed by the Liberty Insurance Company. Its giving program has declined precipitously (to only $2.8 million in 2010, for example).[38] Microsoft, like Boeing, has a significant philanthropic giving program, but it channels its giving through its corporate giving program rather than through a corporate foundation.

The last major category of foundations, community foundations, is most visibly represented by the Seattle Foundation, a community foundation ranked in the top ten in Washington State for both assets and total giving, as indicated in tables 10.2 and 10.3. Moreover, it ranks in the top twenty for community foundations nationally. In 2010, 69.5 percent of all foundations in Washington State were located within the Seattle metropolitan area. While the majority of the foundation community is located in Seattle, foundations with substantial assets are also located outside the Seattle-King County area. Indeed, three of the top ten Washington foundations by assets are outside Seattle (rank in parentheses): the M. J. Murdock Charitable Trust in Vancouver, WA (third); the Gary E. Milgard Family Foundation in Tacoma (seventh); and the Russell Family Foundation in Tacoma (ninth). The M. J. Murdock Charitable Trust and the Gary E. Milgard Family Foundation also ranked third and tenth, respectively, in total giving among Washington State foundations in 2010.

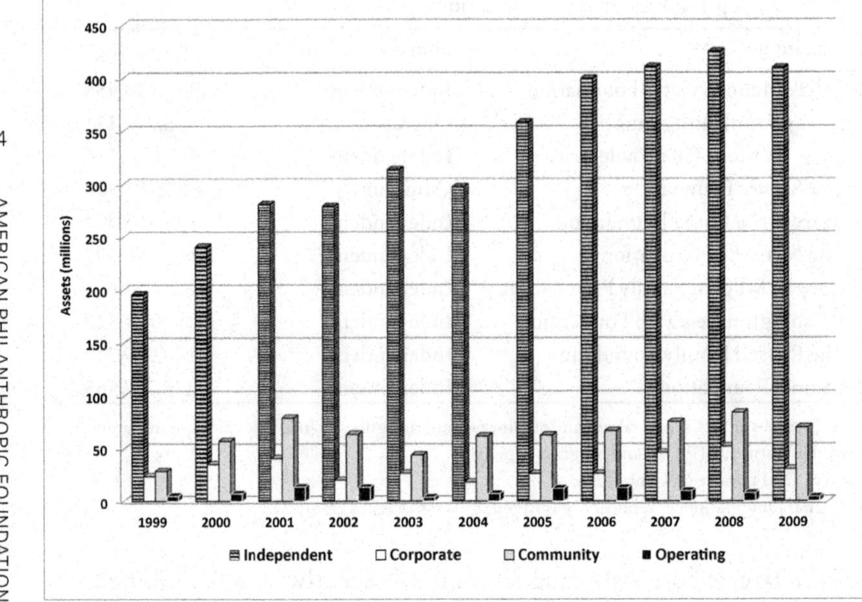

Figure 10.2. Giving by Foundation Type, 1999–2009 (Excluding Gates Foundation) (Foundation Center, FC Stats, Excludes Bill & Melinda Gates Foundation).

Table 10.3. Top Ten Washington Foundations by Total Giving, 2010

Foundation Name	Foundation Type	Total Giving
1. Bill & Melinda Gates Foundation	Independent	$2,486,342,209
2. The Seattle Foundation	Community	52,117,881
3. M. J. Murdock Charitable Trust	Independent	31,663,378
4. Marguerite Casey Foundation	Independent	20,976,412
5. The Paul G. Allen Family Foundation	Independent	14,693,342
6. Charles Simonyi Fund for Arts and Sciences	Independent	11,424,062
7. Community Foundation for Southwest Washington	Community	10,324,502
8. The Wilburforce Foundation	Independent	9,914,366
9. The Norcliffe Foundation	Independent	9,526,239
10. Gary E. Milgard Family Foundation	Independent	6,860,340

Note: Includes grants, scholarships, and employee matching gifts; excludes set-asides, loans, PRIs, and program expenses.

Source: The Foundation Center, 2010.

http://data.foundationcenter.org/?_ga=1.170078 5.1275628255.1477281855.

Patterns and Trends in Washington Foundation Philanthropy

Size, Assets and Giving

The foundation community in Washington State had been growing steadily until the 2008 recession hit. For example, between 1999 and 2007, Washington saw an increase of 71.2 percent in the number of foundations, from 824 to 1,411, as indicated in figure 10.3. This growth was spread almost evenly across foundation types (independent 41.5 percent, corporate 40 percent, community 38.9 percent, operating 44.2 percent).[39] During that period, the number of Washington foundations increased more than the overall rate for foundations nationally (49.8 percent). In addition, foundation growth in Washington outpaced the growth in the number of public charities in Washington, which increased by 30.3 percent, similar to the national public charity growth trend (31.3 percent).[40] However, the number of foundations declined to 1,330 by 2010.

The significant influence of the Gates Foundation on foundation philanthropy in Washington is vividly evident in figures 10.4 and 10.5. For example, 78.3 percent of assets and 83.4 percent of giving in 2010 were from the Gates Foundation. Figure 10.4 illustrates the difference in the Washington asset growth with and without the Gates Foundation. Washington assets more than doubled (104 percent) between 1999 and 2007, from $22 billion to $50.2 billion. Excluding the Gates Foundation, overall Washington foundation assets grew from $6.4 billion to $11.3 billion (76.6 percent) from 1999 to 2007 but experienced a decline of $498.2 million or 6.7 percent between 2000 and 2002. Even without the influence of the Gates Foundation, assets in Washington grew faster than the national average (52.1 percent) between 1999 and 2007, from $6.4 million to $11.3 million (43.4 percent) excluding Gates Foundation. However, from 2007 to 2008 Washington foundation assets saw a significant decrease from $11.3 billion to $8.9 billion (21.7 percent). In 2010, total assets in Washington (excluding the Gates Foundation) increased only 2 percent to $10 billion. Gates Foundation assets more than doubled from $15.5 billion to $38.9 billion (a 151 percent increase) from 1999 to 2007, but experienced a decline, similar to the rest of Washington foundations, of 23.2 percent from 2007 to 2008. From 2008 to 2010, Gates Foundation assets increased to $37.4 billion.[41]

As indicated in figure 10.5, the Washington foundation-giving trend between 1999 and 2007 was similar to the asset trend. Overall, Washington giving more than tripled (a 224 percent increase) from $803.2 million to

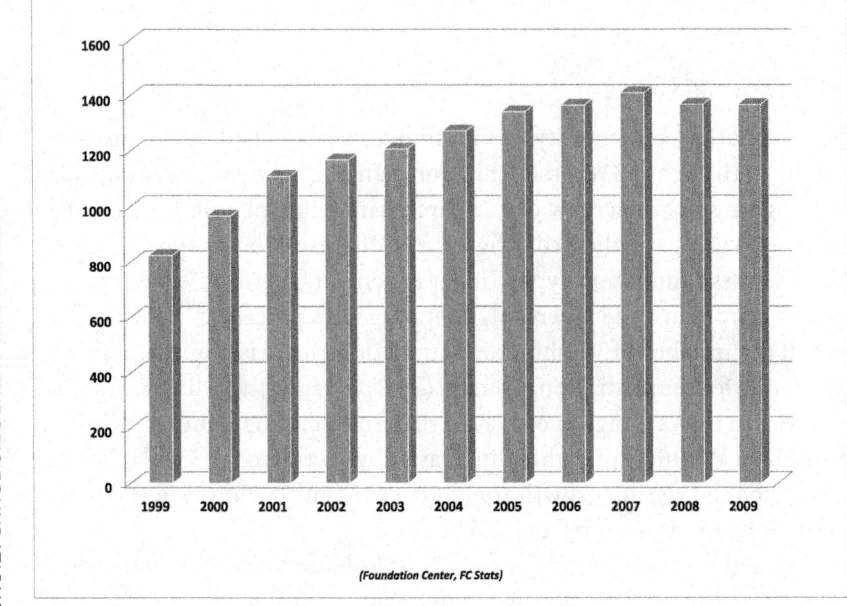

Figure 10.3. Number of Foundations, 1999–2009 (Foundation Center, FC Stats).

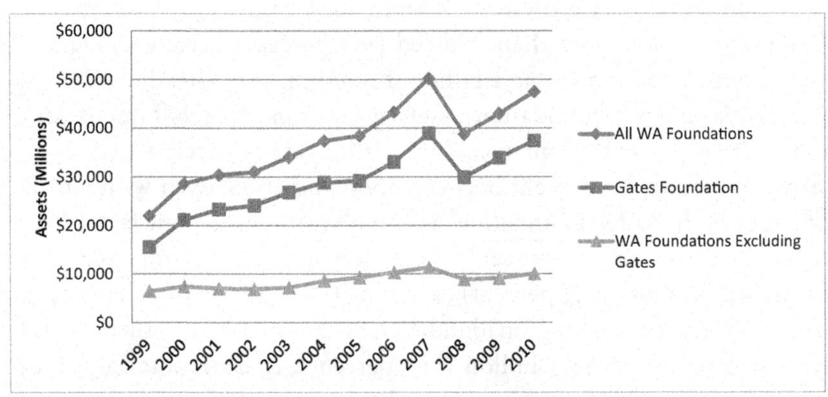

Figure 10.4. Asset Growth Trend for Washington Foundations, 1999–2010 (Foundation Center, FC Stats).

$2.6 billion during this period. Giving increased every year except for a very slight decline of $27.3 million or 1.7 percent between 2000 and 2001. Excluding the Gates Foundation, giving more than doubled (114 percent increase) between 1999 and 2007, from $253.8 million to $543.2 million.

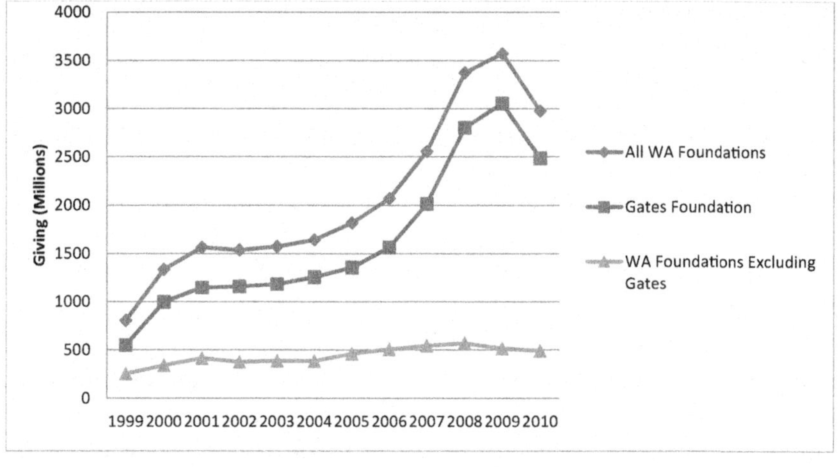

Figure 10.5. Giving Growth Trend for Washington Foundations, 1999–2010.

Similar to asset growth, Washington foundation giving, without the influence of the Gates Foundation, outpaced the percentage increase in national giving (46.3 percent excluding the Gates Foundation). Washington's foundation giving, exclusive of the Gates Foundation, declined by 9.3 percent or 38.6 million in 2001, most likely in response to the corresponding drop in assets. In line with its assets, the Gates Foundation's giving steadily increased from $549 million to $1.6 billion (64.8 percent) between 1999 and 2007. The Gates Foundation's giving between 2007 and 2009 still increased overall by 1.1 billion (55 percent), from $2 billion to $3.1 billion. Washington foundation-giving trends, excluding the Gates Foundation, closely mirrored the national trend between 2007 and 2008 (about 3.6 percent). Total giving by the Gates Foundation increased by 28.3 percent during that time, which accounted for most of the overall giving increase in Washington. This increase, even in the face of significant reductions in Gates Foundation assets, is likely due to the stipulation that the full dollar amount of the Buffet gift be spent annually in addition to regular Gates Foundation grant distributions.[42] More current data from the NCCS indicates a significant slowdown in formation of new foundations after 2007. Moreover, foundation assets dropped by almost 25 percent from 2008 to 2010.[43] Thus, giving by Washington State foundations continued to decline through 2010. Even the Gates Foundation experienced a significant decline in their giving (almost $500 million) from its 2009 peak of about $3 billion.

Giving Characteristics

This section evaluates giving characteristics of the Washington foundation community, including grant size, distribution, recipient type, and subject area. In order to isolate the specific influence of the Gates Foundation, the following data are presented in two parts: Washington foundations excluding the Gates Foundation, followed by the Gates Foundation. The analysis was conducted using data from two sets of Foundation Center grants: 3,361 grants made in 2001 by twenty Washington State foundations (found in the 1,007 largest foundations in the United States that are tracked by the Foundation Center), and 2,883 grants made in 2005 by fifteen Washington State foundations (found in the 1,154 largest foundations in the United States that are tracked by the Foundation Center). These data represent a little more than 80 percent of the total foundations assets and giving in Washington State for 2001 and 2005. Grant distribution data is from FoundationSearch, and includes 11,549 grants of $4,000 or more given in 2003 by Washington foundations locally, nationally, and internationally, as well as grants given to charities in Washington by foundations elsewhere.[44] The total giving by Washington foundations for 2003 as reported by FoundationSearch was $1.3 billion, which represents 66 percent of the total giving for 2003 as reported by the NCCS.[45] We have also supplemented this information with survey data from Philanthropy Northwest, the Regional Association of Grantmakers based in Seattle. Philanthropy Northwest is a member organization of foundations and other private philanthropic funders such as Boeing, Microsoft, and the United Way of King County; its member are from the six-state Northwest region of Montana, Idaho, Wyoming, Oregon, Washington, and Alaska.

Washington Foundations Excluding the Gates Foundation

Grant Size, Recipient Type, and Support Type

In 2005, Washington foundations gave a larger number of small grants than in 2001, which was also the case nationwide. During this time period, the number of grants in Washington State increased by 4.7 percent, while total amount of grants declined by 13.6 percent and average grant amount declined by 17.4 percent. The median grant size remained at $25,000 for both years.[46] Nationally, a 5.5 percent increase occurred in the number of grants given, in addition to a 7 percent decline in amount of grants given, a decline

Table 10.4. Top Ten Types of Organizations (Recipient Type) that Received Funding from Washington Foundations (excluding the Gates Foundation), 2005

Rank	Recipient Type	% of Total Grant Funding
1	Education	21.3%
2	Arts and Culture	10.9%
3	Environment	10.2%
4	Human Services	9.4%
5	Community Improvement	7.8%
6	Philanthropy, Volunteerism	5.8%
7	Healthcare	5.1%
8	International, Foreign Affairs, and National Security	4.5%
9	Religion-Related	4.2%
10	Youth Development	3.6%

Table 10.5. Top Ten Types of Organizations (Recipient Type) that Received Funding from National Foundations (excluding the Gates Foundation), 2005

Rank	Recipient Type	% of Total Grant Funding
1	Education	32.6%
2	Arts, Culture, and Humanities	13.2%
3	Healthcare	8.3%
4	Human Services	7.2%
5	Philanthropy, Volunteerism, and Grantmaking Foundations	5.2%
6	Environment	4.7%
7	Community Improvement and Capacity Building	4.5%
8	International, Foreign Affairs, and National Security	3.3%
9	Public Societal Benefit	3.2%
10	Religion-Related	2.4%

in average grant size of 11.8 percent, and a decline in median grant size of 16.2 percent.[47]

Washington State foundations appear to have similar funding priorities as national foundations overall, with the exception of healthcare and environmental funding. In 2005, Washington foundations contributed 10.2 percent of total funding to environmental organizations and only 5.1 percent to health care (table 10.4) organizations, compared to 4.7 percent environmental and 8.3 percent health care nationally (table 10.5). While

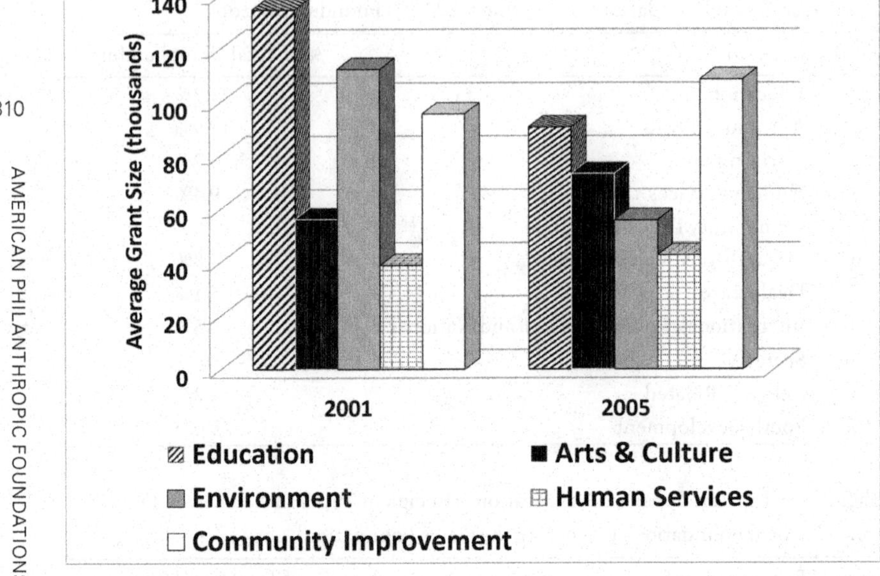

Figure 10.6. Average Washington Foundations Grant by Five Major Recipient Types (excluding Gates Foundation grants), 2001 and 2005.

the overall average grant amount declined, three of the five major recipient types showed increases in average grant size (figure 10.6). The arts and culture category increased by 30.1 percent, community improvement and capacity building increased by 13.6 percent, and human services increased by 9.7 percent, with a larger portion of grants overall going to human services in 2005 (9.4 percent) compared to 2001 (6.6 percent). Giving to environmental organizations declined by 50.3 percent and giving to education declined by 32.7 percent.

Table 10.6 shows the four major support type categories for Washington State and national foundations. Washington foundation giving by support type parallels giving at the national level. In both cases, the vast majority of grants by total amount given and total number given are devoted to program development and general/operating support. More recently, a 2014 Philanthropy Northwest survey of philanthropic giving in the six-state Northwest region concluded that giving grew more than 19 percent from 2004 to 2012. (It experienced a 34 percent rise with the Gates Foundation grants excluded.) However, grants have dropped from a peak of $859 million in 2008 to $590 million in 2012.[48]

Table 10.6. Percent of Total Amount Given, Average Grant Size, and Percent of Total Number of Grants for Washington and the United States by Support Type (excluding the Gates Foundation), 2005

Support Type	**Percent of Total Amount Given**		**Average Grant Size**		**Percent of Total Number**	
	WA	US	WA	US	WA	US
Program Development	30.9%	35.1%	69,721	117,206	30.6%	37.8%
General/ Operating Support	21.4%	22.6%	52,086	95,909	28.4%	29.8%
Building/ Renovation	12.6%	12.2%	110,361	256,483	7.9%	6%
Research	4.5%	5.3%	56,275	180,457	3.1%	3.7%

Grant Distribution

The majority of grants received by charities in Washington (67 percent) in 2003 came from Washington foundations, with an average grant size of $35,843 ($54,742 including the Gates Foundation). These grant funds went to support a variety of purposes separated into the following ten categories: arts and culture, community development, education, environment, health, international giving, miscellaneous philanthropy, religion, social and human services, and sports and recreation. Of these ten categories, only sports and recreation (32.9 percent) and international giving (30.8 percent) received less than half of their funding from Washington foundations. The majority of funding given by Washington foundations went to education (28.3 percent), social and human services (20.7 percent), and arts and culture (15 percent). The single largest grant, for $4.1 million, went to education. The majority of Washington foundation grants to out-of-state organizations went to education (28.5 percent), social and human services (25.1 percent), and environment (11.5 percent). The largest single grant for $8.3 million went to social and human services.

Washington charities received 33 percent of grant funding in 2003 from foundations outside of Washington with an average grant size of $38,123, roughly the same as the average grant size from Washington foundations (excluding the Gates Foundation). International giving (62.9 percent) and sports and recreation (67.1 percent) are the two grant purpose categories that received more than half of their funding from imported grants. The majority of imported grants went to education (36.3 percent), miscellaneous philanthropy (14.5 percent), and health (14.2 percent). The largest single imported grant of $3 million went to health.

Bill & Melinda Gates Foundation

Grant Size, Recipient Type, and Support Type

As a single entity, it is expected that the Gates Foundation's individual focus and goals would set it apart from national giving trends. This section offers specific comparisons in order to identify and portray the specific influence that the Gates Foundation wields as the largest foundation in the world. In comparing the Gates Foundation grant data to national data, it is interesting to note that in 2001 the Gates Foundation did not appear to have a significant impact on the average grant size (3.6 percent increase) and that median grant size was the same with and without the Gates Foundation. However, it is significant that 4.5 percent of the total grants given are attributed to the Gates Foundation. In 2005, the inclusion of the Gates Foundation in the national sample increased the average grant by 9 percent and the median grant by 3.4 percent. Furthermore, 9.4 percent of total grant dollars were attributed to the Gates Foundation.

Unlike foundations on the state and national level, the Gates Foundation gave fewer but substantially larger grants in 2005 than in 2001 (even compared to national data including the Gates Foundation). The total number of grants from the Gates Foundation during this period declined by 48.5 percent, while total giving increased by 106 percent. Average grant size increased by 301.1 percent and median size by 1,121.3 percent.

The proportion of grants given to education organizations increased by 15.1 percent from 2001 to 2005. The proportion given to health care was relatively the same (1.1 percent increase), while the proportion for international, foreign affairs, and national security declined by 8.9 percent, and diseases, disorders, and medical disciplines declined by 10.3 percent. It is important to note that, in this data set, if a grant goes to a healthcare organization, it is coded as healthcare even if the grant has an international purpose. Therefore, international giving will be evaluated separately later in this chapter.

The Gates Foundation's work reflects national priorities around giving to education and healthcare, but due to its international focus it gives a much higher proportion of grants to international, foreign affairs, and national security, and to diseases, disorders, and medical disciplines (see tables 10.7 and 10.8) and a very small proportion to arts and culture (1 percent).

The average grant for three of the major recipient types decreased in 2005 compared to 2001. The average grant to education dropped by the substantial percentage of 243 percent, and average grants also decreased to international, foreign affairs, and national security (47 percent), and

Table 10.7. Top Ten Types of Organizations (Recipient Type) that Received Funding from the Gates Foundation, 2005

Rank	Recipient Type	% of Total Grant Funding
1	Education	44.3%
2	Health Care	24%
3	International, Foreign Affairs, and National Security	8.7%
4	Diseases, Disorders, and Medical Disciplines	6.7%
5	Public Societal Benefit	3.2%
6	Medical Research	3%
7	Social Science	2.2%
8	Science and Technology	1.7%
9	Food, Agriculture, and Nutrition	1.4%
10	Human Services	1.2%

Table 10.8. Top Ten Types of Organizations (Recipient Type) that Received Funding from National Foundations, 2005

Rank	Recipient Type	% of Total Grant Funding
1	Education	33.7%
2	Arts, Culture, and Humanities	12.1%
3	Healthcare	9.8%
4	Human Services	6.7%
5	Philanthropy, Volunteerism, and Grantmaking Foundations	4.8%
6	Environment	4.3%
7	Community Improvement and Capacity Building	4.2%
8	International, Foreign Affairs, and National Security	3.8%
9	Public Societal Benefit	3.2%
10	Religion-Related	2.2%

diseases, disorders, and medical disciplines (23 percent). Average grants to healthcare were significantly higher in 2005 by 97 percent (as indicated in figure 10.7).

The majority of Gates Foundation grants went to program development, which typically meant grants for new initiatives such as school reform or the eradication of a deadly disease. (As an alternative, the foundation could for example dedicate funding to supporting the operating expenses of existing organizations.) This grant focus is evident in their grant distributions. For example, 85.3 percent of total funding went to program development in 2001

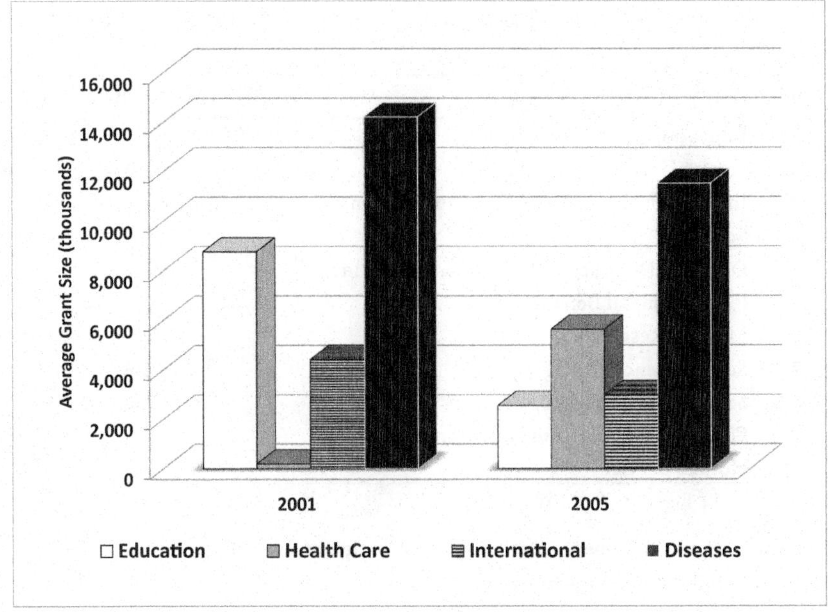

Figure 10.7. Average Gates Foundation Grant by Four Major Recipient Types, 2001 and 2005.

and 63.7 percent went to this area in 2005. By contrast, 32.3 percent nationally went to program development in 2001 and 38.3 percent in 2005, as noted in table 10.9. The reduced share of program development grants is mostly explained by a single $20 million grant by the Gates Foundation for research funding. The largest average grant went to scholarship funds ($15.5 million) in 2005. Given the source of Gates Foundation revenue, it is not surprising that the second-largest support type by number of grants behind program development (49.6 percent) was computer systems, which accounted for 13.5 percent of the total number of grants.

Grant Distribution

Charities in Washington received 25.8 percent of their total grant funding from the Gates Foundation, which accounted for 38.5 percent of grant funding provided by Washington foundations. Similar to the rest of the foundation community, the majority of Gates Foundation funding went to education (35.8 percent), social and humans services (11.1 percent), and arts and culture (12.5 percent). The single largest grant given by the Gates Foundation ($12 million) and the largest average grant ($1.2 million) both went to arts and culture.[49]

The vast majority of Gates Foundation grant funding (90 percent), however, went to charities outside of Washington, which matches the

Table 10.9. Percent of Total Amount Given, Average Grant Size, and Percent of Total Number of Grants for Gates Foundation by Support Type, 2005

Rank	Support Type	Percent of Total Amount Given	Average Grant Size	Percent of Total Number
1	Program Development	63.7%	3,497,732.07	49.6%
2	Research	15%	6,452,290.14	6.3%
3	Scholarship Funds	6%	15,467,497.00	1.1%
4	Capital Campaigns	4.1%	1,720,281.54	6.5%
5	Endowment	3.1%	12,137,500.00	0.7%
6	Seed Money	2.5%	4,793,742.75	1.4%
7	General/Operating Support	1.9%	709,953.46	7.2%
8	Management Development	1.4%	1,795,100.08	2.1%
9	Computer Systems/Equipment	0.6%	129,015.39	13.5%
10	Building/Renovation	0.4%	690,277.78	1.6%

Gates Foundation's national and international focus. The majority of the Gates Foundation grants went to international giving (60.1 percent) and community development (28.3 percent). The largest single grant, for $350 million, went to international giving, while the largest average grant went to community development at $6.6 million.

The Gates Influence

In addition to the sheer size of the Gates Foundation, its involvement as a key stakeholder in large initiatives in the state has shaped the focus of philanthropy in Washington. Most notable is the United Way of King County's Gates Endowment Challenge. In December 1999, the Gates Foundation seeded the United Way of King County's endowment with a $30 million gift and a challenge to raise an additional $55 million that the Gates Foundation would match. The result was the successful completion of the $140 million endowment two years ahead of schedule. This endowment, the largest United Way operating endowment in the country, enables the United Way of King County (UWKC) to offset overhead costs to 3.8 percent annually,[50] although some local commentators have wondered if the UWKC is understating its actual overhead.[51] Regardless of the actual overhead costs, the Gates grant to UWKC greatly accelerated a shift of the UWKC from the traditional model of a United Way chapter—reliant on payroll giving, an annual campaign, and grants to member organizations—to a new model in which the UWKC resembles a community foundation with no specific member requirements for a grant, a dependence on individual donations especially from wealthy individuals, and a substantial endowment. The Gates grant also encouraged the adoption by UWKC of its focused outcome orientation for local grantees.

The Gates Foundation was also a key player in three statewide initiatives: Thrive by 5, Sound Families, and the Washington Families Fund. Thrive by 5 Washington was a public–private initiative to promote, through grants to local organizations, "positive early learning experiences for every child, from birth to age 5, so that they are ready to succeed in school and thrive in life."[52] William H. Gates Sr., Bill Gates's father, served as one of the original chairs of the initiative. Since 2006, the Gates Foundation has made more than $25 million in grants to Thrive by 5 Washington.[53] In fiscal year 2013, Thrive by 5 awarded over $8.6 million in grants to Washington State organizations to promote early learning (approximately 90 percent went to home visiting programs across the state, 7 percent to regional early learning coalitions, and 2 percent to advancing racial equity and other programs).[54] Many other foundations in Washington State have joined this effort.[55] While the annual grants are quite modest compared to the need, Thrive by 5 has certainly contributed to the widespread attention that the issue of early learning now enjoys. The Gates grant to Thrive by 5 also facilitated the consolidation of funder effort on early learning in one organization, as exemplified in the recent merger of Thrive by 5 and the Foundation for Early Learning, a much older Seattle-based organization, into a new public–private partnership called Thrive Washington (beginning in 2015).

The Gates Foundation has been equally involved in Building Changes, an organization that brings together public and private partners to end homelessness. In partnership with the Gates Foundation, Building Changes has launched two initiatives: Sound Families and the Washington Families Fund. Sound Families was a multiyear initiative launched in 2000 that received $40 million from the Gates Foundation to "triple the number of service-enriched housing units for homeless families in Pierce, King, and Snohomish counties in the state of Washington."[56] The success of Sound Families led to the Washington Families Fund (WFF), a public–private partnership created by the Washington State legislature in 2004 to "reduce the number of homeless families in Washington State by 50 percent by the year 2019."[57] The WFF is administered by Building Changes, but has received over $12 million from the state and significant support from a variety of local foundations including Boeing, the Campion Foundation, and the Greater Tacoma Community Foundation. In 2009, the Gates Foundation pledged up to $60 million to support the WFF.[58] A high priority of the WFF is to supply grants to local housing organizations for innovative strategies to reduce homelessness, especially among homeless individuals who also suffer from mental health and substance abuse problems.[59]

International Giving

Since its inception, the Gates Foundation has been at the forefront among foundations in its international giving program. Indeed, according to Philanthropy Northwest's 2012 *Trends in Northwest Giving,* Northwest foundations (including foundations in Alaska, Idaho, Montana, Oregon, Washington, and Wyoming) gave $3.1 billion in international grants in 2008, $2.9 billion of which came from the Gates Foundation.[60] This funding represents 49.4 percent of the $6.2 billion in total international grants reported by Foundation Center for 2008.[61] Of this grant funding, 42 percent was given directly to organizations headquartered outside of the United States (direct) and 58 percent was given to organizations within the United States which serve an international purpose (indirect). Seven percent of funding went through organizations based in the Northwest. The majority of these grant dollars supported health (52 percent direct and 72 percent indirect).

However, this international giving declined by 45 percent among funders reporting in both 2008 and 2010, to $1.65 billion. Excluding Gates Foundation funding, the decline was only 9 percent. While the vast majority of Northwest international funding comes from Gates Foundation, 103 additional foundations contributed $102.6 million in international grants, which account for 1.7 percent of total international giving on a national basis. Excluding Gates Foundation funding, the majority of these grants supported international development (23 percent). Eight of the top ten Pacific Northwest foundations supporting international work are located in Washington, including the Seattle Foundation and Seattle International Foundation. As mentioned previously, the Seattle Foundation is a community foundation, which by definition usually has a local giving focus. Seattle International Foundation was founded in 2007 "as a supporting organization to the Seattle Foundation for the purpose of increasing and enhancing international philanthropy efforts from the Pacific Northwest."[62] The establishment of organizations like Seattle International Foundation, and more recently Global Washington (2010), a public charity that gives grants with an international focus, seem to indicate that international giving will continue to be an important part of foundation philanthropy in Washington.

Washington State and the New Philanthropy

Washington State is famously home to many younger and very wealthy philanthropists from the high-tech industry who are very invested in product innovation and taking good ideas to scale. In general, many of these newer philanthropists have been attracted to a model of philanthropy known as "venture philanthropy" that evolved in the late 1990s. Heavily influenced by thinking from the world of venture capital and the high-tech industry, this model strives to engage philanthropists more deeply in the operations of their grantees, in the hope of improving the overall effectiveness and efficiency of nonprofit agencies. Funding strategies associated with venture philanthropy include greater receptivity to grants for operating expenses, longer term grants, ongoing technical assistance to grantees by foundations, and a focused attention to outcomes and evaluation.[63] The Gates Foundation certainly embodies some of the precepts of this venture philanthropy movement: it is very focused on outcomes and evaluation; however, most of its funding is for project grants rather than ongoing operational support.

Another expression of the venture philanthropy movement are "donor giving circles." Giving circles are typically structured as a 501(c)3 public charity, rather than a private foundation. Donors are members of these organizations and are expected to donate a minimum amount every year. Members are then expected to contribute volunteer time and their expertise to help nonprofit recipient agencies. In this sense, these new organizations are an effort to offer high-engagement philanthropy where members are actively involved in the recipient organizations. Good examples in the Seattle area include Social Venture Partners (SVP), started in part through the efforts of Paul Brainard, with many chapters around the country; and the Washington Women's Foundation. Both organizations are registered as public charities. SVP has garnered widespread support from local philanthropists and garnered national and international attention due to its innovative approach to philanthropic investing that entails direct and ongoing involvement with grantee organizations. Indeed, donors to SVP are expected to give time and money to their grantee organizations. Like the Gates Foundation, SVP is also very interested in outcomes and evaluation and supporting the capacity and infrastructure development of their grantees. Two other notable examples of grant-giving public charities in Washington State are the Wilburforce Foundation and the Social Justice Fund (SJF). The former focuses on supporting conservation-related nonprofits and causes in the West and the SJF supports social change organizations in the Northwest region. Both of these organizations are very modest in size. For example, SJF awarded about $540,000 in grants in 2013.[64]

The interest in outcomes and leverage of grant funds is evident at the United Way of King County (UWKC) and at the Medina Foundation, a family foundation established in 1947. The former has faced substantial competition for charitable contributions given the decline in workplace giving and the rise of donor-designated funds. Further, UWKC also faces competition from the Seattle Foundation and other philanthropic institutions. In an effort to remain relevant in a rapidly changing environment, UWKC has refocused its giving programs to emphasize a more outcomes-oriented approach to grantmaking, including the extensive use of logic models, which are usually a graphic representation of the relationship between what is put into the program in the way of resources and activities and what is expected to result (outputs and outcomes). The organization has also tried to address urgent public problems such as homelessness with larger grants and external funding in the hope of having more impact. Consequently, UWKC, like many United Way chapters, has largely abandoned the unrestricted grants for operating costs of its grantee agencies that were typical of the United Way in earlier eras. To support its new approach to grantgiving, UWKC has received substantial funding from the Gates Foundation and individual members of the Gates family including William Gates, Sr.

The Medina Foundation for many years supported an array of local nonprofit organizations in the Puget Sound region. However, a few years ago, through leadership of its then executive director Tricia McKay, the foundation decided to support a major new innovation: the establishment of a low-income credit union and an affiliated nonprofit that will provide affordable financial products to low-income individuals in King County. This effort fits with the growing emphasis on more market-oriented approaches to address social problems and the desire for greater impact in foundation grantmaking. The Medina Foundation does, however, continue to support an array of local organizations in the region, albeit at modest levels, with direct operating support.

Philanthropy Northwest, the prominent regional association of grantmakers based in Seattle, supports capacity building and technical assistance efforts for local foundations and helps members build the infrastructure of their grantees. It has also promoted learning and practice on the mission investing model for foundations. This model is based on the idea that foundations should maximize all of their assets, including their investments, to attain their programmatic and mission-related goals. Thus, foundations should invest in companies, for example, that are in alignment with their goals or loan their assets to nonprofits and for-profit companies that fit their goals. Philanthropy Northwest also hosts the Mission Investors Exchange, a national organization dedicated to supporting mission investing by foundations.

Despite these noteworthy developments, the data suggest that many local foundations continue with their traditional grant-making approaches. Most foundations in Washington provide project-related funding and most grants are short-term and relatively small in size, with the median grant about $5,000, according to Philanthropy Northwest, for foundations in Washington State.[65] Instead, local foundations in Washington State tend to fund a wide array of different types of organizations. Many of these organizations have longstanding connections to the local foundation community and often provide routine services such as emergency relief and foster care. Many foundations also support different types of cultural institutions. And many foundations are relatively small, so they do not have the capacity to invest substantial resources in evaluation. Overall, then, the data indicate that most foundations in Washington State, aside from the Gates Foundation, tend to play fairly traditional foundation grantgiving roles.

The Gates Foundation receives a lot of well-deserved attention given its size and ambition, but it is also noteworthy that the many other high-tech millionaires and billionaires in the Puget Sound region have not chosen to exercise their influence and reach through a foundation. Although Bezos (Amazon), Glaser (Real Networks), Brotman (Costco), and Allen (Microsoft) have created foundations of varying size, their philanthropic efforts have been relatively modest or idiosyncratic compared to the Gates Foundation. They have also tended to pursue their social and personal goals through a wide variety of investment strategies. For example, Allen has literally transformed vast areas of downtown Seattle into a modern, mixed-use walkable community through his company's investment and development policies. Bezos recently purchased the *Washington Post*.

Conclusion

In sum, foundations in Washington State are comparable to foundations in other regions in that they are linked to the institutional and economic development of the state. With a relatively sparse population and a natural resources-based economy in the nineteenth and early twentieth centuries, foundations developed very slowly during the early history of Washington State, especially compared with the Northeast and the Midwest regions of the country. The rapid post–World War I growth of Boeing led to a significant role for the corporation in the philanthropic giving in the state, albeit through the company rather than a foundation. The much more recent growth of Microsoft and other high-tech companies has in turn profoundly affected the foundation landscape in Washington State, especially with the establishment of the Bill & Melinda Gates Foundation. But the attention accorded the Gates Foundation has also masked the actual similarity between Washington State foundations and foundations in other parts of the country. Washington's foundation giving to various program fields like education is quite similar to national patterns and many foundations have tended to continue their traditional priorities of supporting local agencies with modest grants on a short-term basis; scant money is given to operating expenses.

Yet, the trends evident in the pattern of engagement of Washington State philanthropists in foundations, local nonprofits and other social causes may also augur future developments in other parts of the country. That is, the decline in foundation formation, despite substantial wealth in the region, would suggest that wealthy individuals are turning away from foundation formation and choosing other vehicles to pursue their social goals. SVP, the Washington Women's Foundation, and Global Washington are good examples of new innovative initiatives that support nonprofits but are registered as public charities. The sharp rise in donor-advised funds, as exemplified in the impressive growth of the Seattle Foundation and the Greater Tacoma Community Foundation, are other examples of alternative philanthropic investments to foundations.[66] Also, the rise of third-party intermediaries such as Thrive Washington and Building Changes, who use a pool of foundation and public funds, is a trend evident in many other parts of country.

Overall, foundations in Washington State underscore both the great potential of foundations as innovators and the obstacles faced by them in achieving social change and policy reform. Washington State foundations, especially the Gates Foundation, have invested in a wide variety of program innovations. In some cases, these innovations—such as education reform and homelessness policy—have been replicated elsewhere in the country. Yet, foundations also face a wide array of headwinds: resources have failed to keep pace with need; foundations face competition from other philanthropic instruments; and foundations in Washington State, with some exceptions, are ill-suited to support the infrastructure needs of local community agencies. The Gates Foundation has impressively chosen to spend down its significant assets over the course of the next several decades, but most Washington State foundations remain committed to building their assets and a cautious philosophy on their grantgiving. One of the key challenges facing foundations in the coming years will be their ability to innovate in their own programming and relationship to their community, including other foundations, in support of important community needs.

Natalie C. Alm is the Andes-Amazon Program Officer with the Wildlife Conservation Society, focusing on international development and conservation in Latin America.

Kate Anderson is Project Director and Associate Fellow in the Center for Universal Education at the Brookings Institution, focusing on international education policy and metrics in Africa, South Asia, and Latin America.

Beth L. Lovelady is Fund Development Director for Children's Alliance, a public policy advocacy organization focused on children and families in Washington State.

Steven Rathgeb Smith is Executive Director of the American Political Science Association. He has taught at several universities, including the University of Washington, where he was the Nancy Bell Evans Professor of Public Affairs. His most recent book is *Nonprofits and Advocacy: Engaging Community and Government in an Era of Retrenchment* (with Robert Pekkanen and Yutaka Tsujinaka). He is currently president of the International Society for Third Sector Research.

Notes

1. The authors are indebted to many people in the philanthropic community in Washington State for their support and assistance in our research. We also would like to express our appreciation to the following individuals for their comments on earlier drafts of this paper: Putnam Barber, Paul Beaudet, David Hammack, and Cory Sbarbaro. Meghan McConaughey provided excellent editorial and research support.

2. Paul Brest, "A Decade of Outcome-Oriented Philanthropy," *Stanford Social Innovation Review,* Spring 2012, retrieved from http://ssir.org/articles/entry/a_decade_of_outcome_oriented_philanthropy; Christine Letts, William Ryan, and Allen Grossman, *High Performance Nonprofit Organizations: Managing Upstream for Greater Impact* (New York: Wiley, 1999), 15–28; Joel L. Fleishman, *The Foundation: A Great American Secret; How Private Wealth Is Changing the*

World (New York: Public Affairs, 2009) 45–48, 57–161; Mario Morino, "Leap of Reason: Managing to Outcomes in an Era of Scarcity," *Innovations* 6, no. 3 (2011): 167–77; Leslie Crutchfield and Heather McLeod Grant, "Share Leadership," in *The Jossey-Bass Reader on Nonprofit and Public Leadership*, ed. James L. Perry (New York: John Wiley and Sons, 2009), 124–49.

3. Foundation Center, "Fiscal Data of Grantmaking by Region and State, 2008," retrieved from http://foundationcenter.org/findfunders/statistics/pdf/01_found_fin_data/2008/01_08.pdf.

4. US Census, "Washington Quick Facts" (2016), https://factfinder.census.gov/faces/nav/jsf/pages/community_facts.xhtml.

5. "History," Weyerhaeuser website, http://www.weyerhaeuser.com/Company/CorporateAffairs/History.

6. "History of NWAF," Northwest Area Foundation, http://www.nwaf.org/about/history-nwaf/.

7. "History Narrative," Boeing, http://www.boeing.com/history/narrative/n001intro.html.

8. Bill Virgin, "Boeing Move Was Worthy of Uproar," *Seattle Post-Intelligencer*, March 26, 2002, retrieved from http://www.seattlepi.com/virgin/63787_virgin27.shtml.

9. *International Directory of Company Histories, Vol.63* (Farmington Hills, MI: St. James Press, 2004), retrieved from http://www.fundinguniverse.com/company-histories/Microsoft-Corporation-Company-History.html.

10. CNNMoney.com, *Fortune 500* (2010), http://money.cnn.com/magazines/fortune/fortune500/2010/states/WA.html.

11. US Census. "State rankings: Statistical abstract of the United States," accessed September 23, 2010, https://www.census.gov/library/publications/2009/compendia/statab/129ed/rankings.html.

12. Corporation for National and Community Service, Office of Research and Policy Development, *Volunteering in America 2010: National, State, and City Information* (Washington, DC: Author).

13. Corporation for National and Community Service, Office of Research and Policy Development, *Volunteering in America 2010.*

14. All subsequent data in this section are from Foundation Center FC Stats at www.foundationcenter.org.

15. The Foundation Center, "Foundation Stats" (2014), http://data.foundationcenter.org/#/foundations/all/state:WA/total/list/2014.

16. The Foundation Center, "Foundation Stats" (2014), http://data.foundationcenter.org/#/foundations/all/state:WA/total/list/2014.

17. For more information on the Global Corporate Citizenship program see http://www.boeing.com/companyoffices/aboutus/community/.

18. The Foundation Center, "Foundation Stats" (2014), http://data.foundationcenter.org/#/foundations/all/state:WA/top:assets/list/2013.

19. Heim, Kristi, "Seattle Foundation names Norm Rice as new CEO", *Seattle Times*, June 11, 2009, retrieved from https://www.seattletimes.com/business/seattle-foundation-names-norm-rice-as-new-ceo/.

20. Seattle Foundation, "About GiveBIG," http://givebig.wordpress.com/about/.

21. Bill & Melinda Gates Foundation, "Foundation Timeline," http://www.gatesfoundation.org/about/Pages/foundation-timeline.aspx.

22. American Library Association, "Gates Learning Foundation Gets a Billion," http://americanlibrariesmagazine.org/gates-learning-foundation-gets-a-billion/.

23. Foundation Search, "Bill & Melinda Gates Foundation," http://www.foundationsearch.com/.

24. Bill & Melinda Gates Foundation, "Foundation Timeline."

25. Bill & Melinda Gates Foundation, "Foundation Timeline."

26. Bill & Melinda Gates Foundation, "Warren Buffet," http://www.gatesfoundation.org/Who-We-Are/General-Information/Leadership/Executive-Leadership-Team/Warren-Buffett.

27. Carol J. Loomis, "Warren Buffet Gives Away His Fortune," *Fortune Magazine*, June 25, 2006, http://archive.fortune.com/2006/06/25/magazines/fortune/charity1.fortune/index.htm.

28. Bill & Melinda Gates Foundation, "About the Bill & Melinda Gates Foundation Asset Trust," retrieved from http://www.gatesfoundation.org/about/Pages/gates-foundation-asset-trust.aspx.

29. Bill & Melinda Gates Foundation, "Foundation Timeline."

30. Bill & Melinda Gates Foundation, "Bill & Melinda Gates Foundation Asset Trust."

31. "Form 990 received from IRS–2007," GuideStar website, http://www2.guidestar.org/ReportNonProfit.aspx?ein=91-1663695&Mode=GxLite&lid=513097&dl=False.

32. Unless otherwise noted, all data in this section are from Foundation Center FC Stats at www.foundationcenter.org.

33. Data retrieved from National Center for Charitable Statistics, "US Nonprofit Sector," retrieved from http://nccs.urban.org/statistics/.

34. US Census Bureau, "US Population Projections," http://www.census.gov/population/www/projections/projectionsagesex.html.

35. Bill & Melinda Gates Foundation, "Foundation Timeline."

36. The Foundation Center, "Foundation Stats" (2014), http://data.foundationcenter.org/#/foundations/all/state:WA/top:assets/list/2011.

37. The Foundation Center, "Foundation Stats" (2014), http://data.foundationcenter.org/#/foundations/all/state:WA/top:assets/list/2009.

38. The Foundation Center, "Foundation Stats" (2014), http://data.foundationcenter.org/#/foundations/all/state:WA/top:giving/list/2011.

39. Unless otherwise noted, all data in this section are from Foundation Center FC Stats at www.foundationcenter.org.

40. Data retrieved from the National Center for Charitable Statistics, "NCCS Data Archive," http://nccs-data.urban.org/data.php?ds=core.

41. All figures in this paragraph are derived from data from The Foundation Center, "Foundation Stats" (2014), http://data.foundationcenter.org/#/foundations/all/state:WA/total/trends:giving/2014.

42. These figures are derived from data from The Foundation Center, "Foundation Stats" (2014), http://data.foundationcenter.org/#/foundations/all/state:WA/total/trends:giving/2014.

43. Putnam Barber, *Nonprofits in Washington: A Statistical Profile* (Seattle: Evans School of Public Affairs, University of Washington, 2009). http://evans.uw.edu/sites/default/files/public/NPinWA2009.pdf.

44. Foundation Search, "FoundationSearch," http://www.foundationsearch.com/index.aspx.

45. Data retrieved from the National Center for Charitable Statistics, "NCCS Data Archive," http://nccs-data.urban.org/data.php?ds=core.

46. The Foundation Center, "Foundation Data" (2014), http://foundationcenter.org/gain-knowledge/foundation-data.

47. All national data presented in this section exclude Gates Foundation.

48. Philanthropy Northwest, *Trends in Northwest Giving 2014*, 22, https://philanthropynw.org/sites/default/files/resources/Trends_in_Northwest_Giving_2014-Philanthropy_Northwest-2.0.pdf.

49. All data in this paragraph derives from Foundation Search, "FoundationSearch," http://www.foundationsearch.com/index.aspx.

50. United Way of King County, *Gates Endowment Report*, http://uwkc.pub30.convio.net/assets/files/major-gifts/the-gates-endowment.pdf.

51. William Barrett, "Big Seattle Charity Uses Accounting Magic to Look Better," retrieved from http://newtoseattle.wordpress.com/2012/03/14/big-seattle-charity-uses-accounting-magic-to-look-better/.

52. Thrive by 5, "Annual Report for FY 2012," https://thrivewa.org/wp-content/uploads/Thrive_by_Five_annual_report_FY12.pdf.

53. Bill & Melinda Gates Foundation, "2013 Bill & Melinda Gates Foundation Annual Report," 3, http://www.gatesfoundation.org/Who-We-Are/Resources-and-Media/Annual-Reports/Annual-Report-2013.

54. Thrive Washington, "Investing and Working Statewide Fiscal Year 2013 Report" https://thrivewa.org/wp-content/uploads/FY13_annual_report.pdf.

55. Thrive by 5, "Annual Report for FY 2012."

56. Northwest Institute for Children and Families, *Evaluation of the Sound Families Initiative* (Seattle: University of Washington School of Social Work, 2008), http://www.soundfamilies.org/uploads/scms/files/Sound%20Families%20Early%20Exits%20Report%20FINAL.pdf; http://www.buildingchanges.org/images/documents/library/2008%20Sound%20Families%20Final%20Findings%20Report.pdf.

57. Kristi Heim, "Gates Foundation Joins Others in Goal to Cut Homelessness," *The Seattle Times*, March 19, 2009, http://seattletimes.com/html/businesstechnology/2008884912_gateshomeless19.html.

58. Kristi Heim, "Gates Foundation Joins Others in Goal to Cut Homelessness," *The Seattle Times*, March 19, 2009, http://seattletimes.com/html/businesstechnology/2008884912_gateshomeless19.html; Kristi Heim, "Seattle Foundation Names Norm Rice as New CEO," *The Seattle Times*, June 11, 2009. http://seattletimes.com/html/thebusinessofgiving/2009327878_seattle_foundation_names_as_ne.html.

59. Building Changes, "Washington Families Fund: High-Needs Families," http://www.buildingchanges.org/images/documents/library/2013WFFBriefHighNeedsFamilies.pdf.

60. Unless otherwise noted, all data in this section are from Philanthropy Northwest, *Trends in Northwest Giving 2012*, https://philanthropynw.org/sites/default/files/resources/Trends%202012_FNL_071812.pdf.

61. Foundation Center, "Fiscal Data 2008"; Foundation Center, "Summary of Domestic and International Grant Dollars, circa 2008," http://foundationcenter.org/findfunders/statistics/pdf/03_fund_geo/2008/09_08.pdf.

62. Seattle International Foundation, http://www.seaif.org/index.asp.

63. Letts, Ryan, and Grossman, *High Performance Nonprofit Organizations*; Venture Philanthropy, *High-Engagement Philanthropy: A Bridge to a More Effective Social Sector, Philanthropy News Digest*, July 10, 2004, http://www.vppartners.org/sites/default/files/reports/report2004.pdf; Morino, "Leap of Reason."

64. Social Justice Fund, "Annual Financial Report 2014," http://socialjusticefund.org/annual-financial-reports#overlay-context=about.

65. Philanthropy Northwest, *Trends in Northwest Giving 2014*, 22, https://philanthropynw.org/sites/default/files/resources/Trends_in_Northwest_Giving_2014-Philanthropy_Northwest-2.0.pdf.

66. Seattle Foundation, *Powerful and Rewarding: Equal Values in Philanthropy. Report to the Community, 2013–14*, http://www.seattlefoundation.org/aboutus/annualreport/Documents/2013/TSF_AR2013_web.pdf.

67. Data incomplete for the period 2004–07.

BY WAY OF A CONCLUSION: REGIONS, FOUNDATIONS, AND POLICY

David C. Hammack and Steven Rathgeb Smith

As we noted on the first page of this book, foundations and endowments face contradictory demands: that they should be bolder, more energetic, more venturesome, and more demanding; should do more to relieve immediate need and reduce inequality; and should defer to activists, professionals, and ordinary citizens. Our chapters on foundations in different places reveal other demands: that foundations should focus on their home locales, should build up important local institutions, should move resources from wealthy places to poor ones, should promote national standards and international competitiveness—or reinforce a local culture.

Against the background of such contradictory and conflicting demands, we have asked more specifically whether foundations differ from one part of the United States to another. The essays we have assembled can suggest partial answers and raise questions both about foundations and regions, and about the chances that foundations will be able to respond to the demands they confront.

Collectively, our various studies (and our appendices on very large foundations and community foundations) make it clear, first, that foundations do have at least this to do with region: most US charitable foundations are local. They devote themselves to a specific geographic area, most often a county, a metropolitan area, or a state. Only a relatively small minority gives nationally; only a tiny minority gives across national borders. Most foundation grants stay local—and most go to local institutions. In the Northeast, well-endowed private institutions (colleges and universities, hospitals and medical research centers, libraries and museums), supported by donors in past generations as well as by alumni, former patients, and other strong friends, approach the size of the biggest foundations.

In New England, no foundation challenges the size or influence of the dozen largest endowed institutions. Across the Midwest and much of the West, many of the best-endowed universities are flagship state institutions; these, like Cornell University, the University of Pennsylvania, and the University of Virginia, are also supported by state legislatures as well as by alumni and friends. When legislatures provide funds, they also insist on imposing constraints. On the Pacific Coast, very large foundations outnumber the few highly endowed private universities.

Second, our studies confirm that foundations often do take advantage of their ability to provide sources of initiative that are independent of current political majorities, though broadly tied to local cultures—notably religious cultures. In the first decades after independence, when most state legislatures resisted efforts to give official priority to any single Protestant group, distinctive and competing Protestant denominations created notable foundations and endowments in several cities, including New York and Baltimore. Jewish funds quickly appeared in those cities, as did nonsectarian and sometimes freethinking endowments devoted to books, science, and the arts. Throughout the nineteenth century, Northeastern foundations committed to distinctive religious and cultural traditions helped build churches and schools in newly growing places, as described in our studies of Cleveland, Chicago, and Atlanta.

After the Civil War, funds and foundations based in New York, Baltimore, Chicago, and other cities in the Northeast and around the Great Lakes sought to renew their aid to like-minded churches and schools in the South. Black southerners accepted aid for their churches and schools, even as they insisted that their institutions aid their own communities and protested against the meddling of wealthy outsiders. White southerners rejected northern offers. They preferred to redouble efforts to build and endow institutions and foundations committed to their own communities of white southern Baptists, Methodists, and Presbyterians. Over the course of the twentieth century, these southern religious communities fostered many large private foundations, endowed public charities, and endowed schools and retirement communities. By the last decades of the century, some denominational and religious foundations and funds had relocated from New York and Philadelphia to the Midwest and the South. The essays on New York, Baltimore, Atlanta, and Cleveland in this volume begin to explore religious foundations, but the other essays do not: clearly, religious foundations deserve more consistent attention.

Not all distinctive foundations devote themselves to religion. Foundations committed to civil liberties in the United States and in other parts of the world cluster in New York City. Self-identified progressive foundations also favor New York, but they often appear in Chicago and the San Francisco Bay area—and many other places as well. Proudly conservative foundations can be found in many places, including New York, Ohio, and Wisconsin, as well as Texas and California. Foundations committed to the arts—and to science—also cluster in the Northeast and California, but have many counterparts in every part of the nation.

Most generally, foundations committed to every kind of distinctive religious or cultural purpose distribute themselves widely across the nation. And over time, most regional specializations have declined. Foundations that promote self-help and individual initiative are notable in the Midwest but have always been equally prominent in the Northeast, and have so many counterparts in so many other regions that they cannot be said to give the Midwest a distinctive philanthropic character. Southern foundations and endowments increasingly underwrite the arts, science, medical research, Catholic and Jewish concerns, civil rights and civil liberties: many states outside the South have notable Protestant funds. Across the United States, Catholic dioceses have been building substantial endowed public charities to complement the occasional private foundations whose donors emphasize Catholic causes. Where there are large Jewish communities, there are numbers of private foundations and endowed public charities devoted to Jewish causes. Where smaller religious communities are locally notable, they often receive foundation support.

Everywhere, foundations underwrite colleges and universities, the arts, science, and medical research. Many private foundations, as well as many supporting foundations and funds held by community foundations and other public charities, give chiefly to specific schools, research institutes, orchestras, and museums. In every locality, at least a few foundations underwrite environmental causes, public health, sports and recreation—and the numbers of foundations that pay attention to these topics is everywhere increasing.

As our chapters on Cleveland, Baltimore, Chicago, and Atlanta indicate, across the nation foundations underwrite a wide range of ideas about how to support and reform elementary and secondary education and about what schools should teach. Foundations also support a myriad of different programs and initiatives related to private schools and to local social welfare institutions. Since the 1950's, foundations have been significant sponsors of public radio and television. Though our studies did not focus on this development, in very recent years some foundations have also moved to underwrite local reporting, the publication of local newspapers or their online equivalents, and the development of documentaries for television.

Most foundations are created to advance beliefs, values, and achievements; donors rarely intend to redistribute wealth to the poor.[1] Evaluating the effectiveness of foundation efforts to advance cherished values is a difficult task, one that none of the research reported in this volume was designed to undertake. Yet foundations and endowed funds provide important continuing support for the education of religious leaders as well as for advocates for many secular causes, from secular humanism to libertarian economics to music and other arts. Foundations and endowed funds also do much to underwrite research and scholarship, especially in fields outside healthcare and defense-related science that cannot win significant federal funding.

This volume's chapters on Cleveland, Atlanta, Los Angeles, and the greater San Francisco Bay area illustrate how foundations have been supporting prominent institutions. In one metropolitan region after another, foundations have helped to build high-quality research universities, medical centers, and arts organizations. Their aim is to create clusters of elite institutions comparable to those noted in our chapters on New York, Baltimore, Washington DC, and Chicago. In the United States, such institutions must win sustenance from private donors, in contrast to the continuing reliance on government aid of counterparts in Europe and much of the rest of the world.

These lists of foundation purposes and accomplishments do not begin to cover all the activities of all foundations. Health conversion foundations, class action lawsuit-resolution funds, and the foundations created by pharmaceutical companies to manage distribution programs for expensive drugs must respect constraints imposed by legal authorities. Not a few foundations pursue idiosyncratic projects important above all to their donors. No doubt many donors aim chiefly to advance their own fame, to win a positive reputation for their family name, to impress rivals or members of their own immediate community.

Localism, donor control, commitment to a wide range of distinctive values and purposes, and a solid tradition of underwriting elite (and thus hopefully influential) institutions characterize American foundations. These qualities pose tough challenges to reformers who would like to use public policy to push for change. Most foundations are already committed to home locales, in ways defined by their donors. Many foundations are already committed to particular values, often religious, always strongly held. Foundations are devoted to specific fields of action, and not infrequently to certain institutions. Such commitments are broadly protected under American laws of property, of contract, and of the freedom of religion and speech. These commitments are also defended by the claims of those who live in their home communities who share their values, who work in their chosen fields, or who represent or rely on their favored institutions.

Foundation resources are, moreover, quite limited. Foundations certainly reflect the inequality in American society. Rising inequality has made it possible for foundations to grow, but foundations are minor and subordinate factors in creating inequality, and in shaping the public policies that fail to discourage and may even foster inequality. Most US charitable foundations are small, especially considered in relation to the large aims they espouse. Even taken as a group, American foundations are smaller than observers generally assume. Two-thirds of all foundations have so little money to distribute that they could hardly cover the modest compensation of a single church worker, or public university tuition and living expenses for a single student, or health insurance or a new set of kitchen appliances for three families.[2]

Foundations are not a notable source of the rising inequality of US incomes and wealth.[3] Yet to the struggling half of the population, the numbers do not look insignificant. If the government seized and redistributed all the assets of US foundations equally among all the nation's 116 million households, each household would get just under $6,000. Such an amount would equal 18 percent of the net worth of the quarter of all households below the middle level of wealth but only 3.5 percent on average to those in the quarter above.[4] Given these limits, it is not surprising to discover that foundations in New York, Baltimore, Cleveland, Chicago, and Los Angeles have found it difficult to interject significant resources into local struggles against poverty. Not only are foundations mostly devoted to other purposes; their assets, substantial though they are, would not go far to reduce inequality and poverty even if they were immediately redistributed.

Recognizing the limitations of their resources in relation to the challenges of inequality and poverty (and of health and education), many of America's foundations are currently emphasizing what Paul Brest and others call strategic philanthropy.[5] Often, this is because of the approach to giving: looking to intervene where it is possible to make the biggest difference, employing a carefully considered cause-and-effect analysis, and asking grantees to evaluate outcomes. It can also lead to efforts to improve the delivery of services by governments as well as private nonprofit providers—to employ the "new public administration."[6]

The strategic philanthropy perspective has reverberated widely throughout the foundation sector. Yet the research reported in this book suggests that in recent years, at least, most local (rather than national) foundations—regardless of region—provide relatively modest grants that do not reflect the classic strategic philanthropy considerations. Instead, local foundations give to local nonprofit institutions, usually for specific programs or for capital improvements rather than ongoing operational expenses. As a result, much foundation giving reinforces local religious or other cultural arrangements, and local elite institutions.

When foundations undertake broad social initiatives, their choices often resemble one another across foundations, and even across regions that differ measurably in cultural character. In this sense, our research indicates that the old cliché about foundations—"if you have seen one foundation, you have seen one foundation"—may need to be revised. A few adventurous foundations have worked to empower the marginalized, though as the essays on Washington, DC, Cleveland, Chicago, and Los Angeles make all too clear, foundation efforts in that direction have so far met with very limited success.[7] American foundations often seek—though with decidedly incomplete success—to bring people from underrepresented groups into the flagship civic institutions they support. In pursuit of this aim, foundations subsidize admission fees, transport school children to museums and concerts, sponsor public performances and exhibitions, and underwrite scholarships. In Los Angeles as in other cities, health conversion foundations promote public health and access to medical care. As our chapters on Cleveland and Chicago emphasize, both national and local foundations have joined more powerful American institutions (including major business associations, state governments, and the federal government) in promoting the reform of elementary and secondary education. Although foundations' educational initiatives have been quite varied, they have often emphasized the same elements—local decentralization on the one hand, and state or national standards and testing on the other.[8]

As we read them, the studies in this book suggest that critics, policymakers, and philanthropic leaders should recognize that foundations cannot solve the woes of the public sector and cannot easily address such serious social problems as substance abuse, mental illness, prisoner reentry, workforce development, and homelessness. Foundations are strongly inclined to support other priorities—some of which they see as having higher profiles, some as less controversial, and some as involving core values that are themselves difficult to sustain.

Given their assets and their visibility, both locally and nationally, foundations are still important as catalysts for policy change. Some individual foundations, small and local as well as very large, will surely continue to take on some of the biggest public challenges. But it would take changes in donor priorities and in public regulation that are very unlikely to appear for most foundations to abandon their existing commitments and change their giving in fundamental ways.

DAVID C. HAMMACK is the Haydn Professor of History at Case Western Reserve University. He has held Guggenheim, Russell Sage Foundation, and Yale Program on Nonprofit Organization fellowships and has been president both of the Association for Research on Nonprofit Organizations and Voluntary Action and of Greater Cleveland Community Shares. His books include *Making The Nonprofit Sector in the United States* (1998) and, with Helmut Anheier, *A Versatile American Institution*, a history of foundations (2013).

STEVEN RATHGEB SMITH is the executive director of the American Political Science Association. He has taught at several universities including the University of Washington, where he was the Nancy Bell Evans Professor of Public Affairs. His most recent book is *Nonprofits and Advocacy: Engaging Community and Government in an Era of Retrenchment* (with Robert Pekkanen and Yutaka Tsujinaka). He is currently president of the International Society for Third Sector Research.

NOTES

1. David C. Hammack and Helmut K. Anheier, *A Versatile American Institution: The Changing Ideals and Realities of Philanthropic Foundations* (Washington, DC: Brookings Institution Press, 2013), 152.

2. Total foundation assets have grown along with wealth inequality in the past thirty years, and as a result a few thousand foundations do have significant wealth. Yet the costs of elementary, secondary, college, and professional education, of healthcare, and of medical and scientific research have grown even faster. In 2012, total foundation giving, at $52 billion, amounted to less than one-third of 1 percent of gross domestic product (GDP), or 1.5 percent of all spending by the federal government (Foundation Center, "Key Facts on US Foundations" (2014), 3, http://www.bea.gov/national/; https://www.cms.gov/research-statistics-data-and-systems/statistics-trends-and-reports/nationalhealthexpenddata/nationalhealthaccountshistorical.html). In 2012, the nation spent more than 17 percent of its GDP on healthcare (https://www.cms.gov/research-statistics-data-and-systems/statistics-trends-and-reports/nationalhealthexpenddata/nationalhealthaccountshistorical.html), and 7 percent on education (http://nces.ed.gov/programs/coe

/indicator_cmd.asp). State spending on all purposes (excluding federal funds) was steady at 11 percent of GDP (http://www.brookings.edu/research/papers/2012/03/states-budgets-gordon).

3. Foundation resources remain modest in relation to America's striking inequality in income and wealth. In 2012, the assets of US foundations (including not only private foundations but also operating, corporate, and community foundations) totaled $715 billion, just over 1 percent of total US wealth of $64,482 billion. Careful, cautious estimates of total US financial assets held in overseas tax havens in 2012—assets that are unreported, unaccountable, and out of reach of US tax collectors—come to more, possibly much more, than $1,000 billion (see Gabriel Zucman, *The Hidden Wealth of Nations: The Scourge of Tax Havens* [Chicago: University of Chicago Press, 2015], 53). Separate estimates suggest that US corporations legally avoid $130 billion in US taxes annually by establishing corporate subsidiaries in such tax haven locales (Ibid., 106).

4. Population information from the US Census at https://factfinder.census.gov/faces/nav/jsf/pages/index.xhtml and at http://www.census.gov/quickfacts/table/PST045215/00.

5. Paul Brest and Hal Harvey, *Money Well Spent: A Strategic Plan for Smart Philanthropy* (New York: John Wiley and Sons, 2010), 3–21.

6. Stephen P. Osborne, ed., *The New Public Governance: Emerging Perspectives on the Theory and Practice of Public Governance* (New York: Routledge, 2010), 105.

7. For a study arguing that foundations significantly affected race relations in the San Francisco Bay area and in Cleveland, see Jiannbin Lee Shiao, *Identifying Talent, Institutionalizing Diversity: Race and Philanthropy in Post–Civil Rights America*. (Durham, NC: Duke University Press, 2005).

8. In our view, the evidence supports the conclusion that business and government pressures, not foundations, account for most of the controversial aspects of the recent campaign to reform elementary and secondary education. Widely noted studies that emphasize the responsibility of foundations include Diane Ravitch, *Reign of Error: The Hoax of the Privatization Movement and the Danger to America's Public Schools* (New York: Knopf Doubleday, 2013), and Sarah Reckhow, *Follow the Money: How Foundation Dollars Change Public School Politics* (New York: Oxford University Press, 2013).

APPENDIX A: THE BIGGEST FOUNDATIONS, 1946, 1979, 2012

America's largest charitable foundations attract attention because they hold a very substantial share of all foundation assets. Although they appear to be solid, likely to perpetuate their donors' preferences long into the future, the top foundations often fade with time, whether by design, by a board's decision to deploy the funds in a different way, or because their investments do not do well. Over time, new foundations join the list of the largest, pushing others down the list.

This appendix offers an estimate of the changes in the list of the fifty biggest charitable foundations in the United States at three points in time. We chose 1946 as the first year because that is the year of publication of *American Foundations for Social Welfare*—the first substantially comprehensive list of foundations, a list put together by Shelby M. Harrison and F. Emerson Andrews of the Russell Sage Foundation. Some years later, Andrews would go on to found the Foundation Center, which in 1960 would take up the task of gathering and publishing information about foundations. In 1946, and until the Tax Reform Act of 1969 was fully implemented in the late 1970s, the law allowed foundations to report financial information as they pleased. For various reasons, many preferred not to disclose any numbers at all; in 1946, many foundations refused to provide any information to Harrison and Andrews. Funds that did provide asset values no doubt followed what was then the common practice of naming not a current market value, but rather the number assigned when a donation was made.

Once the Tax Reform Act of 1969 was implemented in the late 1970s, the task of identifying the largest foundations became easier, because all large foundations then had to submit audited financial statements every year. In 1979 for the first time, the Foundation Center was able to base its *Foundation Directory* on the annual, audited statements the Tax Reform Act of 1969 required of every foundation. Since religious institutions could

Table A.1. Fifty Largest US Foundations, 1979, 2012

	1979			2012		
	Name	State	Assets $Billion	Name	State	Assets, $Billion
1.	*Ford Foundation*	NY	2.8	**Bill & Melinda Gates Foundation**	WA	37.2
2.	*W. K. Kellogg Foundation*	MI	1.0	*Ford Foundation*	NY	11.2
3.	Robert Wood Johnson	NJ	1.0	**J. Paul Getty Trust**	CA	10.5
4.	*The Andrew W. Mellon Foundation*	NY	0.9	Robert Wood Johnson Foundation	NJ	9.5
5.	John D. and Catherine T. MacArthur Foundation	IL	0.9	*W. K. Kellogg Foundation*	MI	8.2
6.	*Lilly Endowment Inc.*	IN	0.9	**William and Flora Hewlett Foundation**	CA	7.7
7.	Pew Memorial Trust	PA	0.8	*Lilly Endowment Inc.*	IN	7.3
8.	*The Rockefeller Foundation*	NY	0.8	**The David and Lucile Packard Foundation**	CA	6.3
9.	*The Kresge Foundation*	MI	0.7	The John D. and Catherine T. MacArthur Foundation	IL	6.0
10.	*Charles Stewart Mott Foundation*	MI	0.4	**Gordon and Betty Moore Foundation**	CA	5.7
11.	*The Duke Endowment*	NC	0.4	*The Andrew W. Mellon Foundation*	NY	5.6
12.	San Francisco Foundation	CA	0.3	**Bloomberg Philanthropies**	NY	4.2
13.	*Carnegie Corporation of New York*	NY	0.3	**The Leona M. and Harry B. Helmsley Charitable Trust**	NY	4.2
14.	*The New York Community Trust*	NY	0.3	**Tulsa Community Foundation**	OK	3.7

(continued)

Table A.1. *(continued)*

	1979			2012		
	Name	State	Assets $Billion	Name	State	Assets $Billion
15.	*The James Irvine Foundation*	CA	0.3	*The Rockefeller Foundation*	NY	3.7
16.	Richard King Mellon Foundation	PA	0.3	**The California Endowment**	CA	3.6
17.	*Alfred P. Sloan Foundation*	NY	0.3	*The Kresge Foundation*	MI	3.3
18.	*Houston Endowment Inc.*	TX	0.2	**Margaret A. Cargill Foundation**	MN	3.0
19.	<u>J.E. and L.E. Mabee Foundation Inc.</u>	OK	0.2	*The Duke Endowment*	NC	2.9
20.	*The Cleveland Foundation*	OH	0.2	**Silicon Valley Community Foundation**	CA	2.9
21.	<u>Bush Foundation</u>	MN	0.2	**Robert W. Woodruff Foundation, Inc.**	GA	2.8
22.	<u>Edna McConnell Clark Foundation</u>	NY	0.2	*Carnegie Corporation of New York*	NY	2.8
23.	<u>*Gannett Foundation, Inc.*</u>	NY	0.2	**Foundation to Promote Open Society**	NY	2.7
24.	<u>*The Moody Foundation*</u>	TX	0.2	**The Annie E. Casey Foundation**	MD	2.7
25.	<u>Samuel Roberts Noble Foundation</u>	OK	0.2	**John Templeton Foundation**	PA	2.6
26.	<u>Henry J. Kaiser Family Foundation</u>	CA	0.2	**The Susan Thompson Buffett Foundation**	NE	2.4
27.	<u>Brown Foundation, Inc.</u>	TX	0.2	*Charles Stewart Mott Foundation*	MI	2.3
28.	<u>J. Howard Pew Freedom Trust</u>	PA	0.2	Kimbell Art Foundation	TX	2.3
29.	<u>Weingart Foundation</u>	CA	0.2	**Conrad N. Hilton Foundation**	CA	2.2

Table A.1. *(continued)*

	1979			2012		
	Name	State	Assets $Billion	Name	State	Assets $Billion
30.	*Surdna Foundation, Inc.*	NY	0.2	**Charles and Lynn Schusterman Family Foundation**	OK	2.2
31.	Norton Simon Foundation	CA	0.2	*The New York Community Trust*	NY	2.1
32.	The McKnight Foundation	MN	0.2	John S. and James L. Knight Foundation	FL	2.1
33.	*Rockefeller Brothers Fund, Inc.*	NY	0.2	**The Simons Foundation**	NY	2.1
34.	Ahmonson Foundation	CA	0.2	The McKnight Foundation	MN	2.1
35.	Joyce Foundation	IL	0.1	**Casey Family Programs**	WA	2.1
36.	Starr Foundation	NY	0.1	Richard King Mellon Foundation	PA	2.1
37.	*The Commonwealth Fund*	NY	0.1	**The Harry and Jeanette Weinberg Foundation, Inc.**	MD	2.0
38.	Robert A. Welch Foundation	TX	0.1	**The William Penn Foundation**	PA	2.0
39.	De Rance, Inc.	WI	0.1	**Walton Family Foundation, Inc.**	AR	2.0
40.	Meadows Foundation, Inc.	TX	0.1	*The Cleveland Foundation*	OH	1.9
41.	Sherman Fairchild Foundation, Inc.	CT	0.1	**Ewing Marion Kauffman Foundation**	MO	1.9
42.	Norton Simon, Inc.	CA	0.1	The Chicago Community Trust	IL	1.8
43.	*Amherst H. Wilder*	MN	0.1	Alfred P. Sloan Foundation	NY	1.7
44.	*The John A. Hartford Foundation, Inc.*	NY	0.1	**Doris Duke Charitable Foundation**	NY	1.7
45.	Herbert H. and Grace A. Dow Foundation	MI	0.1	The James Irvine Foundation	CA	1.7

(continued)

Table A.1. *(continued)*

	1979			2012		
	Name	State	Assets $Billion	Name	State	Assets $Billion
46.	Alcoa Foundation	PA	0.1	**Eli & Edythe Broad Foundation**	CA	1.7
47.	Mabel Pew Myrin Trust	PA	0.1	Greater Kansas City Community Foundation	MO	1.6
48.	M. J. Murdoch Charitable Trust	WA	0.1	**Annenberg Foundation**	CA	1.6
49.	*The Clark Foundation*	NY	0.1	**The Wyss Foundation**	DC	1.6
50.	*Northwest Area Foundation*	MN	0.1	Houston Endowment Inc.	TX	1.5

Note: Foundations in *italics* were among the fifty largest in 1946; underlined foundations are not among the fifty largest in 2012; foundations in **boldface** were not on the list of fifty largest in 1979. For purposes of comparison, the value of the Ford Foundation's $11.2 billion endowment in 2012 was similar to, or somewhat less than, the $2.8 billion it held in 1979.[1]
Sources: Foundation Center data 1979, 2014.

declare themselves exempt from these rules, however, some religious funds were omitted. The Foundation Center's recent 2012 list of the largest foundations reflects a peak of foundation value, at a time just past the interruption in foundation growth imposed by the Great Recession of 2008.

The Russell Sage Foundation intended its 1946 book as a contribution to the reconstruction necessary after the Great Depression and World War II. Harrison and Andrews sought to list not all US foundations for all purposes, but rather, all foundations for social welfare. The book included some religious and operating foundations, but mainly those that gave for social welfare or educational as well as strictly religious purposes. The list for 1946 offered here is based on the uncertain information about assets included in *American Foundations for Social Welfare*, but we also based our estimates on information reported in the first *Foundation Directory*, edited by Anna D. Walton and F. Emerson Andrews (New York: Foundation Center, 1960); Joseph Goulden's *The Money Givers* (New York: Random House, 1971); Merrimon Cuninggim's *Private Money and Public Service* (New York: McGraw-Hill, 1972); and the 1979 data published in the eighth edition of *The Foundation Directory* (New York: Foundation Center, 1981). Because we had to make many estimates, this list is much less definitive than the lists provided by the Foundation Center data for 1979 and 2012.[2]

New York was home to nearly half of the fifty largest foundations in 1946, including not only the famous funds created by Carnegie, Rockefeller, and the Guggenheims, but also a dozen less-well-known large funds, including the James—which also focused on Missouri—Charles Hayden, Surdna, John A. Hartford, F. W. Olin, and Field Foundations, among others. A considerable number of funds were scattered around the Great Lakes region, including W. K. Kellogg, Kresge, and Mott in Michigan; the Lilly Endowment in Indianapolis; the Field Foundation in Illinois; the Hill Family (later Northwest Area) and Amherst Wilder Foundations in Minneapolis; and the Kettering Foundation in Dayton. The Cleveland Foundation was in 1946 perhaps a little smaller than those in the top fifty. The small number of large funds located outside New York City in the Northeast included the City Trusts of Philadelphia and the Longwood and Nemours Foundations of Delaware. Those in the South included the Duke Endowment for the Carolinas (managed at the time from New York City); the Danforth Foundation of St. Louis; the Houston Endowment; and the M. D. Anderson Foundation of Houston. Nearly all of the funds based outside New York City in 1946 (as well as the city's Hayden, Surdna, Hartford, and others) chiefly supported home region causes and placed more emphasis on local economic development and opportunity, health, and popular education—and on their notions of religion and ethics—than on scientific research and professional education.

If we add fifty more names to this group—many of which may well have held more assets than some that we estimate to have been in the top group—we would see that several of the largest in 1946 emphasized religion, sometimes supporting religious workers and religious communities by combining charitable activities with insurance operations, as the law then allowed. These included the Jarvie Commonweal Service of the Board of National Missions of the Presbyterian Church in the USA, the Presbyterian Foundation, the United Church Foundation (Congregationalist), the Methodist Foundation, the J. Bulow Campbell and the Callaway Foundations (then respectively emphasizing Southern Presbyterian and Southern Baptist purposes in Georgia), the American Missionary Foundation, the Texas Baptist Foundation, the Raskob Foundation for Catholic Activities, the Board of Education of the Methodist Church Student Loan Fund, the Alabama Educational Foundation, John D. Rockefeller Jr.'s Sealantic Fund, Inc., the evangelical LeTourneau Foundation (based successively in Illinois, Texas, and California), and, in Southern California, the George Pepperdine Foundation (later the base of the endowment for Pepperdine University; Disciples of Christ).

Although religion was not emphasized in *American Foundations for Social Welfare*, quite a few of the foundations it listed, especially those located in the South and the West, specified their support for Baptist, Methodist, Presbyterian, or other religious causes. Other funds, such as the Board of Directors of the City Trusts of Philadelphia, the Knights Templar Educational Foundation, the Elks National Foundation, the American Association of University Women (AAUW) Fellowship Fund, and most community foundations, emphasized comparable commitments to secular or nonsectarian values.

Altogether, at the end of World War II more than half of the fifty largest American foundations worked from locations on the East Coast, mostly in New York City. A dozen more clustered in the largest cities around the Great Lakes and the upper Mississippi. A few (e.g., Irvine in California, the Bishop Estate in Hawaii, and El Pomar in Colorado) were located in the West. Five focused on the South (Duke, then operating from New York City; and the Houston Endowment, M. D. Anderson, Moody, and Le Tourneau in Texas). The Carnegie Institute, Hawaii's Bishop Estate, Minnesota's Wilder Charity, the Wisconsin Alumni Fund, the Longwood Foundation, the Mayo Properties Association, and the Juilliard Musical Foundation each supported a single institution; the Duke Endowment and the City Trusts of Philadelphia supported just a few.[3]

Constant turnover has characterized the list of fifty largest US foundations since 1946. In 1979, twenty-seven of the largest fifty had not been on the list at the earlier date; of the fifty largest in 2012, twenty-eight had joined the list after 1980, and several were no longer among the top one hundred.[4] Foundations were now more evenly distributed across the nation, with a dozen on the West Coast, eight in a South defined to include Oklahoma and Arkansas, fourteen in the Midwestern and Great Lakes states (including Missouri), and sixteen in the Northeast (including the District of Columbia). Technology had produced at least half a dozen (e.g., Gates, Hewlett, Packard, Moore, Silicon Valley); pharmaceuticals accounted for two, and the conversion of a nonprofit health insurance company for another. Overall, insurance, finance, publishing, and home building had joined manufacturing, oil, and mass distribution as ways to great foundation wealth.

Increasingly diverse geographic origins were associated with increasingly diverse foundation purposes. The largest recent source of new foundation contributions has been the big pharmaceutical companies, which decided in the 1980s to channel through charitable foundations their aid to those who need but cannot afford expensive new lifesaving drugs.[5] Several creators of very large new foundations were relatively young entrepreneurs who had gained great wealth through the entrepreneurial development of technology; unsurprisingly, several of their foundations have sought measurable, material impact through entrepreneurial means. In 2012 six of the largest foundations (located, in order of size, in Tulsa, Silicon Valley, New York, Cleveland, Chicago, and Greater Kansas City) were community foundations—public charities that raise money each year from new gifts—most of which pay very close attention to popular public concerns in their home regions, and concentrate their giving there. Increasingly, community foundations cater to the donors who provide the funds they must continually raise. Courts, regulators, and other social entrepreneurs have also been creating new varieties of grant-making foundation—notably the hospital or health insurance conversion fund (including the very large California Endowment) and the class-action lawsuit resolution fund—to direct charitable assets toward specified purposes determined through formal procedures.

Finally, an additional note on religious foundations is in order. While tax reform legislation both before and after 1969 led many of the old divinity-school-scholarship and clergy retirement funds to shift from foundation to insurance- or investment-corporation status, religion remains a very important foundation purpose. Several of the largest of all foundations, including Lilly, Duke, Weinberg, Templeton, Walton, and Anschutz, put notable, though certainly not exclusive, emphasis on religious causes. In 2013–2014 one hundred or more private foundations and public charities strongly affiliated with religious causes in the southern states held assets of more than $20 million each, totaling over $26 billion in all. Most of these funds register as public charities because they raise money annually from many individual donors to support religious and other charitable purposes. A few of these—the Baptist Foundation of Texas, Christus Health of Texas, and the National Christian Charitable Foundation, Inc.—all public charities—and the private Robert W. Woodruff and Joseph B. Whitehead Foundations of Georgia, the Duke Endowment, and the Walton Family Foundation—held more than $1 billion (the Texas Presbyterian Foundation, a public charity, was not far behind at more than $800 million). Substantial religious foundations are found in most states, but they constitute a strikingly large share of the field in the South.[6]

Notes

1. The useful calculators at measuringworth.com put the 2012 value of the Ford Foundation's 1979 endowment, $2.8 billion, at one of these numbers, in billions: $7.24, $9.11, $9.38, or $17.20.

2. Fuller study might conclude that some the following were larger than some of the fifty listed here: the A.W. Mellon Charitable Trust (Pennsylvania), the National Foundation for Infantile Paralysis (New York), the American Missionary Association (New York), the Milbank Memorial Fund (New York), the W. R. Nelson Trust (Missouri), the Z. Smith Reynolds Foundation (North Carolina), the Cleveland Foundation (Ohio), the Hyams Trust (Massachusetts), the Texas Baptist Foundation (Texas), the Murry and Leonie Guggenheim Foundation (New York), and the George F. Baker Charity Trust (New York).

3. In creating this list, the numbers provided by Shelby M. Harrison and F. Emerson Andrews, *American Foundations for Social Welfare* (New York: Russell Sage Foundation, 1946); Foundation Center Library, *The Foundation Directory* (New York: Russell Sage Foundation, 1960); Joseph C. Goulden, *The Money Givers* (New York: Random House, 1971); and Merrimon Cuninggim, *Private Money and Public Service: The Role of Foundations in American Society* (New York: McGraw-Hill, 1972) were considered in the light of the assets reported by the Foundation Center in 1979, when the more accurate reporting requirements of the Tax Reform Act of 1969 had gone generally into effect. Information about the dates of major additions to the assets of individual foundations through gifts, the maturing of trusts, or exceptional increases in asset values (much of which appears in Cuninggim) was also taken into account.

4. Of those among the fifty largest in 1979 that were not in the top one hundred in 2012, De Rance, Inc., had become a fund of the Catholic Diocese of Milwaukee in 1992, two Norton Simon funds had consolidated into the notable Pasadena museum of that name, and three Pew funds had joined the Pew Charitable Trusts, which converted into a nonprofit corporation in 2004. Of the others, all but four were located in the Northeast or Midwest and were still among the larger and more active foundations nationally: Alcoa (Pennsylvania), Amherst H. Wilder (Minnesota), Clark (New York), Gannett (now Virginia), Henry J. Kaiser Family (California), Herbert H. and Grace A. Dow (Michigan), John A. Hartford (New York), Joyce (Illinois), M. J. Murdock Charitable Trust (Washington), Northwest Area (Minnesota), Robert A. Welch (Texas), Rockefeller Brothers Fund (New York), and Sherman Fairchild (Connecticut).

5. Steven Lawrence, Algernon Austin, and Reina Mukai, "Foundation Growth and Giving Estimates" (New York: Foundation Center, 2007), available at http://foundationcenter.org/gainknowledge/research/pdf/fgge07.pdf; Tina Shah, "Copayment Foundations: Help for the Underinsured," *Biotechnology Healthcare* (November–December, 2008): 41–43.

6. Guidestar and other sources list thirty-three Baptist, Methodist, and Presbyterian foundations in the states of the Northeast, Midwest, and West in 2013. Just two of these had assets of more than $100 million: the Presbyterian Foundation of Philadelphia, with assets of $223 million, and the California Baptist Foundation (Southern Baptist), with $127 million.

APPENDIX B: COMMUNITY FUNDS AND THE DISTRIBUTION OF SMALLER FOUNDATIONS

SMALLER FOUNDATIONS ARE LITTLE STUDIED, partly because it is difficult to gather information about them (for one effort to do so, see chapter 10 on Washington State in this book). Although some community foundations are very large,[1] most are small. Like most religious funds and colleges, most community foundations have built up their endowments through accretion of small funds. As donor-advised or as part of field-of-interest funds within a community foundation, those small funds often bear some resemblance to independent foundations. Community foundations have collected and published a good deal of basic information about their assets and grants since the 1930s, and this allows us to say something about the locations of smaller funds, and about the limits of their wealth, though it cannot answer many questions about their operations or impact.

The 1969 Tax Reform Act distinguished quite sharply between private foundations that simply hold funds and public charities that raise money and directly provide educational, health, social, religious, and other services. The act imposed an annual tax on private foundation assets, and it subjected their advocacy, policy work, investments, and disclosures—and their tax advantages and relationships with donors and donor families—to tighter regulation. The 1969 act treated community foundations like other public charities, requiring them to raise new funds from multiple donors each year but exempting them from the new tax and from some of the more onerous regulations. Responding to the demand for disclosure behind the 1969 Act, community foundations significantly increased their effort to gather and make public information about themselves.

Geographically based nonsectarian community foundations date from the creation of the Cleveland Foundation in 1914 (the City Trusts of Philadelphia constituted in many ways an antecedent the dated from the mid-nineteenth century). Very similar funds supporting specific religious denominations and traditions date back to the aftermath of the American Revolution; in the nineteenth century, religious funds became quite substantial, especially in the Northeast and around the Great Lakes.[2] Community foundations proliferated in the 1920s, especially around the Great Lakes, in Connecticut, and in Boston, New York, Philadelphia, and Chicago. They also grew early in Winston-Salem, Kansas City, and other places whose entrepreneurial Protestant and Jewish elites shared many qualities with those in the Midwest, and in Dallas-Fort Worth and Tulsa, where sudden oil wealth made possible the expression of civic ambition and community leadership. Before the 1960s, community foundations continued to be rare and small in the South, Southwest, and Mountain regions; as table B1 suggests, that pattern generally persists.

It is important here to emphasize the nonsectarian commitment of most community foundations. The founders of the Cleveland and other early community foundations well understood that many religious groups had created endowments to support their religious workers, teachers, houses of worship, seminaries, schools, medical facilities, and retirement homes. Those who invented the community foundation aimed to create funds that would serve the community as a whole, indirectly as well as directly encouraging inter-faith tolerance, respect, and cooperation. Initially, community foundations flourished in places where large Protestant, Catholic, and Jewish populations found themselves in close proximity, and where some leaders of each community placed a high priority on avoiding, or at least on managing, conflict along religious lines.[4] In most places where Catholics and Jews were few, the most notable endowments—usually built up through an accretion of modest gifts and individual funds but sometimes including private foundations—were devoted to Protestant religious denominations or their schools and other institutions.

Growing more rapidly than other foundations after the full implementation of the 1969 act in the late 1970s, community foundations now constitute a widespread and distinctive element in the foundation world. They continue to be most notable around the Great Lakes and in New England, but they have also grown considerably in the Great Plains and Pacific Coast regions. By 2014 community foundations numbered 763 and, with $64.9 billion, held about 9 percent of all foundation assets, and accounted for gifts of $5.5 billion, over 10 percent of all foundation giving.[5] To continue to qualify as public charities and avoid the restrictions private foundations must observe, community foundations raise in new donations for their endowments even more than they give away; in 2014 they took in $8.3 billion, making them formidable competitors to other charitable

Table B.1. Community Trusts with Assets Greater than $100,000 in 1930, by Region and Date of Origin[3]

Year		Reported Assets (*$1,000*)			
Region/City	Formed	1930	1949	1960	1979
Midwest					
Cleveland	1914	3,000	11,100	26,000	202,390
Chicago	1915	5,100	10,800	31,000	104,878
Detroit	1915	200	300	600	*
Milwaukee	1915	700	300	1,100	12,599
Minneapolis	1915	200	1,900	4,600	16,886
Indianapolis	1916	1,900	3,200	8,100	19,221
Youngstown	1918	700	800	2,200	4,017
Dayton	1921	300	300	700	3,272
Grand Rapids	1922	100	400	4,100	17,062
Northeast					
Boston	1915	4,800	8,700	36,600	71,896
Cambridge	1916	200	400	600	1,579
Williamsport	1916	200	700	1,100	NA
Philadelphia	1918	600	1,500	3,800	30,279
Buffalo	1920	1,000	1,600	4,800	11,031
New Yor	1920	8,700	18,700	30,100	245.649
Hartford	1925	100	1,700	11,600	45,775
New Haven	1927	100	1,700	9,000	39,415
South					
Winston-Salem	1919	400	3,700	9,700	24,939
Tulsa	1919	100	20	200	NA
West					
Los Angeles	1915	300	4,300	8,700	23,365
Denver	1925	1,000	200	–	3,307

*Defunct after 1985; assets of about $1 million turned over to the Community Foundation of Southeastern Michigan.

nonprofits in their neighborhoods.[6] Individual community foundations differ widely in assets, and, as with private foundations, the largest hold most of the money. In 2014 the one hundred largest community foundations, each with more than $150 million, managed 89 percent of all community foundation assets. The Silicon Valley Community Foundation, bolstered by several large donor-advised funds deriving from technology companies, held $6.5 billion; Tulsa Community Foundation, unusual for the extraordinary influence of the leadership and gifts of a single donor, oil and gas investor George W. Kaiser,[7] held nearly $4.4 billion; another fifteen held between $1 and $2 billion each.

However, most community foundations remain small, and many of the larger ones hold many small donor-advised funds that resemble small foundations. In 2014, according to the Foundation Center, 243 community foundations held assets of $10 million or more, down from 265 in 2010. At the low end of the scale, in a number reported in 2010, 257 held less than $5 million. In many cases the tiny endowments of such funds earned less income than needed to pay for the smallest possible office, staffed only by a director and a single office assistant.[8]

In most states where large private foundations cluster, community foundations remain minor factors. In 2010 they accounted for less than 5 percent of the money granted by foundations in New York, New Jersey, Delaware, Maryland, Arkansas, and Washington. But in forty of the fifty states, a community fund was among the five largest foundations of all kinds. In Oklahoma, Ohio, and Oregon a community foundation that held between $1.3 and $3.5 billion surpassed all other foundations, and a community foundation also topped the list in Connecticut, New Hampshire, Rhode Island, Vermont, South Carolina, Tennessee, Louisiana, and South Dakota.[9] Community foundation assets are in most cases very limited, averaging across the nation in 2014 just $222 per capita. On this basis, as figure B1 shows, community foundations are larger around the Great Lakes and New England and smaller in most southern, southwestern, and mountain states.[10]

The numbers of community foundations vary widely from state to state—from just one each in Vermont and Rhode Island to seventy-six in Indiana, sixty-eight in Ohio, sixty-five in Michigan, fifty in California, and twenty-six in Florida. In relation to the population, community foundations are most numerous around the Great Lakes and in the Plains region; they are least numerous in New England, the south Atlantic, the southeast, the southwest, and the mountain states.[11] In nearly all low-population states,[12] a single statewide community foundation dominated the field by 2010. Of the thirty-six states whose populations exceeded two million, only New Jersey, Arkansas, New Mexico, Arizona, Utah, and Oregon had statewide funds, and on a per capita basis only Oregon had a large endowment. In New England, Delaware, Oregon, and Hawaii, statewide community funds reinforced regional strengths in foundation activity (figure B2).

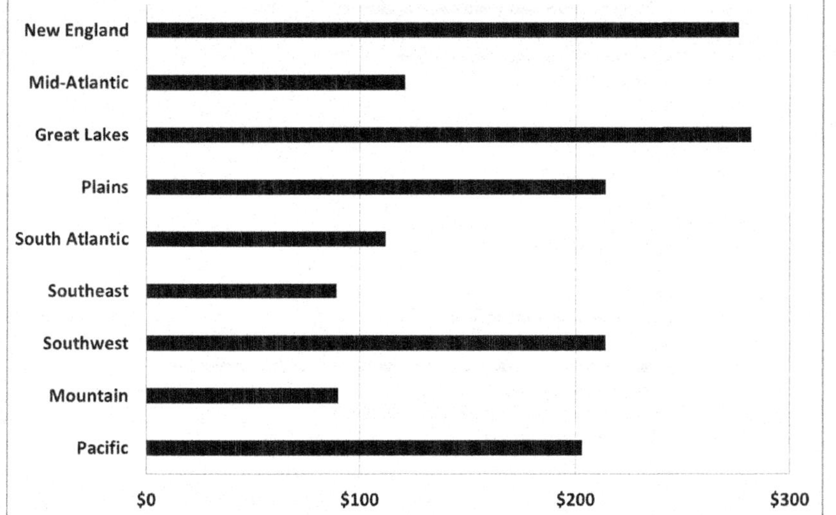

Figure B.1. Community Foundation Assets per capita, 2010 by Region

Although statewide funds in Arkansas, Alaska, and the mountain states of Wyoming, Montana, and Arizona have created many local "affiliates" or special community accounts or field-of-interest funds designed to appeal to donors in small communities, to date they have not attracted significant funds.

Funds and foundations associated with religious communities balance, to some extent, the relatively small presence of community foundations in several states. In Texas in 2013, fifteen such funds held $35 million; one of the oldest, the Baptist Foundation of Texas, held $1.9 billion; the Texas Presbyterian Foundation held $810 million; and the Texas Methodist Foundation held more than $500 million. In Georgia, nearly twenty religious foundations held more than $35 million, including the National Christian Foundation with more than $1.2 billion and two Baptist foundations holding together almost $450 million. Ten religious-affiliated funds with more than $35 million in assets located in North Carolina; four in Alabama; half a dozen in Arkansas; and three each in Missouri and Louisiana. Across the South, large numbers of smaller public charities and independent foundations support religious causes.

The gross evidence of community foundation numbers suggests that in the Great Lakes region and in New England, and perhaps in the northern plains and Pacific Coast regions, there is something about the cultural values and the local sense of community, as well as the wealth, of

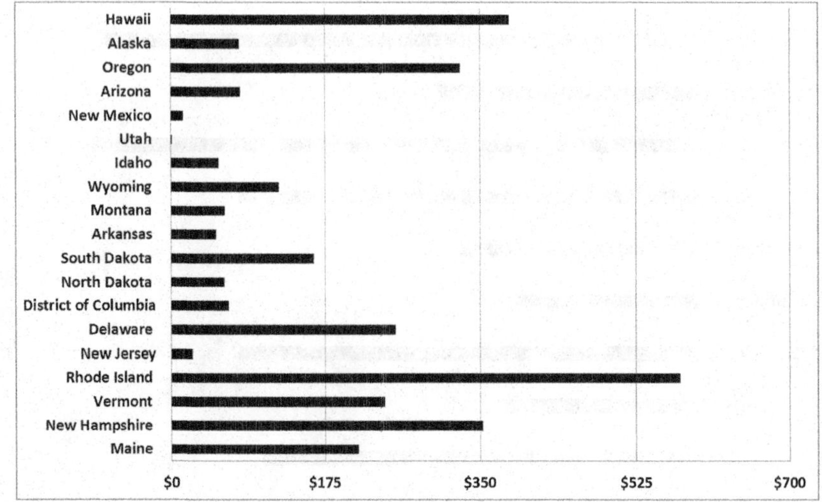

Figure B.2. Statewide Community Foundations Assets *per capita*, 2010. *Sources*: US Census Bureau, Table 14, US Census by State, 1960–2010 (12s0014) and Table 20 Large Metropolitan Statistical Areas—Population (12s0020); cf. INSIGHTS; FY 2011, Columbus Survey of Community Foundations; Foundation Center.

significant numbers of people that encourages numbers of people to give through secular, civic-minded foundations.[13]

Metropolitan versus Rural Location

Wealth, investment facilities, expertise, and communications concentrate in large cities; it is no surprise that community foundations, which require assets of all these kinds, are also found in urban locations. By the 1980s, several of the largest metropolitan areas claimed more than one community foundation. In the three-state New York City region, these included the New York Community Trust; the large community foundations of New Jersey and Greater New Haven; and smaller funds in Plainfield and Westfield (New Jersey) and in Bridgeport, Fairfield, Greenwich, New Canaan, Waterbury, and Meriden (Connecticut). Greater Los Angeles included the large California Community Foundation, a substantial fund in Santa Barbara, and others in Riverside, Pasadena, Glendale, and Ventura. In 1987, the Marin Foundation was almost three times as large as the big San Francisco Foundation; the nearby East Bay, Peninsula, Santa Clara, and Santa Cruz Funds joined them. The Boston Foundation had a large neighbor in the New Hampshire Community Foundation. Dallas-Fort Worth sported the Texas, Dallas, Tarrant County, and other community funds. Reflecting the prominence of the Great Lakes region, in 2001 the largest community foundation was in Cleveland, and in assets others nearby ranked thirty-five (Stark County), forty-three (Richland County), sixty-three (Akron), sixty-four (Canton), and sixty-nine (Loraine).[14] The Minneapolis fund then held the eleventh-largest endowment; the St. Paul fund, the twelfth.

The concentration of community foundation assets in many of the largest metropolitan areas has persisted. In 2001, when community foundation assets averaged $106 per capita for the United States as a whole, they exceeded $200 in the Midwestern metro areas of Cleveland, Columbus, Cincinnati, Indianapolis, Minneapolis–St. Paul, and Kansas City.[15] Among the other metro areas with populations above one million, community foundation assets also exceeded $200 per capita in Pittsburgh (adjacent to Cleveland), in Hartford and Providence in New England,[16] in Greensboro and Winston-Salem in the South, in Oklahoma City in the Southwest, and in the San Francisco Bay and Portland, Oregon, areas on the north Pacific Coast. Community foundations held only $50 per capita or less in several southern and southwestern metro areas: Washington–Baltimore, Tampa–St. Petersburg, Orlando, Miami–Fort Lauderdale, Houston–Galveston, Austin–San Marcos, St. Louis, Salt Lake City, Las Vegas, the greater Los Angeles area, and Sacramento.[17] By 2015, as table B2 makes clear, community foundation assets—driven to a considerable extent by the popularity of donor-advised funds—had increased rapidly in Northern California and in the high-tech areas of Portland Oregon and Boston. They continued to be strong in several metropolitan regionsincluding Kansas City, Cleveland, Columbus, Minneapolis-St. Paul, and in North Carolina—and also (though not included in table B2, in western Michigan. The areas where these funds had always struggled continued to lag.

Rural areas have been slow to adopt community foundations—which is not surprising, given their lower average incomes and the scattered locations of their wealthier residents and of experts and communications. Some city-based foundations have always paid attention to the countryside: the nineteenth century Smith Charity had almost entirely to do with rural Massachusetts; the post–Civil War Peabody Fund focused on education in the deeply rural South. Among the best-known foundation efforts of the early twentieth century were the public health and basic education initiatives for the rural South mounted by the Rockefeller Foundation, Rockefeller's General Education Board, and the Rosenwald Fund.[19] From the 1930s the W. K. Kellogg Foundation invested in public health

Table B.2. Community Foundation Assets per capita, Largest US Metropolitan Regions, ca 2015[18]

Primary Statistical Area	Assets per Capita	Total Assets of Community Foundations	Population
San Francisco-Oakland–San Jose	$1,511.83	$13,013,000,000	8,607,423
Kansas City	$981.91	$2,368,000,000	2,411,635
Cleveland-Akron-Lorain-Elyria-Canton	$769.04	$2,690,000,000	3,497,851
Portland, Oregon	$610.98	$1,931,000,000	3,160,488
Columbus	$575.83	$1,381,000,000	2,398,297
Charlotte-Gastonia–Rock Hill	$540.98	$1,373,000,000	2,537,990
Minneapolis–St. Paul	$480.05	$1,841,000,000	3,835,050
Pittsburgh	$455.20	$1,208,000,000	2,653,781
Milwaukee-Racine	$430.55	$880,000,000	2,043,904
Boston-Worcester-Lawrence-Manchester	$400.02	$3,240,000,000	8,099,575
San Antonio	$386.49	$900,000,000	2,328,652
Indianapolis	$329.24	$775,000,000	2,353,935
Denver-Boulder-Greeley	$327.93	$1,097,000,000	3,345,261
Cincinnati-Hamilton	$260.82	$576,000,000	2,208,450
Chicago-Gary-Kenosha	$258.96	$2,571,000,000	9,928,312
Dallas–Fort Worth	$227.67	$1,674,000,000	7,352,613
Seattle-Tacoma-Bremerton	$213.83	$968,000,000	4,526,991
Detroit	$209.96	$1,116,000,000	5,315,251
San Diego	$205.92	$672,000,000	3,263,431
Atlanta	$168.88	$1,057,000,000	6,258,875
Phoenix-Mesa	$166.18	$746,000,000	4,489,109
New York City	$160.24	$3,787,000,000	23,632,722
Los Angeles-Riverside–Orange County-Santa Barbara	$128.08	$2,376,000,000	18,550,288
St. Louis	$119.02	$346,423,401	2,910,738
Washington-Baltimore	$105.80	$1,010,000,000	9,546,579
Philadelphia-Wilmington–Atlantic City	$94.35	$676,000,000	7,164,790
Tampa-St. Petersburg–Clearwater	$91.23	$266,000,000	2,915,582

Table B.2. *(continued)*

Primary Statistical Area	Assets per Capita	Total Assets of Community Foundations	Population
Miami–Fort Lauderdale	$90.28	$607,000,000	6,723,472
Houston-Galveston	$80.16	$536,000,000	6,686,318
Las Vegas	$54.42	126,000,000	2,315,324
Sacramento-Yolo	$47.75	$120,000,000	2,513,103
Orlando	$21.67	66,000,000	3,045,707
Salt Lake City–Ogden	$13.61	$33,000,000	2,423,912

and education in farming communities in its western Michigan home and beyond, while Chicago's Farm Foundation, supported by leaders of the International Harvester Corporation and a number of others, focused on both public policy and private action concerning farm tenancy and ownership as well as education and health in rural communities.[20] A few years after the end of World War II, the Louis W. and Maud Hill Family Foundation (St. Paul; renamed the Northwest Area Foundation in 1975) gained the resources to make grants to rural as well as urban nonprofits, church-based service organizations, colleges, and researchers in the eight states once served by the Great Northern Railway.[21] The Oldham Little Church Foundation's construction funds, initially focused on its home town of Houston, now go to small, often rural, Protestant churches located across the nation.[22]

At the end of the twentieth century a heightened belief that foundations can be useful led to a number of campaigns to increase community foundation activity in rural areas. Taking a positive view of the uses of foundations and noting both the growing wealth of some rural families and the way the digital revolution was breaking down big-city advantages in access to financial and other expertise, influential foundation and community development leaders saw these campaigns as ways to generate new support for civil society generally. The Ford Foundation–sponsored Local Initiatives Support Corporation (LISC) and its partners, working with the Ford, Mott, Kellogg, John D. and Catherine T. MacArthur, and Annie E. Casey foundations, moved in the 1990s to increase community foundation work for economic and social development in America's rural areas (and also, in the case of Ford, Mott, and MacArthur, in several places overseas).[23] The Lilly Endowment in Indiana and the Irvine Foundation, the California Endowment, and others on the West Coast also joined the effort to increase the numbers of community foundations in rural areas.

When in 2007 Montana Senator Max Baucus became chairman of the US Senate's Banking Committee (which handles tax-exemption legislation), he encouraged foundations to make rural places a priority.[24] The Council on Foundations agreed to pursue the matter, in large part by promoting community foundation initiatives.

As with independent foundations, it continues to be true that the numbers of community foundations are so small that a single actor can make a substantial difference in a particular area.[25] Seeking to expand rural community foundations, the Council on Foundations and several big funds have worked through expert consultants and staff training to subsidize startup expenses, sometimes contributing a substantial initial endowment. The results have been mixed. Relatively large numbers of new and still-small community foundations can now be found in the rural counties of Michigan, Indiana, and West Virginia.[26] In California the number of community foundations has risen and their average size has declined,[27] even as the Silicon Valley, California, Marin, and San Francisco Funds have grown to constitute the largest group of billion-dollar community foundations in any state. In South Dakota, Arkansas, and Montana statewide community foundations set up large numbers of affiliate programs for small communities; Arizona, Wyoming, and Alaska took similar action; and such metropolitan community foundations as that of Columbus, Ohio, followed suit in their own areas.[28] To date, most of the new rural funds have remained very small, with the sponsoring funds still seeking ways to help them grow to sustainable size. Accordingly, a key study group in this movement focused not on assets but on non-grant-making roles and produced a booklet titled *Beyond Money & Grantmaking: The Emerging Role of Community Foundations.*[29]

Notes

1. In 2011–12 the community foundations of Tulsa, Cleveland, New York, Silicon Valley, and Chicago ranked among the nation's fifty largest by assets; see Foundation Center, "50 Largest Foundations by Assets, 2013," foundationcenter.org/findfunders/statistics/.

2. David C. Hammack and Helmut K. Anheier, *A Versatile American Institution: The Changing Ideals and Realities of Philanthropic Foundations* (Washington, DC: Brookings Institution Press, 2013), chap. 2.

3. David C. Hammack, "Community Foundations: The Delicate Question of Purpose," in *An Agile Servant*, ed. Richard Magat (New York: The Foundation Center, 1989); Foundation Center (1980).

4. David C. Hammack, "Community Foundations," in Dwight Burlingame, editor, *Philanthropy in America: A Comprehensive Historical Encyclopedia*, vol. 1 (ABC-CLIO, 2004). 91–95.

5. Foundation Center, *Key Facts on US Foundations,* http://foundationcenter.org/gainknowledge/research/keyfacts2014/ (accessed October 27, 2017).

6. Foundation Center, *Key Facts On Community Foundations,* http://foundationcenter.org/gainknowledge/research/pdf/keyfacts_comm2012.pdf; Foundation Center, "Aggregate Fiscal Data by Foundation Type, 2010," http://data.foundationcenter.org/#/foundations/all/nationwide/total/list/2010 (accessed October 27, 2017).

7. https://tulsacf.org/about-tcf/then-and-now/ (accessed February 9, 2016).

8. Foundation Center, "FY 2014 Columbus Survey of Community Foundations", http://cfinsights.org/Portals/0/Uploads/Documents/2014_Top_100_Rank_By_Assets.pdf (accessed October 27, 2017).

9. In Massachusetts, six states in the Midwest and seven states in the South, a community foundation was second-largest by assets. The Foundation Center lists the fifty largest foundations by assets for each state for recent years at http://data.foundationcenter.org/ (accessed October 27, 2017).

10. Assets per capita ranged from $282 for the states around the Great Lakes and $276 in New England to $112 in the south Atlantic states, $89 in the Southeast, and $90 in the mountain states. At the high end, Oklahoma was off the charts with $1,210, but this was an anomaly: the next-largest state numbers were $545 in Rhode Island and $449 in Ohio. At the low end, Utah's community foundations had $2 per capita, Mississippi's $27, New Jersey's $32, those in Arkansas, $51. Community foundations accounted for a fifth or more of the funds granted by foundations in the less populated states in New England, the northern plains, and the Pacific Coast, as well as in Ohio, Iowa, South Carolina, Kentucky, Tennessee, Mississippi, Louisiana, and Oklahoma. Community foundation asset numbers and grants, and state grant totals, from http://data.foundationcenter.org/; population from US Census.

11. Numbers of community foundations by state http://data.foundationcenter.org/.

12. The exceptions are Nebraska and West Virginia, with populations between one and two million.

13. If we exclude the exceptionally large and single-donor–dominated Tulsa Community Foundation, the southwestern states have significantly smaller than average assets per capita.

14. Hammack, "Community Foundations," 93.

15. The remarkably large funds in Grand Rapids and Kalamazoo gave their western Michigan areas a still higher per capita concentration.

16. New Haven, if considered separately from New York, also had more than $200 per capita in 2001.

17. Hammack, "Community Foundations," 93.

18. Metropolitan region population from https://en.wikipedia.org/wiki/List_of_primary_statistical_areas_of_the_United_States checked against 2014 estimates at https://factfinder.census.gov/faces/nav/jsf/pages/index.xhtml. Assets of all community foundations located within each metropolitan region for dates in 2015 or 2016, as available, from http://www.guidestar.org/search?q=, and from http://www.cfinsights.org/Portals/0/Uploads/Documents/Columbus%20Survey/Access_the_Data_FY_2016_Columbus_Survey.xlsx?cpgn=FY%202016%20Access%20the%20Data. (Acessed October 30, 2017).

19. John Ettling, *The Germ of Laziness: Rockefeller Philanthropy and Public Health in the New South* (Cambridge, MA: Harvard University Press, 1981); Eric Anderson and Alfred A. Moss, *Dangerous Donations: Northern Philanthropy and Southern Black Education, 1902–1930* (Columbia: University of Missouri Press, 1999); Jonathan Engel, *Doctors and Reformers: Discussion and Debate over Health Policy, 1925–1950* (Columbia: University of South Carolina Press, 2002); Peter Max Ascoli, *Julius Rosenwald: The Man Who Built Sears, Roebuck and Advanced the Cause of Black Education in the American South* (Bloomington: Indiana University Press, 2006).

20. Horace B. Powell, *The Original Has This Signature—W. K. Kellogg* (Englewood Cliffs, NJ: Prentice-Hall, 1956); https://www.wkkf.org/who-we-are/history-legacy (accessed October 27,

2017); David P. Ernstes, R. J. Hildreth, and Ronald D. Knutson, *Farm Foundation: 75 Years as a Catalyst to Agriculture and Rural America* (Oak Brook, IL: Farm Foundation, 2007).

21. For an historical overview, see the Minnesota Historical Society's finding aid for the Northwest Area Foundation's records at http://www.mnhs.org/library/findaids/00669.xml (accessed October 26, 2017). For a discussion of the Northwest Area Foundation's history designed to advance the perspective of its leaders at the turn of the twenty-first century, see Karl N. Stauber, "Mission-Driven Philanthropy: What Do We Want to Accomplish and How Do We Do It?" *Nonprofit and Voluntary Sector Quarterly* 30, no 2 (2001): 393–99.

22. "The Story of Morris Calvin Oldham and Oldham Little Church Foundation," Oldham Little Church Foundation website, http://oldhamlcf.org/history (accessed October 26, 2017).

23. See, for example, http://www.ruralamerica.org/; W.K. Kellogg Foundation, "Rural People, Rural Policy: Initiative Overview," at https://www.wkkf.org/~/media/813779035EA94E65BA60C84133C78517.ashx, andhttp://ruralassembly.org/about/ (accessed October 26, 2017). Also http://www.dailyyonder.com/about-daily-yonder; Gabriel Kasper, Justin Marcoux, and Jess Ausinheiler, "What's Next For Community Philanthropy: Making the Case for Change," http://monitorinstitute.com/communityphilanthropy/site/wp-content/uploads/2014/07/Overview.pdf; Avila Kilmurray and Lewis Feldstein, "Beyond Money and Grantmaking: The Non-Grantmaking Role of Community Foundations," The Transatlantic Community Foundation Network, http://kopienufondi.lv/res/docs/beyond-money-and-grant-making_EN.pdf; http://irvine.org/grantmaking/our-programs/specialinitiatives/1204; http://www.lillyendowment.org/cd_gift.html; http://www.mott.org/news/news/2012/20121122-Communiy-Foundations-Support-Organizations-Article6 (accessed April 29, 2016).

24. Baucus began by saying, "I understand that each foundation has particular funding guidelines, regions of focus, and priorities," and stressed that his aim was only to "encourage." *The Chronicle of Philanthropy*, August 10, 2007, http://philanthropy.com/article/Key-Senator-Has-No-Plans-for/62675/ (accessed October 27, 2017). For an argument that rural areas receive "equitable" attention and resources from foundations, see S. R. Ashley, "Is the Inequality Equitable? An Examination of the Distributive Equity of Philanthropic Grants to Rural Communities," *Administration and Society* 46, no. 6 (2014): 684–706.

25. Frederick H. Goff did much to start the first community foundation in 1914. Because he was John D. Rockefeller's Cleveland tax and investment advisor and attorney, Goff would have acted only with Rockefeller's approval. Very large gifts from single individuals launched the community foundations of Dayton and Kalamazoo. A 1986 court decision took the Buck Trust from the San Francisco Foundation and made it the basis of the then larger Marin Community Foundation. And in 1998 George B. Kaiser decided to launch the Tulsa Community Foundation, for a few years the largest of all. Private foundations have also intervened in the community foundation field at least since the 1960s, when Ford Foundation funds helped bring several separate trusts together into what is now the Greater Kansas City Community Foundation.

26. www.lillyendowment.org/cd_gift.html; Karen Tice, "Strategies to Develop Sustainable Community Foundations: Lessons Learned," http://webcache.googleusercontent.com/search?q=cache:X7IxzoGOj48J:growingcf.org/wp-content/uploads/Strategies_to_Develop_Sustainable_Community_Foundations_Lessons_Learned_00024_00116.pdf+&cd=1&hl=en&ct=clnk&gl=us; Claude Worthington Bedenum Foundation, Annual Report 2002, http://www.benedum.org/resources/2002AR.pdf; Charles Stewart Mott Foundation, several entries at https://www.mott.org/news/articles/programs/civil-society/page/5/ and other pages in this series; and http://maps.foundationcenter.org/home.php. All sites accessed Oct. 27, 2017.

27. http://philanthropynewsdigest.org/news/irvine-foundation-awards-4-million-to-california-community-foundations (accessed October 26, 2017).

28. cf INSIGHTS, FY 2011 Columbus Survey of Community Foundations, List of Top 100 Community Foundations by Asset Size, FY 2011 Data as of May 1, 2012; 2011 Columbus Foundation

Survey of Community Foundations, Participant Data as of March 23, 2012, CF Insights. See http://www.cfinsights.org/Knowledge/ViewArticle/ArticleId/28/Top-100-Community-Foundations-by-Assets.aspx (accessed October 27, 2017).

29. Eds. Avila Kilmurray & Lew Feldstein (The Transatlantic Community Foundation Network, 2005), and was available at http://www.globalfundcommunityfoundations.org/information/beyond-money-grantmaking-the-emerging-role-of-community-foun.html. See also the Community Foundation Series from the James Irvine Foundation at https://www.cof.org/page/community-foundations-series-james-irvine-foundation, and, "Growing Community Foundations," on a website © 2003 by the Council of Michigan Foundations, created by Donnell Snite Mersereau and Karin E. Tice and funded by the Kellogg Foundation, at *www.GrowingCF.org*. For a comprehensive discussion, see Lisa Ranghelli, Andrew Mott, and Elizabeth Banwell, "Measuring Foundations' Impact," Nonprofit Sector Research Fund Working Paper Series, (The Aspen Institute, 2006), at https://www.michiganfoundations.org/sites/default/files/resources/CF-Measuring-Community-Foundations-Impact-NSRF-Aspen.pdf. All websites in this note accessed Oct. 27, 2017.

INDEX

Page numbers in *italics* refer to tables and figures.

Difference between a community chest and a community foundation?

CPSIA information can be obtained
at www.ICGtesting.com
Printed in the USA
LVOW13s0756220418
574378LV00016B/19/P